SOMETHING ABOUT THE AUTHOR

something about the author

Facts and Pictures about Authors
and Illustrators of Books for Young People

EDITED BY
ANNE COMMIRE

volume 52

GALE RESEARCH COMPANY
BOOK TOWER
DETROIT, MICHIGAN
48226

Editor: Anne Commire

Associate Editors: Agnes Garrett, Helga P. McCue

Senior Assistant Editor: Dianne H. Anderson

Assistant Editors: Elisa Ann Ferraro, Eunice L. Petrini, Linda Shedd

Sketchwriters: Marguerite Feitlowitz, Rachel Koenig

Researcher: Catherine Ruello

Editorial Assistants: Catherine Coray, Joanne J. Ferraro, Dieter Miller, Karen Walker

Permissions Assistant: Susan Pfanner

In cooperation with the staff of *Something about the Author Autobiography Series*

Editor: Joyce Nakamura

Assistant Editors: Carolyn Chafetz, Laurie Collier

Research Assistants: Shelly Andrews, Carolyn Kline

Production Manager: Mary Beth Trimper

External Production Assistants: Linda Davis, Patty Farley

Internal Production Associate: Louise Gagné

Internal Senior Production Assistant: Sandy Rock

Internal Production Assistant: Candace Cloutier

Layout Artist: Elizabeth Lewis Patryjak

Art Director: Arthur Chartow

Special acknowledgment is due to the members of the *Contemporary Authors* staff
who assisted in the preparation of this volume.

Contents

Introduction

As the only ongoing reference series that deals with the lives and works of authors and illustrators of children's books, *Something about the Author (SATA)* is a unique source of information. The *SATA* series includes not only well-known authors and illustrators whose books are most widely read, but also those less prominent people whose works are just coming to be recognized. *SATA* is often the only readily available information source for less well-known writers or artists. You'll find *SATA* informative and entertaining whether you are:

—a student in junior high school (or perhaps one to two grades higher or lower) who needs information for a book report or some other assignment for an English class;

—a children's librarian who is searching for the answer to yet another question from a young reader or collecting background material to use for a story hour;

—an English teacher who is drawing up an assignment for your students or gathering information for a book talk;

—a student in a college of education or library science who is studying children's literature and reference sources in the field;

—a parent who is looking for a new way to interest your child in reading something more than the school curriculum prescribes;

—an adult who enjoys children's literature for its own sake, knowing that a good children's book has no age limits.

Scope

In *SATA* you will find detailed information about authors and illustrators who span the full time range of children's literature, from early figures like John Newbery and L. Frank Baum to contemporary figures like Judy Blume and Richard Peck. Authors in the series represent primarily English-speaking countries, particularly the United States, Canada, and the United Kingdom. Also included, however, are authors from around the world whose works are available in English translation, for example: from France, Jean and Laurent De Brunhoff; from Italy, Emanuele Luzzati; from the Netherlands, Jaap ter Haar; from Germany, James Krüss; from Norway, Babbis Friis-Baastad; from Japan, Toshiko Kanzawa; from the Soviet Union, Kornei Chukovsky; from Switzerland, Alois Carigiet, to name only a few. Also appearing in *SATA* are Newbery medalists from Hendrik Van Loon (1922) to Russell Freedman (1988). The writings represented in *SATA* include those created intentionally for children and young adults as well as those written for a general audience and known to interest younger readers. These writings cover the spectrum from picture books, humor, folk and fairy tales, animal stories, mystery and adventure, science fiction and fantasy, historical fiction, poetry and nonsense verse, to drama, biography, and nonfiction.

Information Features

In *SATA* you will find full-length entries that are being presented in the series for the first time. This volume, for example, marks the first full-length appearance of Daniel J. Boorstin, Laura Z. Hobson, Elizabeth James, Eros Keith, Lilian Moore, Judith Sachs, and Isaac Watts.

Brief Entries, first introduced in Volume 27, are another regular feature of *SATA*. Brief Entries present essentially the same types of information found in a full entry but do so in a capsule form and without illustration. These entries are intended to give you useful and timely information while the more time-consuming process of compiling a full-length biography is in progress. In this volume you'll find Brief Entries for Carolyn Croll, Patrick C. Dorin, Peter Eyvindson, Lucy Fuchs, Victor Kelleher, Suse MacDonald, Jacqueline Wilson, and Phoebe Worthington, among others.

Obituaries have been included in *SATA* since Volume 20. An Obituary is intended not only as a death notice but also as a concise view of a person's life and work. Obituaries may appear for persons who have entries in earlier *SATA* volumes, as well as for people who have not yet appeared in the series. In this volume Obituaries mark the recent deaths of Bil Baird, Frank H. Forrester, Margaret Leighton, Andrés Segovia, and others.

Revised Entries

Since Volume 25, each *SATA* volume also includes newly revised and updated entries for a selection of *SATA* listees (usually four to six) who remain of interest to today's readers and who have been active enough to require extensive revision of their earlier biographies. For example, when Beverly Cleary first appeared in *SATA* Volume 2, she was the author of twenty-one books for children and young adults and the recipient of numerous awards. By the time her updated sketch appeared in Volume 43 (a span of fifteen years), this creator of the indefatigable Ramona Quimby and other memorable characters had produced a dozen new titles and garnered nearly fifty additional awards, including the 1984 Newbery Medal.

The entry for a given biographee may be revised as often as there is substantial new information to provide. In this volume, look for revised entries on Quentin Blake, Thor Heyerdahl, Ursula K. Le Guin, and Marilyn Sachs.

Illustrations

While the textual information in *SATA* is its primary reason for existing, photographs and illustrations not only enliven the text but are an integral part of the information that *SATA* provides. Illustrations and text are wedded in such a special way in children's literature that artists and their works naturally occupy a prominent place among *SATA*'s listees. The illustrators that you'll find in the series include such past masters of children's book illustration as Randolph Caldecott, Walter Crane, Arthur Rackham, and Ernest H. Shepard, as well as such noted contemporary artists as Maurice Sendak, Edward Gorey, Tomie de Paola, and Margot Zemach. There are Caldecott medalists from Dorothy Lathrop (the first recipient in 1938) to John Schoenherr (the latest winner in 1988); cartoonists like Charles Schulz, ("Peanuts"), Walt Kelly ("Pogo"), Hank Ketcham ("Dennis the Menace"), and Georges Rémi ("Tintin"); photographers like Jill Krementz, Tana Hoban, Bruce McMillan, and Bruce Curtis; and filmmakers like Walt Disney, Alfred Hitchcock, and Steven Spielberg.

In more than a dozen years of recording the metamorphosis of children's literature from the printed page to other media, *SATA* has become something of a repository of photographs that are unique in themselves and exist nowhere else as a group, particularly many of the classics of motion picture and stage history and photographs that have been specially loaned to us from private collections.

Indexes

Each *SATA* volume provides a cumulative index in two parts: first, the Illustrations Index, arranged by the name of the illustrator, gives the number of the volume and page where the illustrator's work appears in the current volume as well as all preceding volumes in the series; second, the Author Index gives the number of the volume in which a person's biographical sketch, Brief Entry, or Obituary appears in the current volume as well as all preceding volumes in the series. These indexes also include references to authors and illustrators who appear in *Yesterday's Authors of Books for Children* (described in detail below). Beginning with Volume 36, the *SATA* Author Index provides cross-references to authors who are included in *Children's Literature Review*.

Starting with Volume 42, you will also find cross-references to authors who are included in the *Something about the Author Autobiography Series* (described in detail below).

Character Index—New Feature

If you're like many readers, the names of fictional characters may pop more easily into your mind than the names of the authors or illustrators who created them: Snow White, Charlotte the Spider, the Cat in the Hat, Peter Pan, Mary Poppins, Winnie-the-Pooh, Brer Rabbit, Little Toot, Charlie Bucket, Lassie, Rip Van Winkle, Bartholomew Cubbins—the list could go on and on. But who invented them? Now these characters, and several thousand others, can lead you to the *SATA* and *YABC* entries on the lives and works of their creators.

First published in Volume 50, the Character Index provides a broad selection of characters from books and other media—movies, plays, comic strips, cartoons, etc.—created by listees who have appeared in all the published volumes of *SATA* and *YABC*. This index gives the character name, followed by a *"See"* reference indicating the name of the creator and the number of the *SATA* or *YABC* volume in which the creator's bio-bibliographical entry can be found. As new *SATA* volumes are prepared, additional characters will be included in the cumulative Character Index and published annually in *SATA*. (The cumulative Illustrations and Author Indexes will continue to appear in each *SATA* volume.)

It would be impossible for the Character Index to include every important character created by *SATA* and *YABC* listees. (Several hundred important characters might be taken from Dickens alone, for example.) Therefore, the *SATA* editors have selected those characters that are best known and thus most likely to interest *SATA* users. Realizing that some of your favorite characters may not appear in this index, the editors invite you to suggest additional names. With your help, the editors hope to make the Character Index a uniquely useful reference tool for you.

What a *SATA* Entry Provides

Whether you're already familiar with the *SATA* series or just getting acquainted, you will want to be aware of the kind of information that an entry provides. In every *SATA* entry the editors attempt to give as complete a picture of the person's life and work as possible. In some cases that full range of information may simply be unavailable, or a biographee may choose not to reveal complete personal details. The information that the editors attempt to provide in every entry is arranged in the following categories:

1. The "head" of the entry gives

    —the most complete form of the name,
    —any part of the name not commonly used, included in parentheses,
    —birth and death dates, if known; a (?) indicates a discrepancy in published sources,
    —pseudonyms or name variants under which the person has had books published or is publicly known, in parentheses in the second line.

2. "Personal" section gives

    —date and place of birth and death,
    —parents' names and occupations,
    —name of spouse, date of marriage, and names of children,
    —educational institutions attended, degrees received, and dates,
    —religious and political affiliations,
    —agent's name and address,
    —home and/or office address.

3. "Career" section gives

    —name of employer, position, and dates for each career post,
    —military service,
    —memberships,
    —awards and honors.

4. "Writings" section gives

    —title, first publisher and date of publication, and illustration information for each book
    written; revised editions and other significant editions for books with particularly long
    publishing histories; genre, when known.

5. "Adaptations" section gives

    —title, major performers, producer, and date of all known reworkings of an author's material
    in another medium, like movies, filmstrips, television, recordings, plays, etc.

6. "Sidelights" section gives

    —commentary on the life or work of the biographee either directly from the person (and often
    written specifically for the *SATA* entry), or gathered from biographies, diaries, letters,
    interviews, or other published sources.

7. "For More Information See" section gives

    —books, feature articles, films, plays, and reviews in which the biographee's life or work has
    been treated.

How a *SATA* Entry Is Compiled

A *SATA* entry progresses through a series of steps. If the biographee is living, the *SATA* editors try to
secure information directly from him or her through a questionnaire. From the information that the
biographee supplies, the editors prepare an entry, filling in any essential missing details with research. The
author or illustrator is then sent a copy of the entry to check for accuracy and completeness.

If the biographee is deceased or cannot be reached by questionnaire, the *SATA* editors examine a wide
variety of published sources to gather information for an entry. Biographical sources are searched with the
aid of Gale's *Biography and Genealogy Master Index*. Bibliographic sources like the *National Union
Catalog*, the *Cumulative Book Index*, *American Book Publishing Record*, and the *British Museum
Catalogue* are consulted, as are book reviews, feature articles, published interviews, and material
sometimes obtained from the biographee's family, publishers, agent, or other associates.

For each entry presented in *SATA*, the editors also attempt to locate a photograph of the biographee as
well as representative illustrations from his or her books. After surveying the available books which the
biographee has written and/or illustrated, and then making a selection of appropriate photographs and
illustrations, the editors request permission of the current copyright holders to reprint the material. In the
case of older books for which the copyright may have passed through several hands, even locating the
current copyright holder is often a long and involved process.

We invite you to examine the entire *SATA* series, starting with this volume. Described below are some of
the people in Volume 52 that you may find particularly interesting.

Highlights of This Volume

QUENTIN BLAKE......remembers "drawing on the back of...exercise books as far back as primary
school." Today he collaborates on books with such well-known authors as Roald Dahl and John Yeoman.
"It's interesting to discover someone who is different from you, but with whom you feel a rapport and a
sense of humor," says Blake. Besides illustrating text, he also produces his own books, including *Mister
Magnolia,* his favorite. "It's not autobiographical," writes Blake, "but reflects the things I like in *pictures.*"
He believes that the secret of his success in the children's book market lies in the fact that he "keeps in touch
with the child" within himself.

LÁSZLÓ GÁL......immigrated to Toronto from Hungary because career choices were very limited for an
aspiring artist under a Communist regime. Although he has had to take more commercial jobs to support
himself, Gál is dedicated to producing quality illustrations for children's books in his free time. He

demands perfection. "When I start to paint, I always find it isn't the way I thought it would be.... As each day passes I want to make it better and better."

THOR HEYERDAHL......made his first expedition to Polynesia in 1939, with nothing but a knife and a tea kettle. Convinced that the Polynesians were descended from two groups of settlers, one from Peru and another from British Columbia, he decided to prove his theory by reenacting the voyage. With six men—only one who knew how to sail—Heyerdahl made a 4,300-mile trip on a 45-foot balsa raft, the *Kon-Tiki*. Publications about the journey made him internationally famous, with countless commercial products named after the expedition. With the money earned from his books and films, Heyerdahl was able to finance more expeditions to such remote places as the Galapagos Islands and Easter Island and to sail on such primitive vessels as a papyrus boat and a reed boat, using multinational crews to prove his theory that "no space is too small, no stress too great, if men will only join hands for common survival."

URSULA K. LE GUIN......wrote her "first story at the age of nine about a man persecuted by invisible elves. Speculative fiction." By twelve she was convinced that the lands of fantasy and science fiction were one and the same—her own "native country." Several years and stories later, she was able to separate her "pure fantasy vein...from my science fiction one, and the separation marked a large advance in both skill and content." Her ability to write realistically about invented worlds and times lies in the fact that she visits them "as in a dream. I don't see things and then stop and describe them," she says. "I am *there.*"

LILIAN MOORE......loved her "neighborhood library on Tremont Avenue in the Bronx....I would come [home] with an armful of books—reading all the way...." Her passion for books eventually led to careers as a reading specialist, as the first editor of Scholastic Book Services' Arrow Book Club, and as editor of Grosset and Dunlap's "Wonder Books," of which she wrote eleven. Her *Little Raccoon* books for children grew out of stories that she wrote as a reading consultant for *Humpty Dumpty* magazine. She began to write poetry for children in 1967, finding the experience "so exhilarating...that I went on writing poetry. What I love to see happen...is to have poetry become as much a part of [children's] lives as cereal in the morning."

MARILYN SACHS......was a "very skinny, cowardly kid" who found safe harbor from neighborhood bullies in her branch library in the Bronx. "It's the weaklings who become the writers, not the bullies," she says. By 1964 she had published her first book, which was followed with a book every year. *Veronica Ganz, Fourteen, Almost Fifteen,* and *Dorrie's Book* are just a few of her popular titles. Although she is routinely praised by critics for her handling of social consciousness and bigotry, Sachs' books have also been banned by local school boards. She believes that parents ought to take an interest in their children's books, but that censorship is wrong. "Those of us who feel strongly about it," says Sachs, "have a responsibility to speak out."

ERIC SLOANE......began his art career as a "lowly sign painter," traveling cross-country in his Model-T. "An itinerant sign painter could enter a tiny midwest village in the morning and leave by evening some fifty dollars richer, which was really something in those days." From sign-painting Sloane progressed to landscapes and "cloudscapes." His first business card identified him as an "aviation artist." Sloane's interest in "sky-painting" led to an in-depth study of meteorology, which produced six books about weather. "I even tried my hand at being the first weatherman on T.V.," he said. As a writer and painter, he attempted to depict the American past, producing numerous books in the process.

These are only a few of the authors and illustrators that you'll find in this volume. We hope you find all the entries in *SATA* both interesting and useful.

Yesterday's Authors of Books for Children

In a two-volume companion set to *SATA, Yesterday's Authors of Books for Children (YABC)* focuses on early authors and illustrators, from the beginnings of children's literature through 1960, whose books are still being read by children today. Here you will find "old favorites" like Hans Christian Andersen, J. M. Barrie, Kenneth Grahame, Betty MacDonald, A. A. Milne, Beatrix Potter, Samuel Clemens, Kate Greenaway, Rudyard Kipling, Robert Louis Stevenson, and many more.

Similar in format to *SATA*, *YABC* features bio-bibliographical entries that are divided into information categories such as Personal, Career, Writings, and Sidelights. The entries are further enhanced by book illustrations, author photos, movie stills, and many rare old photographs.

In Volume 2 you will find cumulative indexes to the authors and to the illustrations that appear in *YABC*. These listings can also be located in the *SATA* cumulative indexes.

By exploring both volumes of *YABC*, you will discover a special group of more than seventy authors and illustrators who represent some of the best in children's literature—individuals whose timeless works continue to delight children and adults of all ages. Other authors and illustrators from early children's literature are listed in *SATA*, starting with Volume 15.

Something about the Author Autobiography Series

You can complement the information in *SATA* with the *Something about the Author Autobiography Series (SAAS)*, which provides autobiographical essays written by important current authors and illustrators of books for children and young adults. In every volume of *SAAS* you will find about twenty specially commissioned autobiographies, each accompanied by a selection of personal photographs supplied by the authors. The wide range of contemporary writers and artists who describe their lives and interests in the *Autobiography Series* includes Joan Aiken, Betsy Byars, Leonard Everett Fisher, Milton Meltzer, Maia Wojciechowska, and Jane Yolen, among others. Though the information presented in the autobiographies is as varied and unique as the authors, you can learn about the people and events that influenced these writers' early lives, how they began their careers, what problems they faced in becoming established in their professions, what prompted them to write or illustrate particular books, what they now find most challenging or rewarding in their lives, and what advice they may have for young people interested in following in their footsteps, among many other subjects.

Autobiographies included in the *SATA Autobiography Series* can be located through both the *SATA* cumulative index and the *SAAS* cumulative index, which lists not only the authors' names but also the subjects mentioned in their essays, such as titles of works and geographical and personal names.

The *SATA Autobiography Series* gives you the opportunity to view "close up" some of the fascinating people who are included in the *SATA* parent series. The combined *SATA* series makes available to you an unequaled range of comprehensive and in-depth information about the authors and illustrators of young people's literature.

Please write and tell us if we can make *SATA* even more helpful to you.

Acknowledgments

Grateful acknowledgment is made to the following publishers, authors, and artists for their kind permission to reproduce copyrighted material.

ALGOL PRESS. Sidelight excerpts from *Dreams Must Explain Themselves* by Ursula K. Le Guin. Reprinted by permission of Algol Press.

GEORGE ALLEN & UNWIN LTD. Illustration from *The Kon-Tiki Expedition* by Thor Heyerdahl. Translated by F. H. Lyon. Copyright under the Berne Convention. Reprinted by permission of George Allen & Unwin Ltd.

ARBOR HOUSE PUBLISHING CO. Photographs from *Laura Z: A Life* by Laura Z. Hobson. Copyright © 1983 by Laura Z. Hobson. Reprinted by permission of Arbor House Publishing Co.

ATHENEUM PUBLISHERS. Illustration by Quentin Blake from *How Tom Beat Captain Najork and His Hired Sportsmen* by Russell Hoban. Text copyright © 1974 by Yankee Rover, Inc. Illustrations copyright © 1974 by Quentin Blake./ Detail of jacket illustration by Trina Schart Hyman from *The Watchers* by Jane Louise Curry. Copyright © 1975 by Jane Louise Curry./ Jacket illustration by Allen Davis from *Very Far Away from Anywhere Else* by Ursula K. Le Guin. Copyright © 1976 by Ursula K. Le Guin./ Illustration by Gail Garraty from *Tombs of Atuan* by Ursula K. Le Guin. Copyright © 1970, 1971 by Ursula K. Le Guin./ Jacket illustration by Dennis Luzak from *Aren't You the One Who...?* by Frances A. Miller. Copyright © 1983 by Frances A. Miller. Jacket illustration copyright © 1983 by Dennis Luzak./ Illustration by Gioia Fiammenghi from *Papa Albert* by Lilian Moore. Text copyright © 1964 by Lilian Moore. Illustrations copyright © 1964 by Gioia Fiammenghi./ Illustration by Diane Dawson from "Johnny Drew a Monster" in *See My Lovely Poison Ivy and Other Verses about Witches, Ghosts and Things* by Lilian Moore. Text copyright © 1975 by Lilian Moore. Illustrations copyright © 1975 by Diane Dawson./ Cover design by Alexi Brodovitch from *The Image: A Guide to Pseudo-Events in America* by Daniel J. Boorstin. Copyright © 1961 by Daniel J. Boorstin. All reprinted by pemission of Atheneum Publishers.

BERKLEY PUBLISHING GROUP. Sidelight excerpts from *The Language of the Night: Essays on Fantasy and Science Fiction,* edited by Susan Wood. Reprinted by permission of Berkley Publishing Group.

BRADBURY PRESS. Illustration by Denys Cazet from *Big Shoe, Little Shoe* by Denys Cazet. Copyright © 1984 by Denys Cazet./ Illustration by Eros Keith from *The King's Falcon* by Paula Fox. Text copyright © 1969 by Paula Fox. Illustrations copyright © 1969 by Eros Keith. Both reprinted by permission of Bradbury Press.

CAROLRHODA BOOKS, INC. Illustration by Peter E. Hanson from "Luck" in *The Cat Walked through the Casserole and Other Poems for Children* by Pamela Espeland and Marilyn Waniek. Text copyright © 1984 by Pamela Espeland and Marilyn Nelson Waniek. Illustrations copyright © 1984 by Carolrhoda Books, Inc. Reprinted by permission of Carolrhoda Books, Inc.

CHATHAM HOUSE PUBLISHERS, INC. Photograph by David Plowden from *The Hand of Man on America* by David Plowden. Copyright © 1971 by David Plowden. Reprinted by permission of Chatham House Publishers, Inc.

CHILDRENS PRESS. Illustration by Paul Sharp from *Dirty Larry* by Bobbie Hamsa. Copyright © 1983 by Regensteiner Publishing Enterprises, Inc. Reprinted by permission of Childrens Press.

COLLIER MACMILLAN LTD. Illustration by Emanuel Schongut from *John Henry McCoy* by Lillie D. Chaffin. Copyright © 1971 by Lillie D. Chaffin and The Macmillan Co. Reprinted by permission of Collier Macmillan Ltd.

THOMAS Y. CROWELL, INC. Illustration by Eric Sloane from *Recollections in Black and White* by Eric Sloane. Copyright © 1974, 1978 by Eric Sloane. Reprinted by permission of Thomas Y. Crowell, Inc.

CROWN PUBLISHERS, INC. Jacket illustration by Diane de Groat from *Fly Away Paul* by Peter Davies. Copyright © 1974 by Peter Davies. Reprinted by permission of Crown Publishers, Inc.

DELL PUBLISHING CO., INC. Illustration by Quentin Blake from *Agaton Sax and the Diamond Thieves* by Nils-Olof Franzén. Translated from the Swedish by Evelyn Ramsden. Copyright © 1959 by Nils-Olof Franzén. English translation copyright © 1965 by André Deutsch Ltd. Copyright © 1967 by Dell Publishing Co., Inc./ Jacket illustration by Emanuel Schongut from *The Talking Table Mystery* by Georgess McHargue. Text copyright © 1977 by Georgess McHargue. Both reprinted by permission of Dell Publishing Co., Inc.

J. M. DENT & SONS LTD. Illustration by Philippe Dumas from *Lucy, Edward's Daughter* by Philippe Dumas. Copyright © 1977 by Flammarion. Reprinted by permission of J. M. Dent & Sons Ltd.

ANDRÉ DEUTSCH LTD. Illustration by Quentin Blake from *You Can't Catch Me!* by Michael Rosen. Text copyright © 1981 by Michael Rosen. Illustrations copyright © 1981 by Quentin Blake. Reprinted by permission of André Deutsch Ltd.

DIAL BOOKS. Illustration by László Gál from *The Enchanted Tapestry* by Robert D. Sans Souci. Text copyright © 1987 by Robert D. Sans Souci. Illustrations copyright © 1987 by László Gal. Reprinted by permission of Dial Books.

DODD, MEAD & CO., INC. Illustration by Emanuel Schongut from *Elidor and the Golden Ball* by Georgess McHargue. Text copyright © 1973 by Georgess McHargue. Illustrations copyright © 1973 by Emanuel Schongut. Reprinted by permission of Dodd, Mead & Co., Inc.

DOUBLEDAY & CO., INC. Illustration by Quentin Blake from *Arabel's Raven* by Joan Aiken. Copyright © 1972, 1973, 1974 by Joan Aiken./ Photographs from *The Ra Expeditions* by Thor Heyerdahl. Translated by Patricia Crampton. Copyright © 1971 by George Allen & Unwin Ltd. Translation from the Norwegian copyright © 1970 by Thor Heyerdahl./ Illustration by Louis Glanzman from *Marv* by Marilyn Sachs. Copyright © 1970 by Marilyn Sachs./ Illustration by Louis Glanzman from *Veronica Ganz* by Marilyn Sachs. Copyright © 1968 by Marilyn Sachs./ Illustration by Eric Sloane from *ABC Book of Early Americana: A Sketchbook of Antiquities and American Firsts* by Eric Sloane. Copyright © 1963 by Eric Sloane. All reprinted by permission of Doubleday & Co., Inc.

DOUGLAS & McINTYRE. Illustration by László Gál from "Ti-Jean Brings Home the Moon" in *Canadian Fairy Tales,* retold by Eva Martin. Text copyright © 1984 by Eva Martin. Illustrations copyright © 1984 by by László Gál. Reprinted by permission of Douglas & McIntyre.

THE DRYDEN PRESS. Sidelight excerpts from *Isaac Watts: His Life and Works* by Arthur Paul Davis. Reprinted by permission of The Dryden Press.

E. P. DUTTON, INC. Illustration by Diane de Groat from *I Don't Live Here!* by Pam Conrad. Text copyright © 1984 by Pam Conrad. Illustrations copyright © 1984 by Diane de Groat./ Illustration by Diane Goode from *I Go with My Family to Grandma's* by Riki Levinson. Text copyright © 1986 by Riki Friedberg Levinson. Illustrations copyright © 1986 by Diane Goode./ Illustration by Simms Taback from *Fishy Riddles* by Katy Hall and Lisa Eisenberg. Text copyright © 1983 by Katy Hall and Lisa Eisenberg. Illustrations copyright © 1983 by Simms Taback./ Photograph by David Plowden from *Desert and Plain, the Mountains and the River: A Celebration of Rural America* by Berton Roueché and David Plowden. Text copyright © 1970, 1972, 1975 by Berton Roueché. Photographs copyright © 1975 by David Plowden./ Jacket illustration by Helen Cogancherry from *Almost Fifteen* by Marilyn Sachs. Copyright © 1987 by Marilyn Sachs./ Jacket illustration by Jim Spence from *Fourteen* by Marilyn Sachs. Copyright © 1983 by Marilyn Sachs./ Illustration by Amy Rowen from *Bus Ride* by Marilyn Sachs. Text copyright © 1980 by Marilyn Sachs. Illustrations copyright © 1980 by Amy Rowen./ Illustration by Joan Drescher from *Not Even Mrs. Mazursky* by Jane Sutton. Text copyright © 1984 by Jane Sutton. Illustrations copyright © 1984 by Joan Drescher./ Illustration by Pamela Johnson from *Hello...Wrong Number* by Marilyn Sachs. Text copyright © 1981 by Marilyn Sachs. Illustrations copyright © 1981 by Pamela Johnson. All reprinted by permission of E. P. Dutton, Inc.

FARRAR, STRAUS & GIROUX, INC. Illustration by Doug Panton from *The Violin-Maker's Gift* by Donn Kushner. Text copyright © 1981 by Donn Kushner. Illustrations copyright © 1981 by Doug Panton. Reprinted by permission of Farrar, Straus & Giroux, Inc.

FUNK & WAGNALLS, INC. Illustration by Eric Sloane from *Diary of an Early American Boy, Noah Blake, 1805* by Eric Sloane. Copyright © 1962 by Wilfred Funk, Inc./ Illustration by Eric Sloane from *A Reverence for Wood* by Eric Sloane. Copyright © 1965 by Wilfred Funk, Inc./ Illustration by Eric Sloane from *A Museum of Early American Tools* by Eric Sloane. Copyright © 1964 by Wilfred Funk, Inc./ Illustrations by Eric Sloane from *American Yesterday* by Eric Sloane. Copyright © 1956 by Wildred Funk, Inc. All reprinted by permission of Funk & Wagnalls, Inc.

GOLDEN PRESS. Illustration by Susan Perl from *Too Many Bozos* by Lilian Moore. Copyright © 1960 by Western Publishing Co. Reprinted by permission of Golden Press.

GREENWILLOW BOOKS. Jacket illustration by Joseph A. Smith from *The Ship from Simnel Street* by Jenny Overton. Copyright © 1986 by Jenny Overton. Reprinted by permission of Greenwillow Books.

HARCOURT BRACE JOVANOVICH, INC. Illustration by Charles Robinson from *Mindy's Mysterious Miniature* by Jane Louise Curry. Text copyright © 1970 by Jane Louise Curry. Illustrations copyright © 1970 by Harcourt Brace Jovanovich, Inc./ Illustration by Charles Robinson from *The Daybreakers* by Jane Louise Curry. Text copyright © 1970 by Jane Louise Curry. Illustrations copyright © 1970 by Harcourt Brace & World, Inc./ Illustration by Harold Jones from *Bless This Day: A Book of Prayer for Children,* compiled by Elfrida Vipont. Copyright by Harcourt Brace & Co., Inc. Illustrations copyright © 1958 by Harold Jones. All reprinted by permission of Harcourt Brace Jovanovich, Inc.

HARPER & ROW, PUBLISHERS, INC. Illustration by Emily Arnold McCully from *Jam Day* by Barbara M. Joosse. Text copyright © 1987 by Barbara M. Joosse. Illustrations copyright © 1987 by Emily Arnold McCully./ Illustration by Eros Keith from *Ivanov Seven* by Elizabeth Janeway. Text copyright © 1967 by Elizabeth Janeway. Illustrations copyright © 1967 by Eros Keith./ Jacket photograph by John Wagner from *Always Coming Home* by Ursula K. Le Guin. Text copyright © 1985 by Ursula K. Le Guin. Jacket photograph copyright © by John Wagner./ Jacket illustration by Griesbach Martucci from *The Beginning Place* by Ursula K. Le Guin. Copyright © 1980 by Ursula K. Le Guin./ Jacket illustration by Jon Weiman from *The Eye of the Heron and Other Stories* by Ursula K. Le Guin. Text copyright © 1978 by Ursula K. Le Guin. Jacket illustration copyright © by Jon Weiman./ Illustrations by Margaret Chodos from *Always Coming Home* by Ursula K. Le Guin. Copyright © 1985 by Ursula K. Le Guin./ Sidelight excerpts from *I Remember America* by Eric Sloane. All reprinted by permission of Harper & Row, Publishers, Inc.

HASTINGS HOUSE, PUBLISHERS. Illustration by Quentin Blake from *Willie the Squowse* by Ted Allan. Text copyright © 1973 by Ted Allan. Illustrations copyright © 1977 by Quentin Blake. Reprinted by permission of Hastings House, Publishers.

HENRY HOLT & CO. Jacket illustration by Wendell Minor from *Gone the Dreams and Dancing* by Douglas C. Jones. Copyright © 1984 by Kemm, Inc. Jacket illustration copyright © 1984 by Wendell Minor. Reprinted by permission of Henry Holt & Co.

HOUGHTON MIFFLIN CO. Illustration by Normand Chartier from *The Great Ringtail Garbage Caper* by Timothy Foote. Copyright © 1980 by Timothy Foote./ Jacket illustration by Ruth Robbins from *A Wizard of Earthsea* by Ursula Le Guin. Text copyright © 1968 by Ursula K. Le Guin. Illustrations copyright © 1968 by Ruth Robbins. Both reprinted by permission of Houghton Mifflin Co.

ALFRED A. KNOPF, INC. Illustration by Quentin Blake from *The Story of the Dancing Frog* by Quentin Blake. Copyright © 1984 by Quentin Blake./ Illustration by Emily Arnold McCully from *Fourth of July* by Barbara M. Joosse. Text copyright © 1985 by Barbara M. Joosse. Illustrations copyright © 1985 by Emily Arnold McCully. Both reprinted by permission of Alfred A. Knopf, Inc.

L'ÉCOLE DES LOISIRS. Illustrations by Philippe Dumas from *La Maison* by Philippe Dumas. Copyright © 1979 by L'École des Loisirs./ Illustration by Philippe Dumas from *Il Pleut, Il Pleut, Bergère* by Philippe Dumas. Copyright © 1985 by L'École des Loisirs./ Illustration by Philippe Dumas from *La Petite Géante* by Philippe Dumas. Copyright © 1977 by L'École des Loisirs. All reprinted by permission of L'École des Loisirs.

LITTLE, BROWN & CO., INC. Illustration by Quentin Blake from "The Big Tent under the Roof" in *Custard and Company,* selected by Quentin Blake. Copyright © 1980 by Quentin Blake. Reprinted by permission of Little, Brown & Co., Inc.

1970 by Daniel J. Boorstin./ Illustration by Leonard Shortall from *The Terrible Mr. Twitmeyer* by Lilian Moore and Leone Adelson. Copyright 1952 by Lilian Moore and Leone Adelson. All reprinted by permission of Random House, Inc.

SIMON & SCHUSTER, INC. Frontispiece by Eros Keith from *Twenty-Two Russian Tales for Young Children* by Leo Tolstoy. Translated by Miriam Morton. Translation copyright © 1969 by Miriam Morton. Reprinted by permission of Simon & Schuster, Inc.

THE UNGAR PUBLISHING CO., INC. Sidelight excerpts from *Ursula K. Le Guin* by Barbara Bucknall. Copyright © 1981 by The Frederick Ungar Publishing Co. Reprinted by permission of The Ungar Publishing Co., Inc.

VANGUARD PRESS, INC. Illustration by Hilary Knight from *Speaking of Mrs. McCluskie* by Cecil Maiden. Text copyright © 1962 by Cecil Maiden. Illustrations copyright © 1962 by Hilary Knight. Reprinted by permission of Vanguard Press, Inc.

VIKING PENGUIN, INC. Illustration by László Gál from *The Moon Painters and Other Estonian Folk Tales,* retold by Selve Maas. Copyright © 1971 by Selve Maas. Reprinted by permission of Viking Penguin, Inc.

VINTAGE BOOKS. Jacket illustration from *The Discoverers* by Daniel J. Boorstin. Copyright © 1983 by Daniel J. Boorstin. Reprinted by permission of Vintage Books.

FREDERICK WARNE CO. Illustration by Nancy Winslow Parker from *My Mom Travels a Lot* by Caroline Feller Bauer. Text copyright © 1981 by Caroline Feller Bauer. Illustrations copyright © 1981 by Nancy Winslow. Reprinted by permission of Frederick Warne Co.

FRANKLIN WATTS, INC. Illustration by Evadne Rowan from *Children of the Mayflower* by Elfrida Vipont. Text copyright © 1969 by Elfrida Vipont. Illustrations copyright © 1969 by William Heinemann Ltd. Reprinted by permission of Franklin Watts, Inc.

WESTERN PUBLISHING CO., INC. Illustration by Tom Cooke from *Bialosky's Best Behavior* by Leslie McGuire. Copyright © 1986 by Workman Publishing, Peggy and Alan Bialosky. Reprinted by permission of Western Publishing Co., Inc.

Sidelight excerpts from *Laura Z., a Life: Years of Fulfillment* by Laura Z. Hobson. Reprinted by permission of Donald I. Fine./ Sidelight excerpts from an article "The Heyerdahl Paradox," by Karl E. Meyer, Spring, 1972 in *Horizon.* Reprinted by permission of *Horizon.*/ Illustration by Roberta MacDonald from *Translations from the English* by Robert Paul Smith. Copyright © 1956, 1958 by Robert Paul Smith. Reprinted by permission of International Creative Management./ Sidelight excerpts from *Senõr Kon-Tiki: The Biography of Thor Heyerdahl* by Arnold Jacoby. Copyright by Arnold Jacoby. Reprinted by permission of Arnold Jacoby./ Sidelight excerpts from *Laura Z: A Life* by Laura Z. Hobson. Copyright © 1983 by Laura Z. Hobson. Reprinted by permission of The Lantz Office./ Sidelight excerpts from an article "How Do You Print So Small?" by Barbara Joosse, May, 1984 in *Milwaukee.* Reprinted by permission of *Milwaukee.*/ Illustration by Gioia Fiammenghi from *Little Raccoon and the Thing in the Pool* by Lilian Moore. Copyright © by Lilian Moore and Gioia Fiammenghi. Reprinted by permission of Lilian Moore.

Sidelight excerpts from an article "The Voyage of Ra II," by Thor Heyerdahl, January, 1971 in *National Geographic.* Copyright © 1971 by National Geographic Society. Reprinted by permission of National Geographic Society./ Sidelight excerpts from an article "The Librarian of Congress," by Lincoln Caplan in "The Talk of the Town," January 5, 1981 in *The New Yorker.* Copyright © 1981 by *The New Yorker* Magazine, Inc. Reprinted by permission of *The New Yorker* Magazine, Inc./ Sidelight excerpts from an article "PW Interviews: Laura Z. Hobson," by Sybil S. Steinberg, September 2, 1983 in *Publishers Weekly.* Copyright © 1983 by Reed Publishing. Reprinted by permission of *Publishers Weekly.*/ Sidelight excerpts from *Recollections in Black and White* by Eric Sloane. Reprinted by permission of the Estate of Eric Sloane./ Sidelight excerpts from an article "History Teaches 'We Don't Know What We Think We Know,'" by Daniel Boorstin, March 5, 1984 in *U.S. News & World Report.* Reprinted by permission of *U.S News & World Report.*

Appreciation also to the Performing Arts Research Center of the New York Public Library at Lincoln Center for permission to reprint the film stills from "The Tenth Month" and "The Lathe of Heaven," and the theater still from "The Tender Trap."

PHOTOGRAPH CREDITS

Denys Cazet: Rank Rodriguez; Pam Conrad: Jon Stampf; Chris Crutcher: Paula L. Whitson; Philippe Dumas: Laurence Henderycksen; Timothy Foote: Martha Holmes; Elfrida Vipont Foulds: Don Jarvis of Michael Boys Ltd; László Gál: Rolf Kalman; Laura Z. Hobson: Alex Gotfryd; Douglas C. Jones: Andrew Kilgore; Barbara M. Joosse: Peter C. Joosse; Ursula Le Guin: Lisa Kroeber; Riki Levinson: Gerry Levinson; Kate McMullan: Jerry Orabona; Louise Meriwether: James E. Hinton; Frances A. Miller: John A. Miller; Lilian Moore: Joan Glazer; Nancy Correll Roberts: Jeep Hunter; Eric Edward Rofes: copyright © by Kent Garvey; Marilyn Sachs: Morris Sachs; Isaac Watts: National Portrait Gallery, London.

something about the author

ALTER, Judith (MacBain) 1938-
(Judy Alter)

PERSONAL: Born July 22, 1938, in Chicago, Ill.; daughter of Richard Norman (a physician) and Alice (Peterman) MacBain; married Joel Alter (a physician), May 16, 1964 (divorced August, 1982); children: Colin, Megan, Jamie, Jordan. *Education:* University of Chicago, B.A., 1961; Northeast Missouri State University, M.A., 1964; Texas Christian University, Ph.D., 1970. *Religion:* Protestant. *Residence:* Fort Worth, Tex. *Office address:* Texas Christian University Press, Box 20783, Fort Worth, Tex. 76129. *Agent:* Ray Peekner Literary Agency, 3210 S. Seventh St., Milwaukee, Wis. 53215.

CAREER: Chicago Osteopathic Center, Chicago, Ill., typist and secretary, 1954-61; Kirksville College of Osteopathic Medicine, Kirksville, Mo., writer and editor in public relations, 1962-64; Fort Worth Osteopathic Hospital, Fort Worth, Tex., secretary, 1965-66, editor of employee publication, 1965-73, public relations consultant, 1971-73; Texas College of Osteopathic Medicine, Fort Worth, director of publications, 1972, acting director of public information, 1977-78, associate director of news and information, 1978-80; free-lance writer, 1973-75; Texas Christian University, Fort Worth, instructor in English as a second language, 1975-76, editor of Texas Christian University Press, 1982-87, director of Texas Christian University Press, 1987—. *Member:* Western Writers of America (member of board of directors, 1976-77; president, 1985-86), Authors Guild, Western American Literature Association, Southwestern American Literature Association. *Awards, honors:* Texas Institute of Letters Award, 1984, for *Luke and the Van Zandt County War.*

WRITINGS—Under name Judy Alter: (With Phil Russell) *The Quack Doctor,* Branch-Smith, 1974; *Stewart Edward White* (pamphlet), Boise State University, 1975; *Dorothy Johnson*

JUDITH ALTER

1

(pamphlet), Boise State University, 1975; *After Pa Was Shot* (juvenile), Morrow, 1978; (with Sam Pearson) *Single Again,* Branch-Smith, 1978.

The Texas ABC Book, Branch-Smith, 1981; (with Joyce Roach) *Texas and Christmas,* Texas Christian University Press, 1983; *Luke and the Van Zandt County War* (illustrated by Walli Conoly), Texas Christian University Press, 1984; *Mattie* (novel), Doubleday, 1988.

Author of book reviews and of two columns, "Along Publishers' Row," for *Roundup,* and "Women's Lit.," a review column in *Fort Worth Star Telegram,* 1974-75.

WORK IN PROGRESS: So Far from Paradise, a novel about the establishment of a ranching empire in North Central Texas, was commissioned by the *Fort Worth Star-Telegram* as a project for the Sesquicentennial celebration in Texas and ran in that newspaper in the spring of 1986—it is currently under consideration by a commercial publisher; two "first readers": *Growing Up in the Old West* and *Women in the Old West* for F. Watts; a book about a girl on a Texas ranch, circa 1895, who wants to join a wild west show, entitled *The Girl Who Could Beat Annie Oakley; A Ballad for Sallie* is based on available material about street children in the Hell's Half Acre of Fort Worth in the 1880s.

SIDELIGHTS: "I always wanted to write—I feel as if publication has come after years of paying dues. I am very interested in Texas history as a viable subject for juvenile and adult fiction. I am most grateful to contacts made through Western Writers of America. I see discouragement for the new writer with no contacts, and wish the system could be changed.

"My interest in Western literature grew out of American literature studies in graduate school but gradually I have become more interested in popular literature rather than academic studies. My first juvenile novel, *After Pa Was Shot,* grew out of scraps of a story in the memoirs of a long-time Texas resident. It is, to me, the work which really justified my calling myself a writer. My writing began as strictly non-fiction, and it was a long, slow transition. For a long time, I thought I simply couldn't write fiction, and lots of short story manuscripts buried in my files seem to support that idea. But the idea for this novel just seemed suddenly right and I tried it. I was most fortunate to have an editor who really worked with me in revisions and rewrites.

"Now I see myself, both as editor and author, as more and more interested in the undeveloped potential of regional fiction for.young adult readers. Both my juvenile novels are rooted in Texas, growing out of actual historical events. Somehow, all my novels are told in the first person by a female narrator— it's a voice I'm most comfortable with."

HOBBIES AND OTHER INTERESTS: Cooking, gardening, reading.

FOR MORE INFORMATION SEE: Fort Worth Star Telegram, May 9, 1978.

BAILEY, John (Robert) 1940-

PERSONAL: Born November 4, 1940, in Grantham, England; son of Arthur Edwin (a draper) and Florence Edith (a housewife; maiden name, Adnitt) Bailey; married Susanne Lysbeth Waddams (a music teacher), May 19, 1970; children: Martin

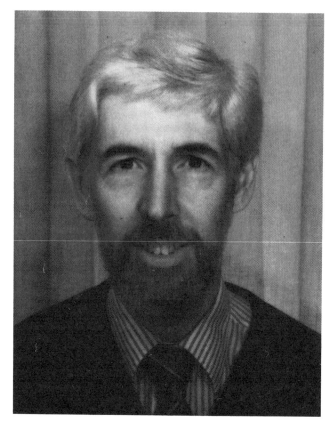

JOHN BAILEY

John, Simon Robert. *Education:* St. John's College, Cambridge, M.A., mechanical science, M.A., theology, 1965; University of Nottingham, M.Ed., 1977. *Religion:* Christian. *Office:* County Hall, Bedford, England.

CAREER: Inner London Education Authority, London, England, advisory teacher of religious studies, 1969-71; writer and editor, 1969—; Lincolnshire County Council, Lincolnshire, England, religious education advisor, 1972-79; Manchester, England, district inspector of education, 1980-83; Bedfordshire, England, county chief inspector of education, 1983—.

WRITINGS—Juvenile: (Editor) *New Life: Songs and Hymns for Assemblies, Clubs and Churches* (music and words), Galliard, 1971; (editor) *Folk Sound* (folk song collection; with tape), Galliard, 1971; (editor) *Blue-print: A Series of Reference Books for Use in Secondary School Assemblies . . . ,* Galliard, Books 1 and 2: 1976, Books 3 and 4: 1977; (reteller with Kenneth McLeish and David Spearman) *Gods and Men: Myths and Legends from the World's Religions* (illustrated by Derek Collard, Charles Keeping, and Jeroo Roy), Oxford University Press, 1981; (with Marian Collihole) *Themework: Assembly Material for Junior, Middle and Lower Secondary Schools,* Stainer & Bell, 1981; *Stories from the Old Testament,* Beaver Books, 1982; *Stories from the New Testament,* Beaver Books, 1982; *Religion in Life: Religious Buildings and Festivals,* Schofield & Sims, 1984; *Founders, Prophets, and Sacred Books,* Schofield & Sims, 1985; *Worship: Ceremonial and Rites of Passage,* Schofield & Sims, 1986; *Religious Leaders and Places of Pilgrimage,* Schofield & Sims, 1987; *Religious Beliefs and Moral Codes,* Schofield & Sims, 1988.

WORK IN PROGRESS: Hymns and Hymnwriters, in collaboration with wife, Susanne, a music teacher.

SIDELIGHTS: Bailey's writing career began as the result of his interest in folk songs. "In 1969 I was a teacher of religious education and my hobby was folksinging. I began to use folk songs in my teaching, and new Christian songs in school assembly. I happened to meet the managing editor of Galliard (Stainer & Bell), the firm which held the copyright to many contemporary Christian songs and hymns. I persuaded Bernard Braley, managing director of Galliard, that there was a need for an inexpensive collection of hymns and songs for use in school assembly. He agreed, and asked me to edit it. This I did, and *New Life* appeared in 1971. I also edited a collection of folk songs for use in religious education, *Folk Sound,* which appeared together with a tape of forty-seven songs in 1971. Soon after this, I became editor of a collection of stories, readings, and resources for school assembly called *Blueprint.* This appeared in four volumes in 1976 and 1977. By this time I was beginning to enjoy writing the occasional article or story, as well as just editing other people's words."

By 1977 Bailey was becoming increasingly intrigued with the subject of world religions in religious education. A meeting with the deputy publisher at Oxford University Press resulted in his fourth book. "I suggested that there was a need for a collection of myths and legends about creation and flood, drawn from the major religions of the world, and Oxford University Press asked me to edit and write it. I involved two friends as co-authors—Kenneth McLeish, an experienced writer of Greek myths and legends, and David Spearman, an English adviser who was an expert in Anglo Saxon and Norse mythology. I wrote most of *Gods and Men* and did much of the research for it, but Kenneth McLeish deserves the credit for shaping and polishing my writing style. I have the happy facility of writing clear, simple, straightforward accounts of existing stories; Kenneth, the professional writer, added the gloss.

"*Themework,* at about the same time, continued my association with Stainer & Bell, and again I wrote many of the stories and readings, this time in association with Marian Collihole, a primary teacher and fertile source of children's stories.

"In 1981 I was discussing the dearth of good, clear, well-illustrated text books for religious education with one of the directors of Schofield & Sims, and once again found myself talked into writing a series to 'plug the gap.'" Bailey described this series as "an attempt to explain clearly and simply the main themes of the major religions of the world."

"I write mainly in the school summer holidays, either at home or at a campsite in France, as this is my main period of 'spare time.'"

She was a lioness, the size of a house, with sharp teeth and rending claws. ■ (From "Ra and Sekhmet" in *Gods and Men: Myths and Legends from the World's Religions,* retold by John Bailey, Kenneth McLeish, and David Spearman. Illustrated by Charles Keeping.)

BAIRD, Bil 1904-1987

OBITUARY NOTICE—See sketch in *SATA* Volume 30: Given name William Britton Baird; born August 14, 1904, in Grand Island, Neb.; died of pneumonia, March 18, 1987, in New York, N.Y. Puppeteer and author. During a career that spanned nearly six decades, Baird became famous for the multitude of puppets that he created and the variety of ways in which they performed. He began his professional career in 1928, working for celebrated puppeteer Tony Sarg. Eventually, Baird went into business for himself, passing on his knowledge to younger puppeteers such as Jim Henson of "Muppets" fame. In collaboration with his wife Cora, Baird governed nearly every aspect of his puppet performances, often choreographing, composing music, staging productions, and filming in addition to building and operating the marionettes. His puppet creations include Snarky Parker, Slugger Ryan, the Spider Lady, and Charlemane the Lion. The Baird marionettes appeared in Broadway musicals and films—notably, "The Sound of Music"—as well as television shows like "Life with Snarky Parker," "The Whistling Wizard," and "The Bil Baird Show." Baird's book *The Art of the Puppet* is considered by many to be a classic in its field. He also wrote *Puppets and Population* and *Schnitzel, the Yodeling Goat.*

FOR MORE INFORMATION SEE: Current Biography, H. W. Wilson, 1954; *Contemporary Authors,* Volume 106, Gale, 1982; *Who's Who in America,* 44th edition, Marquis, 1986. Obituaries: *Los Angeles Times,* March 20, 1987; *New York Times,* March 20, 1987; *Chicago Tribune,* March 21, 1987; *Facts on File,* March 27, 1987; *Newsweek,* March 30, 1987; *Time,* March 30, 1987; *Current Biography,* May, 1987.

Fairy land,
Where all the children dine at five,
And all the playthings come alive.
—Robert Louis Stevenson

CAROL BARKIN

BARKIN, Carol 1944-
(Elizabeth Carroll, Beverly Hastings)

PERSONAL: Born December 22, 1944, in Fort Worth, Tex.; daughter of C. Knight (a physician) and Julie (a nurse; maiden name, Murphy) Aldrich; married Coleman Barkin (a music and special event producer), August 31, 1969; children: David Knight. *Education:* Radcliffe College, B.A. (cum laude), 1965.

CAREER: Editor. Abelard-Schuman, London, England, editor, 1965-67; Follett Publishing Co., Chicago, Ill., editor, 1967-69; Elk Grove Press, Los Angeles, Calif., editor, 1969-70; Sullivan Educational Systems, Los Angeles, editor, 1970-72; Lothrop, Lee & Shepard Co., New York, N.Y., editor, 1973-76; author, 1975—; free-lance editor, 1976—. *Member:* Authors Guild, Society of Children's Book Writers, Mystery Writers of America. *Awards, honors: I'd Rather Stay Home* and *The Simple Facts of Simple Machines* were both chosen one of Child Study Association of America's Children's Books of the Year, 1975, *Slapdash Cooking,* 1976; *Slapdash Decorating* was chosen one of New York Public Library's Books for the Teen Age, 1980, 1981, and 1982, and *How to Write a Term Paper,* 1981, and 1982.

WRITINGS—Juvenile; all with Elizabeth James; all published by Lothrop, except as noted: *The Simple Facts of Simple Machines* (illustrated with photographs by Daniel Dorn, Jr. and with diagrams by Susan Stan), 1975; *Slapdash Sewing* (illustrated by Rita Flodén Leydon), 1975; *Slapdash Cooking* (illustrated by R. F. Leydon), 1976; *Slapdash Alterations: How to Recycle Your Wardrobe* (illustrated by R. F. Leydon), 1977; *Slapdash Decorating* (illustrated by R. F. Leydon), 1977; *How to Keep a Secret: Writing and Talking in Code* (illustrated by Joel Schick), 1978; *What Do You Mean by "Average"? Means, Medians, and Modes* (illustrated by J. Schick), 1978; *How to Grow a Hundred Dollars* (illustrated by J. Schick), 1979.

How to Write a Term Paper, introduction by Leland B. Jacobs, 1980; *The Complete Babysitter's Handbook* (illustrated by R. F. Leydon), (paperback) Wanderer, 1980, (hardcover) Messner, 1981; *A Place of Your Own* (illustrated with photographs by Lou Jacobs, Jr.), Dutton, 1981; *How to Write a Great School Report,* introduction by M. Jean Greenlaw, 1983; *The Scary Halloween Costume Book* (illustrated by Katherine Coville), 1983; (under joint pseudonym Elizabeth Carroll) *Summer Love,* Wanderer, 1983; (under joint pseudonym Beverly Hastings) *Watcher in the Dark,* Pacer, 1986; *How to Write Your Best Book Report* (illustrated by Roy Doty), 1986; *Happy Thanksgiving!* (illustrated by Giora Carmi), 1987; *School Smarts: How to Succeed at Schoolwork,* 1988.

"Transition" series; all with E. James; all illustrated with photographs by Heinz Kluetmeier; all published by Raintree, 1975: *Are We Still Best Friends?; Doing Things Together; I'd Rather Stay Home; Sometimes I Hate School.*

"Money" series; all with E. James; all published by Raintree, 1977: *Managing Your Money* (illustrated by Santos Paniagua); *Understanding Money* (illustrated by D. Hockerman); *What Is Money?* (illustrated by Dennis Hockerman).

Other; all with E. James: (Under joint pseudonym Beverly Hastings) *Don't Talk to Strangers* (novel), Jove, 1980; *Helpful Hints for Your Pregnancy,* Fireside, 1984; (under joint pseudonym Beverly Hastings) *Don't Walk Home Alone* (novel), Jove, 1985; (under joint pseudonym Beverly Hastings) *Don't Cry, Little Girl* (adult novel), Pocket Books, 1987.

WORK IN PROGRESS: Several juvenile and adult projects, both fiction and nonfiction.

SIDELIGHTS: "When people ask me how I came to be an author, I tell them it was because I love books! As a child I was a voracious reader, and I still read too late into the night and sneak in another chapter of a book when I should be doing something else. In school I enjoyed the process of writing—even term papers.

"I also liked editing—fiddling around with other people's writing to see if I could make it clearer or more interesting to read—and when I finished college I was fortunate enough to find work as a children's book editor, first in London and then in Chicago. I had never thought about writing for children until then, but working on the books made me aware of how much expertise and care goes into every one of those volumes on the library and bookstore shelves.

"When I married and moved to Los Angeles, I met Elizabeth James and after working together on a short-lived magazine for children, we decided to try to collaborate on writing a book. Our first effort, *The Simple Facts of Simple Machines,* was published in 1975, and although I now live on the other side of the country, we have published nearly thirty books together—fiction and nonfiction for both children and adults. In addition, I continue to work as a free-lance editor; I find that working on other people's books gives me a very different and valuable perspective.

"Certainly no one could truthfully say that writing books is easy—sometimes it doesn't even seem like much fun! But for the most part I enjoy the process of trying to communicate the ideas or the story I have in mind to other people in the way that will work best. I think one of the reasons I enjoy it so much is that I only write about things that interest me. Whether it's fiction or nonfiction, for adults or for young children or in between, the idea has to be exciting to me or the writing

When you deposit money in a savings account, you are really lending your money to the bank. The bank in turn lends your money to other people and businesses. ■ (From *How to Grow a Hundred Dollars* by Elizabeth James and Carol Barkin. Illustrated by Joel Schick.)

comes out flat and plodding. And when an idea does grab me, it's very satisfying to keep working at it until the words on the page reflect as exactly as possible the thoughts I want to convey.

"What do I do when I'm not writing? My husband and I both love to travel and, along with our son, we squeeze in as many trips as we can around work and school schedules. We love poking around in the back streets and the flea markets as well as seeing the famous sights. There's something magical in immersing yourself in a new and unfamiliar place—it's almost like trying out a completely different life. And there's also something reassuring in discovering over and over again that despite the differences in culture and surroundings, people are as kind and helpful on the other side of the world as they are right next door. Though I don't write travel books, I think exploring new places and experiencing all the vast and subtle differences that make new surroundings so fascinating helps me to observe and describe things better when I do sit down to write."

BATEY, Tom 1946-
(Jasper Tomkins)

PERSONAL: Born December 19, 1946, in Des Moines, Iowa; son of Harry H. (a university professor) and Katherine (a university professor; maiden name, Marshall) Batey; married Marcia Keizer (an artist), August 16, 1984. *Education:* Attended Washington State University, 1965-67; University of Washington, Seattle, B.F.A., 1971. *Home:* Route 1, Box 914, Eastsound, Wash. 98245.

CAREER: Bantam Books, Inc., New York, N.Y., staff artist, 1971-74; Great Northwest Publications, Bellevue, Wash., art director, 1974-78; free-lance writer and artist, 1978—. *Awards, honors: The Catalog* was listed among the five best children's books in the world at the International Children's Book Fair, Bologna, Italy, 1981, and received the Pacific Northwest Booksellers Prize, 1982; *The Catalog* was selected a Children's Choice by the Children's Book Council, 1981, and *The Sky Jumps into Your Shoes at Night,* 1986; Parents' Choice Award from the Parents' Choice Foundation, 1984, for *The Hole in the Ocean!;* Washington Children's Choice Picture Book Award from the Washington Library Media Association, 1985, for *Nimby.*

WRITINGS—Juvenile; under pseudonym Jasper Tomkins; all self-illustrated; all published by Green Tiger Press: *The Catalog,* 1981; *Nimby: A Remarkable Cloud,* 1982; *The Hole in the Ocean! A Daring Journey,* 1984; *The Sky Jumps into Your Shoes at Night,* 1986; *When a Bear Bakes a Cake,* 1987; *The Mountains Crack Up!,* 1987; *The Balancing City,* 1988.

WORK IN PROGRESS: "All the work I will ever do is currently in progress. I am always collecting bits and pieces of thought in the form of words and drawings. When I finish a book it simply means that part of the collection of ideas has come together to form a single unit."

TOM BATEY

SIDELIGHTS: "When I was a child I thought I would be a scientist like my father. I was always very curious and liked to find out how things worked. I loved taking clocks apart and putting them back together. One day I was sent to the principal's office in grade school because I was caught giving electric shocks to students during recess. I had batteries in my pockets and wires running down my sleeves.

"In high school I took all the math and science classes possible. But in college my life suddenly changed after I took an art class. From then on I just had to be an artist. Once I had my art degree I went to New York City and began to work as a designer at a large publishing house. I began to see famous authors bringing in their latest books. And then I knew I had to be an author in addition to being an artist. Several years later my first book, *The Catalog,* came out in the book stores. What a thrill it was to fly to Italy to receive an award for that book at the International Children's Book Fair!

"Now I look back and realize that everything I have done in my whole life has led perfectly to this moment. The books I make are all little containers of my life experiences. I take great delight in the wondrous world around me. Behind every tree, flower, rock, and snail is a lurking surprise. The earth is alive with great majesty and charm. All that there is, down to the smallest raindrop or grain of sand is alive with the joy upon which we are based. If my books can convey some of this joy, I am pleased.

"For me the great bonus in doing these books has been the chance to do programs in schools across the country. What a

real pleasure it has been to share my life with the children who read my books and are beginning to write their own.

"When I write, I draw. I draw what I see and feel. Then I think of the words. *The Mountains Crack Up!* is the sequel to *The Catalog.* My latest book, *The Balancing City,* will be quite a departure for me. Normally, I whittle my words down to the bare minimum and allow the illustrations to tell much of the story. *The Balancing City,* however, will be far more elaborate than my previous books and have much more text than illustration.

"I am curious to see how my new home affects my books in the future. My wife and I recently moved to Orcas Island off the coast of Washington State. It is wild and wonderful here. We are very isolated on the side of a mountain up over the ocean. There are deer munching around the house every day and eagles flying overhead. There are ferocious winds and there is absolute silence. It is the best dream ever."

BAUER, Caroline Feller 1935-

PERSONAL: Born May 12, 1935, in Washington, D.C.; daughter of Abraham (a lawyer) and Alice (an adviser of foreign students; maiden name, Klein) Feller; married Peter A. Bauer (president of White Stag), December 21, 1968; children: Hilary. *Education:* Sarah Lawrence College, B.A., 1957; Columbia University, M.L.S., 1958; University of Oregon, Ph.D., 1971. *Politics:* Democrat. *Religion:* Jewish. *Home:* 6892 Sea-

CAROLINE FELLER BAUER

The good thing about it is sometimes I get to stay up late. ■ (From *My Mom Travels a Lot* by Caroline Feller Bauer. Illustrated by Nancy Winslow Parker.)

way Circle, Huntington Beach, Calif. 92648; and 12 rue Andre Fleury 60500, Chantilly, France.

CAREER: New York Public Library, New York, N.Y., children's librarian, 1958, 1959, 1961; Colorado Rocky Mountain School, Carbondale, Colo., librarian, 1963-66; University of Oregon, Eugene, associate professor of library science, 1966-79. Lecturer, educational consultant. Producer of "Caroline's Corner" for KOAP-TV, 1973-74. *Member:* American Library Association, Society of American Magicians, Puppeteers of America, Bedlington Terrier Club of America. *Awards, honors:* Ersted Award, 1968, for distinguished teaching; *My Mom Travels a Lot* was chosen one of *New York Times* Best Illus-

trated Books of the Year, included in the American Institute of Graphic Arts Book Show, both 1981, and received the Christopher Award, picture book category, 1982; Dorothy McKenzie Award from the Southern California Council on Literature for Children and Young People, 1986, for distinguished contribution to children's literature.

WRITINGS: Children's Literature: A Teletext, Oregon Educational Public Broadcasting Service, 1973; *Getting It Together with Books,* Oregon Educational Public Broadcasting Service, 1974; *Storytelling,* Oregon Educational Broadcasting Service, 1974; *Caroline's Corner,* Oregon Educational Broadcasting Service, 1974; *Handbook for Storytellers,* American

Library Association, 1977; *Children's Literature,* Oregon Educational Broadcasting Service, 1978; *My Mom Travels a Lot* (illustrated by Nancy W. Parker), Warne, 1981; *This Way to Books* (illustrated by Lynn Gates), H. W. Wilson, 1983; *Too Many Books!* (illustrated by Diane Paterson), Warne, 1984; *Celebrations: Read-Aloud Holiday and Theme Book Programs,* H. W. Wilson, 1985; (editor) *Rainy Day: Stories and Poems* (illustrated by Michele Chessare), Lippincott, 1986; (editor) *Snowy Day: Stories and Poems* (illustrated by Margot Tomes), Lippincott, 1986; *Presenting Reader's Theater Plays and Poems to Read Aloud* (illustrated by Lynn Gates Bredeson), H. W. Wilson, 1987; *Midnight Snowman* (illustrated by Catherine Stock), Atheneum, 1987; *Halloween: Stories and Poems* (illustrated by Peter Sis), Lippincott, 1988; *Windy Day: Stories and Poems* (illustrated by Dirk Zimmer), Lippincott, 1988.

Also author of educational aids such as teletexts and videocassettes, including "Take a Poetry Break!" and "Creative Storytelling Techniques," and a sound recording, "What's So Funny? Humor in Children's Literature." Contributor to periodicals, including *Cricket* and *International Quarterly.*

ADAPTATIONS: "My Mom Travels a Lot" (cassette; sound filmstrip), Live Oak Media, 1982.

WORK IN PROGRESS: Storytellng book for children; professional book for early childhood educators.

SIDELIGHTS: "*Peripatetic* was a word that described the Mom in my book *My Mom Travels a Lot.* It means 'to there and elsewhere,' and it describes me perfectly. I travel a lot and when I'm home I go from one activity to the other all day long.

"If I'm at home I get up early and jog two miles, then I get in my car and drive along the ocean to where my horse lives. I ride around an oil field, the home of rabbits, skunks and foxes right in the middle of the bustle of a heavily populated suburb of Los Angeles. After I walk my dog, a Bedlington terrier, I'm finally ready to get to work.

"It's hard to describe what I do because besides being an author, I travel much of the time lecturing to teachers, librarians and parents and I speak to children, too. I had an ambition to lecture in all fifty states and have now achieved that goal. I've been lucky enough to speak at conferences and international schools in many foreign countries. Some of the more exotic places I've been are: Saudi Arabia, Sri Lanka, and Bangladesh. I love to travel and especially enjoy it if I'm going for a reason, such as telling people my ideas for bringing children and books together.

"I guess I don't want the same thing that happened to me to happen to other children. I didn't read for fun until I was in the sixth grade. In fact, I was passed on probation from the second to the third grade because of my poor (non-existent?) reading skills. I'm not sure why I didn't read. My mother and father read all the time, big fat tomes like *The Rise and Fall of the Roman Empire* and they discussed what they read at the dinner table. They also discussed world politics and philosophical and ethical questions. My mother took me to the library every week and we had our own home library, too. I loved to hear books read aloud and I listened to stories on the radio in the form of children's adventure series ('Superman,' 'Terry and the Pirates,' 'Captain Midnight') and adult soap operas. I drew lots of pictures, played with paper dolls and woodcrafting sets while I listened.

"I liked sports too. I ice-skated, rode a bike, played softball, and swam whenever I had the chance. I loved exploring. My dog and I went by ourselves through the neighborhood, across the golf course, or through the woods pretending we were the characters we heard about on radio.

"We moved to different cities, different schools because my father was a lawyer for the government and then the United Nations. Lots of famous people came to our house for dinner and they had wonderful discussions about everything—art, music, politics. I always thought my Dad said the most intelligent things in the wittiest way. My Mom was very curious about people so she was a terrific hostess. She didn't fuss with fancy food or place settings. She just made sure everyone was comfortable so they could talk.

"Somehow in the sixth grade I discovered books and read everything I could. My favorites in those days are still in print; The 'Freddy the Pig' books by Walter Brooks, *Mary Poppins, Dr. Dolittle,* and any story about dogs or horses.

"I'm still reading and my own family reads, too. My husband, Peter, and my daughter, Hilary, and I always take a book with us wherever we go. We read at meal times, on planes, and in the bathtub.

"Now you know why I wrote the books called *My Mom Travels a Lot* and *Too Many Books!* I travel a lot and I have lots and lots of books—but never too many."

Bauer's works are included in the de Grummond Collection at the University of Southern Mississippi.

HOBBIES AND OTHER INTERESTS: Travel (Europe, the Far and Near East, India), skiing (member of National Ski Patrol), jogging, tennis, ice skating, swimming, kayaking, horses, dogs, cooking (and eating), puppetry, magic, drawing, crafts.

BAUM, Louis 1948-

BRIEF ENTRY: Born March 15, 1948, in South Africa. Editor and author of books for young readers. Baum began his university studies at the South African College School, later transferring to the University of Cape Town where he received his B.A. He served as director of two associations and since 1980 has edited for the *Bookseller,* a London-based publication. Baum's first children's book, *Juju and the Pirate* (Andersen Press, 1983), illustrated by Phillipe Matter, tells the story of a parrot in search of a pirate friend. *School Library Journal* commended Baum for evoking in his readers "a feeling of caring and fondness . . . for . . . Juju so that the last scene will produce a sense of satisfaction as well as a few chuckles." *Are We Nearly There Yet?* (Bodley Head, 1986), addresses the sensitivity of families affected by divorce. According to the *Bulletin of the Center for Children's Books,* this work "subtly . . . says volumes about paternal love, and poignancy of the father/son relationship is heightened by the cool restraint of Baum's treatment." His other works include *I Want to See the Moon* (Bodley Head, 1984) and *After Dark* (Andersen Press, 1984).

The Love of Books, the Golden Key
That opens the Enchanted Door.
         —Andrew Lang

DELL BETHEL

BETHEL, Dell   1929-

PERSONAL: Born November 22, 1929, in Chicago, Ill.; son of Earl Francis (a sports artist) and Dolly (Bethel) Cowgill; married Pauline Dorothy Halter (a nursery school teacher), August 30, 1953; children: William Dell. *Education:* University of Minnesota, A.A., 1949; St. Cloud State College, B.S., 1955; Central Washington State College, M.Ed., 1964, and additional graduate study. *Politics:* Democrat. *Religion:* Lutheran. *Home:* North Ridgeville, Ohio.

CAREER: Professional baseball player with New York Giants, 1949-53; coach and teacher in Pine City, Minn., Sunnyside, Wash., and Banning, Calif., 1953-66; Olivet College, Olivet, Mich., associate professor of physical education, head of department, and head baseball coach, 1966-71; City College of the City University of New York, New York, N.Y., assistant professor of physical education and head baseball coach, 1971-73; Lake Ridge Academy, North Ridgeville, Ohio, athletic director, baseball and lacrosse coach, 1973-77; North Ridgeville High School, North Ridgeville, teacher and baseball coach, 1977-85. Has been a major league baseball scout for five years with the New York and San Francisco Giants. Technical director and an actor for the movie, ''Bang the Drum Slowly,'' 1972-73. Has taught baseball and English in Japanese schools. *Military service:* U.S. Army, Infantry and Rangers, 1951-53; served in Korea; became sergeant; received Bronze Star and Purple Heart. *Member:* American Association of College Baseball Coaches (member of international committee), Lions Club, Knife and Fork Club.

WRITINGS: (Contributor) Stephen Jones and Marion Murphy, *Geography and World Affairs,* 2nd edition, Rand McNally, 1962; *Inside Baseball: Tips and Techniques for Coaches and Players,* Reilly & Lee, 1969, revised edition, Contemporary

Books, 1980; (contributor) *The Best in Baseball,* Scholastic Athletic Services, 1970; *The Complete Book of Baseball Instruction,* Contemporary Books, 1978; *Coaching Winning Baseball,* Contemporary Books, 1979; *The Men of Old Baldy* (illustrated by son, William Bethel), Spectrum, 1987. Contributor to coaching periodicals.

WORK IN PROGRESS: Baseball the Major League Way; Green Peanuts and Blue Glue, a book for children ages five to twelve with illustrations by W. Bethel.

SIDELIGHTS: In 1953 Bethel's promising major league pitching career was ended by the Korean War. Bethel, who had been drafted into the army suffered serious head, leg, and hand injuries during a mission. Returning stateside, he went back to college, becoming a teacher and coach. His avid interest in baseball eventually led to writing books on the game. ''I have enjoyed writing because it gives me an opportunity to tell a story or to add to a person's ability by stretching his mind, expanding his horizon, and sharing an experience with him. I minored in journalism at the University of Minnesota, and wrote for the school paper, mainly human interest stories and character sketches.

''Basically, I've written from a lifetime of experiences in baseball from the sandlots to the major leagues. I try to share with young people great players' ways of thinking, playing and excelling at this splendid game and to show how they have reached the top in their profession. I want every young person who reads my books to go away with some definite tips and ways of making himself a better player or coach.

''Each person, as he reads and studies the pages of my books, will, hopefully, gain some inspiration, desire for the hard work needed to accomplish his goal, and a blueprint for getting the most out of his natural ability. I combine these objectives with the teaching of baseball, 'the major league way,' and never losing sight of the fact that baseball should be fun. I feel that this all adds up to a winning formula for the reader and for myself.

''Baseball has been good to me and my family and this is one of the ways I have of paying the game and the great people I've worked with back. This is my way of making a contribution to the game of baseball and the young people I've worked with over the years.

''I write in longhand on legal pads. I will interview people all over the world in their special area of baseball. I will tap my own experiences. I use illustrations, pictures, and drawings to teach specific aspects of the game of baseball or to illustrate a definite technique or mechanic.

''I usually write from 6:00 a.m. to 12:00 noon. You must be disciplined in your writing, writing every day about the things you know and have experienced. I feel everyone has a story to tell and something worthwhile to share with other people, but many lack the discipline and willingness to put in the 'hard work' needed to be a writer.

''When working with young, aspiring writers, I ask them, 'Do you think you can write one page of a story each day?' 'Why of course!' is the usual answer. 'Well then, at the end of a year, you will have a 365-page book,' I tell them. This is the real secret of unlocking the story in a writer's mind and heart.''

HOBBIES AND OTHER INTERESTS: Fishing, wilderness trips, chess, reading books of all types with special emphasis on the study of great people.

FOR MORE INFORMATION SEE: Strength and Health, April, 1962; *Saturday Review,* June 28, 1969; *Library Journal,* July, 1978.

BLAKE, Quentin 1932-

PERSONAL: Born December 16, 1932, in Sidcup, Kent, England; son of William (a civil servant) and Evelyn Blake. *Education:* Downing College, Cambridge, M.A., 1956; University of London Institute of Education, PGCE, 1956-57; attended Chelsea School of Art, 1958-59. *Home:* Flat 8, 30 Bramham Gardens, London SW5 0HF, England. *Agent:* Georges Borchardt, Inc., 136 East 57th St., New York, N.Y. 10022; and A. P. Watt Ltd., 26-28 Bedford Row, London WC1R 4HL, England.

CAREER: Illustrator, drawing for *Punch,* beginning 1948, and other British magazines, including *Spectator,* and illustrating children's and educational books; free-lance illustrator, 1957—; Royal College of Art, London, tutor in School of Graphic Design, 1965-78, head of Illustration Department, 1978-86, visiting tutor, 1986—. Has also worked as an English teacher at Lycee in London, 1962-65. *Exhibitions:* Work has been exhibited at the London Group, England, 1987 and Royal Academy, 1984, 1986, 1987. *Military service:* Served in the Army Education Corps, 1951-53.

AWARDS, HONORS: Put on Your Thinking Cap was selected one of Child Study Association of America's Children's Books

QUENTIN BLAKE

At three o'clock in the afternoon of Saturday 6th June 1959, Agaton Sax, Editor-in-Chief of the *Bykoping Post,* was sitting at his desk in the editorial office of that paper. ■ (From *Agaton Sax and the Diamond Thieves* by Nils-Olof Franzén. Illustrated by Quentin Blake.)

of the Year, 1969, *Arabel's Raven,* 1974, *Custard and Company,* 1985, and *The Giraffe and the Pelly and Me,* 1986; Hans Christian Andersen honor book for illustration from the International Board on Books for Young People, 1976, for *How Tom Beat Captain Najork and His Hired Sportsmen,* and 1982, for *Mister Magnolia; A Near Thing for Captain Najork* was selected one of *New York Times* Best Illustrated Books of the Year, 1976.

Kate Greenaway Medal from the British Library Association, and Children's Book Award from the Federation of Children's Book Groups, both 1981, both for *Mister Magnolia;* Kate Greenaway Medal high commendation, 1980, for *The Wild Washerwomen;* elected to Royal Designer for Industry, 1980; Kurt Maschler Award runner-up from the National Book League (England), 1982, for *Rumbelow's Dance; The Witches* was selected one of *New York Times* Outstanding Books of the Year, 1983; *The Rain Door* and *Cyril Bonhamy and Operation Ping* were exhibited at the Bologna International Children's Book Fair, 1985; awarded the Silver Brush (Holland), 1986.

WRITINGS—Self-illustrated children's books: *Patrick,* J. Cape, 1968, Walck, 1969; *Jack and Nancy,* J. Cape, 1969; *A Band of Angels* (picture book for adults), Gordon Fraser, 1969; *Angelo,* J. Cape, 1970; *Snuff,* Lippincott, 1973; *Lester at the Seaside,* Collins Picture Lions, 1975; *Lester and the Unusual Pet,* Collins Picture Lions, 1975; (compiler with John Yeoman) *The Puffin Book of Improbable Records,* Puffin, 1975, published in America as *The Improbable Book of Records,* Atheneum, 1976; *The Adventures of Lester,* B.B.C., 1978; (compiler) *Custard and Company: Poems by Ogden Nash,* Kestrel, 1979, Little, Brown, 1980; *Mister Magnolia,* Merrimack, 1980; (with J. Yeoman) *Rumbelow's Dance,* Hamish Hamilton, 1982; *Quentin Blake's Nursery Rhyme Book,* J. Cape, 1983, Harper, 1984; *The Story of the Dancing Frog,* J. Cape, 1984, Knopf, 1985; *Mrs. Armitage on Wheels,* Cape, 1987.

Illustrator: Evan Hunter, *The Wonderful Button,* Abelard, 1961; Frances Gray Patton, *Good Morning, Miss Dove,* Penquin,

1961; John Moore, editor, *The Boys' Country Book,* Collins, 1961; Rosemary Weir, *Albert the Dragon,* Abelard, 1961; Edward Korel, *Listen and I'll Tell You,* Blackie, 1962, Lippincott, 1964; John Moreton, *Punky: Mouse for a Day,* Faber, 1962; Ezo, *My Son-in-Law the Hippopotamus,* Abelard, 1962; Rupert Croft-Cooke, *Tales of a Wicked Uncle,* Cape, 1963; Richard Schickel, *The Gentle Knight,* Abelard, 1964; Joan

The new aunt's name was Bundlejoy Cosysweet. ■ (From *How Tom Beat Captain Najork and His Hired Sportsmen* by Russell Hoban. Illustrated by Quentin Blake.)

Tate, *The Next-Doors,* Heinemann, 1964; R. Weir, *Albert the Dragon and the Centaur,* Abelard, 1964; R. Weir, *The Further Adventures of Albert the Dragon,* Abelard, 1964; Fred Loads, Alan Gemmell and Bil Sowerbutts, *Gardeners' Question Time,* BBC Publications, 1964, second series, 1966; Ennis Rees, *Riddles, Riddles Everywhere,* Abelard, 1964; James Britton, editor, *The Oxford Books of Stories for Juniors,* 3 volumes, Oxford University Press, 1964-66.

E. Rees, *Pun Fun,* Abelard, 1965; Bill Hartley, *Motoring and the Motorist,* BBC, 1965; Charles Connell, *Aphrodisiacs in Your Garden,* Mayflower, 1965; Barry Ruth, *Home Economics,* Heinemann Educational, 1966; Jules Verne, *Around the World in Eighty Days,* Chatto, 1966; Thomas L. Hirsch, *Puzzles for Pleasure and Leisure,* Abelard, 1966; Robert Tibber, *Aristide,* Hutchinson, 1966, Dial, 1967; Marjorie Bilbow and Antony Bilbow, *Give a Dog a Good Name,* Hutchinson, 1967; J. Tate, *Bits and Pieces,* Heinemann, 1967; E. Rees, *Tiny Tall Tales,* Abelard, 1967; J. Tate, *Luke's Garden,* Heinemann, 1967; Helen J. Fletcher, *Put on Your Thinking Cap,* Abelard 1968; G. Broughton, *Listen and Read with Peter and Molly,* BBC, 1968; Gordon Fraser, editor, *Your Animal Book,* Gordon Fraser, 1969; H. P. Rickman, *Living with Technology,* Zenith Books, 1969; G. Broughton, *Success with English: The Penguin Course,* Penguin, 1969; Nathan Zimelman, *The First Elephant Comes to Ireland,* Follett, 1969; James Reeves, *Mr Horrox and the Gratch,* Abelard, 1969; E. Rees, *Gillygaloos and the Gollywhoppers: Tall Tales about Mythical Monsters,* Abelard, 1969.

We got some other things from automatic machines too. ■ (From *Arabel's Raven* by Joan Aiken. Illustrated by Quentin Blake.)

I put out to sea
in a wooden row-boat
with a cheese and pickle sandwich
and a yellow hat and coat.

(From *You Can't Catch Me!* by Michael Rosen. Illustrated by Quentin Blake.)

Gillian Edwards, *Hogmanay and Tiffany: The Names of Feasts and Fasts,* Geoffrey Bles, 1970; D. Mackay, B. Thompson and P. Schaub, *The Birthday Party,* Longman, 1970; Elizabeth Bowen, *The Good Tiger,* J. Cape, 1970; H. J. Fletcher, *Puzzles and Quizzles,* Platt, 1970; Thomas Corddry, *Kibby's Big Feat,* Follett, 1970; H. Thomson, *The Witch's Cat,* Addison-Wesley, 1971; J.B.S. Haldane, *My Friend Mr Leakey,* Puffin, 1971; Ruth Craft, *Play School Play Ideas,* Penguin, 1971; Aristophanes, *The Birds,* translated by Dudley Fitts, Royal College of Arts, 1971; G. Broughton, *Peter and Molly,* BBC, 1972; Sid Fleischman, *McBroom's Wonderful One-Acre Farm,* Chatto & Windus, 1972; Natalie Savage Carlson, *Pigeon of Paris,* Blackie, 1972, Scholastic, 1975; Norman Hunter, *Wizards Are a Nuisance,* British Broadcasting Corp., 1973; Julia Watson, *The Armada Lion Book of Young Verse,* Collins, 1973; R. C. Scriven, *The Thingummy-jig,* BBC, 1973; F. Knowles and B. Thompson, *Eating,* Longman, 1973; Clement Freud, *Grimble,* Penguin, 1974; Dr. Seuss (pseudonym of Theodor Seuss Geisel), *Great Day for Up!,* Random House, 1974; Bronnie Cunningham, editor, *The Puffin Joke Book,* Penguin, 1974.

Willis Hall, *The Incredible Kidnapping,* Heinemann, 1975; W. Hall, *Kidnapped at Christmas,* Heinemann Educational, 1975; G. Broughton, *Peter and Molly's Revision Book,* BBC, 1975; Lewis Carroll, *The Hunting of the Snark,* Folio Society, 1976; Sylvia Plath, *The Bed Book,* Faber, 1976; Adele De Leeuw, *Horseshoe Harry and the Whale,* Parents Magazine Press, 1976; Ellen Blance and Ann Cook, *Monster Books,* 24 Volumes, Longman, 1976-1978; S. Fleischman, *Here Comes*

He was very depressed. ■ (From *Willie the Squowse* by Ted Allan. Illustrated by Quentin Blake.)

McBroom!, Chatto, 1976; Margaret Mahy, *The Nonstop Nonsense Book,* Dent, 1977; Sara Brewton and others, *Of Quarks, Quasars and Other Quirks: Quizzical Poems for the Supersonic Age,* Crowell, 1977; Ted Allan, *Willie the Squowse,* McClelland & Stewart, 1977, Hastings House, 1978; Carole Ward, *Play School Ideas 2,* BBC, 1977; Stella Gibbons, *Cold Comfort Farm,* Folio Society, 1977; B. Cunningham, editor, *Funny Business,* Penguin, 1978.

Helen Young, *What Difference Does It Make, Danny?,* Deutsch, 1980; Evelyn Waugh, *Black Mischief,* Folio Society, 1981; S. Fleischman, *McBroom and the Great Race,* Chatto & Windus, 1981; Jonathan Gathorne-Hardy, *Cyril Bonhamy v. Madam Big,* J. Cape, 1981; Tony Lacey, editor, *Up with Skool!,* Kestrel, 1981; Tim Rice and Andrew Lloyd Webber, *Joseph and the Amazing Technicolor Dreamcoat,* Holt, 1982; J. Gathorne-Hardy, *Cyril Bonhamy and the Great Drain Robbery,* J. Cape, 1983; E. Waugh, *Scoop,* Folio Society, 1983; Rudyard Kipling, *How the Camel Got His Hump,* Macmillan (England), 1984, Bedrick Books, 1985; J. Gathorne Hardy, *Cyril Bonhamy and Operation Ping,* J. Cape, 1984; Jeff Brown, *A Lamp for the Lambchops,* Methuen, 1985; M. Mahy, *The Great Piratical Rumbustification and the Librarian and the Robbers,* Godine, 1986; Jan Mark, *Frankie's Hat,* Kestrel, 1986; Dr. Pete Rowan, *"Can You Get Warts from Touching Toads?",* Messner, 1987.

All by Joan Aiken, all published by BBC Publications, except as noted: *The Escaped Black Mamba,* 1973; *Tales of Arabel's Raven,* J. Cape, 1974, published as *Arabel's Raven,* Doubleday, 1974; *The Bread Bin,* 1974; *Mortimer's Tie,* 1976; *Mortimer and the Sword Excalibur,* 1979; *The Spiral Stair,* 1979; *Arabel and Mortimer* (includes *Mortimer's Tie, The Spiral Stair,* and *Mortimer and the Sword Excalibur*), J. Cape/BBC Publications, 1979, Doubleday, 1981; *Mortimer's Portrait on Glass,* 1980; *The Mystery of Mr. Jones's Disappearing Taxi,* 1980; *Mortimer's Cross* (Junior Literary Guild selection), J. Cape, 1983, Harper, 1984; *Mortimer Says Nothing,* Harper, 1987.

All by Patrick Campbell, all published by Hutchinson, except as noted: *Come Here Till I Tell You,* 1960; *Constantly in Pursuit,* 1962; *Brewing Up in the Basement,* 1963; *How to Become a Scratch Golfer,* Blond, 1963; *The P-P-Penguin Patrick Campbell,* Penguin, 1965; *Rough Husbandry,* 1965; *A Feast of True Fandangles,* W. H. Allen, 1979.

All by Roald Dahl: *The Enormous Crocodile,* Knopf, 1978; *The Twits,* Knopf, 1980; *George's Marvellous Medicine,* J. Cape, 1981, published in America as *George's Marvelous Medicine,* Knopf, 1982; *The BFG,* Farrar, Straus, 1982; *Roald Dahl's Revolting Rhymes,* J. Cape, 1982, Knopf, 1983; *The Witches* (ALA Notable Book), Farrar, Straus, 1983; *The Giraffe and the Pelly and Me,* Farrar, Straus, 1985; *Dirty Beasts,* Penguin, 1986; *Matilda,* Cape, 1988.

All by Nils-Olof Franzen: *Agaton Sax and the Diamond Thieves,* Deutsch, 1965, Delacorte, 1967; *Agaton Sax and the Scotland Yard Mystery,* Delacorte, 1969; *Agaton Sax and the Incredible Max Brothers,* Delacorte, 1970; *Agaton Sax and the Criminal Doubles,* Deutsch, 1971; *Agaton Sax and the Colossus of Rhodes,* Deutsch, 1972; *Agaton Sax and the London Computer Plot,* Deutsch, 1973; *Agaton Sax and the League of Silent Exploders,* Deutsch, 1974; *Agaton Sax and the Haunted House,* Deutsch, 1975; *Agaton Sax and the Big Rig,* Deutsch, 1976; *Agaton Sax and Lispington's Grandfather Clock,* Deutsch, 1978.

All by Russell Hoban: *How Tom Beat Captain Najork and His Hired Sportsmen* (ALA Notable Book; *Horn Book* honor list),

Atheneum, 1974; *A Near Thing for Captain Najork*, J. Cape, 1975, Atheneum, 1976; *The Twenty Elephant Restaurant*, J. Cape, 1980; *Ace Dragon Ltd.*, J. Cape, 1980, Merrimack, 1981; *The Marzipan Pig*, Farrar, Straus, 1986; *The Rain Door*, Crowell, 1987.

All by J. P. Martin: *Uncle*, J. Cape, 1964, Coward, 1966; *Uncle Cleans Up*, J. Cape, 1965, Coward, 1967; *Uncle and His Detective*, J. Cape, 1966; *Uncle and the Treacle Trouble*, J. Cape, 1967; *Uncle and Claudius the Camel*, J. Cape, 1969; *Uncle and the Battle for Badgertown*, J. Cape, 1973.

All by Michael Rosen: *Mind Your Own Business*, S. G. Phillips, 1974; *Wouldn't You Like to Know?*, Deutsch, 1977; *The Bakerloo Flea*, Longman, 1979; *You Can't Catch Me!*, Deutsch, 1981; *Quick, Let's Get Out of Here*, Deutsch, 1984; *Don't Put Mustard in the Custard*, Deutsch, 1986; *Under the Bed*, Prentice-Hall, 1986; *Smelly, Smelly Jellyfish*, Prentice-Hall, 1987.

All by John Yeoman: *A Drink of Water and Other Stories*, Faber, 1960; *The Boy Who Sprouted Antlers*, Faber, 1961, revised edition, Collins, 1977; *The Bear's Winter House*, World, 1969; *Alphabet Soup* (poem), Faber, 1969, Follett, 1970; *The Bear's Water Picnic*, Blackie, 1970, Macmillan, 1971; *Sixes and Sevens*, Blackie, 1971, Macmillan, 1972; *Mouse Trouble*, Hamish Hamilton, 1972, Macmillan, 1973; *Beatrice and Vanessa*, Hamish Hamilton, 1974, Macmillan, 1975; *The Young Performing Horse*, Hamish Hamilton, 1977, Parents Magazine Press, 1978; *The Wild Washerwomen: A New Folktale* (*Horn Book* honor list), Greenwillow, 1979; *Rumbelow's Dance*, Hamish Hamilton, 1982; *The Hermit and the Bear*, Deutsch, 1984; *Our Village*, Walker Books, 1988.

Also illustrator of *Is That So?* by Peter Rowan, 1986.

Also illustrator of numerous other children's books. Illustrator for "Jackanory," BBC-TV. Contributor of illustrations to periodicals, including *Punch* and *Spectator*.

ADAPTATIONS: "Patrick" (filmstrip), Weston Woods, 1973; "Snuff" (filmstrip with record or cassette), Weston Woods, 1975; "Great Day for Up!" (filmstrip), Random House.

WORK IN PROGRESS: "I'm working on a book about the creative process of illustration, an autobiographical work which I hope will be interesting to children, adults and especially to art students."

SIDELIGHTS: Born December 16, 1932 in England, Blake is the son of a civil servant. "I grew up in Sidcup, near Kent, a suburb of London. I can remember drawing on the back of my exercise books as far back as primary school. I wasn't especially encouraged by anyone.

"Aside from children's comics, there wasn't a great deal of illustrated material available when I was a young boy. If you were growing up in a wealthy family, you would perhaps be conscious of Arthur Rackham. But in general, children had no notion of 'an illustrator.' Once I got past children's books, I became an omnivorous reader. I read anything and everything.

"I submitted drawings and wrote for the Chislehurst Grammar School magazine, *The Chronicle*. My most significant experience at Chislehurst was meeting Alfred Jackson, a cartoonist for *Punch* and other magazines. His wife, my Latin teacher, took an interest in my drawings, and arranged a meeting between us. I was fifteen at the time, and had no idea how one went about submitting drawings to magazines. After my informative meeting with Jackson, however, I began to send my work to *Punch*. For two years they quite rightly rejected my work. But eventually they accepted a few small drawings. I was drawn to the work of Ronald Searle and Andre Francois. I was influenced by them, not in terms of style, but because each in his own way seemed to be absolutely unrestricted by the conventions of illustration.

"After Chislehurst I did my national service, becoming a soldier of sorts for two years." As a national serviceman Blake taught English at Aldershot and illustrated a reader for illiterate soldiers.

"Then I went to Cambridge University to read English. I had decided against art school because I wanted an education in literature. Had I enrolled in art school I knew that I would lose the opportunity to study literature, whereas in my pursuance of literature, I could still continue to draw. I spent three years at Cambridge, where I drew for their undergraduate magazines, and occasionally for *Punch*. Then I did a year of teacher's training at London University. On the verge of becoming a teacher, I quit the training program and went back to what I had always intended for myself—art and illustration.

Lovely girls in spangled pants
Ride on gilded elephants.

■ (From "The Big Tent under the Roof" in *Custard and Company*, poems by Ogden Nash. Selected and illustrated by Quentin Blake.)

"I began freelancing, and was soon hired to do one drawing per week for *Punch*. I also worked for the *Spectator*, a major literary magazine. I became a part-time student at Chelsea College of Art, because I wanted to learn more about life drawing and painting. I chose Chelsea because I was familiar with the work of Brian Robb, a painter/illustrator/cartoonist who lectured there. I had read an article about him, and felt he was the type of artist with whom I would like to study. He did, in fact, influence my attitude toward work, especially toward book illustration. He later left Chelsea for the Royal College of Art where he became head of the illustration department. Years later, he invited me to teach there.

"I attended Chelsea for eighteen months. The experience gained in life drawing and painting was very important, and as a result my drawings became richer. I have always liked economical, reduced drawings. A possible analogy is soup—the more ingredients you add to the broth, the better the taste. So it is with my drawings. It is my diverse background knowledge and experience that has made the simplicity of my drawings possible. I also discovered that when working in black and white, you can actually paint out or correct mistakes. That was an enormously liberating discovery and helped free me from a lot of inhibitions.

"My early cartoons were funny, which was their main objective. I was not at all interested in political satire, which is probably why my career developed more in the direction of book illustration than cartooning. I was drawn to the drama of illustration and the theatricality of it. Books offered a continuity of narrative, which was very important to me. I was interested in storytelling and in showing how people react, how they move, and how they're placed in a scene. I was fascinated with the way one could tell a story by visually portraying the action of the characters. Of course, I didn't identify this as a motive at the time, but it certainly had a lot to do with my development in the direction of book illustration.

"For *Punch* I had to think up funny things and invent visual jokes. Whereas for the *Spectator* I was briefed once a week when I went to the office and expected to come up with something by the next day. One week it was Krushchev, the next it was French cooking. I liken this kind of work, and the versatility it demands, to repertory acting: one week you're Ophelia and the next Macbeth."

Blake never uses models for his work. "If I want to draw a character pulling on his trousers, I would never have someone pose, or check the gesture in the mirror. I try to *remember* what an action looks like. Perhaps my drawing will not reflect the action with absolute precision, but it will reflect how the action *feels*. When I imagine the feeling as I draw it, the emotion becomes part of the illustration. I draw gesture, and gesture is not a fixed moment in time. Pulling on trousers can take several minutes. There is an early part, a middle and a late part of any action or movement. This is why I try to identify with the *feeling* of doing something. In this sense,

A talking dog had been taken ill with a sore throat and they were desperate for a replacement. ■
(From *The Story of the Dancing Frog* by Quentin Blake. Illustrated by the author.)

illustration is like mime. Of course you must have knowledge of anatomy to make things look real, but all of my drawing is a mixture of knowledge and feeling.''

Blake works in pen and ink and watercolor. ''Over the years I have evolved a distinct style, a 'handwriting' which is recognizable. My work has developed in two ways. When I started drawing, I was either tight and nervous or so relaxed that I lost part of the drawing. Now I am able to relax in the work and draw well. I can be loose, but accurate. I have also learned quite a bit about book design, how a book flows from beginning to end. I am better at pacing now and have come to understand how a *whole* book works.

''My drawings are meant to look as though they are easy to execute. That, however, is rarely the case; they are carefully planned. Going back to the theater analogy, I would say the drawings are well rehearsed. When an actor comes onstage and falls over dead, the audience believes he just fell over, not thinking how he rehearsed his fall sixty, seventy times to make it look perfectly natural. Likewise, I make a lot of drawings before I get to the one which feels right.''

Blake works a schedule of regular hours each day. ''I get things *ready,* and, eventually, start drawing. Once you begin to draw, you start solving problems. As soon as you make a mark, life flows into the drawing and forces you on. If I have a set of thirty drawings to do, I usually complete a set of rough sketches first before I do any one finished drawing. Sometimes I start at the beginning, other times I begin with a drawing I especially want to do. I keep sketching until I have a feeling for the way the whole book ought to look. I prefer to immerse myself in one book at a time to gain a feeling for the whole by relating to all the drawings.

''I often do the easy drawings first because if I get them right, I tend to feel better about the rest. I don't adhere to that old adage offered to children, 'Carry on and do the next in line, however difficult.' Once I do the easy drawings, I feel better and can go back and face the difficult ones with confidence.

''I'm not one of those artists who require absolute silence in order to work. I can live with interruption—perhaps because of the kind of drawing I do. I draw quite rapidly, so the most difficult bits, such as the expression, don't actually take very long to do.''

Blake has illustrated books for such well-known authors as Roald Dahl and John Yeoman. ''I work in different ways with different authors. I know John Yeoman very well, he is an old friend, and I would call our working relationship a collaboration. It's easy to talk to him about illustration. I also take drawings to Roald Dahl for his reactions. 'What you've drawn is what I wrote,' Dahl will say. 'But it might be better if we did it another, less literal way.' That is collaboration.

''I approached the illustration of Dahl's work as if I were working on the artificial world of a Samuel Beckett play. Many of Dahl's characters embody awfulness and have no redeeming features. I must keep in mind that, like Beckett's worlds, Dahl's stand above all *literary* worlds. This is what I tried to convey in my drawings.

''J. P. Martin's 'Uncle' books were lots of fun to illustrate. His proliferative imagination provided a constant supply of new characters and bizarre situations. Every time I turned the page, there was something new to draw, resulting in very stimulating and lively work.

My grandmother was the only grandmother I ever met who smoked cigars. ■ (From *The Witches* by Roald Dahl. Illustrated by Quentin Blake.)

''Once I accept a manuscript, I read it intensively and then start drawing, capturing my surge of response to the text. One shouldn't start off with 'What does the author want?' or consult with him in the beginning. The first collaboration is with the story. If you're the right illustrator for the text, you get a rush of ideas and feelings from the story itself. Then you can go to the author and confer. If you're not the right illustrator, I don't believe the collaboration will ever be fruitful.

''Collaboration must be team work, but it can be a funny sort of team. It's interesting to discover someone who is different from you, but with whom you feel a rapport and a common sense of humor. Russell Hoban and Roald Dahl are quite different from me. I have to make an effort to adapt my way of drawing and my way of thinking to theirs. If the gap is too great, I obviously can't serve the text. If there is a genuine lack of sympathy, there is no point in going on.''

About his own books, Blake observed, ''Most of the books I've written are really just sequences of drawings with text added for necessary explanations. My urge is to draw, and the story is worked out later. The illustrations are, so to speak, *leading* the story. *The Story of the Dancing Frog* was my only book not written like this. Illustrating it was a bit like working on someone else's manuscript. I'm delighted that I can do both, but if I had to give up one, I would give up writing.

"Working on my own books is often more of a headache. When you illustrate someone else's text, that text is well defined when you start. You get the manuscript, you start, you find the structure, think about the mood, the characters and how to fit them into the illustration. You want to do well by the story, but there are limits. When you work on your own text, however, you can change the pictures, or change the text at will. Everything is up for negotiation. The possibilities are infinite. It's like swimming in mud; all I can think about is, 'Where's the shore?'"

Of his own books, his favorite is *Mister Magnolia*. "It's not autobiographical, but reflects the things I like in *pictures*."

Blake lives in a flat in London and owns a fifteenth-century seaside house in Hastings, on the south coast of England. "The house was built about 1450, when Henry VI was king of England, and about a hundred years before Shakespeare was born. It's made of oak beams with the spaces in between filled with mud.

"What's nice about having two places is that they are very different. My London flat is large and overlooks a garden with trees. A young friend who came to visit put it best when he said, 'It's just the kind of place Sherlock Holmes would live in.' The point of having a place outside of London is that it enables me to go somewhere peaceful without distractions when I have a lot of work to do. The house is near the sea, so no matter how much work I bring, I feel I'm on holiday."

Blake has won many prestigious awards for his work. "I do cherish the Kate Greenaway Medal for *Mister Magnolia*. My favorite, however, was the Children's Book Award from the Federation of Children's Book Groups, which is actually awarded by children—their vote decides the winner. What you win is not a medal or money, but a book filled with their own writing and drawing, all in response to your books. Quite a marvelous prize indeed!

"I don't have children, but am still in touch with the child in me, and this has been immensely important to me as an artist. Part of keeping one's child-self alive is not being embarrassed to admit it exists."

Blake, head of the illustration department at the Royal College of Art from 1978-1986, offered the following advice to young artists: "You must want to draw all the time, because that is the only way you can get good at it. You can study a certain amount of technique, but *doing it* is the key element. Beyond this, I am disinclined to prescribe anything because one of the main aspects of being an illustrator or children's author is that you are a hybrid, a mixture of many elements. I've met other illustrators and have observed that none of us are the same. Some illustrators place an emphasis on color or texture, some on landscape, others on the light or the season in which the illustrations take place. I tend to be concerned with people— the faces they make and the way they move. If you have the instinct to want to draw and to tell stories in pictures, there are many ways to approach illustration and many different things one might contribute. Look at other artists' work but don't be too influenced by them. Go on drawing, go on doing the job, and you will find out what you really like, and what you have to contribute. In this sense, there are no rules. Everybody's got to find out for himself."

—*Based on an interview by Kathleen Betsko.*

FOR MORE INFORMATION SEE: *Punch*, December 15, 1965; *Graphis*, number 131, 1967, (children's book edition) September, 1975; Lee Kingman and others, compilers, *Illustrators of*

Children's Books: 1957-1966, Horn Book, 1968; *New Statesman*, October 31, 1969, November 9, 1973, November 21, 1980; *Spectator*, December 5, 1970, April 16, 1977; *Puffin Post*, Volume 17, number 8, 1973; *Horn Book*, February, 1974; *New York Times Book Review*, November 3, 1974; *Signal*, January 16, 1975; Martha E. Ward and Dorothy A. Marquardt, *Illustrators of Books for Young People*, Scarecrow, 1975; *Folio*, autumn, 1976; L. Kingman and others, compilers, *Illustrators of Children's Books: 1967-1976*, Horn Book, 1978; *Times Literary Supplement*, March 28, 1980, November 26, 1982; *Times Educational Supplement*, March 28, 1980, October 31, 1980; *Books for Keeps 1*, March, 1980; *Cricket*, April, 1980; Sally Holmes Holtze, editor, *Fifth Book of Junior Authors and Illustrators*, H. W. Wilson, 1983; Brigid Peppin and Lucy Micklethwait, *Book Illustrators of the Twentieth Century*, Arco, 1984.

BOORSTIN, Daniel J(oseph) 1914-

PERSONAL: Born October 1, 1914, in Atlanta, Ga.; son of Samuel Aaron (an attorney) and Dora (Olsan) Boorstin; married Ruth Carolyn Frankel, April 9, 1941; children: Paul, Jonathan, David. *Education:* Harvard University, B.A. (summa cum laude), 1934; Oxford University, Balliol College (Rhodes Scholar), B.A. (first class honors), 1936, B.C.L. (first class honors), 1937; Yale University (Sterling fellow), J.S.D., 1940. *Politics:* Independent. *Religion:* Jewish. *Home:* 3541 Ordway St. N.W., Washington, D.C. 20016.

CAREER: Admitted as barrister-at-law, Inner Temple, London, England, 1937, admitted to the Massachusetts Bar, 1942; Harvard University, Cambridge, Mass., history instructor, 1939-

DANIEL J. BOORSTIN

The whole idea of "separate but equal"—even if it could have been enforced—was wrong. ■
(From *The Landmark History of the American People: From Appomattox to the Moon* by
Daniel J. Boorstin. Photograph courtesy of Fred Ward.)

42; Office of Lend-Lease Administration, Washington, D.C., senior attorney, 1942; Swarthmore College, Swarthmore, Pa., assistant professor of history, 1942-44; University of Chicago, Chicago, Ill., 1944-69, began as assistant professor, became Preston and Sterling Morton Distinguished Professor of History, 1956-69; Smithsonian Institution, Washington, D.C., director of National Museum of History and Technology, 1969-73, senior historian, 1973-75; appointed Librarian of Congress, Washington, D.C., 1975-87. Fulbright visiting lecturer at University of Rome, 1950-51, and Kyoto University, 1957; lecturer for U.S. Department of State in Turkey, Iran, Nepal, India, and Ceylon, 1959-60. First occupant of chair of American history at the Sorbonne, Paris, 1961-62; fellow of Trinity College, and Pitt Professor of American History and Institutions at Cambridge University, 1964-65; Shelby and Kathryn Cullom Davis Lecturer, Graduate Institute of International Studies, Geneva, Switzerland, 1973-74.

MEMBER: American Studies Association (president, 1969-70), American Historical Association, American Academy of Arts and Sciences, American Antiquarian Society, Authors Guild, National Press Club, American Philosophical Society, International House of Japan, Colonial Society of Massachusetts, Phi Beta Kappa, Elizabethan Club (Yale University), Cosmos Club (Washington, D.C.). *Awards, honors:* Bancroft Prize from Columbia University, and Friends of American Literature Prize, both 1959, both for *The Americans: The Colonial Experience;* Francis Parkman Medal of American Society of Historians, and Patron Saints Award of Society of Midland Authors, both 1966, both for *The Americans: The National Experience;* D.Litt. from Cambridge University, 1968, and numerous other honorary degrees; Dexter Prize from the Society for the History of Technology, and Pulitzer Prize for history, both 1974, both

for *The Americans: The Democratic Experience;* La decoration d'Officier de l'Ordre de la Couronne from His Majesty the King of the Belgians, 1980; Chevalier de l'Ordre de la Legion de'Honneur presented by the French government, 1984; Grand Officer of the Order of Prince Henry the Navigator by the government of Portugal, 1985, and the Watson-Davis Prize of the History of Science Society, 1986, both for *The Discoverers: A History of Man's Search to Know His World and Himself;* First Class Order of the Sacred Treasure from the government of Japan, 1986.

WRITINGS: The Mysterious Science of the Law, Harvard University Press, 1941, reissued, Peter Smith, 1973; (editor) *Delaware Cases, 1792-1830,* three volumes, West, 1943; *The Lost World of Thomas Jefferson,* Holt, 1948, reissued, University of Chicago Press, 1982; *The Genius of American Politics,* University of Chicago Press, 1953; *The Americans: The Colonial Experience,* Random House, 1958, new edition published as *The Americans 1: The Colonial Experience,* 1985.

America and the Image of Europe: Reflections on American Thought, Meridian, 1960; (editor) *A Lady's Life in the Rocky Mountains,* University of Oklahoma Press, 1960; *The Image: What Happened to the American Dream,* Atheneum, 1962, new edition published as *The Image: A Guide to Pseudo-Events in America,* Harper, 1964; *The Americans: The National Experience,* Random House, 1965, new edition published as *The Americans 2: The National Experience,* 1985; (editor) *An American Primer,* two volumes, University of Chicago Press, 1966; (with Ruth F. Boorstin) *The Landmark History of the American People* (juvenile), Random House, Volume I: *From Plymouth to Appomattox,* 1968, Volume II: *From Appomattox to the Moon,* 1970, new edition, two volumes, Random House,

Hundreds of thousands of young Americans gathered near Woodstock, New York, in August 1969. ■ (From *The Landmark History of the American People: From Appomattox to the Moon* by Daniel J. Boorstin. Photograph courtesy of Wide World Photos.)

1987; *The Decline of Radicalism: Reflections of America Today,* Random House, 1969.

The Sociology of the Absurd; or, The Application of Professor X, Simon & Schuster, 1970; (editor) *American Civilization,* McGraw, 1972; *The Americans: The Democratic Experience,* Random House, 1973, new edition published as *The Americans 3: The Democratic Experience,* 1985; *Democracy and Its Discontents: Reflections on Everyday America,* Random House, 1974; *The Exploring Spirit: America and the World, Then and Now,* Random House, 1976; (editor) *America in Two Centuries: An Inventory,* Arno, 1976; *Visiting Our Past: America's Historylands,* National Geographic Society, 1977; *The Republic of Technology: Reflections on Our Future Community,* Harper, 1978.

(With Brooks Kelley) *A History of the United States,* Ginn, 1980; *The Discoverers: A History of Man's Search to Know His World and Himself,* Random House, 1983; *Hidden History: Exploring Our Secret Past,* Harper, 1987.

Editor of the thirty-volume *History of American Civilization,* University of Chicago Press. Former editor of American history for *Encyclopaedia Britannica.* Contributor to *Harper's, Newsweek, U.S. News & World Report, Commentary, New York Times Book Review, Fortune, Esquire, Life,* and *Look.*

WORK IN PROGRESS: The Creators—a companion volume to *The Discoverers*—to be published by Random House. "Just as *The Discoverers* was a history of man's search to know the world and himself, *The Creators* will be a history of man's search to fulfill himself in the arts—architecture, sculpture, painting, music, drama, and literature."

SIDELIGHTS: **October 1, 1914.** Born in Atlanta, Georgia, Boorstin's grandparents were Jewish immigrants from Russia. "Long ago, I fell in love with fact. Nothing in the world is as divine as fact. Being an American and a Jew is a great advantage in studying history. As a Jew, I am somewhat peripheral to the Christian world—as Veblen said, we are 'clay pots put among iron vessels.' As an American, I am grateful to history and to our ancestors for the unexpected. History, as I have said, is largely the study of the unexpected. Because of that, I believe that the dogmatic theories of history are false and corrupting. They prevent us from being ready for the unexpected." [Michael Ryan, "GEOConversation: Daniel J. Boorstin," *GEO,* May, 1982.[1]]

1916. Family moved to Tulsa, Oklahoma after Boorstin's father, a young attorney, helped defend Leo Frank, a factory supervisor who was wrongly accused of murder and lynched. A wave of anti-Semitism followed the case, and the family relocated to the pioneer town of Tulsa, where young Boorstin was raised.

1930. Entered Harvard University at the age of fifteen. "I went to high school—a good high school in Tulsa—during the Depression, and I got into Harvard on the 'highest seventh' plan. That was a scheme that made it possible for the top students from schools in the sticks to get into Harvard without

(From *The Landmark History of the American People: From Plymouth to Appomattox* by Daniel J. Boorstin.)

taking the college entrance examinations; the assumption was that they wouldn't pass, and that was probably true. The only college entrance examination I took was in English composition, to try to get out of a freshman writing course. I failed it.''¹

During his Harvard undergraduate years, Boorstin was an editor of the *Crimson* and won the Bowdoin Prize for an essay on Gibbon's *Rise and Fall of the Roman Empire.* ''Well, in those days there was an anti-Semitic tinge to the place. But I wouldn't say that anti-Semitism was at all dominant. There were some great figures on the faculty then—Alfred North Whitehead, John Livingston Lowes and Irving Babbitt. It was a great time to be there.''¹

1934. Graduated summa cum laude from Harvard. ''I intended to go to law school, perhaps because my father was a lawyer. But there were some fine courses offered in history and literature. Then, at the beginning of my junior year, my grandfather died. It was the first experience I had had with death, and it impelled me toward science. I thought I should be a doctor. I switched to biochemistry. In a year and a half, I realized that I wasn't made for science. I was miserable in the laboratory. I switched back to English history and literature.''¹

Accepted a Rhodes scholarship to study law at Oxford University. ''I won a Rhodes scholarship from Tulsa. I went to

(Cover design by Alexi Brodovitch from *The Image: A Guide to Pseudo-Events in America* by Daniel J. Boorstin.)

Balliol College, Oxford, and studied law; I thought that if I stayed in England, I might want to become a barrister. I received a Bachelor of Civil Law degree and went to the Inner Temple until I was called to the bar. I never practiced. When I returned to this country, I went to Yale law school, then back to Harvard to teach English and law.''¹

1936-37. Earned Oxford's most prestigious academic honor—a double first—when awarded a B.A. in jurisprudence and a B.C.L. (Bachelor of Civil Law). In 1937 Boorstin also passed the English bar examination, thus becoming a barrister-at-law. ''There were serious problems in this country; it was the Depression. But the more time I spent in England, the more I became interested in this country, in its culture and history and civilization.''¹ Returned to the United States.

1939. Taught American literature and history at Harvard University. Member of the Communist party until Hitler's rise to power in 1939.

April 9, 1941. Married Ruth Carolyn Frankel. The couple had three sons, Paul, David and Jonathan. Ruth Boorstin has edited all her husband's books.

1942. Admitted to the Massachusetts bar and two years later began a twenty-five-year career teaching American history at the University of Chicago. While on the faculty, Boorstin spent considerable time traveling as a consultant, researcher, and visiting professor to universities throughout the world. He also began to write during his tenure at the University. ''I loved the University of Chicago; it's the greatest university in the world. Still one of the peculiarities of American civilization is the fluidity of institutions. We're not good at distinctions, and there aren't sharp boundaries in our culture between anything and anything else. This is true of institutions as well, and the distinctions between being in a library and being in a university aren't that sharp either.

''In this country, we don't have an intelligentsia. We have an educated group and a semieducated group and a quasieducated group. Do you realize that we have twelve million students in so called institutions of higher learning? Twelve million! We have more faculty members in the country than there are students in all the British universities. There is a creative chaos in this country that blurs the distinction between intellectuals and nonintellectuals.''¹

1969. Left Chicago to assume the directorship at the Smithsonian Institution's National Museum of History and Technology.

1974. Awarded the Pulitzer Prize in history for the third volume of *The Americans.* ''. . . Any history is impossible to write. There is an infinite number of facts about anything. . . . You have to decide what to cut away. You simply have to approach the writing of history with a curiosity and a passion for what interests you. If other people don't agree with you, too bad. When I wrote *The Americans,* I devoted a large amount of attention to the history of packaging; I was interested in how people persuade people to make decisions and purchases. I was criticized for that, but epistemologically speaking, I think it's one of the most important subjects in the history of this nation. I've always believed in the cosmic significance of trivia.

''The world's a very interesting place. As I've studied it, I've focused more and more on individual people rather than on the history of ideas. I've found that *things* predominate over ideas as well, and that technology itself is fascinating. I've also concentrated on the experience of the peoples: you know, the word *experience* occurs in the subtitle of each volume of *The Americans*.

"I deal only with civilizations, not with prehistory. I don't go back to prehistory, as H. G. Wells did in his *Outline of History*. He was much more interested in empires and civilizations than I am. I'm more interested in the great openings of the mind and the great experiences of mankind.''[1]

1975. President Ford asked Boorstin to accept the position of Librarian of Congress; Boorstin's presidential appointment was opposed, however, by the American Library Association because he was not a professional librarian, and by the Congressional Black Caucus because of his stand toward affirmative action. "Before I accepted President Ford's nomination, my wife and I needed a month to reflect on the offer. I considered myself a writer. Still do. I want to be a *writer* when I grow up—I consider that my ambition. I had launched on a world history, partly as a project of self-education, and I wondered if I should not devote full time to it. My wife and I wandered anonymously in the Library. In the manuscript room—this seems as if it were scripted, but it's true—we came on an exhibit about the selection of Librarians by Presidents. In it was an exchange of correspondence on the selection of Archibald MacLeish. F.D.R. wrote to Felix Frankfurter asking for help in the matter: 'I have had a bad time picking a Librarian to succeed Putnam. What would you think of Archie MacLeish?' MacLeish, you know, was not a professional librarian. Frankfurter wrote back, 'What is wanted in the directing head of a great library [is] imaginative energy and vision. He should be a man who knows books, loves books, and makes books.'' I knew Felix Frankfurter and admired him—found him a stirring man—and I decided to accept the President's nomination.'' ["The Talk of the Town," *New Yorker*, January 5, 1981.[2]]

November 12, 1975. Became the twelfth Librarian of Congress directing a \$200-million-dollar organization that is housed in three buildings on Capitol Hill in Washington, D.C. The national library has the largest known collection (twenty million books) and is staffed by 5,800 people. "The library is the greatest cultural resource in the world—and that's an understatement. In the United States, it fulfills a much broader function than the national libraries of other countries do: it is both a parliamentary library and a national library. In most countries, those are separate—France and Great Britain, for example. The one major exception is the National Diet Library in Japan, set up after World War II and modeled on the Library of Congress.

"In most countries, the parliamentary library is focused on politics, economics and statistics. The combination of a national and a parliamentary library here provides Congress with a wider context. It gives our lawmakers access to a whole world of culture—history, literature and philosophy.''[1]

"I was aware that the Library had great treasures. One of the themes of my books is that culture in a democratic society has a special role to play—especially in the New World—as a catalyst for learning. I wanted to make certain that the Library was more than a warehouse—that it was also a wellspring for the discovery of culture. My first object was not to make things worse. The Library was a sound institution, with good staff. But I wanted to open it up. When I opened the front doors, which had been closed for some time, so the public could come into the Great Hall of this beautiful building instead of coming into the basement, some people objected. 'You'll create a draft,' they said. That's *just* what I wanted to do. I wanted to draw people in!''[2]

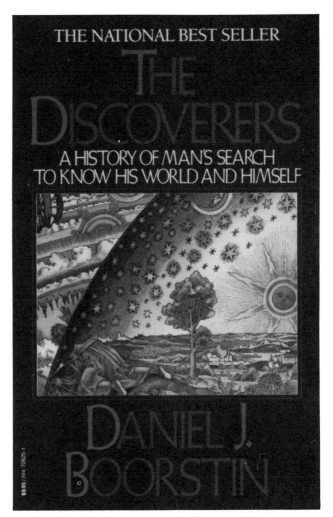

(Jacket illustration from *The Discoverers* by Daniel Boorstin. Early sixteenth-century woodcut reprinted courtesy of The Bettmann Archive.)

"We've coined the phrase 'multimedia encyclopedia' to describe this institution. Most national libraries are confined to works on paper. Here, we have collected still photographs, posters, graphic designs, recorded music on discs and tapes, and films—both fictional and documentary. Some of these come to us through the copyright process—every document copyrighted in the United States is received here. We also seek out gifts of materials that are peculiar to American civilization. But we must not confine ourselves simply to works on paper. This is a versatile and fidgety civilization we live in; without materials in other media, the record would not be complete.

"Anybody can use the Library of Congress. To get into the British Library, you need a letter of introduction. At the Bibliothèque Nationale in Paris, it's even harder. But if you're wearing shoes and you behave yourself, you can use the Library of Congress.''[1]

1983. Continued to write from his home in the early mornings before going to work. "In my confirmation hearings, before the Rules Committee, Senator Claiborne Pell, who has been chairing the Joint Committee on the Library, said he hoped that I would not write another book while I was Librarian. I told him I saw nothing wrong with the Librarian of Congress being involved with scholarly pursuits, and I got confirmed. Before I accepted President Ford's nomination, I called Archie

MacLeish and asked, 'Should I take the job?' He asked me, 'How much sleep do you need? I need eight hours a night, which is too much if I am to write and do anything else.' It's a piece of luck that I don't need much sleep. I take little naps, and I've always been an early riser—. . . at my desk at six o'clock . . .—which is early, but not as early as Jefferson. Anyway, I was determined to write after I came here. I do all my writing before I come in to the Library. . . ."[2]

Historians admired by Boorstin include: ". . . Huizinga and R. H. Tawney and J. B. Bury and Samuel Eliot Morison—but Edward Gibbon is my idol. *The Decline and Fall of the Roman Empire* was the first book I read that interested me in the study of history. If anybody led me into the study of history, it was Gibbon, because he practiced history as a literary art.

"It's been my observation that professionalization tends to be the enemy of literary art in history. It allows people to put jargon in the place of elegance. The literary artist has to take care to find exactly the right word; jargon provides an easy substitute. It removes precisely the iridescence and ambiguity that are wonderful in literature and language and history."[1]

1985. The government of Portugal made Boorstin a Grand-Officer of the Order of Prince Henry the Navigator for his work on his historical book, *The Discoverers: A History of Man's Search to Know His World and Himself.* "Every great discovery discloses hitherto unimagined realms of ignorance. That's why one of the themes of my new book is that the great obstacle to progress is not ignorance but the illusion of knowledge.

"Those who said that we didn't know as much as we thought were the prophets, the discoverers. The courage to believe that we don't know what we think we know is the first stage in discovery. This was the courage of such men as Copernicus, Galileo and Magellan.

"If there is a lesson for us in examining the history of discovery, it is that the increase of our knowledge and the increasing reverence for science may lead us to underestimate the amount of our ignorance.

"History reminds us that every supposedly complete discovery has been incomplete. Newton was adored for having *at last* discovered the laws of the movement of the spheres and the earth. But Newton's work was not the ending; it was only a new beginning.

"People like to think that discoveries provide the final answer, but usually what they provide is a new question.

"In my research, I came very quickly to the conclusion that there is no such thing as a typical discoverer.

"For example, Paracelsus, who played a leading role in the history of medicine, was a mystic and so disrespectable that he was driven from the town where he was trying to practice medicine. But another medical discoverer, William Harvey, was the king's physician; he was eminently respectable.

"Christopher Columbus was passionately religious and to some extent a mystic, while Amerigo Vespucci, who followed Columbus, was a much more open and tentative person.

"There turns out to be an unpredictable spectrum of possibilities among those who were discoverers. There's no pattern.

"The ironies and the unpredictability that I came upon confirmed my notion that history is not the search for laws but the science of uniqueness. It's the way of discovering the spectrum of human possibilities so that we don't get stuck in the rut of the familiar." [Daniel Boorstin, "History Teaches 'We Don't Know What We Think We Know,'" *U.S. News & World Report,* March 5, 1984.[3]]

On June 15, 1987, Boorstin left his position as Librarian of Congress to devote more time to writing and lecturing. In his spare time, he enjoys outdoor activities, including tennis, swimming, hiking, bird watching, and gardening on his nine-acre place, "Mount Vernon View," in southern Maryland. "I probably wouldn't have written most of my books if I had been properly trained as a historian. But I didn't know what the ruts were, and I didn't know where the highway was. And the highway usually becomes a rut for any profession. So I had to do what interested me." ["Interview: Daniel J. Boorstin," *Omni,* May, 1986.[4]]

Boorstin's books have been translated into thirteen languages.

FOR MORE INFORMATION SEE: Newsweek, February 26, 1962; *American Historical Review,* April, 1962, February, 1971; *Kenyon Review,* January, 1966; Robert A. Skotheim, *American Intellectual Histories and Historians,* Princeton University Press, 1966; *Book Week,* March 5, 1967; *Current Biography,* September, 1968, January, 1984; *Best Sellers,* November 1, 1968; *Children's Book World,* November 3, 1968; *New York Times Book Review,* November 24, 1968; Marcus Cunliffe and Robin W. Winks, editors, *Pastmasters: Some Essays on American Historians,* Harper, 1969; *Village Voice,* October 2, 1969; *Vital Speeches of the Day,* October 15, 1969; *Washington Star,* November 9, 1969, July 27, 1975; *Washington Post,* November 18, 1969, January 29, 1984.

New York Review, February 12, 1970; *National Review,* April 7, 1970; *Nation,* March 6, 1971; John Wakeman, editor, *World Authors: 1950-1970,* H. W. Wilson, 1975; *Publishers Weekly,* November 29, 1976, March 21, 1986; *Authors in the News,* Volume II, Gale, 1976; *U.S. News & World Report,* May 15, 1978, March 17, 1980, March 5, 1983, March 5, 1984; *Christian Science Monitor,* December 5, 1978, December 14, 1979, March 18, 1987.

Smithsonian, April, 1980; "The Talk of the Town," *New Yorker,* January 5, 1981; *People,* April 19, 1982; "Daniel J. Boorstin: Historian, Teacher, the Librarian of Congress," *GEO,* May, 1982; Larry Van Dyne, "Daniel Boorstin Remembers," *Washingtonian,* June, 1982; *New York Times,* July 8, 1983, November 16, 1983, January 31, 1987; Frank Annunziata, "Daniel J. Boorstin," *Dictionary of Literary Biography,* Volume 17, Gale, 1983; "Interview: Daniel J. Boorstin," *Omni,* May, 1986; *The Atlanta Constitution,* January 15, 1987; "Boorstin to Leave LC after 12 Years in Post," *School Library Journal,* February, 1987.

BOWEN, R(obert) Sydney   1900-1977   (James Robert Richard)

PERSONAL: Born in 1900, in Boston, Mass.; died of cancer, April 11, 1977, in Honolulu, Hawaii; married wife, Mary Ann; children: three sons, one daughter. *Residence:* Honolulu, Hawaii.

CAREER: Author, editor, and journalist. Began working as a journalist, 1918, for *London Daily Mail, Chicago Tribune* in

Paris, and for two Boston newspapers; served as editorial director for the International Civil Aeronautics Conference in Washington, D.C.; editor-in-chief, *Aviation* magazine; also editor of *Flying News* and several motor magazines; free-lance writer of fiction, 1930-77. *Military service:* U.S. Aviation Service, 1914-18; qualified as ace fighter pilot by shooting down eight enemy aircraft. *Member:* American Society for Promotion of Aviation (publicity director). *Awards, honors:* Junior Book Award from the Boys' Clubs of America, 1950, for *Fourth Down; Infield Flash* was selected one of Child Study Association of America's Children's Books of the Year, 1969.

WRITINGS—All published by Lothrop, except as noted: *Flying from the Ground Up,* McGraw, 1931; *Make Mine Murder,* Crown, 1946; *The Winning Pitch,* 1948; *Player, Manager,* 1949; *Fourth Down,* 1949; *Ball Hawk,* 1950; *Blocking Back,* 1950; *Hot Corner,* 1951; *Touchdown Kid,* 1951; *Canyon Fury,* 1952; *Pitcher of the Year,* 1952; *Behind the Bat,* 1953; *Infield Spark,* 1954; *The Million-Dollar Fumble,* 1954; *The Big Inning,* 1955; *The Last White Line,* 1955; *The 4th Out,* 1956; *No Hitter,* 1957; *The Big Hit,* 1958; *Triple Play,* 1959.

Hot Rod Angels, Chilton, 1960; *Pennant Fever,* 1960; *Million-Dollar Rookie,* 1961; *Bat Boy,* 1962; *Flight into Danger,* Chilton, 1962; *Wings for an Eagle,* Chilton, 1962; *Perfect Game,* 1963; *Dirt Track Danger,* Doubleday, 1963; *They Found the Unknown: The Stories of Nine Great Discoveries in the Field of Medical Knowledge,* Macrae, 1963; *Hot Corner Blues,* 1964; *Hot Rod Rodeo,* Criterion, 1964; *Rebel Rookie,* 1965; *They Flew to Glory: The Story of the Lafayette Flying Corps,* 1965; *Hot Rod Patrol,* Criterion, 1966; *Man on First,* 1966; *Hot Rod Showdown,* Criterion, 1967; *Lightning Southpaw,* 1967; *Hot Rod Outlaws,* Chilton, 1968; *Wipeout,* Criterion, 1969; *Infield Flash,* 1969; *Born to Fly,* Criterion, 1971; *Hot Rod Doom,* Criterion, 1973.

"Dave Dawson" series; all published by Crown: *Dave Dawson at Dunkirk,* 1941; . . . *in Libya,* 1941; . . . *on Convoy Patrol,* 1941; . . . *with the Pacific Fleet,* 1942; . . . *at Singapore,* 1942; . . . *with the Commandos,* 1942; . . . *on the Russian Front,* 1943; . . . *at Casablanca,* 1944; . . . *at Truk,* 1946.

"Red Randall" series; all published by Grosset & Dunlap: *Red Randall at Midway,* 1944; . . . *on New Guinea,* 1944; . . . *at Pearl Harbor,* 1944; . . . *in Burma,* 1945; . . . *in the Aleutians,* 1945; *Red Randall's One-Man War,* 1946.

Under pseudonym James Robert Richard; all published by Lothrop, except as noted: *The Club Team,* 1950; *Fighting Halfback,* 1952; *Quarterback, All-American,* 1953; *Phantom Mustang,* 1954; *The Purple Palomino,* 1955; *The Appaloosa Curse,* 1956; *Snow King,* Lippizan Horse, 1957; *Double M for Morgans,* 1958; *Joker, the Polo Pony,* 1959.

SIDELIGHTS: During World War I, fourteen-year-old R. Sydney Bowen enlisted in the United States Aviation Service. He distinguished himself by shooting down eight enemy aircraft, thus qualifying him as an ace fighter pilot. The experience left Bowen with a life-long interest in aviation.

After the war, Bowen began working as a journalist, writing articles for the Paris edition of the *Chicago Tribune* and the *London Daily Mail,* as well as for two Boston newspapers. He eventually combined aviation with journalism as editor-in-chief of *Aviation Magazine,* editor of *Flying News,* and publicity director of the American Society for Promotion of Aviation.

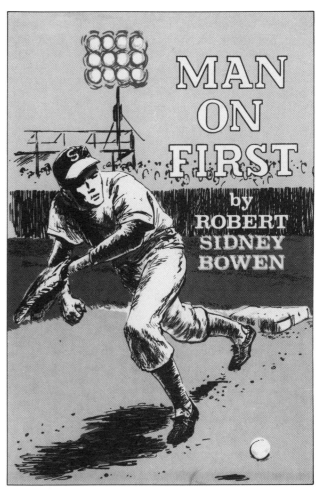

It was the tenth game of the season, and a Friday night crowd of some thirty-five hundred people had come to Honolulu Stadium. ■ (Jacket illustration by Richard W. Lewis from *Man on First* by Robert Sidney Bowen.)

He turned to fiction writing in 1930, writing for the next forty years numerous adventure novels, adventure stories for popular magazines of the day, and adventure series for boys. Shortly after the invasion of Poland during World War II, Crown Publishers commissioned Bowen to write an adventure story based on the war. The result was the first "Dave Dawson" adventure book. Dawson, a seventeen-year-old American-born R.A.F. ace, became a popular war hero with teenagers in England and the United States, netting Bowen about $10,000 in royalties each year. The closest rival was another teenage ace, Red Randall, whom Bowen also created. The "Red Randall" series, published by Grosset and Dunlap, sold about 200,000 copies in its first year.

To help him with the technical accuracy of the stories, Bowen compiled an enormous file on aviation during World War II by clipping newspaper articles and articles from over twenty magazines. He also read nonfiction books on the war as a hobby.

Writing boys' thrillers required a rigid working schedule as well as research. He wrote seven days a week, nine-to-five, from a rented office in Wilton, a Connecticut town where he and his family lived. In a good working day, he averaged 10,000 words. He refused to revise his writing, believing that any tampering with a story would spoil it.

In later years, Bowen abandoned his series books to write adventure stories about sports, horses, cars—almost any subject that interested young people. He died at the age of seventy-six of cancer in 1977 in Honolulu, Hawaii.

FOR MORE INFORMATION SEE: Oden Meeker and Olivia Meeker, "For Boys Only," *Collier's,* November 24, 1945; Martha E. Ward and Dorothy A. Marquardt, *Authors of Books for Young People,* 2nd edition, Scarecrow, 1971. Obituaries: *New York Times,* April 14, 1977.

BOWMAN, Kathleen (Gill) 1942-

PERSONAL: Born December 19, 1942, in Minneapolis, Minn.; daughter of Albert (a postman) and Inga (a nurse; maiden name, Thompson) Gill; married Daniel Clifford Bowman (an archaeologist), June 12, 1974; children: Susan, William, Geoffrey. *Education:* Attended Lawrence University, 1960-61; University of Minnesota, B.S. (with high distinction), 1964, M.A., 1967, Ph.D., 1977.

CAREER: Junior High School teacher of English and Spanish, Robbinsdale, Minn., 1964-66; University of Minnesota, Minneapolis, instructor in education, 1968-71; Hamline University, St. Paul, Minn., director of human relations, 1972-75; Minnesota Department of Education, St. Paul, program consultant, 1976-77; Legislative Advisory Council on the Economic Status of Women, research associate, 1977—. *Member:* American Civil Liberties Union, National Organization for Women, Women's Equity Action League, Women in State Employment, Phi Beta Kappa, Eta Sigma Epsilon.

WRITINGS—All for young people; all published by Creative Education, 1976: *New Women in Media; New Women in Entertainment; New Women in Social Sciences; New Women in Medicine; New Women in Art and Dance; New Women in Politics; On Stage: Johnny Cash* (biography); *On Stage: Elvis Presley* (biography). Also author of monographs, *Minnesota Women: State Government Employment* and *Minnesota Women: Education, Training and Job Market Reentry.* Editor of "New Women" series, Creative Education Press, 1976. Contributor to *Insports.*

WORK IN PROGRESS: Research on women in Minnesota state government employment, the status of the family, and women as homemakers.

SIDELIGHTS: "I have been trained as an academician, but I am most comfortable writing for young people and the general public, specifically on issues of a social or political nature. The driving force behind much of my work is the notion that equality requires not sameness, but *diversity,* along dimensions of age, sex, race, religion, and life-style."

HOBBIES AND OTHER INTERESTS: Weaving, classical piano.

CAUDELL, Marian 1930-

PERSONAL: Surname is pronounced "caw-*dell*"; born October 8, 1930, in Mitchell, Ind.; daughter of Samuel Wendell (a merchant) and Mildred (a homemaker; maiden name, Ridge) Holmes; married Don W. Caudell (a merchant), June 30, 1952; children: Don II, Kurt, Kelly, Klay. *Education:* Indiana University, A.B., 1952, M.S., 1967. *Home:* 821 West Oak St., Mitchell, Ind. 47446.

MARIAN CAUDELL

CAREER: Homemaker, 1952-63; Mitchell Community Schools, Mitchell, Ind., English teacher, 1963-76, 1983-84, chairperson of English department, 1972-74, junior high school librarian, 1976-79, junior high school reading teacher, 1980-83; Mitchell Community Public Library, Mitchell, clerk-treasurer, 1984-85; full-time writer, 1985—. *Member:* Indiana Retired Teachers' Association, National Writers Club.

WRITINGS—Young adult romances: *One Boy Too Many,* Bantam, 1985; *Listen to Your Heart,* Bantam, 1986. Contributor of a short story to *Young World.*

WORK IN PROGRESS: Doing My Thing, a young adult humor novel featuring four twelve-year-old boys, completed; a series of mysteries involving fourteen-year-old twin girls, of which four stories have been completed.

SIDELIGHTS: "I became interested in writing for young adults while working in the junior high. My books do not contain sex or violence. I think young people are already exposed to too much of that at a time when they are least able to handle it. I prefer to leave the reader feeling good about himself and his fellowman."

CAZET, Denys 1938-

PERSONAL: Born March 22, 1938, in Oakland, Calif.; son of Alex Denys (in finance and banking) and Yvonne (Aye) Cazet; married Carol Hesselschwerdt, August 8, 1958 (divorced); married Donna Maurer, 1982; children: Craig, Robert, Scott, Michelle. *Education:* St. Mary's College, Moraga, Calif., B.A., 1960; attended Fresno State College (now California State University, Fresno), 1960-61; San Francisco State College (now San Francisco State University), Teaching Credential, 1961; attended University of California, Berkely, 1962; Sonoma State College (now California State College, Sonoma), M.A., 1971; Pacific Union College, Librarian Credential, 1974. *Politics:* "People." *Religion:* "Occasionally." *Home and office:* 1300 Ink Grade Rd., Pope Valley, Calif. 94567.

CAREER: Worked as gardener, writer, mail carrier, warehouse worker, cable line worker, cook, stock clerk, and process server, 1955-60; taught school in Corcoran, Calif., and in St. Helena, Calif., 1960-75; writer, 1973—; Elementary School, St. Helena, librarian and media specialist, 1975-85; University of California, Davis, extension classes, member of faculty, 1976-78; St. Helena School District Media Centers, St. Helena, director, 1979-81; California College of Arts and Crafts, instructor, 1985-86. Founder of Parhelion & Co. (printers and designers of educational materials), 1972-73.

WRITINGS—For children; self-illustrated except as noted; all published by Bradbury, except as noted: *Requiem for a Frog*, Sonoma State College, 1971; *The Non-Coloring Book: A Drawing Book for Mind Stretching and Fantasy Building*, Chandler & Sharp, 1973; *The Duck with Squeaky Feet*, 1980; *Mud Baths for Everyone*, 1981; *You Make the Angels Cry*, 1983; *Lucky Me*, 1983; *Big Shoe, Little Shoe*, 1984; *Christmas Moon*, 1984; *Saturday*, 1985; *December Twenty-fourth*, 1986; *Frosted Glass*, 1987; *A Fish in His Pocket*, Orchard Books, 1987; *Sunday*, 1988; *Great-Uncle Felix*, Orchard Books, 1988; *Mother Night*, 1988.

ADAPTATIONS: "Big Shoe, Little Shoe" (cassette), Random House, 1985.

SIDELIGHTS: "Every moment in a writer's life exerts some influence on his work.

"I was raised in a traditional 'first American' French family. They were a strange mix of features—European with a touch of American. Our extensive family possessed varied qualities, or inequalities, that made for impossible personality situations, and never duplicated. They were a lively and noisy cast of characters.

"Family gatherings were often. Meals began at one and ended at six. They were followed by card-playing, drinking, and arguments that ranged from current political conflicts to how many layers of custard in a proper Napoleon. A few hours later, soup was served and the ritual began all over again.

Grandpa shuffled downstairs and picked up the laundry. ■ (From *Big Shoe, Little Shoe* by Denys Cazet. Illustrated by the author.)

DENYS CAZET

"Family functions were like participating in a Renaissance fair, held in the middle of a Barnum and Bailey freak show. Everyone had a position to maintain and a point to get across. The intellectuals got theirs across by dismissing everyone else's arguments as so much rubbish, and those less endowed, by not knowing the difference. Stories were told with great gusto, laughter, and animation. Each version became more elaborate than the last. Children walked and talked with adults. They were treated with care, respect, and above all, were listened to. For a child, it was like being at the bottom of the funnel of love.

"The characters in my books are animals. But, the truth is, they are all based on the wonderful people who influenced my life. They gave me much, and I try not to forget them. By putting them in my books, I hope to make them live forever."

CHIN, Richard (M.) 1946-

PERSONAL: Born December 9, 1946, in Canton, China; son of James C. and Mary Y. (Bow) Ming. *Education:* Long Island University, B.S., 1970; Goddard College, M.A., 1974; Far Eastern University, M.D., 1980; University of Hong Kong, O.M.D. *Politics:* "None." *Religion:* "None." *Home:* 5 Richards Ave., Dover, N.J. 07801. *Office:* American Medical Association, 346 Lexington Ave., New York, N.Y. 10016.

CAREER: Martial arts instructor, acupuncturist, psychiatrist. Asian Martial Arts Studio, New York, N.Y., director, 1972—;

Asian American Medical Research Institute, New York City, director, 1974—, serving as dean for the College of Oriental Medicine at the University of Aruba, professor of health education at C. W. Post College of the Long Island University, and senior research assistant at New York University College of Medicine. *Member:* Association for Advancement of Behavior Therapy, Center for Chinese Medicine, American Association of Acupuncture and Oriental Medicine, North American Acupuncture Association, Asian Martial Arts Association (president, 1984-85). *Awards, honors:* Named best instructor, Asian Martial Arts Studio, 1974; *The Martial Arts* was one of New York Public Library's Books for the Teen Age, 1980, 1981, and 1982.

WRITINGS: (With Susan Ribner) *The Martial Arts* (juvenile; illustrated by Melanie Arwin), Harper, 1978; *Acupressure in Sports Medicine,* Simon & Schuster, 1987. Contributor of regular column to *Karate Illustrated;* contributor to *Inside Kung Fu* and *International Journal of Chinese Medicine.*

SIDELIGHTS: "I came to write about the martial arts because of my long experience in the field," said Chin, a student of karate and kung fu for more than thirty years. A teacher of the martial arts for the past fifteen years, Chin was all Asian champion in kung fu three times and has performed at Madison Square Garden. He was featured on the television show "A.M. New York" and later made three karate movies—two in the United States and one in Hong Kong.

Chin's *Acupressure in Sports Medicine,* a book for active people such as tennis players and runners, will cover western treatment of sports injuries, Chinese acupressure methods for prevention of injuries, and rehabilitation of old and new sports injuries.

Aiming to explore current trends in art and literature, Chin is producing two television talk shows: "The Voice of Professionals" and "Newstyle." He is working with the American Medical Association in the hope of bringing eastern medicine together with western medicine to work and exchange ideas.

FOR MORE INFORMATION SEE: New York Times, February, 1965; *New Yorker,* July, 1976; *People and Places,* Volume 9, number 4, 1983.

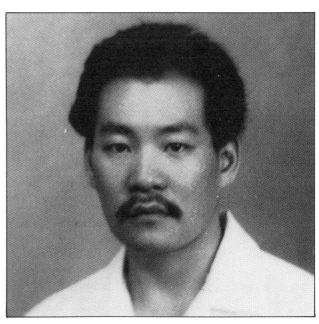

RICHARD CHIN

CLARK, Ronald William 1916-1987

OBITUARY NOTICE—See sketch in *SATA* Volume 2: Born November 2, 1916, in London, England; died March 9, 1987. Journalist and author. After beginning his career in magazine journalism, Clark became a war and foreign correspondent with the British United Press in 1943. After his first book, *Splendid Hills: The Life and Photographs of Vittorio Sella, 1859-1943*, was published in 1948, writing became his full time profession. Clark wrote several works for young readers, such as *We Go to Switzerland*, *We Go to Scotland*, *Great Moments in Battle*, and *The Air: The Story of the Montgolfiers, the Lilienthals, the Wright Brothers, Cobham, and Whittle*. His other works include the biographies *Freud: The Man and the Cause*, *J.B.S.: The Life and Work of J.B.S. Haldane*, and *Einstein: The Life and Times*. Clark's fascination with the history of mountaineering led him to collect photographs on the subject and produce titles like *The Early Alpine Guides*, *Men, Myths, and Mountains*, and, in collaboration with E. C. Pyatt, *Mountaineering in Britain: A History from the Earliest Times to the Present Day*, a standard reference work.

FOR MORE INFORMATION SEE: Authors of Books for Young People, 2nd edition, Scarecrow, 1971; *Authors and Writers Who's Who*, 6th edition, Hafner, 1971; *Contemporary Authors*, Volumes 25-28, revised, Gale, 1977. Obituaries: *Times* (London), March 14, 1987.

CONRAD, Pam 1947-

PERSONAL: Born June 18, 1947, in New York, N.Y.; daughter of Robert F. (a teacher) and Doris (a businesswoman; maiden name, Dowling) Stampf; married Robert R. Conrad (a designer), June 25, 1967 (divorced, 1982); children: Johanna, Sarah. *Education:* Attended Hofstra University, 1977-79; New School for Social Research, B.A., 1984. *Residence:* Rockville Centre, N.Y. *Agent:* Maria Carvainis, Maria Carvainis Agency, Inc., 235 West End Ave., New York, N.Y. 10023.

CAREER: Writer, 1979—. *Member:* Society of Children's Book Writers. *Awards, honors:* Work-in-Progress Grant from the Society of Children's Book Writers, 1982; *I Don't Live Here* was chosen one of Child Study Association of America's Children's Books of the Year, 1983; Spur Award from the Western Writers of America, Judy Lopez Memorial Award from the Women's National Book Association, named a "best children's book" by the Society of Midland Authors, and one of Child Study Association of America's Children's Books of the Year, all 1985, Children's Book Award from the International Reading Association, Cowboy Hall of Fame Award from the Cowboy Hall of Fame in Oklahoma, *Boston Globe-Horn Book* Award honor book, named a Notable Children's Trade Book in the Field of Social Studies by the joint committee of the National Council for Social Studies and the Children's Book Council, and Golden Kite Award honor book from the Society of Children's Book Writers, all 1986, all for *Prairie Songs*.

WRITINGS: I Don't Live Here! (juvenile; illustrated by Diane de Groat), Dutton, 1983; *Prairie Songs* (young adult; *Horn Book* honor list; illustrated by Darryl S. Zudeck), Harper, 1985; *Holding Me Here* (young adult), Harper, 1986; *What I Did for Roman* (young adult), Harper, 1987; *Seven Silly Circles* (juvenile; illustrated by Mike Wimmer; sequel to *I Don't Live Here!*), Harper, 1987; *Tub People* (picture book; illustrated by Richard Egielski), Harper, 1988; *Machan and the Strawberry Day* (juvenile), Harper, 1988; *Taking the Ferry Home* (young adult), Harper, 1988.

PAM CONRAD

WORK IN PROGRESS—All for Harper: *Staying Nine*, for children: *Kitchen Poem: Waiting for You*, a picture book alphabet poem; biography about Solomon Butcher, the photographer who made a cameo appearance in *Prairie Songs;* nineteenth-century Nebraska book about two children who find dinosaur bones on their farm.

SIDELIGHTS: "I began writing in February of 1957 when I was trapped in bed with the chicken pox. My mother gave me paper, thinking I would draw, but I began writing poetry. From then on, whenever I got a fever, I would write poetry. Luckily as I grew older, I harnassed the talent a bit, and I learned to write even when I felt healthy!

"There were many years during college, my early marriage and in early motherhood when I didn't write anything but letters or journal entries. But when my youngest daughter was three I grew restless, returned to college and began writing once again. It was like discovering a best friend I had forgotten. It's what I love doing most.

"I can write anything—articles, advertising copy, poetry, but I especially love to write stories, to make up people and places and events. I say make them up, but I really have a very private sense of being a receiver, like a television set, and the stories are already out there in the air, and I just pull them in and tell them. Very often my characters take off in their own directions as I sit at my word processor.

"For instance, after writing *Prairie Songs* I spoke to a group of teachers in Nebraska, and afterwards a teacher asked me to

I'll be the spider, Shirl, and you be the fly. ■ (From *I Don't Live Here!* by Pam Conrad. Illustrated by Diane de Groat.)

sign a copy of the book for her neighbor, Solomon Butcher's daughter. I got goose bumps, so sure was I that I had made him up. And yet here I was signing a book for his daughter. Any minute I expected Lester to tug at my skirts.''

HOBBIES AND OTHER INTERESTS: ''I like needlework, quilting, crocheting, and knitting, pug dogs, country music, Ray Charles, jogging, reading, the seashore (including boats, fish, seashells and sand) and the plains (including big skies, fossils, corn, and coal trains).''

FOR MORE INFORMATION SEE: Women's Record, November, 1985; *Grand Island Daily Independent,* December 19, 1985.

CROLL, Carolyn 1945-

BRIEF ENTRY: Born May 20, 1945. Although Croll has been employed as a free-lance illustrator in a variety of areas, including packaging, fashion illustration, and greeting cards, she considers children's books her speciality. After receiving a B.F.A. from the Philadelphia College of Art in 1967, she spent the next seventeen years at that same institution as an instructor in design and illustration. Through the years, Croll has illustrated several titles written by Jane Flory and published by Houghton, including *Ramshackle Roost* (1972), *We'll Have a Friend for Lunch* (1974), *The Unexpected Grandchildren* (1977), and *The Bear on the Doorstep* (1980). She also provided illustrations for Peter R. Limburg's *What's in the Names of Stars and Constellations* (Coward, 1976), Eleanor Coerr's *The Big Balloon Race* (Harper, 1981), and Laurence Santrey's *Music* (Troll Associates, 1985). In 1979 Croll produced *Too Many Babas* (Harper), which she both wrote and illustrated, a simple tale of four peasant women who experience the unfortunate adage of ''too many cooks can spoil the broth.'' *Booklist* described Croll's ''round, bready grannies in traditional dress'' as ''reminiscent of de Paola's simpler realizations.'' She is currently at work on both text and illustrations for another book entitled *The Little Snowgirl. Home:* 1420 Locust St. 22H, Philadelphia, Pa. 19102.

CHRIS CRUTCHER

CRUTCHER, Chris(topher C.) 1946-

PERSONAL: Born July 17, 1946, in Cascade, Idaho; son of John W. (a county clerk) and Jewell (Morris) Crutcher. *Education:* Eastern Washington State College (now University), B.A., 1968. *Politics:* Independent. *Religion:* ''None in particular.'' *Home:* West 730 Carlisle, Spokane, Wash. 99205. *Agent:* Liz Darhansoff, 1220 Park Ave., New York, N.Y. 10028. *Office:* Community Mental Health, South 107 Division, Spokane, Wash. 99202.

CAREER: Teacher of high school dropouts, 1970-73; Lakeside School, Oakland, Calif., teacher, 1973-76, director, 1976-80; Community Mental Health, Spokane, Wash., child protection team specialist, 1980-82, child and family specialist, 1982—. *Awards, honors: Running Loose* and *Stotan!* were chosen one of the American Library Association's Best Books for Young Adults, 1983 and 1986, respectively.

WRITINGS: Running Loose (young adult novel), Greenwillow, 1983; *Stotan!* (novel), Greenwillow, 1986; *The Crazy Horse Electric Game,* Greenwillow, 1987. Contributor to *Spokane.*

WORK IN PROGRESS: Screenplay for *Running Loose; Chinese Handcuffs,* a novel.

SIDELIGHTS: ''It is a joy to write a tale that is believable, that is real. Writing is also a way to express humor and to present different human perspectives. I like to explore the different ways in which people make sense of what goes on around them—ways in which they respond to the wide range of random things that happen, and to the situations they create.

''I am not a well-read writer. I haven't read the classics in any but comic book form and I do a horrible job of keeping up with new writers or literature in general. I have very little formal training and usually feel hopelessly inadequate in the company of other writers. My writing and style come mostly from experience.

''Working in the mental health field provides me with some unique perspectives on the human drama—how people get stuck and how they grow. Every client, man, woman, or child, no matter how damaged, has shown me at least a small glimpse of how we're all connected.

''I am interested in all kinds of sports. I run distances up to half-marathons, play a lot of basketball, and do minimal weight training. Daily, I run my Siberian Husky and my Alaskan Malamute four miles through whatever weather presents itself. My neighbors think I'm a professional dog sled.''

FOR MORE INFORMATION SEE: Idaho Daily Statesman, July 28, 1983.

CURRY, Jane L(ouise) 1932-

PERSONAL: Born September 24, 1932, in East Liverpool, Ohio; daughter of William Jack, Jr. (a ceramic engineer) and Helen (a teacher; maiden name, Willis) Curry. *Education:* Attended Pennsylvania State University, 1950-51; Indiana State College (now Indiana University of Pennsylvania), Indiana, Pa., B.S., 1954; attended University of California, Los Angeles, 1957-59; graduate study at University of London, 1961-62, 1965-66; Stanford University, M.A., 1962, Ph.D., 1969. *Residence:* Menlo Park, Calif. *Address:* c/o Margaret K.

McElderry Books, Macmillan Children's Book Group, 866 Third Ave., New York, N.Y. 10022.

CAREER: Writer and artist. Art teacher in Los Angeles (Calif.) city schools, 1955-59; Vroman's Bookstore, Pasadena, Calif., shop assistant, 1963; Stanford University, Stanford, Calif., teaching assistant, 1959-61, 1964-65, acting instructor in English literature, 1967-68, 1983-84, lecturer, 1987. Paintings shown in London at exhibitions of Royal Society of British Artists and other groups, 1962. *Member:* International Arthurian Society, Authors Guild, Children's Literature Association, Southern California Council on Literature for Children and Young People.

AWARDS, HONORS: Fulbright grant, 1961-62, and Stanford-Leverhulme fellowship, 1965-66, both for study in London; *Book World*'s Children's Spring Book Festival Honor Book, 1970, and Notable Book by a Southern California Author from Southern California Council on Literature for Children and Young People, 1971, both for *The Daybeakers; Der geflügelte Mann (Over the Sea's Edge)* was named Book of the Month by Deutsche Akademie für Kinder- und Jugendliteratur, 1971; *The Watchers* was selected as one of *New York Times* Outstanding Books of the Year, 1975; Ohioana Book Award from the Martha Kinney Cooper Ohioana Library Association, 1978, for *Poor Tom's Ghost;* "Special Award," Mystery Writers of America, 1978, for *Poor Tom's Ghost,* and 1979, for *The Bassumtyte Treasure;* Award for "Distinguished Contribution to the Field of Children's Literature" from the Southern California Council on Literature for Children and Young People, 1979, for body of work; Ohioana Book Award, 1987, for *The Lotus Cup*.

*WRITINGS—*Juvenile: *Down from the Lonely Mountain: California Indian Tales* (illustrated by Enrico Arno), Harcourt,

JANE LOUISE CURRY
THE WATCHERS

(Detail of jacket illustration by Trina Schart Hyman from *The Watchers* by Jane Louise Curry.)

1965, self-illustrated edition, Dobson, 1967; *Beneath the Hill* (illustrated by Imero Gobbato), Harcourt, 1967; *The Sleepers* (illustrated by Gareth Floyd), Harcourt, 1968; *The Change-Child* (ALA Notable Book; illustrated by G. Floyd), Harcourt, 1969; *The Daybreakers* (illustrated by Charles Robinson), Harcourt, 1970; *Mindy's Mysterious Miniature* (illustrated by C. Robinson), Harcourt, 1970, published in England as *The Housenapper,* Longman, 1971; *Over the Sea's Edge* (illustrated by C. Robinson), Harcourt, 1971; *The Ice Ghosts Mystery,* Atheneum, 1972; *The Lost Farm* (illustrated by C. Robinson), Atheneum, 1974.

Parsley Sage Rosemary and Time (illustrated by C. Robinson), Atheneum, 1975; *The Watchers,* Atheneum, 1975; *The Magical Cupboard* (illustrated by C. Robinson), Atheneum, 1976; *Poor Tom's Ghost,* Atheneum, 1977; *The Birdstones,* Atheneum, 1977; *The Bassumtyte Treasure,* Atheneum, 1978; *Ghost Lane,* Atheneum, 1979; *The Wolves of Aam,* Atheneum, 1981; *Shadow Dancers,* Atheneum, 1983; *The Great Flood Mystery,* Atheneum, 1985; *The Lotus Cup* (Junior Literary Guild selection), Atheneum, 1986; *Me, Myself, and I,* McElderry Books, 1987; *Back in the Beforetime: Tales of the California Indians* (illustrated by James Watts), McElderry Books, 1987.

Contributor of notes on Middle English poetry to journals. Book reviewer for *Times Educational Supplement* (London) 1969-70.

JANE L. CURRY

WORK IN PROGRESS: Tippy-Tap; The Shades.

SIDELIGHTS: ''Considering that I was born in East Liverpool, Ohio, the setting of _The Lotus Cup_ and once the foremost pottery center in America, I heard very little as a child about the town's rich past. My mother won awards for her clay sculptures in the local competitions; my father was for a time manager of the Potters Supply. But if the adults talked nostalgically of the town's past glories, I was never listening.

''My imaginative life was elsewhere: in the fairy-tale plays I wrote and dragooned my friends and little sister into playing; in the shows that came to the splendid Ceramic Theatre from the marvelous world 'Outside'; and in books. All sorts of books. Any book.

''Our small school had more a bookcase than a library. And then, in fifth grade, after my father's job took us to Kittanning, Pennsylvania, I found myself in a school with a real _library,_ with children's books. I worked my way up and down the aisles, and stumbled across E. Nesbit's _The Enchanted Castle._ It not only swept me off my feet, but changed my life—though I wasn't to know that for another nineteen years.''

Curry earned a B.S. in art education at Indiana State College, studied English literature at U.C.L.A., and then pursued graduate work at Stanford University. ''[There] I won a Fulbright Award to continue my studies at the University of London, and it was in London, in Foyles' Bookshop, that I unexpectedly found _The Enchanted Castle_ again.

The children had withdrawn as far as the cemetery wall. ■ (From _The Daybreakers_ by Jane Louise Curry. Illustrated by Charles Robinson.)

There's a snag where Papa caught his foot in the runner the night the bat got in and Papa went after it with a shotgun. ■ (From _Mindy's Mysterious Miniature_ by Jane Louise Curry. Illustrated by Charles Robinson.)

''I did not have enough money on hand to buy it, so I _ran_ the five or six blocks to the British Museum Library, put in a book order, found a seat in the Reading Room, and, when _The Enchanted Castle_ came, read it straight through. For almost two hours I was ten again. When I finished, I may not have known it, but I was already on the path to a career in writing for children and young people. I had been working with a company of Girl Guides (the same as our Girl Scouts), and the girls suggested that I make a book of the California Indian tales I had told them. Without having planned it, I was well on my way to _Down from the Lonely Mountain,_ my first book. My second, _Beneath the Hill,_ and many of those that followed, have been fantasies. Here and there, where a talisman makes possible travel back in time, are the echoes of E. Nesbit's _Story of the Amulet,_ and in a number of books I have woven a story around evils done in the past that erupt into the present. Not until _The Lotus Cup_ did I try to explore that theme in a realistic novel.

''_The Lotus Cup_ was many years in the growing. It was not until fifteen years ago that I saw for the first time a piece of the lovely, translucent porcelain Lotus Ware made in East Liverpool back in the 1890s. To think that we had once done work as fine as that! The little filigreed bowl became for me an emblem of a vanished world. I would write, I thought, an historical novel. But the story refused to take shape until at last I realized that it must be set in the present: that someone—Corry Tipson—must recover and understand the town's and her family's past before she can truly know and be herself.

"... My fictional world reflects my understanding of the workings of the real one—complex, organic, and dynamic—in which all human relationships, deep or casual, present and past, can touch or turn, blight or enrich us. Then too, I am always both literally and figuratively crossing and recrossing my own tracks.

"I was born in the Ohio Valley, and we moved to Pennsylvania when I was twelve. Two weeks after graduating from college I transplanted myself to California, teaching art in the Los Angeles schools only long enough to see me to Europe for a summer and back into graduate school. At Stanford, I was a teaching assistant in the English Department, and my M.A. came after the Fulbright year in London, the Ph.D. after a year in London on a Leverhulme Fellowship and another back at Stanford as a full-time acting instructor. The upshot of it all is a transatlantic network of friends and 'family,' an astonishing number of them as improbably acquainted with each other as my Gordian tangle of characters. And I shuttle back and forth.

"For years I had a cherished fantasy: that, hidden under a tangle of rose vines somewhere in the Cotswolds or the south of England, there was a crooked Elizabethan cottage with a walled garden and a tiny orchard that I was *meant* to have. For one long and memorable summer I rented just such a cottage (minus orchard) in a tiny village isolated in the Sussex Downs, but the dream of owning one—or even renting one, now that rents have soared sky-high—has over the years dwindled from a real possibility into a pipe-dream. The realities of property and travel costs in combination with changes in the children's book market mean that if I wish to continue to travel, setting stories in West Virginia or Pennsylvania or London, I must do without a 'home base.' I have been a gypsy now for twenty years, house-sitting and renting—a room or studio or, in a good year, a pleasant cottage—here and there from California to Cambridgeshire. Occasionally I teach a course at Stanford University, but since for me teaching, like writing, absorbs all of my attention, I cannot do both at once. Then too, I am always so pleased to get back to the writing that I am never tempted to stay put and teach full-time. So gypsying it is! And, since all things change and anything can happen, who knows? 'At eighty-three, when the fiddle-footedness has faded,' as I wrote some years ago, I may indeed be home at last in that Elizabethan cottage, 'sleeping in a bedroom four hundred years full of dreams' and writing about those dreams and dreamers. It was and is a happy thought—to be pruning a shaggy garden, and to have room for weekend housefuls of tottering friends, their children, and their children's children."

Curry's works are included in the Kerlan Collection at the University of Minnesota. Some of her works have been translated into German.

HOBBIES AND OTHER INTERESTS: Cooking; gardening; painting; travel; reading mysteries; British and North American Indian history and folklore; pre-Columbian history, religion and art; Shakespeare and his theatre.

FOR MORE INFORMATION SEE: Observer Review, August 4, 1968; *Young Readers' Review,* September, 1968; *Library Journal,* May 15, 1969; D. L. Kirkpatrick, *Twentieth-Century Children's Writers,* St. Martin's Press, 1978; Doris de Montreville and Elizabeth D. Crawford, editors, *Fourth Book of Junior Authors and Illustrators,* H. W. Wilson, 1978.

DAVIES, Peter 1937-

PERSONAL: Born February 22, 1937, in London, England; emigrated to Canada, 1957; son of Tony (a timber merchant) and Joan (Howell) Davies; married Lan Rayside (a teacher), April 27, 1967; children: Wendy, Jonathan. *Education:* Attended schools in Croydon, Surrey, England. *Politics:* "Hard to say! Both liberal and socialist, depending on how I feel on a particular day." *Religion:* Christian. *Home:* 189 Three Valleys Dr., Don Mills, Ontario M3A 3L7, Canada.

CAREER: Held a variety of jobs, including microfilming concentration camp records in West Germany for the Israeli government, working for a lumber company in New Zealand, and as a telephone salesman, clerk, swimming instructor, and lifeguard, 1957-58; supervisor of a home for boys in Montreal, Quebec, 1958-60; Royal Trust Co., Montreal, Quebec, member of staff, 1963-67; full-time writer, 1967—; York Detention Home, Toronto, youth worker, 1977-85.

WRITINGS: Fly Away Paul (novel), Crown, 1974. Contributor to *Chatelaine* and *Weekend.*

WORK IN PROGRESS: Delinquent of the Year/Diary of a Mad Teen-ager, an adult satirical novel about a fifteen year-old boy trapped within the Canadian juvenile correctional system.

SIDELIGHTS: Davies said that his experience as a supervisor in a Montreal boys' home was the catalyst for his writing. "I sympathized with these young people. My parents were di-

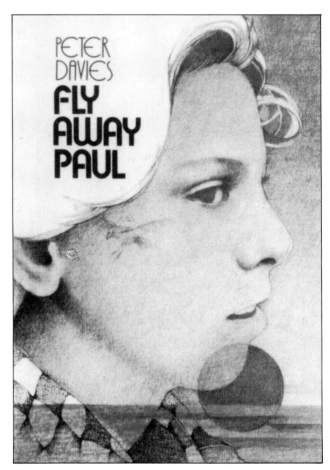

Paul wondered how much time there was left. ■
(Jacket illustration by Diane de Groat from *Fly Away Paul* by Peter Davies.)

vorced while I was still a middle teenager. Though I did not spend any time as a boy in a home, I knew how they felt. The boys in the home were not criminal though they were often treated as such." *Fly Away Paul,* which Davies describes as a "short bitter novel" that nevertheless contains hope, is about such a boy who ultimately gains freedom.

Davies speaks "some French, more German."

HOBBIES AND OTHER INTERESTS: Travel, photography (has a 4,000-slide collection), music ("mostly serious, my current favorite composer being Gustave Mahler"), the supernatural (a "lifelong hobby to gain greater control over my physical body, thus allowing my spirit to develop to its ultimate point"), swimming, ping-pong, tennis, long walks, reading.

FOR MORE INFORMATION SEE: Irma McDonough, editor, *Profiles,* revised edition, Canadian Library Association, 1975.

DIVINE, Arthur Durham   1904-1987
(David Divine, David Rame)

OBITUARY NOTICE: Born July 27, 1904, in Cape Town, South Africa; died April 30, 1987. Journalist, editor, and author of books for children and adults. Divine began his career as a journalist in his native Cape Town, working for the *Cape Times* during the 1920s and 1930s. From 1940 to 1945 he was a war correspondent for the *Sunday Times* in London, England; later, he became the publication's defense correspondent, a post he held until 1975. For his wartime service, Divine received the Distinguished Service Medal and was cited as commander of the Order of the British Empire. A prolific and versatile author, Divine wrote more than forty books, including thrillers, adventure stories, historical accounts, and studies of military politics. Among his numerous titles, some of which were published under the pseudonyms David Divine or David Rame, are the children's adventure stories *Diamond Coast* and *The Three Red Flares.* His other titles include the novel *Boy on a Dolphin,* which was adapted to film and became an American box office hit, *Sea Loot, Road to Tunis, Dunkirk: An Account of the Evacuation of the British Army from Dunkirk in May, 1940,* and *The Broken Wing: A Study in the British Exercise of Air Power.* Divine also edited *My Best Secret Service Story: A Collection of Stories Chosen by Their Own Authors* and was a contributor to magazines and newspapers.

FOR MORE INFORMATION SEE: Contemporary Authors, Volume 103, Gale, 1982; *International Authors and Writers Who's Who,* 9th edition, Melrose, 1982; *Who's Who,* 137th edition, St. Martin's, 1985. Obituaries: *Times* (London), May 2, 1987.

DORIN, Patrick C(arberry)   1939-

BRIEF ENTRY: Born February 12, 1939, in Chicago, Ill. Dorin has held a variety of positions throughout his professional career, including cost analyst in marketing and train operation research, public high school teacher, school principal, community education coordinator, and vice chairman of the transportation committee of the East Central Minnesota Development Council. His memberships include the National Association of Elementary School Principals, Chicago and Northwestern Historical Society, and Lake Superior Transportation Club. Dorin's written works deal primarily with trains and train travel, including *Commuter Railroads, Canadian Pacific Railroad,*

Milwaukee Road East, and *Amtrak Trains and Travel,* all published by Superior. For middle-grade readers, he hopes that *Yesterday's Trains* (Lerner, 1981) will "help preserve some of the history of the railroad as well as help other individuals with their own hobbies." The book gives a brief overview of developments in engines and specialized railroad cars, followed by a description of an overnight trip on a Pullman car. "As an introduction to trains," commented *School Library Journal,* ". . . [this] book can't be beat." Dorin has also written *Young Railroader's Book of Steam* (Superior, 1977) and *Yesterday's Trucks* (Lerner, 1982). *Address:* P.O. Box 667, Superior, Wis. 54880.

FOR MORE INFORMATION SEE: Contemporary Authors, New Revision Series, Volume 15, Gale, 1985.

DUMAS, Philippe   1940-

PERSONAL: Born September 26, 1940, in Cannes, France; son of Robert (a saddler and an amateur artist) and Jacqueline (Hermes) Dumas; married Kay Fender (a singer and writer), January 5, 1969; children: Alice, Emile, Jean, Robert, Louis. *Education:* Attended Ecole des Métiers d'Art, 1958-61, and Ecole Nationale Superieure des Beaux Arts, 1961-66. *Religion:* Protestant. *Home:* 84 rue Chaptal, 92300 Levallois-Perret, France. *Office:* c/o L'Ecole des Loisirs, 11 Rue de Sèvres, 75006 Paris, France.

CAREER: Painter and writer. *Military service:* Served with the French Cavalry, 1961-63. *Member:* Club de Saint Aubrin sur mer. *Awards, honors:* Prix Graphique, and one of *New York Times* Outstanding Books of the Year, both 1977, and *Boston Globe-Horn Book* Award honor book for illustration, 1978, all for *The Story of Edward; New York Times* cited *Odette: A Bird in Paris* as one of the Best Illustrated Children's Books of the Year, 1978; prix de la Fondation de France, 1981, for *Ce Changement-là* and 1985, for *Il Pleut, Il Pleut*

PHILIPPE DUMAS

Bergère; prix Beaugency (Funniest Book of the Year), 1987, for *Victor Hugo s'est égaré.*

WRITINGS—For children; all self-illustrated: *Laura, le terre-neuve d'Alice,* L'Ecole des Loisirs, 1976, translation by wife, Kay Fender, published as *Laura, Alice's New Puppy,* David and Charles, 1979; *Histoire d'Edouard,* Flammarion, 1976, translation by Gwen Marsh published as *The Story of Edward* (Junior Literary Guild selection), Parents Magazine Press, 1977; *Les Avatars de Benoit* (title means "Ups and Downs of Benjamin"), L'Ecole des Loisirs, 1976, Dent, 1980; *La petite géante,* L'Ecole ds Loisirs, 1977, translation by K. Fender published as *The Little Giant,* Dent, 1978; *Lucie, la fille d'E-douard,* Flammarion, 1977, translation by G. Marsh published as *Lucy, Edward's Daughter,* Dent, 1977, translation by Michael Rosenbaum published as *Lucie: A Tale of a Donkey,* Prentice-Hall, 1980; *Ondine au fond de l'eau* (title means "Ondine beneath the Waves"), L'Ecole des Loisirs, 1977; *Le Professeur Ecrouton-Creton* (title means "Professor Ecrouton-Creton"), L'Ecole des Loisirs, 1977; *Menteries et vérités* (title means "Lies and Truths"), L'Ecole des Loisirs, 1978; *Cesar, le coq du village,* Flammarion, 1978, translation by Deirdre Engel published as *Caesar, Cock of the Village,* Prentice-Hall, 1979 (published in England as *Caesar, the Village Cockerel,* Dent, 1979); *Laura et les bandits,* L'Ecole des Loisirs, 1978, translation by D. Engel published as *Laura and the Bandits,* David and Charles, 1980; *Le Maison,* L'Ecole des Loisirs, 1979, translation by Elsie Fender published as *The House,* Dent, 1980; *Laura sur la route,* 1979, translation by D. Engel published as *Laura on the Road,* David and Charles, 1979.

L'Equitation et l'école espagnole de Vienne, Flammarion, 1980, translation by Mariana Fitzpatrick published as *The Lippizaners and the Spanish Riding School of Vienna,* Prentice-Hall, 1981; *Laura perd la tête,* 1981, translation published as *Laura Loses Her Head,* David and Charles, 1981; *Comptines francaises, comptines coquines, jeux de Mots* (title means "French Nursery Rhymes and Naughty Rhymes"), Flammarion, 1981; *Ce Changement-là* (title means "This Change"), L'Ecole des Loisirs, 1981; *Laura fête Noël* (title means "Laura Celebrates Christmas"), L'Ecole des Loisirs, 1982; *Il Pleut, Il Pleut, Bergère,* L'Ecole des Loisirs, 1985; *Péche a Pied* (title means "Fishing in the Rock Pools"), L'Ecole des Loisirs, 1986; *Victor Hugo s'est égaré,* L'École des Loisirs, 1987.

Other writings; all self-illustrated: *Les Rats* (title means "Rats"), Editions de Saint-Aubin, 1971; (with Ionic Parlier) *Robidu,*

Hachette, 1972; *Les brigands calabrais* (title means "The Brigands of Calabria"), L'Ecole des Loisirs, 1977; (with Boris Moissard) *Les contes à l'envers* (title means "Topsy-turvy Fairy Tales"), L'Ecole des Loisirs, 1977; (with B. Moissard) *Les Aventures du Vantard* (title means "Adventures of a Braggart"), L'Ecole des Loisirs, 1978; *Monsieur Menee* (title means "Mr. Menee"), Editions Arthur Hubschmid, 1979; *Coffret de chansons* (title means "Casket of Songs"), Flammarion, 1982; *Coffret d'histoires* (title means "Casket of Stories"), Flammarion, 1983.

Illustrator: Kay Fender, *Odette: A Bird in Paris,* Prentice-Hall, 1978 (published in England as *Odette: A Springtime in Paris,* Gollancz, 1978); Theophile Gautier, *Le Roman de la Momie* (title means "The Story of the Mummy"), L'Ecole des Loisirs, 1979; Charles Dickens, *Captain Boldheart* (juvenile), Dent, 1980; Jan Dutourd, *Oevres romanesques* (title means "Selected Works"), Flammarion, 1980; Marcel Ayme, *Les Contes du chat perché* (juvenile; title means "Tales of a Perched Cat"), Gallimard, 1980; *De nouvelles de Maupassant,* 3 volumes (title means "Short Stories by Maupassant"), L'Ecole des Loisirs, 1981-82; Roger Rudigoz, *Les Contes de la Souris chauve* (juvenile; title means "Tales of a Baldheaded Mouse"), L'Ecole des Loisirs, 1982; André Roux, adapter, *Bible en images: Ancien Testament* (title means "The Bible in Imagee: Old Testament"), L'Ecole des Loisirs, 1982; Jakob Grimm and Wilhelm Grimm, *The Queen Bee,* Creative Education, 1984; Chekhov, *Histoires pour rire et sourire* (title means "Stories to Make You Laugh and Smile"), L'Ecole des Loisirs, 1984; *Haute de Gamme,* Flammarion, 1985. Also illustrator of D. Merimee's *Chroniques du regne de Charles IX* (title means "Chronicles of the Reign of Charles IX"), L'Ecole des Loisirs, Guy de Maupassant's *Histoires fantastiques* (title means "Fantastic Stories"), L'Ecole des Loisirs.

WORK IN PROGRESS: "I have begun illustrating a series of popular songs similar to those I did for *Il Pleut, Il Pleut Bergère.*"

SIDELIGHTS: Dumas was born in 1940, in Cannes, France. "For generations my family has been Parisian and Protestant. There was, however, a break of about a hundred years following the Revocation of the Edict of Nantes, which in 1685 banned Protestantism from France. My ancestors fled their native country and settled in Hamburg, where they could practice their religion freely. The three generations that lived there remained French-speaking, and, with the sole exception of my

After walking for three days they reach their objective. ■ (From *Lucy, Edward's Daughter* by Philippe Dumas. Illustrated by the author.)

On se fourre au lit en quatrième vitesse.

(From *La Petite Géante* by Philippe Dumas. Illustrated by the author.)

grandfather, who wed a German woman, married within the French community there. During the French Revolution, my grandfather returned to Paris where my family has lived ever since.

"To grow up Protestant in a Catholic country makes you feel a bit like an outsider. As part of a minority you develop a pride in being different and apart from the others. This may be especially true for Protestants, whose prime quality is to protest—not a bad trait to have! But seriously, I am grateful to be that way because it makes one comparatively independent.

"Some of my earliest memories center on World War II. I knew early on that my father was taken prisoner and then escaped to unoccupied southern France. My pregnant mother fled to Cannes, where I was born shortly after her arrival in 1940.

"After the German army invaded the unoccupied territory in November 1942, my parents no longer had any reason to hide in Cannes. So we returned to Paris. I was about three years old at the time. Paris was still in a state of great turmoil. There were frequent bomb alerts at night, and I recall many a night waiting in our bathrobes in the basement with the other tenants for the 'all clear' signal. Even before the liberation of Paris by the Allies in 1944, suspected collaborators were being avenged. From our sixth-floor window, I witnessed two women who had their heads shaved—the typical chastisement for women believed to have had friendly relations with the Germans—hustled into a car and driven away. The car was immediately pursued by a German truck. I don't know what eventually happened to the women. As a child I was deeply impressed by the violence which was going on all around me.

"I have four brothers and one sister. It was very important for me to grow up in a large family: it meant many books around the house, many games being played and many stories being told by the elders. I still dream of a big family, although we now have a girl and four boys, and my wife, Kay, is less enthusiastic about further expanding our numbers.

"We were very free in my family. My parents never imposed anything on us except a tremendous moral influence. My brothers and I all branched out in different directions, the result, I think, of our upbringing. If we were interested in something and truly determined, my parents would encourage us even when they disagreed with our ideas. Before it became fashionable, one of my brothers decided to go to India. My father was at first absolutely opposed to the idea, but my brother stood his ground and finally left. Hardly thirty minutes after his departure, my father was already talking about the wonderful trip my brother was undertaking. My parents' trust and emphasis on personal freedom was extremely helpful when I decided to become a painter.

"I have always drawn. My father was an amateur painter and on Sundays when the weather was fine, I would go with him to draw outdoors. Then we would go to Julien's studio and draw a nude female. I was twelve years old and dreamed of becoming Van Gogh. Later, I studied painting at the Métiers

Stephen Dujour, whom I had always thought to be a peace-loving man like all shoemakers, gave me a disappointing welcome. ■ (From *Caesar, Cock of the Village* by Philippe Dumas. Illustrated by the author.)

I soon understood that I was in a magical house. ■ (From *La Maison* by Philippe Dumas. Illustrated by the author.)

d'Art and then attended the Ecole des Beaux Arts. It was a period during which theory was exceedingly important, and big words were used to express simple thoughts. I, on the other hand, prefer people who say important things with simple words. Also, all of my teachers belonged to the abstract art movement. What I've always enjoyed in painting is the anecdotal and a narrative approach. I like art that, while not necessarily naive, is simple.

"Along with my paintings, I have always created half-drawn, half-written little stories. When I was in school, I wrote stories about my life as a pupil. Later I wrote stories about my fortunes or misfortunes in love. And I kept writing and drawing stories about my own life until I had children, at which point I began writing and illustrating stories for them. I've always done painting and illustration side-by-side. Although they are very different, they complement each other and, I'm interested in both mediums.

"I never wanted to be an illustrator. I cannot stand the traditional connotation of illustration: drawings that merely reiterate the text. Unless the illustrator is a genius, he is necessarily going to steal images from the reader's imagination. A good drawing can suggest many things, and I've always tried to accentuate something that is in the text without *specifically* being in it. That's what I call a 'picture-novel.' That's to say a novel where text and drawings are put together to serve a story without redundancies. It's more about annotating than illustrating. The books of the nineteenth century Swiss illustrator Rodolphe Töpffer, who mixes drawings and text is really the model for my work.

"I like to do books in which the 'sacrosanct' quality of illustration is debunked. I have found out that in this regard the use of cartoon bubbles along with text and drawings work well—quite a departure from the self-seriousness of the images of Edmund Dulac or any of the illustrators of the 1920s. This is not to suggest that I want to go to the opposite extreme, namely cartoons. Although I have done comic-strips for the

back covers of a few books, I could never be a cartoonist. It is a very definite and restricted genre. I prefer to do larger, more varied work. With comics, you have to redo the same characters over and over again. You have to be able to draw them from a three-quarter perspective, in profile, etc. The reader/viewer must recognize the characters immediately, otherwise he will have difficulty in understanding the story. Comics are about signs and about dealing with signs. Some comics, like *Tintin* are quite wonderfully done, but they never inspired me to seriously try my hand.

"Before anything else a book is a matter of rhythm. A good book is one you want to pick up again as soon as you finish it. But apart from that, if a book is really fine, you want to keep on turning the pages. Sometimes you should turn the pages fast, at other times you should linger over them. The pacing is very close to that in film. If suddenly in the middle of a book you have an astounding illustration which is more important than the text, it's not good because it means the overall movement of the book has come to a halt.

"With drawing there is an element of surprise, which I experience in my hand, and which doesn't happen with writing. I need that surprise, I need *not to know* where I am going. If I know beforehand where the story will end, the pen literally falls from my hand. It's a thrilling moment when the imagination takes over and carries you. Then I don't feel the tedium of the work. This always happens at the most unexpected moment, and sometimes it doesn't come for a long time.

"I am a graphic person and if I have any kind of intelligence, it's comprised entirely of intuition and sensibility. My work is never based on method or theory. I contradict myself, I flounder, I start afresh many times and finally I create a story. Little by little I express what I want. It's sometimes difficult because I often have the feeling that I am working on an eternal rough draft. Today, with all the means of reproduction available through new technology, we are more free to work and correct at the same time. For example, it's possible to write a story, photocopy it, and start from scratch again.

J'entends sous le feuillage
L'eau qui tombe à grand bruit;

(From *Il Pleut, Il Pleut, Bergère* by Philippe Dumas. Illustrated by the author.)

"I generally devote equal attention to drawings and text. But because I am first and foremost a graphic person, I do like to try my hand at all the functions related to the visuals in a book. For instance, I enjoy color separation. It's the same principle as working on lithographs. Unfortunately, today books are reproduced with the four-color process, which tends to make every reproduction look the same. It has almost become impossible to obtain the subtleties of nuance that existed at the time of the illustrator Boutet de Monvel, for example.

"I use every medium available: water color, gouache, oil paint, crayons, pen and ink, etc. Oil allows a superimposition of colors. You can come back to a painting and work over the surface until you're satisfied. With water color, on the other hand, if it's not good the first time, you have to redo the whole illustration from scratch. But what I like most, is to work with odds and ends. I find it more stimulating if I use a rotten pen on scraps of papers I scrounge here and there. The material I use is always on the verge of decay. I think this comes also from a desire to surprise myself, to start with a handicap and to overcome. It's also much cheaper. In fact, it costs next to nothing. Once in a while, when I walk by a store with fancy boxes of paints or pastels displayed in the window, I dream of having them. But I always think, 'Later, when I am a real professional, I will treat myself to one of those boxes.' And at Christmas, when I see the fancy painter's outfits my nephews receive, my tongue hangs out with pure jealousy. Even so, I know that they might paint only once every six months.

"The first children's book I illustrated [for another author] was *Odette*. We already had our first child, Alice, and my wife wanted to do a story for her. So she wrote the text, and I illustrated it. I showed it to a number of French publishers, none of whom were interested in it. It was finally Gollancz, an English publisher, who first accepted to publish it. At the beginning, it was very difficult for me to be published in France. Publishers were very nice and complimentary, but nobody wanted to publish my books, telling me that there was not yet a market for the kind of books I did, which were not children's books in the traditional sense. Finally, L'Ecole des Loisirs accepted *Laura,* a book I wrote and illustrated in three days. I did the drawings in one shot, and never reworked them. After that publication, I was able to palm off my old 'unsaleable' stories which had been lying around in my closet. It must have appeared as though I was suddenly very prolific because all the books which had previously been rejected were now being accepted and published.

"My first adult novel was *Robidu,* which I illustrated with drawings in black and white. It is a very complicated story, very literary with many symbols, allusions and references, and is admittedly a little difficult to read. It took me ten years to complete it, and I very much enjoyed doing it. I was sure that the book was going to be well received, and yet it was not. The practice of publishing illustrated books for adults no longer exists in France. There are still some illustrated editions of the works of classical writers, but to publish a contemporary illustrated novel is unthinkable.

"I started to have publishing success only when I began to do children's books. Today it is the only domain in which illustration is still respected. There is in France a general contempt for illustration. Apart from Sempé's books, French people don't

Edward has been living very happily with his family in their cottage deep in the woods, where he doesn't have to hide his ears. ■ (From *Lucie: A Tale of a Donkey* by Philippe Dumas. Illustrated by the author.)

Mais bientôt j'ai compris que j'étais dans une maison magique. Elle est pleine de palmiers, avec des singes qui se balancent aux branches, et des perroquets qui vous saluent à grand bruit. Partout sont suspendus des ananas et des noix de coco.

(From *La Maison* by Philippe Dumas. Illustrated by the author.)

buy books with drawings. Konrad Lorenz, who specializes in books on animals, published a book in England about dogs with illustrations showing different canine faces. Well, in the French edition, which was more expensive and luxurious, all the drawings were taken out. There is in England an important illustration tradition, and the work of illustrators like Kate Greenaway is frequently exhibited.

"I like to do books that can be read by adults as well as by children, because it's often adults who read to kids. Children read differently from adults and look for different things in a book. The trick is to write books which can be read on several levels, thus surmounting the obstacle of categories. This is often baffling to editors because they tend to want clear identifications and labels. They are used to books made for particular age groups. This is something I don't understand—it's so superficial. In any case, I have never been able to follow those rules. Take a tree in nature, for example: a child of two, an adolescent and an old man will all perceive it differently. And that's the way it should be with books. To obtain this appeal when making a book is very difficult. One must achieve simplicity. We tend to start out in a complicated and convoluted way. The point is to take out everything that seems unnecessary, until the story is as direct and simple as possible without being puerile or falsely naive. That's the kind of work I am trying to do.

"As readers children are superior to adults. They read and look with an intensity of concentration and a depth of attention that most adults don't have. Instead of discovering, adults are often satisfied with recognizing what they already know and with identifying points of references, 'Oh yes, this reminds me of such and such.' Children don't have that kind of snobbery. When adults read a text by Albert Camus, for example, even if it's boring, they read it respectfully because it belongs to Camus. Children don't work that way—they drop a book right away when it's uninteresting, or they persevere because it's compelling.

"When my father died, it was a shock to me and to my children and nephews. I wanted to tell the story of his death in *Ce changement là*. It is the story of a life. I tell the last moments and the way death happened. I tried to talk about it as simply as possible. Today it seems there are no more grandmothers who pass on family tales, as my grandmother did with me. I keep an illustrated diary wth little texts about my life, and had done the same with my father. When I made a book about his death I naturally talked about memories I had of him and what he meant to me. Writing a book about death was difficult, because it touches a subject that is beyond all of us. I wrote lots and lots of sentences and little by little, succeeded in saying what I wanted to say. My drawings were more immediately successful, and this was a good thing. It meant that I could suggest rather than recount; I could say everything I wanted with very few words.

"I live a secluded life. I'm the kind of guy who is always home. I rarely see anyone except for my wife and kids. I spend a lot of time looking out the window thinking about ideas. In the morning I take one of my children to school on my bicycle, and then return home and work through the morning. I have lunch and then go back to work. I sometimes listen to the radio but on the whole I am quite isolated from the outside world. Unintentionally so, perhaps, but that's the way it is.

"When I'm working on something which is not going well, I keep working because I absolutely must make that drawing or text work. It's like going fishing in the hope that sooner or later you will catch something. I would have a bad conscience if I were to go out. In the first place, it takes me a long time to make a drawing, and I'm always afraid that I am losing time. Also, ideas mature very slowly and I don't want any distraction even when I happen to be down in the dumps. I can go for a week without putting my nose outside. I don't even go out to see exhibitions, and I really should. Once in a while when I walk down the street it suddenly dawns on me how isolated I am, and how difficult it is to talk with others, even with grocers when I shop. In my professional life I don't have to be social. I bring my editors my books when they are finished and ready to be printed. Otherwise we are rarely in touch. I am really not integrated, and this sometimes worries me. Things are going well right now, but a new trend could come along, and if the two or three editors who publish my work suddenly decided not to any more, I really don't know what I would do. I have always painted or illustrated; I have never known how to do anything else. I could never work again in a conventional environment. It's wonderful to be free as a bird, to draw or write and stop when you want to.

"I'm very privileged, but it's sometimes agonizing. There is the pressure of always having to produce a new book, and the fear of doing one which won't work. The further I go, the scarier it becomes. One might think that it would be the opposite, that having done a few books would be reassuring. Well, not at all. If you look back at books you thought were very good, and don't like them anymore, you start thinking, 'God, how awful. And to think that I was pleased with those books!' And if there is a book which you still find truly good, you start worrying that you will never again be able to match that quality. It's a difficult situation—the dilemma, I think, of everyone with an artistic career.

"There is a quote from the poet Paul Valéry which goes 'A good drawing is one which can be continued.' Glorious examples for me are the drawings of Degas. One always feels that they're a study for something else. Maybe he died before achieving what he was looking for, but he was searching till the end. I admire that. There is nothing more irritating than people who are satisfied with themselves and with what they do.

"It is essential to keep a fresh vision. One must guard against repeating oneself. If I find myself settling down in that way, I drop everything. I just stop. That's why I always have several books at once in different stages. I put several aside and when I go back, I find things in some of those projects that I like, and this gives me an incentive to continue.

"The danger of having too many projects at once is spreading yourself too thin. I can spend days and days trying to push along my little piles but with such minimal progress that I often feel that I have not accomplished anything. Another danger is that little by little the drawings shrink and it's good once in a while to go back to a larger, more painterly format. With *Il Pleut, Il Pleut Bergère,* for example, I did relatively large drawings in pen and ink and then in water color.

"Illustrating other people's works is not that different from doing my own stories. For one thing, I only illustrate books that I like. In order to illustrate a book I have to read it at least eight times, so if it's not good I am rapidly bored to death. Most of the time I am the one to propose to an editor that I illustrate a certain author. When you admire an author, it's fantastic to illustrate him. I have also done a number of classics. When we were living in Normandy, I was inspired to do Maupassant because that is where he comes from. I have also done some Chekov, Marcel Ayme and Flaubert's tales.

He fed her breakfast of warm milk through an eye dropper. ■ (From *Odette: A Bird in Paris* by Kay Fender. Illustrated by Philippe Dumas.)

''*Les contes à l'envers,* I did with Boris Moissard. I have known him from childhood and we are very good pals. He wrote two tales and I wrote three. He is a much better writer than I am and as he corrected my text, we don't know anymore what belongs to whom. It was a great collaboration. Moissard has very reliable judgment concerning drawings. We often agree and have similar taste.

''If I have one hero, it's Charlie Chaplin. I love everything he did. Critics have talked about meanness and aggressiveness in his work, but I don't think it's true. The way he talks about himself in his memoirs is absolutely fantastic. He is a man of this century and has experienced practically everything. He was adulated, rejected, and finished his life as a 'grand bour-

geois' pretending to take himself seriously. And the way he fell passionately in love every three months. There is in Chaplin an enormous appetite for life which I admire very much. I would love to have illustrated a book on Chaplin's life, but I gave up the idea after seeing a very good English documentary which used extracts of Chaplin's movies as biographical material. My drawings could never have matched the way he portrayed himself. Still, I was very influenced by him, and like most people of my generation, by cinema in general.

''There are many things I would like to do. My wife is a musician and I hope that some day we will succeed in putting on a theatrical show together. I'd like to do the set and the costumes, Kay would do the music, and Boris Moissard the text. I envision something very simple and light—in the *co-media del arte* style. And hopefully, it will be easy to move around, so we can take it on tour. I really hope the three of us will realize that project one day.''

—Based on an interview by Catherine Ruello.

EDWARDS, Audrey 1947-

PERSONAL: Born April 21, 1947, in Tacoma, Wash.; daughter of Cyril Alfred (a writer) and Bertie (a director of a senior citizens' center) Edwards. *Education:* University of Washington, Seattle, B.A., 1969; Columbia University, M.A., 1974. *Office: Family Circle,* 488 Madison Ave., New York, N.Y. 10022.

CAREER: Redbook, New York City, associate editor, 1970-72; Columbia University, New York City, editor for Urban Center, 1972-73; Fairchild Publications, New York City, promotion editor, 1974-77; *Black Enterprise,* New York City, senior editor, 1977-78; *Family Circle,* New York City, senior editor, 1978—. *Member:* National Association of Black Journalists. *Awards, honors:* Coretta Scott King Fellowship from American Association of University Women, 1969.

WRITINGS—Children's books: (With Gary Wohl) *The Picture Life of Muhammad Ali,* F. Watts, 1976; (with G. Wohl) *The Picture Life of Bobby Orr,* F. Watts, 1976; (with G. Wohl) *The Picture Life of Stevie Wonder,* F. Watts, 1977; *Muhammad Ali: The People's Champ,* Little, Brown, 1977. Contributor to popular magazines, including *Redbook, Essence,* and *Your Place.*

SIDELIGHTS: ''Writing takes many shapes, moods, and routes, touching us in places we know and recognize. As a black writer I attempt to strike the note that is universal, explore the experience which is common, and give expression to the black aesthetic. My writing necessarily reflects a black perspective, and should be about the business of education; informing, illuminating, and transmitting. I strive, always, to be responsible.

''Travels have taken me to Africa (which revealed more about me than about Africans), Japan, the Caribbean, and throughout the United States, and I consider traveling to be the next best thing to reading.''

FOR MORE INFORMATION SEE: Black Enterprise, December, 1978.

ELWOOD, Ann 1931-

BRIEF ENTRY: Born January 3, 1931, in Ridgewood, N.J. From 1967 to 1972, Elwood was employed as advertising manager at Glencoe Press in California. She is the author of *The Macmillan Illustrated Almanac for Kids* (Macmillan, 1981), written in collaboration with Carol Orsag and Sidney Solomon, which provides adolescents with information on a variety of topics, such as animals, science, sports, laws that protect children, and health or emotional problems typically encountered by youths. *Kliatt* observed that ''the text and format are appealing and would engage many young browsers,'' while *New York Times Book Review* advised: ''Open this book to almost any page and be prepared to be amazed, fascinated, or informed.'' Elwood collaborated with Linda C. Wood on *Windows in Space* (Walker, 1982), which was named a Distinguished Work of Nonfiction by the Southern California Council on Literature for Children and Young People in 1983. *Science*

Books and Films noted that this account of the solar system and space travel ''covers a surprisingly large range of material rather well.'' Elwood's other works include the young adult novel *Walking Out* (Tempo, 1980), written with John Raht, and *Brainstorms and Thunderbolts: How Creative Genius Works* (Macmillan, 1983), another collaboration with Orsag. *Home:* 2442 Montgomery Ave., Cardiff, Calif. 92007.

ERLANGER, Ellen (Louise) 1950-

BRIEF ENTRY: Born November 14, 1950, in Canton, Ohio. Erlanger revealed that she writes ''because I feel that thoughtful, creative communication shows the beauty of human capability—and because it's fun!'' She has been variously employed as a history teacher, director of education, camp director, and in a career education program. Erlanger's books for children include *America Is* (C. E. Merrill, 1979) and the biographies *Jane Fonda: More than a Movie Star* (Lerner, 1984) and *Isaac Asimov: Scientist and Storyteller* (Lerner, 1986). *School Library Journal* described the first biography as ''clearly written and informative . . . [it] does justice to the complex, outspoken and talented Fonda,'' while *Bulletin of the Center for Children's Books* noted that the second ''gives good balance of information about Asimov's personal and professional life.'' According to Erlanger, her goal is to ''portray positive role models for young people in the most accurate, interesting way possible.'' *Home:* 213 North Broadleigh, Columbus, Ohio 43209.

FOR MORE INFORMATION SEE: Contemporary Authors, New Revision Series, Volume 15, Gale, 1985.

ESPELAND, Pamela (Lee) 1951-

PERSONAL: Born August 19, 1951, in Oak Park, Ill.; daughter of Jack Ingolf (a carpenter) and Roberta (a housewife; maiden name, Ralls) Espeland; children: Jonah Daniel Klevesahl. *Education:* Attended Harvard University, 1972, and University of Minnesota, 1974; Carleton College, B.A., 1983. *Politics:* Democrat. *Home and office:* 3351 Colfax Ave. South, Minneapolis, Minn. 55408.

CAREER: Free-lance writer and editor in Minneapolis, Minn., 1976—.

WRITINGS—Juvenile, except as noted; all published by Carolrhoda, except as noted: *The Story of Cadmus* (illustrated by Reg Sandland), 1980; *The Story of Arachne* (illustrated by Susan Kennedy), 1980; *The Story of King Midas* (illustrated by George Overlie), 1980; *The Story of Pygmalion* (illustrated by Catherine Cleary), 1981; *The Story of Baucis and Philemon* (illustrated by G. Overlie), 1981; *Theseus and the Road to Athens* (illustrated by R. Sandland), 1981; *Why Do We Eat?* (illustrated by Nancy Inderieden), Creative Education, 1981; (with Marilyn Waniek) *Hundreds of Hens and Other Poems for Children* (illustrated by D. M. Robinson; translated from the Danish by Halfdan Rasmussen), Black Willow Press, 1982; (with M. Waniek) *The Cat Walked through the Casserole and Other Poems for Children* (illustrated by Trina S. Hyman and others), 1984; (with Jacqulyn Saunders) *Bringing Out the Best: A Resource Guide for Parents of Young Gifted Children,* Free Spirit, 1986; (with Evelyn Leite) *Different Like Me: A Book for Teens Who Worry about Their Parents' Use of Alcohol-Drugs,* Johnson Institute, 1987.

I didn't come out of my mother. I don't have my father's green eyes. ■ (From "Luck" in *The Cat Walked through the Casserole and Other Poems for Children* by Pamela Espeland and Marilyn Waniek. Illustrated by Peter E. Hanson.)

Editor: Anne Wilson Schaef, *Women's Reality,* Winston Press, 1979; Milan Dolenc, *Lipizzaner: The Story of the Horses of Lipica,* Control Data, 1980; Gerry Spiess, *Alone Against the Atlantic,* Control Data, 1981; Susan L. Barrett, *It's All in Your Head: A Guide to Understanding Your Brain and Boosting Your Brain Power* (illustrated by Jackie Urbanovic), Free Spirit, 1985; Earl Hip, *Fighting Invisible Tigers: A Student Guide to Life in "The Jungle"* (illustrated by Troy Acker), Free Spirit, 1985; Timmen L. Cermak, *Diagnosing and Treating Co-Dependence: A Guide for Professionals Who Work with Chemical Dependents, Their Spouses and Children,* Johnson Institute, 1986; Vernon E. Johnson, *Intervention: How to Help Someone Who Doesn't Want Help—A Step-by-Step Guide for Families and Friends of Chemically Dependent Persons,* Johnson Institute, 1986; Ellen Sue Stern, *Expecting Change: The Emotional Journey through Pregnancy,* Poseidon/Simon & Schuster, 1986; Miriam Adderholdt-Elliott, *Perfectionism: What's Bad About Being Too Good* (illustrated by Caroline Price), Free Spirit, 1987; James Delisle and Judy Galbraith, *The Gifted Kids Survival Guide II: A Sequel to the Original Gifted Kids Survival Guide (for Ages 11-18)* (illustrated by Harry Pulver Jr.), Free Spirit, 1987; James C. Worthy, *Portrait of a Maverick: William C. Norris and Control Data Corporation,* Ballinger, 1987; Dick Schaefer, *Choices & Consequences: What to Do When a Teenager Uses Alcohol/Drugs: A Step-by-Step System that Really Works,* Johnson Institute, 1987.

Editor with Judy Galbraith of *Free Spirit: News & Views on Growing Up Gifted* (bimonthly newsletter).

WORK IN PROGRESS: Coauthoring a book about peace with futurist Earl Joseph for Free Spirit; editing other books and a new newsletter from Free Spirit; ghostwriting a scary novel set in Minnesota.

SIDELIGHTS: "Many people in my life encouraged me to write—my mom, teachers. . . . But what's kept me going is the simple fact that I like to write—and edit, of course, which is mostly what I do. I also teach with Marilyn Nelson Waniek, my coauthor on two books for children (so far).

"My days are spent in front of my word processor, which enables me to write and edit more and faster. Since I spend so much time in my study, I've tried to surround myself with things that amuse and entertain me. Ralph the full-sized cardboard skeleton hangs in a corner directly in front of me (and sometimes scares me at night—good for when I'm working on the scary novel). There's a poster of William Wegman's dog, Man Ray, with painted fingernails, and another poster by Jonathan Borofsky of himself standing on top of the world and surrounded by the words, 'Art Is for the Spirit.' A stuffed Peter Rabbit stands on a shelf overlooking a Barbie doll and two Kens (one with painted hair and one with real hair). There are pictures of my son, Jonah, and postcards of the Prince and Princess of Wales, the universe, and New York City (in 3D). There's an old National Geographic globe on my file cabinet and a gigantic boom box on my desk—I listen to music all the time. My aged dog, Fante, sleeps at my feet, and my two cockatiels, Birdie and Burdette, fly around my head whenever the spirit moves them. And all around me are books I use in my work—encyclopedias, dictionaries, thesauruses, art books, books about writing and the language, rhyming dictionaries, atlases, almanacs—so I can get answers in the middle of the night, when I need them the most.''

Espeland's works are included in the Kerlan Collection at the University of Minnesota.

HOBBIES AND OTHER INTERESTS: Reading, traveling, and music—jazz, classical, zydeco, country. ''I probably listen to music fourteen hours a day, so my tastes keep broadening.''

TIMOTHY FOOTE

EYVINDSON, Peter (Knowles) 1946-

BRIEF ENTRY: Born January 20, 1946, in Carberry, Manitoba, Canada. Teacher, librarian, storyteller, and author of books for children. Eyvindson received B.A. and B.Ed. degrees from the University of Manitoba. In 1969 he began his teaching career at Melita Composite School where he worked for four years; he then taught at Snow Lake School and Clavet Comprehensive School, where he also held the position of librarian. Eyvindson became a free-lance storyteller in 1984, telling stories to children in several Canadian provinces. To engage the imaginations of his young listeners, he incorporates props and puppets into his stories. Eyvindson feels that his various professions prepared him for the challenge of writing, as he ''became acutely aware of the finely crafted work authors of children's books must use to make their stories effective.'' *Kyle's Bath* (Pemmican, 1984), illustrated by Wendy Wolsak, is based on Eyvindson's own experiences with his young son's reluctance to bathe, while *Old Enough* (Pemmican, 1986) tells the story of a father who eagerly awaits his infant son's growing years only to find that his job prevents him from spending time with the child. *Address:* P.O. Box 51, Clavet, Saskatchewan, Canada S0K 0Y0.

FLEISHER, Robbin 1951-1977

PERSONAL: Born January 6, 1951, in Brooklyn, N.Y.; died April 26, 1977; daughter of Marvin (a teacher) and Phyllis (a teacher; maiden name, Zipkin) Fleisher. *Education:* Hunter College, B.A.; attended Teachers College of Columbia University.

CAREER: Artist, animator, musician, songwriter and author.

WRITINGS: Quilts in the Attic (picture book; Junior Literary Guild selection; illustrated by Ati Forberg), Macmillan, 1977.

SIDELIGHTS: Robbin Fleisher died at the age of twenty-six, after a short illness. She left many notes for future children's books. Primarily an illustrator, she was beginning to develop many ideas for stories for preschool age children. Her pictures, as her plots, were inbred with warmth and caring, and deep sensitivity and respect for the children about whom she wrote. She used her own history—the names of beloved grandparents, stories handed down from generation to generation—to relate her very modern, yet timeless stories of children and their world.

FOOTE, Timothy (Gilson) 1926-

PERSONAL: Born May 3, 1926, in London, England; son of John Taintor (a writer) and Jessica Florence (an actress; maiden name, Todhunter) Foote; married Audrey Chamberlain (a writer and teacher), June 18, 1948; children: Colin, Victoria, Valerie, Andrew. *Education:* Harvard University, A.B., 1949, M.A., 1952. *Politics:* Conservative. *Religion:* Episcopalian. *Home:* 10925 Mariner Dr., Ft. Washington, Md. 20744. *Agent:* Wallace & Sheil Agency, Inc., 177 East 70th St., New York, N.Y. 10021. *Office:* Smithsonian Magazine, 900 Jefferson Dr., S.W. Washington, D.C. 20560.

CAREER: Life, New York City, reporter and writer, 1949-51, assistant editor, 1953-54, associate editor, 1958-61, senior editor, 1961-62; Thomas Jefferson School, St. Louis, Missouri, teacher, 1952-53; Time-Life News Service, Paris, France, foreign correspondent, 1954-58; *Time,* New York City, book reviewer, 1962-64, associate editor, 1968, senior editor and book critic, 1969-77, senior editor for education, religion, law and science, 1977-82; International Book Society, Paris, European editor, 1964-66; *Smithsonian* Magazine, Washington, D.C., board of editors, 1982—. Fiction judge for National Book Awards, 1974. *Military service:* U.S. Navy, 1944-46; served in Pacific theater and Asia; received two battle stars. *Member:* National Book Critics Circle (member of executive board, 1976-82, 1984—), Phi Beta Kappa.

WRITINGS: The World of Peter Bruegel, Time-Life, 1968; *The Great Ringtail Garbage Caper* (illustrated by Normand Chartier), Houghton, 1979. Contributor to popular magazines, including *Esquire, New York, Harper's,* and *Horizon.* Member of advisory board of *Sea History,* 1977—.

ADAPTATIONS: ''The Great Ringtail Garbage Caper'' on ''Storybreak,'' CBS-TV, 1985.

WORK IN PROGRESS: An anthology of fishing stories to be published by David R. Godine; *A Sailors History of the American Revolution* to be published by Knopf; *Ringtails Aweigh.*

SIDELIGHTS: ''The older I get the more clearly I realize how much I still live off a country boyhood, and the emotional capital it provided in love of stories, the turning seasons, and all sorts of animals tame as well as wild.

''The practical details of a story have to be reasonable and logical, or the reader, even the young reader will turn away.

But a story that draws you in, especially a story that involves romance, magic, or adventure, carries its own special truth which often has nothing to do with logic and everyday reality.

"That is one reason why I believe in happy endings, after brave effort. I do not consider them frivolous or misleading, and I think we're wrong to insist that children get drenched in contemporary problem stories, and to make parents feel guilty (as some of them do) about offering tales that feed the imagination.

"Everyone learns all too soon about the harshness of life, its gritty dailiness and unforgiving demands upon us. But we deal with it, in part because of qualities of mind and heart acquired almost unwittingly in childhood. I'm not talking about moral preachment here, or formal religion. I mean the sense of possibility and hopefulness that stories, often labeled escapist, with happy endings coming after struggle in a good cause against apparently overwhelming odds, can provide at a level far below moral precept or worldly reason. In this sense reading *The Lord of the Rings* is not escapism, it is encouragement of the heart.

"In that connection I have a friend who endured prison and much more in the Soviet Union, but in the end escaped from

They drank and shouted and shouted and drank . . . ■
(From *The Great Ringtail Garbage Caper* by Timothy Foote. Illustrated by Normand Chartier.)

imprisonment several times and made his way to the West. He often wonders why he survived among so many others. And he believes that one of the reasons he made it is because as a boy in the late 1920s he read books like *The Three Musketeers, Michael Strogoff* and *The Deerslayer,* tales of adventure and daring, and so carried forward into life some inner, and perfectly irrational hope that a brave attempt might be crowned with success. So when the moment came, the chance to escape presented itself, he took it, where others around him did not.

"It is hard to have that inner lift if you have read only of failure and been told that everyone is a hopeless victim of circumstance."

FORRESTER, Frank H. 1919(?)-1986

OBITUARY NOTICE: Born about 1919, in New York, N.Y.; died by his own hand, May 21, 1986, in McLean, Va. Meteorologist, broadcast weatherman, and author. Forrester, who received his meteorological training during World War II, began his career as a radio and television weatherman in 1949. He broadcast the weather in both New York City and Jacksonville, Florida before joining WRC television and radio in Washington, D.C., in 1960. Two years later, he began working with the U.S. Geological Survey while continuing to broadcast part time at WRC. In his work with the geological survey, first as public information officer and later as chief of public affairs, Forrester provided both the public and the news media with information concerning meteorological phenomenon. After his retirement in 1981, he maintained an interest in meteorology, supplying local radio station WMAL with useful facts about the weather. Forrester wrote *1001 Questions Answered about the Weather* and two books for young readers, *Exploring the Air Ocean* and *The Real Book about the Weather.*

FOR MORE INFORMATION SEE: Authors of Books for Young People, 2nd edition, Scarecrow, 1971. Obituaries: *Washington Post,* May 23, 1986.

FOULDS, Elfrida Vipont 1902-
(Charles Vipont, Elfrida Vipont)

PERSONAL: Born July 3, 1902, in Manchester, England; daughter of Edward Vipont (a physician) and Dorothy (Crowley) Brown; married Robinson Percy Foulds, April 21, 1926 (deceased); children: Robin, Carolyn, Dorothy, Ann. *Education:* Attended Mount School. *Religion:* Society of Friends (Quaker). *Home:* Green Garth, Yealand Conyers, near Carnforth, Lancashire LA5 9SG, England.

CAREER: Writer of children's books. Lecturer on writing children's books and on Quaker history; head of Quaker Evacuation School for young children during World War II. *Member:* P.E.N., Society of Authors. *Awards, honors:* Carnegie Medal from the British Library Association, 1951, for *The Lark on the Wing; Book World*'s Children's Spring Book Festival Honor Book, 1970, for *The Elephant and the Bad Baby.* Honorary Doctorate in Humane Letters, 1984, from Earlham College.

WRITINGS—Children's books, under name Elfrida Vipont, except as indicated: *Good Adventure,* John Heywood, 1931; *Colin Writes to Friends House,* Friends Book Centre, 1934, 3rd edition, Bannisdale Press, 1957; (under pseudonym Charles

Vipont) *Blow the Man Down,* Oxford University Press, 1939, Lippincott, 1951; *The Lark in the Morn,* Oxford University Press, 1948, Bobbs-Merrill, 1950, 2nd edition, Holt, 1970.

Sparks among the Stubble, Oxford University Press, 1950; *The Lark on the Wing* (illustrated by Terence Reginald Freeman),

Oxford University Press, 1950, Bobbs-Merrill, 1951, 2nd edition, Holt, 1970; (under name Elfrida Vipont Foulds) *The Birthplace of Quakerism* (for adults and young people), Friend Home Service Committee, 1952, 3rd edition, 1973, revised edition (photographs by Simon Warner), Quaker Home Service, 1987; *The Story of Quakerism, 1652-1952* (for adults

For Thy many gifts we thank Thee;
For the gift of seeing things and people;
For the gift of hearing loud and soft sounds;
For the gift of tasting food and drink;
For the gift of feeling things we touch;
For the gift of smelling the scent of flowers —
For Thy many gifts we thank Thee.

Bertha C. Krall

(From *Bless This Day,* compiled by Elfrida Vipont. Illustrated by Harold Jones.)

The *Mayflower* rolled to and fro, and shuddered. ■ (From *Children of the Mayflower* by Elfrida Vipont. Illustrated by Evadne Rowan.)

and young people), Bannisdale Press, 1954, 2nd edition published as *The Story of Quakerism through Three Centuries,* 1960, 3rd edition, Friends United Press, 1977; *The Family at Dowbiggins,* Bobbs-Merrill, 1955; (under pseudonym Charles Vipont) *The Heir of Craigs,* Oxford University Press, 1955; *Arnold Rowntree: A Life* (for adults and young people), Bannisdale Press, 1955; *The Spring of the Year,* Oxford University Press, 1957; (editor) *The High Way,* Oxford University Press, 1957; (with others) *Five More,* Basil Blackwell, 1957; *More about Dowbiggins,* Lutterworth, 1958, published as *A Win for Henry Conyers,* Hamish Hamilton, 1969; (editor) *Bless This Day: Anthology of Prayers for Young Children,* Harcourt, 1958; *Changes at Dowbiggins,* Lutterworth, 1958, published as *Boggarts and Dreams,* Hamish Hamilton, 1969; *Henry Purcell and His Times,* Lutterworth, 1959; *Ackworth School* (for adults and young people), Lutterworth, 1959.

Flowering Spring, Oxford University Press, 1960; *The Story of Christianity in Britain,* M. Joseph, 1960; *What about Religion?,* Museum Press, 1961; (editor) *The Bridge,* Oxford University Press, 1962; *Search for a Song,* Oxford University Press, 1962; *A Faith to Live By,* Friends General Conference, 1962 (published in England as *Quakerism: A Faith to Live By,* Bannisdale Press, 1965); *Some Christian Festivals* (for adults and young people), M. Joseph, 1963; *Stevie,* Hamish Hamilton, 1965; *Larry Hopkins,* Hamish Hamilton, 1965; *The Offcomers,* Hamish Hamilton, 1965, McGraw, 1967; *Weaver of Dreams,* Walck, 1966; *Terror by Night,* Hamish Hamilton, 1966, published as *Ghosts' High Noon,* Walck, 1967; *The Secret Passage,* Hamish Hamilton, 1967; (with others) *People*

ELFRIDA VIPONT FOULDS

of the Past, Oxford University Press, 1967; *Children of the Mayflower,* Heinemann, 1969, F. Watts, 1970; *Michael and the Dogs,* Hamish Hamilton, 1969; *The Pavilion,* Oxford University Press, 1969, Holt, 1970; *The Elephant and the Bad Baby* (illustrated by Raymond Briggs), Coward, 1969; *Towards a High Attic,* Hamish Hamilton, 1969, Holt, 1971.

(With others) *My England,* Heinemann, 1973; *Bed in Hell* (for adults and young people), Hamish Hamilton, 1974; *George Fox and the Valiant Sixty* (for adults and young people), Hamish Hamilton, 1975; *A Little Bit of Ivory: A Life of Jane Austen,* Hamish Hamilton, 1977. Also author of short radio plays for school broadcasting. Contributor to periodicals.

WORK IN PROGRESS: A novel for young people set during World War II.

SIDELIGHTS: As a child, Foulds was both an avid storyteller and "a voracious, undiscriminating reader." An early encounter with *Treasure Island* led to the subsequent realization that "a book is a living world, and the characters in it are living people." As she grew older, she continued her storytelling through the written word and credits Latin with helping develop a sense of technique: "The study of Latin taught me to be more concerned with the structure and balance of a sentence, more precise in my choice of the right word or phrase.

"Life is the essential thing. A story, a setting, a group of characters must be given time to come alive; otherwise you have an ephemeral, dead-alive story. They will not come to life of themselves; patient research is needed, until you know your characters and their settings as well as you know your closest friends and probably better. Sloppy thinking is no substitute for exact knowledge.... Characters are like people; they have a life of their own, and once they come alive, you cannot impose your will on them. If you have drawn your plot too tightly, they can make hay of it. I have never forgotten how Judith, in *The Heir of Craigs,* refused to remain a minor character and wilfully played her part in the action whch led to the final tragedy.

"I found out by experience that hard work and self-discipline were essential to my craft. I soon learnt that the humility to take criticism and learn from it was another necessary ingredient, as well as the courage to recognize failure, and pick myself up and begin again. There was, however, another kind of criticism which must be resisted at all costs: the criticism which strikes at what your book has to say about life, which—take it or leave it—is what you were born to say.

"Writing fiction for children and young people has been my main work, but I have always tried to avoid getting into a rut. I also write biography, history and books about religion and, occasionally, music. These are not a whit less exacting, but they involve a different kind of discipline which I seem to need from time to time."

FOR MORE INFORMATION SEE: Library Association Record, May, 1951; *Junior Bookshelf,* July, 1951; *Christian Science Monitor,* January 23, 1956; *Young Reader's Review,* June, 1967; *New York Times Book Review,* July 9, 1967, March 22, 1970; *Books and Bookmen,* July, 1969; *Times Literary Supplement,* October 16, 1969; *Library Journal,* May 15, 1970.

Books should to one of these four ends conduce,
For wisdom, piety, delight, or use.
—Sir John Denham

FUCHS, Lucy 1935-

BRIEF ENTRY: Born April 13, 1935, in Ohio. As a writer, Fuchs observed: "I am interested in just about everything, especially people as they relate to each other." She is the author of four romance novels for young adults, all published by Bouregy: *Wild Winds of Mayaland* (1978), *Dangerous Splendor* (1978), *Shadow of the Walls* (1980), and *Pictures of Fear* (1981). Fuchs has worked as a counselor, social worker, elementary and high school teacher, and college instructor. She is a member of the International Reading Association and, in her spare time, enjoys travel, religion, reading, crafts, gardening, and cooking. *Home and office:* 505 South Oakwood Ave., Brandon, Fla. 33511.

FOR MORE INFORMATION SEE: Contemporary Authors, New Revision Series, Volume 12, Gale, 1984.

GÁL, László 1933-

PERSONAL: Born February 18, 1933, in Budapest, Hungary; came to Canada in 1956, naturalized in 1961; son of Istvan and Anna (Gemes) Gál; married Armida Romano Gargarella, January 20, 1962; children: Anna Maria, Raffaella. *Education:* Attended Academy of Dramatic Arts, Budapest, Hungary, 1951-52; Superior School of Pedagogy, Budapest, diploma, 1955. *Religion:* Roman Catholic. *Home:* Toronto, Ontario, Canada.

CAREER: Teacher of art to children in grades five to eight in Budapest, Hungary, for three years; free-lance artist beginning in the 1950s; *Globe and Mail,* Toronto, Ontario, Canada, artist of political portraits, 1950s; Eatons (department store), Toronto, layout artist, 1950s; Canadian Broadcasting Company (CBC), Toronto, graphic designer, 1958-65, 1977—; Arnoldo Mondadori Editore, Verona, Italy, illustrator, 1965-69; free-

lance illustrator, Toronto, 1969-77. *Exhibitions:* Cedarbrae Library, 1983. *Military service:* Hungarian Army, 1952-54. *Member:* Royal Canadian Academy of Arts.

AWARDS, HONORS: Canadian Library Association Book of the Year for Children Award, 1971, for *Cartier Discovers the St. Lawrence; The Moon Painters, and Other Estonian Folk Tales,* was chosen one of Child Study Association of America's Children's Books of the Year, 1971; Imperial Order of the Daughters of the Empire Best Children's Book of the Year, 1978, for *My Name Is Not Odessa Yarker, The Shirt of the Happy Man/La camicia dell'uomo felice,* and *Why the Man in the Moon Is Happy, and Other Eskimo Tales of Creation,* and 1980, for *The Twelve Dancing Princesses: A Fairy Story;* Amelia Frances Howard-Gibbon Illustrator's Medal from the Canadian Library Association, and Canada Council Children's Literature Prize to the illustrator of an English language publication, both 1980, both for *The Twelve Dancing Princesses: A Fairy Story;* Amelia Frances Howard-Gibbon Illustrator's Award runner-up, and Canada Council Children's Literature Prize for illustration, both 1984, both for *Hans Christian Andersen's "The Little Mermaid";* nominated for the Hans Christian Andersen Award, 1984; *Canadian Fairy Tales* and *The Willow Maiden* were included in the exhibition at the Bologna International Children's Book Fair, 1985.

WRITINGS: (Compiler) Hans C. Andersen, *Fiable de Andersen* (juvenile; self-illustrated), Mondadori, 1967.

Illustrator: Maria Luisa Gefaell de Vivanco, reteller, *Le gesta del Cid,* Mondadori, 1965, English translation published as *El Cid: Soldier and Hero,* Golden Press, 1968; M. L. Gefaell de Vivanco, *I Nibelunghi,* Mondadori, 1966, English translation published as *Siegfried: The Mighty Warrior,* McGraw, 1967; M. L. Gefaell de Vivanco, *Chanson de Roland* (title means "Song of Roland"), Mondadori, 1966; M. L. Gefaell de Vivanco, *Orlando paladino di Francia,* Mondadori, 1968; M. L. Gefaell de Vivanco, reteller, *Aeneide,* Mondadori, 1969.

Ronald Melzack, reteller, *Raven: Creator of the World,* Little, Brown, 1970; William Toye, *Cartier Discovers the St. Lawrence,* H. Z. Walck, 1970; Selve Maas, reteller, *The Moon Painters, and Other Estonian Folk Tales,* Viking, 1971; Leslie M. Frost, *Forgotten Pathways of the Trent,* Burns & MacEachern (Ontario), 1973; Nancy Cleaver, *How the Chipmunk Got Its Stripes,* Clarke, Irwin (Toronto), 1973; Mary Alice Downie, *Scared Sarah,* Nelson (Toronto), 1974; Marion Ralston, *Comparative Mythology,* Heath (Toronto), 1974; Bert Williams, *Sword of Egypt,* Scholastic-TAB, 1976; Edith Fowke, *Folklore of Canada,* McClelland & Stewart (Toronto), 1976; Mariella Bertelli, *The Shirt of the Happy Man/La camicia dell'uomo felice,* Kids Can Press (Toronto), 1977; Marian Engle, *My Name Is Not Odessa Yarker,* Kids Can Press, 1977; R. Melzack, *Why the Man in the Moon Is Happy, and Other Eskimo Tales of Creation,* McClelland & Stewart, 1977, published in England as *Why the Man in the Moon Is Happy and Other Eskimo Creation Stories,* Good Reading, 1979; Janet Lunn, reteller, *The Twelve Dancing Princesses: A Fairy Story,* Methuen, 1979, Braille edition, CNIB (Toronto), 1984.

Catherine Ahearn, *Cristobel: A Story for Young People,* Golden Dog Press (Ottawa), 1982; Margaret Crawford Maloney, reteller, *Hans Christian Andersen's "The Little Mermaid,"* Methuen (Toronto), 1983; Eva Martin, reteller, *Canadian Fairy Tales,* Douglas & McIntyre (Vancouver), 1984; Meghan Collins, *The Willow Maiden,* Dial, 1985, Braille edition, CNIB, 1986; E. Martin, reteller, *Tales of the Far North,* Dutton, 1986; Robert San Souci, *The Enchanted Tapestry,* Dial, 1987.

LÁSZLÓ GÁL

The giant and his wife and little girl were having their supper. The little girl was sitting on the floor, but even so, she was so tall that she towered over Ti-Jean. ■ (From "Ti-Jean Brings Home the Moon" in *Canadian Fairy Tales,* retold by Eva Martin. Illustrated by László Gál.)

As the moon sailed majestically across the sky, the new ladder was raised. ■ (From *The Moon Painters and Other Estonian Folk Tales,* retold by Selve Maas. Illustrated by László Gál.)

Also illustrator of *Illiad* and *Odyssey,* both 1968.

WORK IN PROGRESS: Illustrations for J.R.R. Tolkien's *Farmer Giles of Ham.*

SIDELIGHTS: Born February 18, 1933 in Budapest, Hungary, Gál was the youngest of six children. He showed an early interest and exceptional talent in drawing. By the age of nine he had already decided on a career as illustrator and by thirteen was showing some of his drawings in an international exhibition of children's art in Paris. Music was also an important part of his early life. Everyone in his family sang, with one brother going on to become a professional opera singer.

Gál's interests turned to acting during his teen years. He auditioned and was accepted into the Academy of Dramatic Arts in Budapest. His acting career proved short-lived, however, when he was cut from the program after one year's study.

With the Communist take-over of Hungary, career choices became very limited. The government decided that Gál should use his talents to become a teacher. He subsequently received an Art Education Diploma in 1955 to teach art to children.

He left Hungary during the 1956 Revolution and immigrated to Toronto, Canada where he worked various odd jobs as dishwasher, waiter, sign painter until he was able to put his artistic

(From *The Enchanted Tapestry* by Robert D. Sans Souci. Illustrated by László Gál.)

skills to better use, drawing political portraits for the editorial page of the *Globe and Mail,* as layout artist for Eatons and later as graphic designer for the Canadian Broadcasting Company (CBC).

In 1962 Gál took his new Italian Canadian bride, Armida Romano Gargarella, on a vacation to Italy. Here he took his portfolio to the publishing house of Arnoldo Mondadori, who encouraged him to prepare illustrations for *El Cid* on speculation. It took a year to prepare over sixty illustrations that led to a contract with Mondadori, launching his career as book illustrator. Gál moved to Italy and illustrated two full color books a year. Economic difficulties, however, forced his return to Canada and employment with CBC as well as freelance book illustration. Earning a living exclusively with illustration did not prove possible. "There is no money in it whatsoever.

"*The Little Mermaid* took a year and a half—for five or six thousand dollars. And it's selling very well. Can you imagine if it didn't sell very well?" [Laurie Bildfell, "Keeping the Wolf from the Door: The Financial Drawbacks of Illustrating Children's Books," *Quill & Quire,* November, 1984.[1]]

Gál must find time for his illustrations during lunch hours, in the evenings, or on the weekends. Besides creating certain frustrations, he admits "I have to put away an illustration for two or three weeks and I have to start it all over again. If you aren't practising constantly, you lose the touch."[1]

Gál prefers to illustrate in full color, but the limited budgets of most Canadian publishers have forced him to design in one or two colors. In 1978 he won the Toronto IODE award for his black and white illustration in *My Name Is Not Odessa Yarker, The Shirt of the Happy Man,* and *Why the Man in the Moon Is Happy.* He demands perfection in his work. "When I have the final drawing then I think I know what I am doing; but when I start to paint, I always find it isn't the way I thought it would be. It runs out completely differently. As I work on each painting my eyes become so critical that as each day passes I want to make it better and better and better. Although I might have liked it the day before yesterday and thought 'That's pretty good,' when I see it the next day in a different surrounding I decide it is not good." [Virginia Van Vliet, "Laszlo Gal," *Profiles 2: Actors and Illustrators,* edited by Irma McDonough, Canadian Library Association, 1982.[2]]

Among his many award-winning books was *The Twelve Dancing Princesses,* a personal favorite of his since he used his daughters, Anna Maria and Raffaella, as models. ". . . I said when I finished that if I don't get any results with this book I will never touch another one. One has to be very dedicated or just simply crazy to work for two years for practically nothing as I did for this book. That's why you don't find illustrators in this country because nobody makes sacrifices for what sometimes seems a hopeless cause."[2] The Renaissance style of the paintings evoke the influence of his years in Italy. "In Verona you are living in the midst of so much beauty and art that it would be impossible for it not to seep in."

FOR MORE INFORMATION SEE: In Review, October, 1980; Virginia Van Vliet, "Laszlo Gal," *Profiles 2: Actors and Illustrators,* edited by Irma McDonough, Canadian Library Association, 1982; "Exhibition of Laszlo Illustrations," *Toronto East End News,* May 11, 1983; Laurie Bildfell, "Keeping the Wolf from the Door: The Financial Drawbacks of Illustrating Children's Books," *Quill & Quire,* November, 1984.

GANZ, Yaffa 1938-

BRIEF ENTRY: Born March 26, 1938, in Chicago, Ill. Homemaker, editor, and writer. Ganz received her B.A. from the University of Chicago in 1962. The wife of a Bible and Talmud teacher, she devoted much of her time and energy during the following years to caring for a family of five children. In 1979 she became editor of the Young Reader's Division of Feldheim Publishers in Jerusalem, Israel. Ganz began writing books for children in an effort to bring "even a tiny bit of . . . vast wealth, wisdom, or beauty to light." Her first work, *Savta Simcha and the Incredible Shabbos Bag* (Feldheim, 1980), was described by *Publishers Weekly* as "an unusually appealing book" in its treatment of Jewish customs and holidays. Among Ganz's other titles, also published by Feldheim, are *Yedidya and the Esrog Tree, The Riddle Rhyme Book, The Adventures of Jeremy Levi, Savta Simcha and the Cinnamon Tree, The Story of Mimmy and Simmy, The Gift That Grew,* and *The Terrible Wonderful Day.* In addition, she has contributed several articles on Judaism and Israel to magazines and newspapers in the United States, Canada, England, and Israel. *Office:* Feldheim Publishers, P.O. Box 6525, Jerusalem, Israel.

FOR MORE INFORMATION SEE: Contemporary Authors, Volume 115, Gale, 1985.

GEISERT, Arthur (Frederick) 1941-

BRIEF ENTRY: Born September 20, 1941, in Dallas, Texas. Artist, printmaker, educator, author and illustrator of books for children. Geisert completed graduate study at the Art Institute of Chicago as well as the Otis Art Institute and the Chouinard Institute, and has taught classes in art at Concordia and Clark Colleges. His work has been exhibited at the Minnesota Art Museum, Illinois Art Council Gallery, National Museum of American Art in Washington, D.C., Joslyn Art Museum, and others. Representations of his prints also appear in university and museum collections, including the Museum of Art in Lodz, Poland.

According to Geisert, he began writing and illustrating books for children "to combine a classic etching style with humorous subject matters." His first picture book, *Pa's Balloon and Other Pig Tales* (Houghton, 1984), contains three stories about a lively pig family and their adventures in a hot air balloon. *Booklist* observed: "[The text's] ingenuous simplicity is a good match for the old-fashioned illustrations that were reproduced from copper-plate etchings and painstakingly watercolored." *Pigs from A to Z* (Houghton, 1986) provides an illustrated story about pigs building a treehouse, and, at the same time, presents a challenging alphabet game for preschoolers. The game, which involves finding letters visually embedded in the illustrations, was described by *Booklist* as "an intriguing venture for curious, ambitious browsers." Geisert's third picture book is entitled *The Building of Noah's Ark,* to be published by Houghton. *Address:* P.O. Box 3, Galena, Ill. 61306.

FOR MORE INFORMATION SEE: Who's Who in American Art, 16th edition, Bowker, 1984; *The Printworld Directory,* 3rd edition, Printworld, 1985; *Contemporary Authors,* Volume 120, Gale, 1987.

In silence I must take my seat, . . .
I must not speak a useless word,
For children must be seen, not heard.
—B.W. Bellamy

GOLDSMITH, John Herman Thorburn 1903-1987
(John Thorburn)

OBITUARY NOTICE: Born May 30, 1903, in Manchester, Lancashire, England; died May 31, 1987. Civil servant and author. Under the name John Thorburn, Goldsmith produced the children's books *Three's Company* and *Hildebrand,* both published during the 1930s. In the early days of World War II, Goldsmith aided in the evacuation of Norwegian and Dutch royal families; later, he served in the British National Fire Service. His work on staff selection for this agency eventually led him to join the Civil Services Selection Board in 1945. He became the board's chairman in 1951, and acted as civil service commissioner until his retirement in 1963.

FOR MORE INFORMATION SEE: International Authors and Writers Who's Who, 8th edition, Melrose, 1977; *Who's Who,* 139th edition, St. Martin's, 1987. Obituaries: *Times* (London), June 5, 1987.

GOLDSTEIN, Ernest A. 1933-

BRIEF ENTRY: Born July 13, 1933, in Providence, R.I. After receiving his B.A. from Brandeis University in 1954, Goldstein went abroad for doctoral study at the University of Strasbourg. On returning to the United States, he worked in New Hampshire as a youth counselor and a university lecturer, and, later, in New York in corporate library services. Eventually he became vice-president of New York-based Litton Educational Publishing, Inc. A turning point occurred for Goldstein in 1974 when he began writing full time. Targeted for children in grades four through eight, his "Let's Get Lost in a Painting" series consists of *Winslow Homer: The Gulf Stream, Edward Hicks: The Peaceable Kingdom, Emanuel Leutze: Washington Crossing the Delaware,* and *Grant Wood: American Gothic.* Each book discusses how its title artist fused subject, color, form, line, and movement to create meaning in a particular work. *School Library Journal* commended the author for expressing "through his eloquent apreciation of art and artists, a poetic humanism" and creating "intelligent and interesting books which show . . . a model approach to the study of painting." For young readers, Goldstein also wrote *Teaching through Art* and co-authored, with Robert Saunders, a two-book series titled *Understanding and Creating Art. Home:* 15 West 72nd St., New York, N.Y. 10023.

FOR MORE INFORMATION SEE: Contemporary Authors, Volume 110, Gale, 1984.

GREEN, Roger James 1944-

BRIEF ENTRY: Born in 1944, in Buxton, England. Green received his teaching certificate from the Sheffield College of Education in 1965 and later attended the University of London where he earned a B.S. in economics. Since 1977 he has held the position of deputy headteacher at Wisewood Primary School in Sheffield, England. All three of Green's books for young readers contain an element of the supernatural, flavored with such occurrences as hauntings, devil sightings, and ghosts. Green chooses to write about this realm because "the supernatural is an open-ended question and I like children to be left with a questioning sense of wonder." In his first book, *The Fear of Samuel Walton* (Oxford University Press, 1984), a young boy fears that an old stone situated on his grandfather's

farm possesses the power to commit evil. *School Library Journal* called this work "a super job of blending mysterious legend with an accurate setting of English village life," while *Booklist* commented that "the suspense builds to a redoubtable crescendo, and one waits with bated breath for the finale." The "finale," as it were, runs into Green's sequel entitled *The Lengthening Shadow* (Oxford University Press, 1986), demonstrating the author's intention to keep his books open-ended. Green's third book is *The Devil Finds Work.* He is presently working on additional juvenile books about witchcraft in eighteenth-century England. *Home:* 268 Abbeydale Rd. S, Sheffield, England S17 3LN.

GREENBERG, Polly 1932-

PERSONAL: Born April 21, 1932, in Milwaukee, Wis.; daughter of Lindsay (vice-president and editor-in-chief of *Milwaukee Journal*) and Margaret (an educator; maiden name, Pollitzer) Hoben; married Daniel S. Greenberg (a writer and editor), June, 1953 (divorced, 1964); children: Julie, Margaret, Cathryn, Ellen Elizabeth, Gwen. *Education:* Sarah Lawrence College, B.A., 1954; University of Delaware, M.Ed., 1957; further graduate study at University of Massachusetts. *Politics:* "Active grassrootist." *Religion:* "Ecumenical existential humanist."

CAREER: Author. Worked as an elementary school teacher in Maryland; employed by the U.S. Office of Education, 1963-64, Office of Economic Opportunity, 1964-65, Child Development Group of Mississippi (Head Start program; founder), 1965-67, General Learning Corp., 1968-74, and Human Service Group, 1974-76; U.S. Department of Health, Education & Welfare, Office of Human Development Services, Washington, D.C., staff member, beginning in 1977. Volunteer work includes counseling delinquent boys and teaching learning-disabled children and their parents. Public speaker; consultant. *Awards, honors: Oh Lord, I Wish I Was a Buzzard* was included in the American Institute of Graphic Arts Book Show, 1967-68, and was selected one of Child Study Association of America's Children's Books of the Year, 1968.

WRITINGS: Oh Lord, I Wish I Was a Buzzard (juvenile; illustrated by Aliki), Macmillan, 1968; *The Devil Has Slippery Shoes,* Macmillan, 1969; *Bridge-to-Reading: Comprehensive Early Chidhood Curriculum,* Silver Burdett, 1973; *Day Care Do-It-Yourself Staff Growth Program,* Kaplan Press, 1975; *How to Convert the Kids from What They Eat to What They Oughta,* Kaplan Press, 1978; *Changes and Challenges: Our Children's Future,* Pergamon, 1979; *I Know I'm Myself Because . . .* (juvenile; illustrated by Jennifer Barrett), Human Services Press, 1981; *Birds of the World* (juvenile; illustrated by Philip Rymer), Platt & Munk, 1983. Contributor to professional journals. Editor of *Dimensions,* 1974-76.

WORK IN PROGRESS: How to Be a Better Single Parent; Creative Coping: Single Parenting with Five Daughters, Two Careers, and Serious Cash Flow Problem, an autobiography; a novel; a book "about peace, freedom, and love"; a book of short stories; four juvenile books.

SIDELIGHTS: "I love to write because I have lots to say. I used to be crazy about working all the time; now I get enormous pleasure out of writing as a hobby, even if it is published.

"Over the past few years, however, I find it increasingly frustrating that publishing has become so commercialized and industrialized. An author has to write a 'proposal' almost as long as the book itself in order to get a manuscript read by an editor. Rules about length and other detail have come to outweigh public demand. And it is as time-consuming to 'sell' a manuscript to an agent as it is to sell it directly to a publisher.

"Because of all this, I tend to write, finish, and file books, not bothering with the incredible hassle and expense of marketing manuscripts or story ideas.

"The greatest frustration of all is getting my writing time funded up to the level of my family needs right now. When all my daughters are through college, I hope to buy a mountain farm, write at least three-quarters of the year, revel in nature, read novels, bask in my extended family, take care of my pets, and do challenging other jobs one-quarter of the year anywhere on earth.

"My passionate current interest is public policy pertaining to creating and assisting humane beings. I also want to write fiction.''

Greenberg's works are included in the Kerlan Collection at the University of Minnesota.

HOBBIES AND OTHER INTERESTS: Pets, nature, novels, travel, civic activities.

FOR MORE INFORMATION SEE: Martha E. Ward and Dorothy A. Marquardt, *Authors of Books for Young People,* supplement to the 2nd edition, Scarecrow, 1979.

NEALE HALEY

HALEY, Neale

PERSONAL: Born in Buffalo, N.Y.; daughter of Frederick H. (a research chemist) and Jacqueline (a writer; maiden name, Longaker) Kranz; married Russell I. Haley (a market researcher), May 29, 1948; children: Douglas Frank, Kim Suzanne. *Education:* Barnard College, A.B., 1962. *Politics:* Independent. *Religion:* Christian Scientist. *Agent:* Julie Fallowfield, MacIntosh and Otis, 475 Fifth Ave., New York, N.Y. 10017.

CAREER: Riding director, director at Camp Longacres, East Aurora, N.Y., summers, 1943-68. *Member:* First Church of Christ (first reader). *Awards, honors: Teach Yourself to Ride* was chosen one of New York Public Library's Books for the Teen Age, 1980, 1981, and 1982, and *Birds for Pets and Pleasure,* 1982; Outstanding Science Trade Book for Children from the National Science Teachers Association and Children's Book Council Joint Committee, 1981, for *Birds for Pets and Pleasure.*

WRITINGS: How to Teach Group Riding, A. S. Barnes, 1970; *Judge Your Own Horsemanship,* A. S. Barnes, 1971; *The Schooner Era: A Lost Epic in History,* A. S. Barnes, 1972; *How to Have Fun with a Horse,* A. S. Barnes, 1972; *Understanding Your Horse: Equine Character and Psychology,* A. S. Barnes, 1973; *Grooming Your Horse,* A. S. Barnes, 1974; *Teach Yourself to Ride,* A. S. Barnes, 1974; *Training Your Horse to Show,* A. S. Barnes, 1976; *Birds for Pets and Pleasure: How to Keep Them Alive* (illustrated by Pamela Carroll), Delacorte, 1981. Contributor to *Christian Science Monitor, Christian Science Journal, Christian Science Sentinel, American Cage Bird,* and other periodicals.

SIDELIGHTS: "I want to help people, especially children. . . . You can help a great many children in the riding ring. Horses open their hearts, then you can reach them.

"I have a love for schooners, for the part they played in making America the nation it is today. The pioneers who went West have been glorified, deservedly so, for their courage and persistence, but the men on schooners who faced death at sea in their daily lives and who generally died at sea, the men who worked carrying dull loads up and down a dangerous coast, are almost forgotten.

"One's life changes, a bit like a kaleidoscope, retaining the underlying values, but throwing color and form into new fields. An eighteen-foot aviary with artificial lights and plants behind a glass wall in my living room highlights an interest that rivals my interest in horses. Here twenty species of finches mingle and breed. But I've turned now to my real love, children's fiction.

"My aim is still to reach out to a world that is much in need of love and understanding. My heart yearns to preserve the innocence of childhood and fill it with joy and laughter.

"One of the joys of life is to discern new directions and broader horizons for blessing people. Our great need is for compassion and understanding in our world. Each of us finds his or her own answer of specific means for solutions to the world's problems. We find ways in our own sphere for helping those who need it most. As a Christian Scientist, I have a conviction in the power of prayer, with an understanding of God as Love, can bring peace and comfort to the world.

"As a writer, I am now writing for non-literate adults in New Hampshire. Some of the historical background I use also reaches children. It is exciting to see the response from the material I have written so far. Since this is a new area for me, and I am not doing it for pay, the compensation from the delight of the readers has special significance."

HALLIDAY, William R(oss) 1926-

PERSONAL: Born May 9, 1926, in Emory University, Ga.; son of William Ross (an actuary and executive) and Jane E. (Wakefield) Halliday; married Eleanore Hartvedt, July 2, 1951 (deceased); children: Marcia Lynn, Patricia Anne, William Ross III. *Education:* Swarthmore College, B.A., 1946; George Washington University, M.D., 1948. *Home:* 1117 36th Ave. E., Seattle, Wash. 98112.

CAREER: Private practice of thoracic surgery, Seattle, Wash., 1957-65; Department of Labor and Industries, Olympia and Seattle, Wash., medical consultant, 1965-71, chief medical consultant and medical director, 1971-76; Washington State Division of Vocational Rehabilitation, medical director, 1976-82; in private practice, 1983-84; Middle Tennessee Back Care Center and Comprehensive Medical Rehabilitation Center (Dashville), medical director, 1984-87. Director of Western Speleological Survey, 1955-81; president of International Speleological Foundation, 1981—; assistant director of International Glaciospeleological Survey, 1972—; director of speleological research for Travel Industry for the Environment, 1973-75. *Military service:* U.S. Navy, Medical Corps, 1949-50, 1955-56; became lieutenant commander. *Member:* American College of Chest Physicians (fellow), National Speleological Society (fellow; trustee, 1950-72), American Spelean History Association (president, 1968), Federation of Western Outdoor Clubs (vice-president, 1959-61), North Cascades Conservation Council (vice-president, 1962-63), Explorers Club (fellow), The Mountaineers (trustee), Seattle Free Lances (past president). *Awards, honors:* Certificate of Merit from National Speleological Society, 1960; *Desert Magazine* award, 1960, for *Adventure Is Underground;* Governor's award, 1968, chosen as one of the New York Public Library's Books for the Teenage, 1980, 1981, 1982, all for *Depths of the Earth.*

WRITINGS: Adventure Is Underground, Harper, 1959; *Depths of the Earth,* Harper, 1966; *American Caves and Caving,* Harper, 1974. Author of numerous articles and booklets. Editor of *Journal of Spelean History,* 1967-73.

WORK IN PROGRESS: Systematic research on caves and their interaction with man; research on psychosocial complications of disability programs, disability prevention, and rehabilitation.

HAMSA, Bobbie 1944-

PERSONAL: Born June 14, 1944, in Ord, Neb.; daughter of R. A. (a dentist) and Doris (a writer; maiden name, Sanborn) Hamsa; married Mike Eisenhart, September 20, 1967 (divorced, 1976); married Dick Sullivan (an advertising executive), June 18, 1977; children: (first marriage) John; (second marriage; stepchildren) Kenton, Tracy. *Education:* University of Nebraska, B.A., 1966.

CAREER: First National Bank of Omaha, Omaha, Neb., management trainee, 1966-67; United Airlines, Omaha, reservation agent, 1967-68; Freeman-Thompson Insurance Agency, Omaha, secretary and junior underwriter, 1968-69; Bozell & Jacobs, Inc. (advertising agency), Omaha, copywriter, 1975-80; writer, 1980—. *Member:* Kappa Kappa Gamma (member of alumnae executive board, 1973-75), Junior League of Omaha, Planned Parenthood. *Awards, honors:* Advertising awards include three Cornhusker Addy Awards between 1977 and 1981, for advertising copy.

WRITINGS—Juvenile; ''Far-Fetched Pets'' series; all illustrated by Tom Dunnington; all published by Childrens Press:

**Dirty Larry gets dirty
No matter what the hour.**

■(From *Dirty Larry* by Bobbie Hamsa. Illustrated by Paul Sharp.)

Your Pet Bear, 1980; *Your Pet Beaver,* 1980; *Your Pet Elephant,* 1980; *Your Pet Kangaroo,* 1980; *Your Pet Camel,* 1980; *Your Pet Penguin,* 1980; *Your Pet Gorilla,* 1981; *Your Pet Lion,* 1981; *Your Pet Sea Lion,* 1982; *Your Pet Giraffe,* 1982.

Other—juvenile; *Dirty Larry* (illustrated by Paul Sharp), Childrens Press, 1983; *Fast Draw Freddie: Rookie Readers* (illustrated by Stephen Hayes), Childrens Press, 1984; *Animal Babies* (illustrated by T. Dunnington), Childrens Press, 1985; *Polly Wants a Cracker* (illustrated by Jerry Warshaw), Childrens Press, 1986.

WORK IN PROGRESS: Children's books; parodies and other short pieces.

SIDELIGHTS: ''The idea for my series began when my son asked for a pet lizard. 'If you're going to have a pet, at least choose something that's useful around the house,' I answered, 'like an elephant. At least he could clean your aquarium.' In the series, children learn many otherwise dry vital statistics about animals by imagining what it's like to have them around the house. Needless to say, this leads to some pretty funny stuff!

'' 'Fools rush in . . .' and that I did, busting brazenly 'over the transom' via the U.S. Mails, with three manuscripts for 'Far-Fetched Pets.' I was not afraid of the word 'no' and had even made plans for papering a wall with rejection slips, an idea I thought delightfully camp! This aspect of my career began in 1980 as an extension of—and diversion from—writing advertising copy for a variety of clients, including Mutual of Omaha's 'Wild Kingdom,' sometime source of factual material for the 'Far-Fetched Pets' series.

''If there's any philosophy behind my writings, it's the same philosophy that lies behind my life. . . . I enjoy making light of the world around me, turning the commonplace into the unexpected, observing things in a fresh light. Tongue-in-cheek humor is my forte and, to me, it is not work.

"I stand as proof to aspiring writers that anyone can do it provided they have (1) desire, (2) luck, and (3) talent, named last because it alone is no guarantee of success. You can't lose more than a few bucks postage by trying, by forging ahead, by taking that first awful chance. And if you aren't by nature genuinely self-confident, at least pretend you are until your manuscript is in the mail."

HARRIS, Jonathan 1921-

PERSONAL: Surname legally changed in 1954; born November 13, 1921, in New York, N.Y.; son of Morris (a salesman) and Becky (Plutt) Awerbach; married Martha Sheffer (a school librarian), February 22, 1948; children: Paul Julian, Seth David. *Education:* College of the City of New York (now City College of the City University of New York), B.A., 1941; Institut d'Etudes Politiques, Paris, France, Diploma, 1952; Harvard University, M.A.T., 1962; New York University, Ph.D., 1972. *Home and office:* 78 Hillside Ave., Roslyn Heights, N.Y. 11577. *Agent:* Edite Kroll, 31 East 31st St., New York, N.Y. 10016.

CAREER: Headquarters, Supreme Commander Allied Powers (S.C.A.P.), Tokyo, Japan, editor and writer, 1946-47; International News Service, New York City, foreign news rewriter, 1953-54; advertising copywriter and copy chief for agencies in New York City and Boston, Mass., 1954-60; Paul D. Schreiber High School, Port Washington, N.Y., social studies teacher and department chairman, 1962-83; writer, 1983—. *Military service:* U.S. Army, 1943-46; became technical sergeant. *Member:* Authors Guild, American Civil Liberties Union.

WRITINGS—For young adults: *Hiroshima: A Study in Science, Politics, and the Ethics of War,* Addison-Wesley, 1970; *Scientists in the Shaping of America,* Addison-Wesley, 1971; *Judgment: A Simulated Trial of Harry S. Truman,* Interact, 1977; *The New Terrorism: Politics of Violence,* Messner, 1983; *Super Mafia: Organized Crime Threatens America,* Messner, 1984; *A Statue for America: The First One Hundred Years of the Statue of Liberty* (Junior Literary Guild selection), Four Winds, 1986; *Drugged Athletes: The Crisis in American Sports,* Four Winds, 1987; *The Land and People of France,* Lippincott, 1988.

SIDELIGHTS: "Travel is my chief fascination. I took my Army discharge in Japan and lived there for two years, working as an editor and writer for the Occupation and visiting much of

the country. I lived in France from 1950 to 1953, took a graduate diploma in international relations, and visited several other countries. Since then I've enjoyed shorter trips to Mexico, Canada, Israel, Greece, England, Scotland, and Spain. I've also seen a good deal of the United States.

"Variety in employment has also spiced my life. I've had a few careers, enjoying each until the time came for a change. Now, at last, I'm a full-time writer.

"My first books for teenagers were published during the twenty-one richly rewarding years I spent teaching social studies to high school students. I retired from teaching in 1983 in order to write full time.

"I feel strongly that the conceptual content of books for young people should never be watered down in any condescending way. Any and all ideas, however subtle or complex, can and should be expounded clearly and simply.

"Since my writings tend to deal with broad historical subjects that have been treated by other authors, I get a special kick out of discoveries—which often happen through the mysterious process of serendipity—of precious nuggets of information that have never been published before."

HOBBIES AND OTHER INTERESTS: Jazz and classical music; chess; reading; brisk walking.

HENBEST, Nigel 1951-

BRIEF ENTRY: Born May 6, 1951, in Manchester, England. Editor, consultant, and author. In 1972 Henbest graduated with first class honors from Leicester University with a B.S. in astronomy and physics; three years later, he received his M.S. in radio astronomy from Cambridge University. He has co-written television scripts, acted as a script consultant, and broadcasted for British radio and BBC World Service. In addition, Henbest has served as an on-going contributor to encyclopedias, international publications, and British magazines and newspapers, two of which have enlisted him as a regular columnist. A member of the British Astronomical Association, he has edited the organization's journal since 1985. He also acts as a consultant for the London-based magazine, *New Scientist.*

According to Henbest, "by writing about the sky, its beauty and its mysteries, an author can not only grip his audience, but also impart . . . an understanding of how science, and scientists work." He has produced a number of books on astronomy such as *The Exploding Universe, The Mysterious Universe, Halley's Comet,* and, with Michael Marten, *The New Astronomy.* Many of Henbest's works have been written with Heather Couper, fellow broadcaster and scriptwriter. Among their collaborations, aimed at middle and high school-age readers are *Space Frontiers* (Marks & Spencer, 1978), which was included in a special award from the New York Academy of Sciences for a series of engineering and technology in 1979, *Astronomy* (F. Watts, 1983), *Physics* (F. Watts, 1983), *The Planets* (Pan, 1985), *The Sun* (F. Watts, 1986), and *The Moon* (F. Watts, 1987). In its review on *Physics, School Library Journal* commended the authors for "simplifying without encouraging . . . misapprehensions," and, in essence, creating "a good appetite-whetter for the subject." Presently, Henbest and Couper are working on two new titles, *Guide to the Galaxy* and *The Stars.* When time permits, Henbest enjoys traveling, music, and vegetarian food. *Home:* 55 Colomb St., London SE10 9EZ, England.

JONATHAN HARRIS

HEYERDAHL, Thor 1914-

PERSONAL: Born October 6, 1914, in Larvik, Norway; son of Thor (president of brewery and mineral water plant) and Alison (chairman of Larvik Museum; maiden name, Lyng) Heyerdahl; married Liv Coucheron Torp, December 24, 1936 (marriage ended); married Yvonne Dedekam-Simonsen, March 7, 1949; children: (first marriage) Thor, Bjorn; (second marriage) Anette, Marian, Elisabeth. *Education:* Attended Larvik College; University of Oslo, graduate studies, 1937. *Home:* Colla Micheri, Laigueglia, Italy. *Agent:* Yvonne Heyerdahl, Jonsrudveien 7E, Oslo 2, Norway.

CAREER: Anthropologist, explorer, author. Expeditions to Polynesia, 1938, 1947, British Columbia, 1939-40, Galapagos Islands, 1952, Andes region, 1954, Easter Island and the East Pacific, 1955-56, 1986, Africa and Asia Minor, 1968-70, 1973-77, Atlantic Ocean, 1969, 1970, and Indian Ocean, 1977-78, 1982-84. Producer of documentary film "Kon-Tiki," RKO, 1951, "Galapagos," 1955, "Aku-Aku, the Secret of Easter Island," "The Ra Expeditions," Swedish Broadcasting Corp., 1971, "The Tigris Expedition," British Broadcasting Corp./ National Geographic Society, 1979, and "The Maldive Mystery." Member and lecturer at International Congress Americanists, Cambridge, 1952, Sao Paulo, 1954, San Jose, 1958, Vienna, 1960, Barcelona, Madrid, and Sevilla, all 1964, at International Congress of Anthropology and Ethnology, Paris,

1960, and Moscow, 1964, and International Pacific Science Congress, Honolulu, 1961, Tokyo, 1965, and Vancouver, 1976. Has appeared on radio and television in Europe, United States, and Latin America. Founder and board member, Kon-Tiki Museum, Oslo, Norway, 1948—. International trustee, World Wildlife Fund, 1977; international patron, United World Colleges, 1978. *Military service:* Free Norwegian Forces, 1942-45; became lieutenant. *Member:* Royal Norwegian Academy of Sciences; New York Academy of Sciences (fellow; honorary member); Geographical Societies of Norway, Sweden, Belgium, Brazil, Peru, Russia (honorary member); World Association of World Federalists; Worldview International; Academy of Sciences of the U.S.S.R. (honorary member); Explorers Club (New York); Travellers Club (Oslo); Club des Explorateurs (Paris).

AWARDS, HONORS: Commander, Order of St. Olav (Norway); Officer of Distinguished Merits (Peru); Decorated Grand Officer, Order al Merito della Republica Italiana; Officer of Merit, First Class (Egypt); Great Officer of Royal Alaouites Order (Morocco); Kirll i Metodi, Order of First Class (Bulgaria); Order of the Golden Ark (Holland); Retzius Medal, 1950, and Vega Gold Medal, 1952, both from Royal Swedish Anthropological and Geographical Society; Mungo Park Medal from Royal Scottish Geographical Society, 1951; Prix Bonaparte-Wyse Société de Geographie, 1951 (France); Academy Award for camera achievement from the National Academy

THOR HEYERDAHL

of Motion Picture Arts and Sciences, for documentary film, "Kon-Tiki," 1951; Elish Kane Gold Medal, 1952, from the Geographical Society, Philadelphia; Ph.D. from University of Oslo, 1961; Lomonosov Medal from Moscow University, 1962; Patrons Gold Medal from Royal Geographical Society of Great Britain, 1964; *The Ra Expeditions* was selected one of American Library Association's Best Young Adult Books, 1971; Academy Award nomination for "The Ra Expeditions," 1971; International Pahlavi Environment Prize from United Nations, 1978; Gold Medal from Boston Museum of Science; named honorary professor, El Instituto Politécnico Nacional, Mexico; Magellan Award from the Circumnavigators Club, 1981; *The Tigris Expedition* was selected one of New York Public Library's Books for the Teen Age, 1982.

WRITINGS: Paa jakt efter paradiset (title means "On the Hunt for Paradise"), Gyldendal (Norway), 1938; *Kon-Tiki Ekspedisjonen*, Gyldendal, 1948, translation by F. H. Lyon published as *Kon-Tiki: Across the Pacific by Raft*, Rand McNally, 1950, young people's edition published as *Kon-Tiki for Young People*, Rand McNally, 1960, 2nd edition, G. Allen, 1965, new edition published as *The Kon-Tiki Expedition*, 1968, another edition published as *Kon-Tiki: A True Adventure of Survival at Sea* (illustrated by Ronald Himler), adapted by Lisa Norby, Random House, 1984; *American Indians in the Pacific: The Theory behind the Kon-Tiki Expedition*, Allen & Unwin, 1952, Rand McNally, 1953; *Great Norwegian Expeditions*, Dreyers Forlag, 1956; (with Arne Skjolsvold) *Archaeological Evidence of Pre-Spanish Visits to the Galapagos Islands*, Society for American Archaeology, 1956; *Aku-Aku: The Secret of Easter Island*, Rand McNally, 1958, reissued, Ballantine, 1974.

(Editor and contributor with Edwin N. Ferdon) *Norwegian Archaeological Expedition to Easter Island, and the East Pacific Reports*, Rand McNally, Volume I: *Archaeology of Easter Island*, 1961, Volume II: *Miscellaneous Subjects*, 1965; (coauthor) *Vanished Civilizations*, Thames & Hudson, 1963; *Sea Routes to Polynesia*, Rand McNally, 1968; *The Ra Expeditions*, Doubleday, 1970; *Fatu-Hiva: Back to Nature*, Allen & Unwin, 1974, Doubleday, 1975; *The Art of Easter Island*, Doubleday, 1975; (author of preface with Carl Sagan) Ronald Story, *The Space Gods Revealed: A Close Look at the Theories of Erich Von Daniken*, Harper, 1976; *Early Man and the Ocean: A Search for the Beginnings of Navigation and Seaborne Civilizations*, Doubleday, 1978; *The Tigris Expedition: In Search of Our Beginnings*, Doubleday, 1980; *The Maldive Mystery*, Adler & Adler, 1986.

Contributor of chapters to *The Quest for America*, 1971, and to scientific journals and other periodicals.

SIDELIGHTS: Born **October 6, 1914.** Heyerdahl shared his mother's interest in woodcarving, animals and anthropology. At the age of seven he exhibited his collection of snakes, shells, starfish, crabs, butterflies and insects in a stable behind his family's house, already familiar with the Latin names of even the rarest animals.

An unremarkable student, he became bored with school, dreaming, instead, about faraway places. The great outdoors of fields and forests and ponds became his educational arena. Zoology, an early career ambition, was a field he would pursue at the university. One of his professors recalled his impressions of his young student: "I was at once fascinated by his clearcut face, which suggested determination—there was such sparkling liveliness in his eyes, his questions so concise and to the point, and his range of expressions revealed a quick grasp and appreciation of everything that was said. A resolute,

Heyerdahl as a child in Norway.

almost set expression of his mouth suggested that if this fellow started on a project he would hardly give up until he had reached his aim. That was how the young student Thor Heyerdahl looked as a freshman." [Arnold Jacoby, *Señor Kon-Tiki: The Biography of Thor Heyerdahl*, Rand McNally, 1967.¹]

1938. Made first expedition to Polynesia to study animal and plant life. With his new bride, Liv Torp, Heyerdahl lived for a year on the remote island of Fatu-Hiva in the Marquesas Islands of the Pacific Ocean. Owned by France, the islands are 2,000 miles southeast of Hawaii. "As one island rose from the sea another sank and disappeared, for there was a great distance between the islands in the group. The Pacific stretched between them in varied tints of blue. But the sea round each individual island was green as grass, due to the microorganisms that lived upon what the perpetual succession of waves broke from the brittle rocks of the islands. Shoals of fish were also attracted to this green pasture with dolphins in pursuit of them. Swarms of seabird followed our boat and plunged after the fish which struggled on the line we were towing astern.

"... Here the Pacific reached its highest degree of fertility, putting to shame the finest of hothouses. Deep wild gorges cutting into the central mass of the mountains continually opened before us. The jungle clothed the mountains like giant moss, then flowed down the ledges and clefts in the cliffs, to end in a chaos of luxuriant foliage in the valley, the crowns of the palm trees growing ever higher, striving to outstrip the steep precipices on either side. It seemed as if the green wealth of vegetation was reflected in the sea around, green on green. But the naked rock of mountains was red, and the sky was as blue as the ocean farther off shore.

"It was not the equatorial heat alone which created these floating hothouses. In the interior of the island, peaks soared into the air to intercept the course of the clouds and squeeze the rain out of them before they were able to pass by. The rainwater poured down from the interior parts of the mountains in rushing torrents and rivers, through the jungle and the palm valleys and out into the green sea. And the tooth of time had played with the fragile volcanic rock. Deep caves and subterranean streams, pinnacles and grotesque carvings in the mountains turned the whole picture into a fantastic fairyland. . . . Empty of human life, but full of mystery. . . ."[1]

The two young explorers lived among the natives under primitive conditions, nothing but a knife and a tea kettle. Heyerdahl later recalled his daily life: "Our days begin with a heavenly chorus of joy, after the brightly colored Marquesan cuckoo has awakened the choir of forest birds with his trumpet call. While the cool night wind from the mountains is still blowing through the hut and arousing us with a thrilling joy of life, the sunlight blazes like a revelation through the tops of the palm trees and on the colorful bamboo floor. The bare mountain peaks at the head of the valley, which loomed rust brown in the twilight of dawn, flame out like a cock's comb in the morning sun, and all nature is suddenly turned into a festival, crowded with every kind of sun worshiper rejoicing to welcome the day.

"We two in our green bamboo hut are happy spectators of all this harmonious combination of light, air, and music, which has gone on just like this ever since the Creator started it in the dawn of time. No human beings have had a hand in this performance. Shades seem to fall from our eyes at such a moment. When we go to wash in the spring, hidden among gigantic leaves, every drop of water spilt from our hands can sparkle like a jewel of incomparable beauty. No precious stone polished by human hands can shine with more loveliness than that pure liquid drop beneath the flame of the sun. Here—at the spring—we can bail them up by handfuls and afford to let them trickle by the thousands down toward their reflection and obliteration in the water beneath. And what about the melodious dance of the little stream, and the artistic composition of this frame of green vegetation which surrounds the living water? Can mankind create anything half so beautiful? Here the work of creation is perfect and complete, the masterpiece in which physics and chemistry, art and religion are inextricably blended, to fashion the Creator's great *perpetuum mobile*."

After conquering daily living on Fatu-Hiva, the couple ventured out on expeditions of steadily increasing length discovering the legend of Tiki, the god who brought the first natives to the Polynesian Islands. "I remember how I shocked my father and astonished my mother and her friends when I came back to Norway and handed over my glass jars of beetles and fish from Fatu-Hiva to the University Zoological Museum. I wanted to give up animal studies and tackle primitive peoples. The unsolved mysteries of the South Seas had fascinated me. There must be a rational solution of them, and I had made my objective the identification of the legendary hero Tiki."[1]

1939-1940. Heyerdahl made an expedition to British Columbia with his wife and young son. The income from his first book and from his other writings and lectures gave him enough money for six months' field work in Bella Coola. He wrote

(From *The Kon-Tiki Expedition* by Thor Heyerdahl.)

Heyerdahl with his youngest son, Bjorn.

from Vancouver: "Once more we are on an island in the Pacific—Vancouver Island. We are sitting on a top floor room of an English villa on the outskirts of Victoria. There is a bright moon outside, and we can catch a glimpse of the Pacific. It is a remarkable country, this Pacific coast of Canada. It is midwinter, with glittering ranges of snow-clad mountains, but along the coast here the grass is green. There are roses and fruit. And they are even bathing on the beach! In the parks, bears, bison, and deer are strolling about, and masses of wild duck are swimming along the shore. There are even seals. Of course there are skyscrapers to spoil the whole thing. But all the same, if there must be a town, it can't be more beautiful than Victoria. . . ."[1]

Heyerdahl believed that the Polynesians were descended from two groups of settlers—one group coming east to Polynesia from Peru and another from as far north as British Columbia. In **1941** he first published his theory on the origin of Polynesian culture. "After a year of research along the British Columbian coast I believe that I possessed sufficient material to trace two separate migrations from the American mainland to the Polynesian island world: (a) a pre-Incan civilization, with its center near Lake Titicaca and along the Peruvian coast below, seems to have swept the islands at a comparatively early period, via Easter Island; while (b) a later migration, the descendants of which dominate the present Polynesian race, reached the islands via Hawaii from the Bella Coola area of British Columbia about 1000 A.D.'"[1]

1942-1945. Served with the Free Norwegian Forces during World War II.

1946. Convinced that the inhabitants of the South Sea Islands came from South America on primitive Inca rafts, Heyerdahl decided to prove his theory by reenacting the voyage. Attempting to gain financial backing for his expedition, he approached the United States War Department. ". . . Before it was too late," he wrote in his diary, "I decided on the raft trip and staked my whole life on the plan, leaving no way of retreat open, in order to be able to concentrate on the way forward. I've gone straight ahead as never before in my life, I have *believed* and *willed* and the obstacles have collapsed, one after another, until today. Many are still willing to contribute their name, some are willing to contribute from the government's abundance. But no one is willing to give anything of his own. We have arrived at a point where we have attracted abundant interest, have obtained most of the important equipment, but have not a penny with which to start the expedition. The snowball has rolled too quickly; we could not stop it, for then the whole expedition would crumble to nothing. What has been done hitherto has been necessary to get money and to make the machinery work. Today that side of the proceedings culminated in an official 'release' from the War Department and with a press conference at which all American news agencies were represented.

"After the meeting we all separated: the Americans, the Norwegian military attaché. . . . Back in the hotel I made the following calculation: my cash in hand amounts to $35.35, all that remains of $200 which I borrowed . . . when I ran short of money on my arrival in Washington. I am to return to New York tomorrow evening. My $35.35 is not even sufficient to

[We gave] the boat a curved stem in the Egyptian style. This added section was to prove the boat's weak point. ■ (From *The Ra Expeditions* by Thor Heyerdahl.)

pay the hotel bill here. . . . At the moment I can see no possibility of getting any money at all. . . . This is the day after Christmas, 1946, and I am alone. There is one way forward and none back. I *believe* it will work out; and I am determined that it *shall* work out. But I should like to remember this day, this struggle and this experience for the rest of my life till the day I shall be forced to give up my very breath.''[1]

April 28, 1947. With extremely limited financial backing, set off across the Pacific on the *Kon-Tiki*, a 45-foot balsa raft named after the Incan sun-god, in an attempt to prove his theory that Incan raftsmen had carried their civilization across the Pacific to Polynesia. Of the six men aboard the *Kon-Tiki* only one, Erik Hesselberg, knew how to sail. ''When darkness crept over the waters, our first duel with the elements began. We were still not sure of the sea; we were still uncertain whether it would show itself a friend or an enemy in the intimate proximity we ourselves had sought. When, swallowed up by the darkness, we heard the general noise from the sea around us suddenly deafened by the hiss of a roller close by

and saw a white crest come groping toward us on a level with the cabin roof, we held on tight and waited uneasily to feel the masses of water smash down over us and the raft.

''But every time there was the same surprise and relief. The *Kon-Tiki* calmly swung up her stern and rose skyward unperturbed, while the masses of water rolled along her sides. Then we sank down again into the trough of the waves and waited for the next big sea. The biggest seas often came two or three in succession, with a long series of smaller seas in between. It was when two big seas followed each other too closely that the second broke on board aft, because the first was still holding our bow in the air. It became, therefore, an unbreakable law that the steering watch must have ropes round their waists, the other ends of which were made fast to the raft, for there were no bulwarks. Their task was to keep the sail filled by holding stern to sea and wind.

''We had made an old boat's compass fast to a box aft so that Erik could check our course and calculate our position and

Something about the Author • *Volume 52*   **67**   **Heyerdahl**

speed. For the time being it was uncertain where we were, for the sky was overclouded and the horizon one single chaos of rollers. Two men at a time took turns as steering watch and, side by side, they had to put all their strength into the fight with the leaping oar, while the rest of us tried to snatch a little sleep inside the open bamboo cabin.

''When a really big sea came, the men at the helm left the steering to the ropes and, jumping up, hung on to a bamboo pole from the cabin roof, while the masses of water thundered in over them from astern and disappeared between the logs or over the side of the raft. Then they had to fling themselves at the oar again before the raft could turn around and the sail thrash about. For, if the raft took the seas at an angle, the waves could easily pour right into the bamboo cabin. When they came from astern, they disappeared between the project-

ing logs at once and seldom came so far forward as the cabin wall. The round logs astern let the water pass as if through the prongs of a fork. The advantage of a raft was obviously this: the more leaks the better. Through the gaps in our floor the water ran out but never in.''[1]

Hardly a day passed during the 101 days at sea when the raft was not visited by sea creatures—whales, porpoises, sharks, octopus, and squid, to name a few.

September 29, 1947. Returned to San Francisco after successfully completing his 4,300-mile journey. Publication of the *Kon-Tiki Expedition* and an international lecture tour were efforts to wipe out the enormous debt incurred by the expedition. At first the book was poorly received in Norway, but when it was translated into Swedish, it gained an enthusiastic recep-

The open Atlantic was waiting outside Safi harbor. ■ (From *The Ra Expeditions* by Thor Heyerdahl.)

tion. By the time the book was translated into English it was an international best-seller, having been translated into sixty-three languages. ''It certainly is a wonderful thing'' wrote President Truman in a letter, ''to have people in the world who can still take hardship and do an exploration job just as the one you young men did on that raft. One of the difficulties of civilization is that people become fat and easy-going and can't accept hardships as a part of life. I am hoping that situation will not develop to too great an extent in this Republic of ours.''¹

After the expedition had become famous, ''Kon-Tiki'' fever took over in the form of ''Kon-Tiki'' drinks, chocolate, candy, perfume, souvenirs, porcelain, games, ornaments and ''Kon-Tiki'' hotels and restaurants. When Russia sent up the world's first manned satellite, it contained ''Kon-Tiki'' chocolate among its provisions.

First marriage ended in divorce. Married second wife, Yvonne Dedekam-Simonsen, in **1949.**

1951. Received an Academy Award for camera achievement for his documentary film, ''Kon-Tiki.''

1952. Lectured at the International Congress Americanists, held in Cambridge. With the money earned from his books and films, Heyerdahl led an expedition to the Galapagos Islands. ''The plan and purpose of the expedition is to carry out the first archaeological survey on the Galapagos islands in the

hope that evidence may be found to show that the group was known even to pre-European people.''¹

1955. Expedition to Easter Island resulted in another best-seller, *Aku-Aku: The Secret of Easter Island,* which was translated into thirty-two languages.

1958. Moved his family onto a medieval estate, Colla Micheri, above the Italian Riviera. ''I knew straightway that I had come to stay. Somehow, I had felt rootless since my attempt to return to nature in the luxuriant jungle of Fatu-Hiva. When in the tropics, I soon longed for the Norwegian mountains, but if I had been back home for awhile, I found myself yearning for the sunshine and exuberance of the southern latitudes. Here, at Colla Micheri was everything I had dreamed of, palms and blue sea, pine and orange groves and, nearby, snow-covered mountains sheltering friendly shepherds and vine cultivators from the northern winds.''¹

1962. Given the Lomonosov Medal from Moscow University. In Scandinavia Heyerdahl was also awarded the highest distinction a scientist could attain—the Vega Gold Medal. ''Today the doctors and psychologists are occupied with curing troubles and diseases which are due to our unnatural way of life—congested living conditions, contamination, noise, rush, sedentary work, and overeating. We are just as careless with our minds as with our bodies. We have no time for artless pleasures and quiet moments. The twilight hour has disappeared, and we no longer sit on our doorstep at sunset chatting

Safi the baby monkey, aboard the Ra, a happy farewell gift from the Pasha of Safi. ■ (From *The Ra Expeditions* by Thor Heyerdahl.)

(Jacket illustration by Gordon Grant from *Kon-Tiki: Across the Pacific by Raft* by Thor Heyerdahl.)

with our neighbor. We suffer from haste, and we have forgotten how to relax. Fortunately we have developed music and art, which compensate to some extent for what we lost when we gave up life within the very heart of the greatest of all art galleries and music halls: Mother Nature. The day we cut down the last tree and pour asphalt and concrete on the last stalk of grass, we shall be left like orphans in the street.''[1]

1964. Awarded the Patrons Gold Medal from the Royal Geographical Society of Great Britain.

1969. Embarked on the *Ra I*, a papyrus boat similar to those used by Egyptian sailors. ''Numerous theories of voyagers drifting from Africa to tropical America have been proposed to explain the sudden blossoming of high culture from Mexico to Peru. Like the ancient peoples of the Old World, Indians of the Americas worshiped the sun, built pyramids and giant stone statues, married brother to sister in royal families, wrote in hieroglyphs, performed cranial surgery, and mummified the dead.

''I resolved to build and sail a reed boat from Africa to the New World to find out if ancient man could have done the same.

''In 1969, on the sands behind the Great Pyramids of Egypt, shipwrights from Lake Chad helped me build *Ra I*. Their system was to lash together many small reed bundles with separate ropes; their design featured a high bow and low stern. At my request, they added a stern to match the bow. But their patchwork method of construction didn't work. Under way, we saw the stern break apart. Waves rolled aboard, like combers onto a beach, tearing away quantities of papyrus. *Ra I* had to be abandoned short of Barbados.'' [Thor Heyerdahl, ''The Voyage of *Ra II*,'' *National Geographic*, January, 1971.[2]]

Undaunted, Heyerdahl had another papyrus boat, the *Ra II*, built by Aymara Indians from Bolivia. *Ra II* sailed from Africa to America; the flag of the United Nations flying from its mast. The men aboard were from eight different countries, including the U.S. and the U.S.S.R. ''. . . It was easier with a crew that had nothing in common—race, religion, class, or nationality. That gave me the most pleasure, to see how well we worked as a team, even though we had to use three common languages [English, French, and Italian].

''It was more difficult on *Kon-Tiki*. . . . On your first day on a raft, you're still a guest, very well-mannered. But this does not last more than three days, and then it is like an unending house party in which you are trapped with the others. After a month, you get what I call 'expedition fever.' You lose all sense of proportion, small irritants blow up into terrible quarrels. In my log, I had to keep detailed records of every minor dispute, so that when a bigger fight came along, I'd know all the facts.

Giant heads of tall statues half buried in silt from the slopes of the Rano-Raraku crater. ■(From *Sea Routes to Polynesia* by Thor Heyerdahl.)

(From *Kon-Tiki* by Thor Heyerdahl.)

''Well, if you're all from the same background, as we were on *Kon-Tiki,* you are too liable to relax. Anger is too easily expressed. With different backgrounds, you stay on guard, almost as if you were an ambassador. It is much, much easier with a multinational crew. . . .'' [Karl E. Meyer, ''The Heyerdahl Paradox,'' *Horizon,* spring, 1972.³]

In the fifty-seven days at sea, the crew of the *Ra II* saw so much human garbage around the boat that they kept a pollution diary. ''It is not the objective of the *Ra* expedition to draw biological or ecological conclusions from our observations. Our intention is merely to call attention to observations virtually forced upon us. Yet there is no doubt that the time is past when ocean pollution is a mere offense to human esthetics; if left unchecked, it can hardly avoid affecting the future world economy.''³

''The voyage has succeeded. But what has it proved? First, we have demonstrated that a papyrus ship, properly built, can cross a major ocean.

''Second, we have shown that a craft of such ancient design—coming from North Africa, a cradle of civilization—could have crossed the Atlantic with a crew to bring cultural influences to the aboriginal population of the Western Hemisphere.

''Finally, we can attribute our success to cooperation among the men of many nations who undertook it, having learned that no space is too narrow, no stress too great, if men will only join hands for common survival.''²

After the voyage, Heyerdahl became a frequent speaker at world conferences on pollution.

1977. Successfully sailed with a multinational crew of eleven a reed boat, the *Tigris,* down the Tigris River in Iraq, through the Persian Gulf, across the Arabian Sea, and into the Gulf of Aden at the African Horn to prove that the ancient people of Mesopotamia, Egypt, and the Indus Valley were united and communicated with each other. ''The success of *Ra II* led to my study of the Sumerians, but here I encountered major differences, both in building materials and in sailing conditions. *Kon-Tiki* and *Ra I* and *Ra II* represented 'drift' voyages—that is, voyages dependent on favorable winds and currents. I found no such reliable 'conveyor belts' in the waters adjacent to Mesopotamia. To ply these waters, one cannot merely drift, one must navigate, utilizing variable winds and currents.

''Based on Mesopotamian carvings and cuneiform records I have seen, I feel that the Sumerians, precursors and contemporaries of the Egyptian pharaohs, were the master builders of reed ships. . . . I decided to construct such a reed vessel and to explore the ancient sea routes of the Sumerians. That is how *Tigris* was born.'' [Thor Heyerdahl, ''Tigris Sails into the Past,'' *National Geographic,* December, 1978.⁴]

The expedition was recorded in a documentary film in 1979 and in a book published in 1980. The income derived from each expedition's books and films made it possible for Heyerdahl to finance his next expedition. ''I enjoy the trips. I enjoy writing the books. I enjoy making the films. I am not

Heyerdahl during a ski exploration of the Norwegian mountains.

primarily an adventurer, but I enjoy adventure when it comes my way....

"... I never undertake a voyage unless I find a scientific reason for it. I have tried the three oldest types of prehistoric vessels that were in dispute among scientists which were supposed to be nonseaworthy. At the moment there are no more vessels like that to test, but that does not mean that if something comes up I might not start another expedition...." [Arthur Unger, "Thor Heyerdahl: The Viking Who Dreaded the Sea," *Christian Science Monitor,* April 10, 1979.⁵]

Heyerdahl's latest expeditions were return trips to the Indian Ocean in 1982 to 1984 and to Easter Islands in 1986. He has also produced a documentary film, "The Maldive Mystery."

His motto is "a united mankind in a healthy biosphere."

HOBBIES AND OTHER INTERESTS: Woodcarving, cartooning.

FOR MORE INFORMATION SEE: National Geographic, January, 1941, January, 1971, December, 1978; *Current Biography,* H. W. Wilson, 1947; *Spectator,* March 31, 1950; *Times Literary Supplement,* April 7, 1950, June 25, 1971, October 17, 1980, September 12, 1986; *Chicago Sunday Tribune,* September 3, 1950, July 26, 1953; *Chicago Sun-Times,* September 5, 1950; *Christian Science Monitor,* September 7, 1950, August 20, 1975, April 10, 1979; *New York Herald Tribune Book Review,* September 10, 1950, October 18, 1950; "Daring 'Kon-Tiki' Adventure to Be Seen in New Dallas Film," *Dallas Morning News,* June 19, 1951; *New York Times,* August 9, 1953, May 26, 1969, July 23, 1969, April 1, 1979; *Booklist,* September 1, 1953.

Stanley J. Kunitz, editor, *Twentieth Century Authors,* H. W. Wilson, 1955; *New Statesman,* April 5, 1958, May 7, 1971;

Manchester Guardian, April 8, 1958; *Kirkus Reviews,* July 1, 1958; *Newsweek,* September 8, 1958, August 7, 1967, May 26, 1969, March 10, 1980; *Time,* September 8, 1958, August 15, 1969, August 30, 1971, November 28, 1977; *Springfield Republican,* September 14, 1958; *Saturday Review,* September 27, 1958, October 4, 1958, May 13, 1961, August 2, 1969, December 6, 1969, October 9, 1971; *Horn Book,* February, 1959; *New York Times Book Review,* November 27, 1960, December 8, 1968, August 22, 1971, August 16, 1981; Bernadine Bailey, *Famous Modern Explorers,* Dodd, 1963; Arnold Jacoby, *Señor Kon-Tiki: The Biography of Thor Heyerdahl,* Rand McNally, 1967; *Washington Post,* May 26, 1969, July 23, 1969, December 9, 1984, August 26, 1986; *Variety,* May 28, 1969, January 12, 1972; *Life,* August 15, 1969, September 24, 1971.

"Heyerdahl's Voyage—Modern Sea Epic," *U.S. News & World Report,* July 27, 1970; *Observer,* August 20, 1970; Karl E. Meyer, "The Heyerdahl Paradox," *Horizon,* spring, 1972; Thor Heyerdahl, "A View from a Raft," *Bulletin of the Atomic Scientists,* September, 1972; *Atlantic,* July, 1976, March, 1979; *Holiday,* March, 1977; "The Tigris Expedition," *American Educator,* spring, 1979; Meg Whitcomb, "Explorer Thor Heyerdahl Won't Quit and He Suggests 8 Trips for You," *50 Plus,* August, 1979; Paul Westman, *Thor Heyerdahl: Across the Seas of Time* (juvenile), Dillon Press, 1982.

HOBSON, Laura Z(ametkin) 1900-1986 (Peter Field)

PERSONAL: Born June 19, 1900, in New York, N.Y.; died of cancer February 28, 1986, in New York; daughter of Michael (an editor and labor organizer) and Adella (Kean) Zametkin; married Francis Thayer Hobson (a publisher), July 23, 1930 (divorced, 1935); children: (adopted) Michael, Christopher. *Education:* Cornell University, A.B., 1921. *Religion:* "My ancestors were Jews; I am an agnostic as were my parents." *Agent:* International Famous Agency, 1301 Avenue of the Americas, New York, N.Y. 10019.

CAREER: Author. George Batten Co., New York City, advertising copywriter, 1923-26; *New York Evening Post*, New York City, reporter, 1926-27; *Time, Life,* and *Fortune* magazines, New York, N.Y., promotion writer, 1934-40, becoming promotion director of *Time* magazine. Consultant, *Time, Fortune,* and *Sports Illustrated*, 1956-62; editorial consultant, *Saturday Review*, beginning 1960. *Member:* Authors League of America (council member, 1970-73), P.E.N., Americans for Democratic Action, American Civil Liberties Union, Regency Whist. *Awards, honors:* New York Film Critics Award, and Academy Award from the Academy of Motion Picture Arts and Sciences for Best Motion Picture, both 1947, both for "Gentleman's Agreement."

WRITINGS: A Dog of His Own (juvenile), Viking, 1941; *The Trespassers,* Simon & Schuster, 1943; *Gentleman's Agreement,* Simon & Schuster, 1947, large print edition, Thorndike Press, 1982; *The Other Father,* Simon & Schuster, 1950; *The Celebrity,* Simon & Schuster, 1951; *First Papers,* Random House, 1964; *"I'm Going to Have a Baby"* (juvenile), Day, 1967; *The Tenth Month,* Simon & Schuster, 1971; *Consenting Adult,* Doubleday, 1975; *Over and Above,* Doubleday, 1979; *Untold Millions,* Harper, 1982, large print edition, G. K. Hall, 1982; *Laura Z: A Life,* Volume I, Arbor House, 1983; *Laura Z, a Life: Years of Fulfillment,* Volume II, Donald I. Fine, 1986.

Other; with Francis Thayer Hobson under joint pseudonym Peter Field: *Outlaws Three,* Morrow, 1933; *Dry Gulch Adams,* Morrow, 1934.

LAURA Z. HOBSON

Columnist for *Saturday Review,* "Trade Winds," summers, 1952, 1953, 1956, International News Service, "Assignment America," 1953-54. *Good Housekeeping* (book page), 1953-56. Contributor of short stories, novelettes, and articles to national magazines, including *Collier's, Ladies' Home Journal, McCall's,* and *Cosmopolitan.*

ADAPTATIONS: "Gentleman's Agreement" (movie), starring Gregory Peck and Celeste Holm, Twentieth Century-Fox, 1947; "The Tenth Month" (television movie), starring Carol Burnett, Joe Hamilton Production, CBS-TV, 1979; "Consenting Adult" (television movie), starring Marlo Thomas and Martin Sheen, Martin Starger Co., ABC-TV, 1985.

SIDELIGHTS: **June 19, 1900.** Born in New York, New York, daughter of Russian-Jewish socialists. Her father was editor of the *Jewish Daily Forward;* her mother was a regular contributor to a Jewish newspaper. "Actually, unlike most mortals, I have *two* birthdays, because my twin was born before midnight on June 18th and I about an hour later on the 19th. This seemed too complex for the people who issued birth certificates, so Alice and I shared ours, which gives June 18 for both of us.

"While we were kids, it was her fancy to announce grandly on June 18th, 'I'm a year older than you are—you have to do what I say.' And later, in our thirties, when we began to worry about advancing age, I got it all back. 'I'm a year younger than you!'

"For years, if the 18th fell on an inconvenient day, we would have our party on the 19th, and for further years, even on passports or driver's licenses, I'd write either the 18th or 19th until I finally decided that, mnemonically, 19 went with 1900 and stuck to 19 ever since." [Laura Z. Hobson, *Laura Z: A Life,* Arbor House, 1983.[1]]

May, 1916. First writing published. "The first time I wrote anything that I thought might be published, I was fifteen and a pupil at Jamaica High School. It wasn't signed, and it wasn't long, but it did see the bright black sheen of printer's ink. For I was assistant editor of *The Oracle,* the school's monthly magazine.

"My name was right up there on the masthead, side by side on the top line with the editor in chief . . . whom I no longer remember. Ranked below us were the seven subeditors whose sections were called Alumni, Art, Assemblies, Boys' Athletics, Gossip, Societies and something called Exchange.

"It was the first public acknowledgment that I had some affinity for the written word, albeit a subordinate affinity. But to be any kind of editor of anything that went regularly to press and sold for ten cents a copy was glory enough in the world as I knew it then.

"I was fifteen, too, when I first earned actual money by writing something for it. Writing for a real honest-to-goodness New York newspaper, what was more. How I got the idea that I might try for any such grandiose role I do not know, but one day I set forth for the city by streetcar, and then by elevated train and subway, with an appointment to see one of the editors of the *Evening Mail* . . . who, in the parlance of the day, 'conducted' the School page in the afternoon and home editions.

"I must have written for an appointment, must have been astonished to receive an answer and more astonished that the well-known editor would actually interview me when I appeared.

"What I was after was permission to send in school news from Jamaica High. She said I could try. If she printed anything, it would be paid for at five dollars a column or twenty-five cents a stick. A stick, she told me, was one inch of type, seven printed lines. If I sent in any items about school elections or dramatics or sports, she would read them herself and decide whether they belonged in a big city newspaper or not.

"Even that much commitment aroused in me the first dazzling thrill of professionalism. Three months before, I had begun a diary—also a first—and part of the entry for May 7, 1916 reads, 'I am writing for a newspaper and getting paid for it! . . . I can't tell yet what the average of pay is, because although it is about a month since it started, I have only gotten two checks—one for 50¢—that was for one day's work—& one for $5.50.'

". . . On and off through my whole writing life, that early need to 'write it down' that impelled me to that little red book remained as some subterranean force in me. Whenever I began thinking out an idea for a story, or, later on, for a novel, I would turn to the typewriter, roll in a sheet of blank paper and head it, 'Possible Plot for Story?' or 'Possible Novel?' and then frequently, 'Notes on Novel?' and subsequently, 'More Notes on Novel?'

"The question mark was an integral part of the phrase until the manuscript, short or long, for magazines or for the publisher of books, frivolous or serious—until that manuscript really got under way. Then, if I needed to 'write it down' the question mark disappeared and the phrase itself changed. It became, quite firmly, 'The Rest of the Story.'"[1]

1921. Graduated from Cornell University. "I was an honor student at Cornell, with an official notification on white vellum to that effect from the dean of the College of Arts and Sciences. But I never made Phi Beta Kappa, and the private story I was told about why not when my grades were so high, was

(From the movie "Gentleman's Agreement," which won three Academy Awards in 1947, including one for Celeste Holm [above] as Best Supporting Actress.)

another facet of my 'education.' In that uncatalogued, un-named course, Antisemitism I.''

"My first real job and my first real love were intertwined experiences, and they both began about two years after I was out of college.

"... In **1923** came the real thing, a job as cub copywriter with George Batten Company at $25 a week, $108 a month. Batten was no little pipsqueak place downtown; it was on Fourth Avenue at about Twenty-eighth Street, in a real office building a few blocks north of the old Madison Square Garden, with big offices and carpeted floors and a reception room and a president and many vice-presidents and copy chiefs and many copywriters, of which I fast became the fair-haired girl. To be writing copy for Batten, even then, before it united with an-other agency to become Batten, Barton, Durstine and Osborne, the prestigious B.B.D. & O., was to have started at the top of the heap. I just knew I was going to make good.

"There was also at Batten a copywriter who was twenty-eight, a Princeton man, handsome, witty, attractive and married, a man named Thomas Ernest Mount. He had already written a short story that Mencken had printed in *Smart Set,* and meant to write others, perhaps even a book. . . .

"At the office all went well. I seemed to have a flair for writing copy, and they kept giving me new assignments, one after another, Cliquot Club Ginger Ale, Dairymen's League, a collective farm group, Lustrite nail polish, half a dozen oth-ers whose names I can't recall. I got my first raise in six months, a jump from twenty-five dollars a week to forty, and I was supposed to be thrilled, for the usual raise for beginners was five a week.

"But instead of being thrilled and silent, I went to the vice-president in charge of most of the accounts I was working on, William J. Boardman, and despite the racing sense of risk, I thanked him for the forty but asked if it 'couldn't possibly be fifty?'

"He was astounded. I explained about my debts, not the long-term Cornell ones, but private ones of ten or twenty or thirty dollars to family friends and even to my mother's pupils, working people all, who had helped me because of their feel-ings for her. I was fast becoming tense and even guilty about those private debts, I told him, not sleeping well, wondering if I might do a little free-lancing to earn more and get free again.

"I got the fifty. But I earned it, and I earned every other raise I was to get at Batten during the three years I stayed there. . . .''[1]

(From the movie "Gentleman's Agreement," starring Dorothy McGuire, Gregory Peck, and John Garfield. Copyright 1947 by Twentieth Century-Fox Film Corp.)

1926. "One day I went down to the offices of the *New York Evening Post,* then a sound liberal newspaper, and saw the book editor.... I asked for a job on the staff, not on that 'business end' I had once thought to settle for, but a real job, right up there with the rest of the reporters.

"I told him I was making about $14,000 a year. I had left Batten by then and was free-lancing full time; my fee was no longer the picayune $10 per piece of copy; I had no trouble getting or holding clients through small agencies; I had begun to carry around a professional proofbook of printed ads I had written. I showed them to him.

"'A cub reporter,' he said, 'starts at twenty-five dollars a week. Even a man.'

"I said I knew it. I knew also that the *Post* had no women reporters at all...."[1]

Hired as a reporter. "By-line after by-line came my way, and frequent small raises, even a few five-dollar prizes for the 'best written story of the week.' For the rest of the year I spent on the *Post,* I was sent out on most of the major stories, to do the 'human interest' side of the news. By the end of the year my pay was fifty dollars.

"By the next summer, in 1927, soon after I had won some more by-lines covering the return of Lindbergh from his solo

Hobson at LaBaule, Brittany, in 1929.

flight to Paris, I began to face up to the fact that the fourth estate was not quite the seventh heaven I had dreamed it would be. I still liked my work, and I had made good friends on the paper. Jim Thurber is the one I remember best, undoubtedly because it was while he was right there on the *Post* that he began to send in the pieces that turned him into James Thurber of the *New Yorker.*"[1]

July, 1930. Married publisher Francis Thayer Hobson, a vice-president at William Morrow, then a small publishing house. "... Thayer, as a publisher, needed an active social life, with authors and agents and editors and other publishers, cocktail parties, lunches, dinners. It seems that I quickly became an easy hostess. We had a maid who was a good cook—I never became a good cook—but I was gregarious, enjoyed meeting people and talking to 'real live authors.'..."[1]

During their marriage, Hobson and her husband wrote two Westerns, *Outlaws Three* and *Dry Gulch Adams* under their joint pseudonym Peter Field.

April 23, 1932. First short story published in the *New Yorker* magazine.

1933. Advertising copywriter for Altman's department store. "Whether or not writing ads can be considered any preparation for real writing has been argued many times, pro and con, but in my opinion *any* kind of daily writing is an invaluable apprenticeship for anybody intending to become a professional writer, not just a hobby writer.

"Good ads have to have headlines that catch the attention; some of them have a story to tell, a mood to set, but more important than any other consideration, they are there to be done every day. Whether you're in a mood to write or not, you go to that typewriter or pick up that pencil; you can't make excuses for skipping a day; you learn to ignore a headache and write; you learn to surmount sadness or worry and write; you grow out of all nonsense about 'not being in the mood,' or waiting until the spirit moves you.

"At Altman I never spent an hour without writing. I didn't keep a proofbook of any of my work there, but there were several highlights that brought raises and advancement."[1]

1935. "And then, suddenly, came divorce. I put it that abruptly because that is how it came to me. There was no warning, no preparation.

"It was like a drawing room comedy by Noel Coward or Frederick Lonsdale, the two of us sitting together on our sofa in our lovely living room, having after-dinner coffee from our small black Wedgwood demitasses, and Thayer quietly saying, 'I have something to tell you.'

"There was a long pause, me looking attentive, expectant. 'I've fallen in love with somebody,' he went on. 'Somebody else. I've tried to fight it for a year, all this past year, but I couldn't. So I have to tell you—I'm so sorry to hurt you, but I want a divorce.'

"Falling in love at first sight may be a myth, but annihilation in one moment is not. It was like a bomb dropping, a bullet to the inner brain.

"I didn't behave well. I wept, I grew hysterical, I couldn't speak in sentences, my breath tore out of my throat in gasps. As he told me—off and on through most of the night—how it had happened, I went through layer after layer of shock, of

Hobson biking in Bermuda, 1937.

disbelief, a shuddering away from this sudden explosion of everything my life had come to be.

"Some people get over shock and grief with enviable celerity. In others the tenacity of pain can be astonishing. I am one of the latter kind. But on the other hand I am fortunate. For me there is one analgesic that can actually cut me away from that area of pain for hours at a time, can give me surcease, make me so absorbed that I don't know what time it is, don't remember to eat, don't know when it is time to go to bed. The name of that kindly drug is writing.''[1]

Began to write and publish stories in magazines under the name Laura Z. Hobson. "By itself, Laura Hobson was a good name for an author, but it was stripped of *me*. The initial Z. would put me back, right into the middle of it. Instinctively I knew that everybody would forever ask me what the Z. stood for, and I also knew I would always tell them not just, 'My maiden name, Zametkin,' but also, 'It's Russian and it's Jewish.''''[1]

1937. Adopted a son, Michael. "Today the 'single-parent adoption' is nearly an everyday matter, but in the middle thirties, it was almost unheard of. Many of my friends said it couldn't be done at all, that I would just risk another period of frustration and heartbreak if I even attempted it.''[1]

1941. First book, a children's story entitled *A Dog of His Own*, was dedicated to her son. "... When *A Dog of His Own* was published in London by Hamish Hamilton, Clare [Booth Luce] wrote for the jacket blurb, 'It gave the most awful pain in the heart, longing for a small boy of my own to go with the book,' while Dorothy [Thompson], printed directly above Clare, went in for a little political fun, unusual for her. 'It preaches the only moral, social and economic lesson, namely: that too much of a good thing is too much. Only think how well-off Mr. Hitler would have been if he had been satisfied with a Dachshund and a Pomeranian, but no, he also had to have a Scotty and a Great Dane, and I give you my word, if we are not careful, he is going to go after a Mexican hairless. And with them all on a lead, he is going to be exactly like Mikey—praying for a policeman to save him.'''[1]

December 27, 1941. Second son, Christopher, was born out of wedlock. ''. . . Back in 1941 there was no such thing as being open and casual about a pregnancy out of wedlock, no liberated attitudes about a woman or girl being unmarried and pregnant and happy all at once.

''My own impulse was to shout it from the rooftops to all the world, but I knew I could never permit myself that luxury. . . .''[1]

1943. First novel, *The Trespassers,* was published. ''Once the corrected galleys were turned in to Dick Simon [of Simon & Schuster] I again set myself to the need for income. I rewrote 'False Witness' and this time it sold, to *Cosmopolitan,* for $1,250. I sold another to *Liberty* for $500, and a wartime novelette, *The Girl I Left,* for a large $1,750 somewhere else. I began 'The Sleepless' and soon wished I hadn't. . . .

''All the while I kept on searching for promotion assignments, and finally landed three magazines all at once, the *American Mercury,* no longer H. L. Mencken's, and on a less lofty plateau, *Mercury Mysteries* and *Ellery Queen's Mystery Magazine.* . . .

''During the summer I also had one of the oddest little writing assignments ever, with one of the strangest 'employers' ever. This was to turn out 'short-short stories,' a few hundred words each, for the nation's thousands of newspapers—three short-shorts every week—whose plots were to appeal especially to women at home or 'women at war.' They ran perhaps six or eight inches down a single newspaper column, and were paid for at a munificent $20 per.

Laura Hobson on a skiing trip in New Hampshire, 1938.

(From the television movie "Consenting Adult," starring Martin Sheen and Marlo Thomas. Produced by Martin Starger Co. Presented on ABC-TV, 1985.)

"And during all the assorted assignments and tasks and stories and novelettes, despite all the seductive early reports on my book, for all the prepublication activity of press releases and interviews, there was one hidden preoccupation of mine which I never spoke of to a soul.

"I had already begun to wonder what my next novel would be about."[1]

1947. *Gentleman's Agreement,* a novel about anti-Semitism, sold over 2,000,000 copies and was translated into a dozen foreign languages.

The movie version of the book was produced by Darryl F. Zanuck for Twentieth Century-Fox, and received the New York Film Critics Award and the Academy Award for Best Motion Picture. "We all cheered when Celeste Holm won an Oscar for Best Supporting Actress, but that was nothing compared to what happened when Kazan won as Best Director. And at long last, when 'Gentleman's Agreement' won as Best Picture of the Year, there was a kind of happy frenzy of kisses and hugs and I-knew-it-all-alongs.

"I can't truly recall what it was I felt in those first moments. I think it was a composite or collage of feelings, pleasure, pride, even a practicality akin to a salesman's with a big order in hand, but no inspired preview came to me that night of what lay ahead for that Best Picture.

"We were all a bit let down that Gregory Peck did not win the Oscar for Best Actor, but were certain that in due time he would collect more than one for other pictures. But it hurt me badly that Moss Hart did not win for Best Screenplay, which went to 'Miracle on Thirty-Fourth Street.' Nobody, least of all me, could figure out how anything could be Best Picture if it hadn't first been Best Screenplay." [Laura Z. Hobson, *Laura Z., a Life: Years of Fulfillment,* Donald I. Fine, 1986.[2]]

1950. "And suddenly I was fifty. I had finally finished my father-daughter novel, *The Other Father,* and it had been published the month before my birthday. I took the title from the court scene in Dostoevsky's *The Brothers Karamazov.*

"I wanted this third novel of mine to contrast a good, normal parent-child relationship with its opposite, the obsessive one. My story line, the vehicle that would explore this theme, was what we today would call a 'father-fixation,' its point being that father fixations and mother fixations are apt to be two-way streets, where if a father falls in love with a woman young enough to be his daughter, he may well be acting out the forbidden love for his real daughter, in which case she, his child, may in turn fall in love with a man old enough to be her father. Part of my intention was to write the entire novel as if I were doing it before Freud was ever heard of, with not a single reference to 'fixation' or neurosis or anything else in the analytic lexicon.

"I may have succeeded. It got fair enough reviews, though some were what is called 'mixed,' it was serialized by *Cosmopolitan* for two-and-a-half times the price I'd been paid for *Gentleman's Agreement,* and it settled down for a while about midway on the best-seller lists.

"But in the long look backward, I can see for myself that it was not what is rated a 'major novel.'

"Neither was the one I had just begun to work on, *The Celebrity*. It was to be my first attempt at social satire in a novel, and it was that same old idea of trying to do an amusing send-

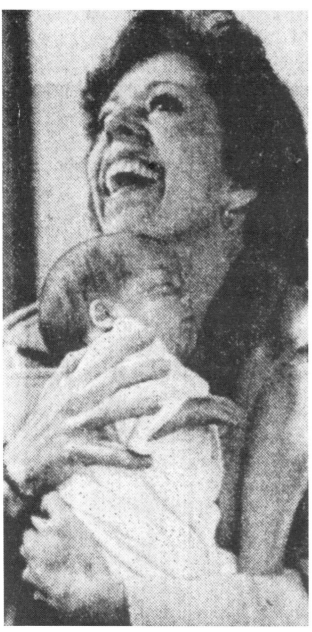

(From the television movie "The Tenth Month," starring Carol Burnett. Presented on CBS-TV, September 16, 1979.)

up of phony celebrity. I had abandoned it years ago, but as many an author can attest, no idea you are attracted to ever remains permanently abandoned. It may be submerged for ages, but it keeps sending up its periscope every so often to have another look around."[2]

1967. Another book for children, *"I'm Going to Have a Baby!"* was written and dedicated to son Chris. "I suppose it's lucky that I didn't have a total of five or six children or I might have turned into a habitual writer of what the trade calls juveniles.

"I enjoyed writing it, as I had enjoyed writing *A Dog of His Own* all those years earlier, and I wrote it almost as swiftly. This one had a title that required quotation marks around it, for it was an account of the last weeks of a pregnancy, told in the first person by none other than a six-year-old named Chris.

"*'I'm Going to Have a Baby!'* has a large picture of an excited kid leaping into the air, face all alight as he makes this announcement, and the picture is not only on the soon-to-be-destroyed jacket, but right on the indestructible binding of the book itself.

"Never before or since did I have a book that was praised both by Dr. Benjamin Spock, the baby guru for so many generations, and the Catholic Library Association, if I am remembering the name correctly. It went very well, in terms of juvenile sales, and I felt that I had squared off whatever debt I had left unpaid to the second child in my small family.

"There was something else in the way of work that I was enjoying, a sort of hobby, more than work: being the anonymous editor of my favorite time-consumer, the weekly Double Crostic in the *Saturday Review*.

"It was a delightful hobby. I would receive the puzzles in manuscript form, everything left blank, just as it would be when the reader faced them in the magazine. I would solve them, reach decisions about the propriety and fairness of the various clues or definitions, check them for accuracy, and then phone in any suggestions for changes to one of the magazine's real editors."[2]

1975. "*Consenting Adult* appeared in June . . . to the best and most widespread reviews I had had on any book since *Gentleman's Agreement*. The lengthy piece in the *Sunday Times*, by Professor of History Martin Duberman, called it 'a milestone in the history of social attitudes,' and said, 'most of the novel's success hinges on the complexities of her two main characters . . . mother and son, and also on her decision—unique in the literature about homosexuality—to tell the story from the parents' point of view.'

"It received various special awards, both in this country and in London when it was published there, won a sizable paperback deal and drew almost at once assorted queries about options for motion picture and television rights.

"But unlike anything I had ever had with any of my books was the quality—the passion—of the letters that poured in with every mail, sometimes as many as eight or ten in a single day. Most of them were from young people who were gay; many of them were from their parents. It is hard to select samples or to excerpt any of them."[2]

Living a lifestyle daringly ahead of its time, Hobson used the episodes in her own life as the basis for her controversial themes. In 1983 her first of a two-volume autobiography, *Laura*

Z: A Life was published. "I have always said to my two sons, 'I'll *never* write an autobiography. I'm not egotist enough to write my life as if it were terribly important.' Besides, I have taken the biggest chunks of my life and based novels on them." [Sybil S. Steinberg, "PW Interviews: Laura Z. Hobson," *Publishers Weekly*, September 2, 1983.[3]]

In an effort to describe her work, Hobson stated that her novels were "the curious amalgam of what happened and what you wish had happened.

"Let's take *Gentleman's Agreement*. Was I ever a young man, a reporter on a magazine? I was never. Was I ever a young widow? Never. Was I ever living in California and suddenly a stranger in New York? *No!* Yet *nothing* is made up—except the stuff that doesn't matter."[3]

In her fiction, she was like an archaeologist on a dig. "I take a part of my life and create a whole other creature around it.

"At times I would sit there at the typewriter and be writing steadily and strongly and suddenly dissolve into tears and be right back where I was thirty-five years ago. I would weep— and then go on. That's when you know you've got it right.

"There are very few honest autobiographies; I'm convinced of it. And as for memoirs, don't ask me because I'll get livid. Memoirs are things that pick and choose. I put in things that I wish I hadn't had to."[3]

1985. In her eighties, Hobson biked regularly. "I was sixty-six when I took that first ride on a bike in Central Park. . . . Now I am just eighty-five, and every one of those intervening years saw me ride a thousand miles, making a note in my log as I crossed each new hundred. . . ."[2]

1986. Son Chris offered the following observations of Hobson's last days: "What I remember about my mother's last year isn't the illnesses and the decline, but her effort to go on: to return to normal health and vigor, and particularly to write, for writing was life to her—it was her greatest pleasure, and in some sense she only felt truly alive when she was writing. As I look over the logs . . . entry after entry shows what those months were like:

"August 31: 5 1/2 m. on bike—first time since illness in Feb!!

"November 5: Worked hard—end of chapter XV p. 432'"[2]

February 28, 1986. Died of cancer in New York. "I've often heard it said that to a novelist, nothing is ever lost, that every scrap of his or her past life somehow finds its way to a future use, large or small, in some piece of work, perhaps half a century in the future."[1]

FOR MORE INFORMATION SEE: Chicago Sun Book Week, March 2, 1947; *New York Herald Tribune Book Week*, March 9, 1947, November 8, 1964; *Time*, May 29, 1950, November 9, 1953; *Life*, November 27, 1964; *Saturday Review*, February 27, 1965; Sybil S. Steinberg, "PW Interviews: Laura Hobson," *Publishers Weekly*, September 2, 1983; Laura Z. Hobson, *Laura Z: A Life*, Volume I, Arbor House, 1983; L. Z. Hobson, *Laura Z., a Life: Years of Fulfillment*, Volume II, Donald I. Fine, 1986. Obituaries: *Variety*, March 5, 1986.

Youth is confident, manhood wary, and old age confident again.
            —Martin Farquhar Tupper

DIANE HOH

HOH, Diane   1937-

PERSONAL: Born April 28, 1937, in Warren, Pa.; daughter of John F. (an electrician) and Regis (a housewife; maiden name, Niver) Eggleston; married William A. Hoh (a financial analyst), August 30, 1958; children: Julie Hoh Nannola, Jenny Hoh Deaton, Martin. *Education:* Attended St. Bonaventure University, 1956-57. *Religion:* Roman Catholic. *Home and office:* 8400 Rockwood Lane, Austin, Tex. 78758.

CAREER: Housewife, 1958-84; writer, 1984—. *Member:* Authors Guild, Austin Writers League. *Awards, honors:* Short Story Award from *Young Miss*, 1975.

WRITINGS—Young adult; all published by Scholastic: *Loving That O'Connor Boy*, 1985; *Flirting*, 1985; *Betrayed*, 1985; *Staying Together*, 1985; *Brian's Girl*, 1986; *Pulling Together*, 1986; *Proving It*, 1986; *A Night to Forget*, 1986; *The Girls of Canby Hall*, 1987; *Spring Fever*, 1987; *The Almost-Summer Carnival*, 1987; *The Ghost of Canby Hall*, 1987.

Work represented in anthologies, including *The Favorites*, edited by Lee Wyndham, Institute of Children's Literature, 1976. Contributor of stories to *Young Miss*.

WORK IN PROGRESS: Three books for "The Stepsisters" series for Scholastic which deal with step-families in today's world.

SIDELIGHTS: "A housewife for twenty-six years, I began writing for teens in 1984. I chose this group as an audience because I never quite grew up, nor do I have any strong inclination to do so. I've never fully understood the world of adults, although I function as one rather well, considering.

"Although there *is* romance in the books I write (what red-blooded American teenager would read them if there wasn't?), that isn't the whole of it. A rather left-handed compliment I often get from adults who've read my books is, 'Gee, I was surprised there was so much in the book!' It's as if they expected only romance, nothing more. There is much more to write about for teenagers because they're just learning about life. All of the books I've written have contained something about loyalty, something about compassion, something about friendship. Keeping in mind, always, that lecturing to teenagers can mean the death of a writer's career, lessons can be finely drawn and handled with humor in order to make them painless and, therefore, acceptable. I don't deny that my values are 'old-fashioned,' which can also be the kiss of death if one is heavy-handed. My own personal feeling is that today's teenagers are smart enough to realize that many old-fashioned values are still valuable and can be incorporated into a modern life without social disaster.

"I really love writing for teenagers, in spite of the people who ask me when I'm going to write a 'real' book. To me the books I write are very real, because the audience is. I see teenagers as fully developed human beings in the process of learning and growing. This is the group I will write for until I'm too grown up to do so.

"I lead a quiet life, spending most of my time writing. What time is left is spent gardening, reading, and with my family. My goal right now is to find the time to volunteer for some kind of work with teenagers. My fan mail suggests that they can use all of the help they can get. These are difficult times for them.

"When people ask me how to become a writer, I always tell them the same thing: by reading. My parents were readers, and so, therefore, were their nine children, one of whom was me. I was, I think, the most 'difficult' among the six girls, and reading calmed me down, took me into another world where I was happy. When I married, I spent many years working like crazy to become Donna Reed, and did a relatively decent job, but always, always, I stole the time to read. I think you can be a reader without ever writing a book, but I don't believe you can be a writer without ever having read one. Obviously, I'm a zealot about reading. It has made all the difference in my life. When I speak to teenagers, I'm very honest about where I come from, about my background—working-class, wrong side of the tracks, etc.—and that if it hadn't been for books and my family's love of them, I might still be on Fifth Street. My father, who worked in a factory, read about better places, better lives, and was determined to provide one for his family. He did exactly that, in time. But unquestionably, the greatest gift both of our parents gave all nine of us, was the example of what books could mean."

HOWE, Fanny   1940-

BRIEF ENTRY: Born October 15, 1940, in Buffalo, N.Y. University lecturer, poet, and author. Since 1961 Howe has lectured in creative writing at Tufts University, Emerson College, and Columbia University. She has also been associated with the Massachusetts Poetry-in-Schools program and, in 1978, served as visiting writer at the Massachusetts Institute of Technology. Among the honors she has received are fellowships from the McDowell Colony and Bunting Institute, as well as

grants from the St. Botolph Society and National Endowment for the Arts. Howe's books for adults include her first, *Forty Whacks* (Houghton, 1969), a collection of six short stories; poetical works like *Eggs* (Houghton, 1970), *For Erato: The Meaning of Life* (Tuumba Press, 1984), and *Introduction to the World* (Figures, 1986); and novels such as *First Marriage* (Avon, 1974) and *In the Middle of Nowhere* (Fiction Collective, 1984). In her young adult novels, Howe deals with black/white racial issues, first from a historical perspective in *The White Slave* (Avon, 1980), and then in a more contemporary setting in *The Blue Hills* (Avon, 1981) and its sequels, *Yeah, But* (Avon, 1982) and *Radio City* (Avon, 1984). In its review of *Yeah, But, School Library Journal* commented on Howe's treatment of a sensitive subject matter: "It is no mean trick to show how races and classes stereotype one another and also develop characters influenced but yet independent of their race and class. This Howe does successfully." Her other young adult novels include *Taking Care* (Avon, 1985) and *Race of the Radical* (Viking/Kestrel, 1985). *Home:* 195 Winthrop Rd., Brookline, Mass. 02146.

FOR MORE INFORMATION SEE: Contemporary Authors, Volume '117, Gale, 1986.

INGMAN, Nicholas   1948-

PERSONAL: Born April 29, 1948, in Richmond, Surrey, London, England; son of Dan Soutter and Vivien (Sutherland) Ingman; married Angella Doyle, April 29, 1978 (divorced November, 1982); married Angela Green (a promotions executive), August 31, 1985. *Education:* Berklee College of Music, graduated, 1967; Guild Hall School of Music and Drama, postgraduate study with Dr. Edmund Rubbra, 1970. *Home:* 10, The Gardens, East Dulwich, London, England.

CAREER: Free-lance musical arranger, composer, and conductor for television films and radio. Norrie Paramor's Independent Record Company, London, England, arranger and producer, about 1969-75.

*WRITINGS—*Young adult, illustrated by Bernard Brett: *The Story of Music,* Ward Lock, 1972, Taplinger, 1976; *What Instrument Shall I Play?,* Ward Lock, 1975, Taplinger, 1976; *Gifted Children of Music: The Young Lives of the Great Musicians,* Ward Lock, 1978.

SIDELIGHTS: Ingman studied privately with jazz composer Graham Collier after graduating from Westminster School and then spent three years studying composition at the Berklee School of Music in Boston. Following postgraduate study with Dr. Edmund Rubbra, Ingman joined Norrie Paramor's Independent Record Company as arranger and producer in 1969. While there, he became musical director for Cliff Richard, Sacha Distel, and Olivia Newton-John, among others. As musical associate, he worked with these and others in their respective television shows for British Broadcasting Corporation television. For Moss Empires, he composed the music for four consecutive Christmas pantomimes at the London Palladium.

In 1974 Ingman signed with Polydor Records to record under his own name, and his records were released internationally. In the same year, he was nominated for an Ivor Novello Award for his theme tune for BBC television's comedy series "Casanova '74." He also completed several film scores for Rank U.K. Ltd. and contributed to "Death Wish," directed by Michael Winner.

NICHOLAS INGMAN

In 1975, he was commissioned by Ward Lock Ltd. to write three books for children; his *The Story of Music* was eventually translated into ten languages. Shortly after, he left the Norrie Paramor organization to work in a free-lance capacity as well as continuing his composing activities. Since then he has been signed to EMI as a recording artist and, as a producer, worked with The Kings Singers and Ken Dodd, with whom he had a top ten hit.

Ingman has subsequently branched out into the jingle field—with more than two hundred campaigns to his credit—and appears regularly as guest conductor with BBC radio orchestra for Radio Two.

Ingman contributes many albums a year to the main music libraries and has worked on Bruton, K.P.M., and de Wolfe labels. Other work for television includes the signature tunes and all incidental music for the BBC 2 series "Hilary," starring Marti Caine.

IVERSON, Genie 1942-

BRIEF ENTRY: Born November 10, 1942, in Newport News, Va. Author of books for children. Following her graduation from the University of California at Berkeley in 1966, Iverson worked as a reporter for the *Contra Costa Times* and *Lesher News Bureau.* Since 1971, she has been promotion director for Iverson Game Bird Calls in San Mateo, California. She is the author of three biographies: *Jacques Cousteau* (Putnam, 1976), *Louis Armstrong* (Crowell, 1975), and *Margaret Bourke-White* (Creative Education, 1980). Iverson's *I Want to Be Big* (Dutton, 1979), aimed at preschoolers, tells the tale of a small girl looking for independence. According to *Bulletin of the Center for Children's Books,* this story "has a theme that should appeal to its audience, and the writing has a direct, ingenuously serious quality." Iverson also wrote two children's plays, *The Goose That Laid Golden Eggs* and *The Robbers and the Fig Tree,* both published by Ginn in 1982. In her spare time, she enjoys tennis, photography, and marine biology. *Address:* P.O. Box 405, San Mateo, Calif. 94401.

FOR MORE INFORMATION SEE: Authors of Books for Young People, supplement to the 2nd edition, Scarecrow, 1979; *Contemporary Authors, New Revision Series,* Volume 9, Gale, 1983.

JAMES, Elizabeth 1942-
(Elizabeth Carroll, Katherine Duval, Beverly Hastings, E. James Lloyd, James Lloyd)

PERSONAL: Born November 5, 1942, in Pittsburgh, Pa.; daughter of Curtis Blakeslee (a salesman) and Sally (a banker; maiden name, Lloyd) James; married J. David Marks (a motion picture executive), June 24, 1973. *Education:* Colorado College, B.A., 1963; graduate study at University of California, Los Angeles, and California State College (now University) at Long Beach. *Residence:* Beverly Hills, Calif.

CAREER: United Air Lines, Los Angeles, Calif., stewardess, 1963-65; Otis Productions, Los Angeles, Calif., writer and female lead in the motion picture "Born Losers," 1965-67; free-lance writer, 1965—. Assistant director, Sullivan Educational Systems (publisher), 1970-72; consultant to Stanford Research Institute in evaluating Project Follow Through, 1972; consultant to Education Commission of the States, Denver, Colo., developing television programs on early childhood development, 1972-73. Member of the board of directors, Neighbors of Watts, 1978. Has written scripts for both theatrical and documentary films. *Member:* Screen Actors Guild, Society of Children's Book Writers, Authors Guild, Women's National Book Association, Writers Guild of America (West), Southern California Council on Literature for Children and Young People, Mystery Writers of America, P.E.N., Southern California Children's Booksellers Association. *Awards, hon-*

ELIZABETH JAMES

ors: Society of Children's Book Writers Member of the Year, 1986.

WRITINGS—Juvenile; all with Carol Barkin, except as noted; all published by Lothrop, except as noted: *The Simple Facts of Simple Machines* (illustrated with photographs by Daniel Dorn, Jr. and with diagrams by Susan Stan), 1975; *Slapdash Sewing* (illustrated by Rita Flodén Leydon), 1975; (with Lee Arthur and Judith B. Taylor) *Sportsmath: How It Works,* 1975; *Slapdash Cooking* (illustrated by R. F. Leydon), 1976; *Slapdash Alterations: How to Recycle Your Wardrobe* (illustrated by R. F. Leydon), 1977; *Slapdash Decorating* (illustrated by R. F. Leydon), 1977; *How to Keep a Secret: Writing and Talking in Code* (illustrated by Joel Schick), 1978; *What Do You Mean by ''Average''? Means, Medians, and Modes* (illustrated by J. Schick), 1978; *How to Grow a Hundred Dollars* (illustrated by J. Schick), 1979.

How to Write a Term Paper, introduction by Leland B. Jacobs, 1980; *The Complete Babysitter's Handbook* (illustrated by R. F. Leydon), (paperback) Wanderer, 1980, (hardcover) Messner, 1981; *A Place of Your Own* (illustrated with photographs by Lou Jacobs, Jr.), Dutton, 1981; (with Malka Drucker) *Series TV: How a Show Is Made,* Clarion, 1983; *How to Write a Great School Report,* introduction by M. Jean Greenlaw, 1983; *The Scary Halloween Costume Book* (illustrated by Katherine Coville), 1983; (under joint pseudonym Elizabeth Carroll) *Summer Love,* Wanderer, 1983; (under joint pseudonym Beverly Hastings) *Watcher in the Dark,* Pacer, 1986;

How to Write Your Best Book Report (illustrated by Roy Doty), 1986; *Happy Thanksgiving!* (illustrated by Giora Carmi), 1987; *School Smarts: How to Succeed at Schoolwork,* 1988.

''Transition'' series; all with C. Barkin; all illustrated with photographs by Heinz Kluetmeier; all published by Raintree, 1975: *Are We Still Best Friends?; Doing Things Together; I'd Rather Stay Home; Sometimes I Hate School.*

''Money'' series; all with C. Barkin; all published by Raintree, 1977: *Managing Your Money* (illustrated by Santos Paniagua); *What Is Money?* (illustrated by Dennis Hockerman); *Understanding Money* (illustrated by D. Hockerman).

Adult: (Under pseudonym Katherine Duval) *Ziegfeld: The Man and His Women* (novelization of screenplay by Joanna Lee), Paradise, 1978; (with C. Barkin, under joint pseudonym Beverly Hastings) *Don't Talk to Strangers* (novel), Jove, 1980; *Secrets* (novel), Berkley, 1983; (with C. Barkin) *Helpful Hints for Your Pregnancy,* Fireside, 1984; (with C. Barkin, under joint pseudonym Beverly Hastings) *Don't Walk Home Alone* (novel), Jove, 1985; (with C. Barkin, under joint pseudonym Beverly Hastings) *Don't Cry, Little Girl* (adult novel), Pocket Books, 1987.

Also author of several screenplays and television dramas, including (under pseudonym James Lloyd) ''Born Losers,'' starring Tom Laughlin and Elizabeth James, American Interna-

(From the movie "Born Losers," starring Tom Laughlin. Copyright © 1974 by American International.)

"We can do a lot of advertising for $2.50," said Danny. ■ (From *How to Grow a Hundred Dollars* by Elizabeth James and Carol Barkin. Illustrated by Joel Schick.)

tional Pictures, 1967, and (under pseudonym E. James Lloyd) "Loose Change," Willgeorge Productions, 1971.

WORK IN PROGRESS: Another adult novel; juvenile and young adult projects.

SIDELIGHTS: "As described to me by college recruiters, jobs in mathematics sounded incredibly boring. So upon graduation I took a job as an airline stewardess in order to see the world.

"I had moved to Los Angeles, and the magic of the movies beckoned. My first screenplay, 'Born Losers,' was produced independently and released by American International Pictures in 1967. It was the first of the 'Billy Jack' films and I played the female lead opposite Tom Laughlin who played Billy Jack.

"After that, I wrote a number of other screenplays for Fox, American International Pictures, and independent producers, as well as a television Movie-of-the-Week.

"I also did some consulting for educational films and then began writing books. The first one was published in 1975.

"For the past several years I have been engaged primarily in writing books and occasional screenplays. I enjoy the different and unique challenges in both collaborative writing and working alone, and I have produced scripts and books both ways.

"My formal education did not include courses in writing. Though writing classes may be helpful, I have found that ex-

tensive reading, life experience, a good grasp of the language, and logical thought processes are invaluable in writing both fiction and nonfiction.

"Every book requires research, but I find it impossible to write from library research alone. For both fiction and nonfiction I must have some sort of intuitive grasp of the subject matter before I can begin. I need to already know something about the topic, to be interested in that theme or problem, to care about it. If parts of the book are set in locations I'm unfamiliar with, I go there. I require the details of ambience from my own experience to provide an environment for my characters; I can't pick up this feel for a setting by reading about it. Similarly, if a book has projects and instructions, I try everything out to make sure it works and that it works by following the directions I've written. I am forced to follow the old adage 'write what you know.'

"In doing travel research, the one item I find indispensable is a good camera. I take terrible notes; my handwriting is almost illegible, even to me. And I can't encompass in a few phrases the wealth of details I recapture in a bunch of snapshots. I don't waste time taking postcard-type pictures; I buy those. Instead, I look for everyday items—street signs, crowds on sidewalks, passing cars and buses and taxis and emergency vehicles, garden arrangements, odd bits of architecture. I find it jarring to read about a city I know and see mistakes in geography or the colors of the police cars or the look of the houses, no matter how interesting the story. I also get comprehensive local maps and mark them as I go. And I save matchbooks, leaflets, and brochures. They bring back all sorts of related memories when I sift through them as I write.

"As to writing itself, I agree with many of my writer friends who say it's always nicest to 'have written.' In retrospect, everything I've done was fairly easy. I tend to forget the time and the agonizing and the rewriting and am always surprised at how difficult it is to face that blank page at the beginning of a project. I have no solutions other than to start at the beginning and just keep plugging along until you reach the end. Whether fiction or nonfiction, working in collaboration or alone, I find it essential to have a mental map of where I'm going and how I plan to get there. However, there is no substitute for that putting of one word after another to create a gripping word-picture that captures the vision of the mind's eye.

"Every experience I have, every place I go, every person I meet, all provide grist for the mill. Everything just gets shoved into the pot we all have bubbling away on the back burner of the brain."

HOBBIES AND OTHER INTERESTS: Reading, traveling, tennis, gardening, and living life.

JOHNSON, Sylvia A.

BRIEF ENTRY: Born in Indianapolis, Ind. Author of science books for young readers. A graduate of Marian College in Indiana, Johnson received her M.A. from the University of Illinois and later worked as a book and free-lance editor in Minneapolis. She has conributed more than two dozen books to Lerner's well-received "Natural Science Books" series, which provides detailed and informative looks at all aspects of natural science from animals to insects to life beneath the sea. The series, which originates in Japan, features scientific terminology in boldface type and appended glossaries that further define words. In addition, texts are accompanied by diagrams and close-up, color photographs of the subject matter. "[These books] are challenging and very informative," observed *School Library Journal,* "technical enough to keep adults amazed and yet written clearly enough for youngsters to follow." As a contributing author to the series, Johnson was included in a special award presented to Lerner in 1983 by the New York Academy of Sciences for "a beautifully photographed series of reference books." Her titles include *Penguins* (1981), *Beetles* (1982), *Crabs* (1982), *Inside an Egg* (1982), *Mushrooms* (1982), *Apple Trees* (1983), *Frogs and Toads* (1983), *Mosses* (1983), *Coral Reefs* (1984), *Morning Glories* (1985), and *Rice* (1985). Johnson also produced six books in Lerner's "Wildlife Library" series, including *Animals of the Deserts, Animals of the Mountains,* and *Animals of the Polar Regions* (all 1976).

JONES, Douglas C(lyde)   1924-

PERSONAL: Born December 6, 1924, in Winslow, Ark.; son of Marvin Clyde (an auto mechanic) and Bethel (Stockburger) Jones; married Mary Arnold (a sales clerk), January 1, 1949; children: Mary Glenn, Martha Claire, Kathryn Greer, Douglas Eben. *Education:* University of Arkansas, B.A., 1949; graduate study at U.S. Army Command and General Staff College, 1961; University of Wisconsin—Madison, M.S., 1963. *Home:* 1987 Greenview Dr., Fayetteville, Ark. 72701. *Agent:* George Wieser, Wieser & Wieser, Inc., Box 608, Millwood, N.Y. 10546.

DOUGLAS C. JONES

CAREER: Writer and artist. U.S. Army, career officer, 1943-68, retiring as lieutenant colonel; served in Pacific Theater during World War II, later as commander of infantry rifle companies in Europe and Korea, and as information officer with Philadelphia Army Air Defense Command; chief of Armed Forces Press Branch, Office of Assistant Secretary of Defense for Public Affairs, The Pentagon, Washington, D.C., 1966-68. University of Wisconsin—Madison, member of faculty in School of Journalism and Mass Communication, 1968-74, visiting lecturer, 1974-78. Has exhibited paintings of Plains Indians in one-man show at Washington Gallery of Art, 1967, Tulsa, Okla., 1979, and in Fayetteville, Ark., 1981. *Awards, honors*—Military: Army Commendation Medal, 1957, 1960, and 1966; Legion of Merit, 1968. Civilian: Golden Spur Award, Western Writers of America, 1976, for *The Court-Martial of George Armstrong Custer,* 1984, for *Gone the Dreams and Dancing,* and 1986, for *Roman; Elkhorn Tavern* was named best novel of 1980 by Friends of American Writers, and was chosen one of New York Public Library's Books for the Teen Age, 1981 and 1982; *The Barefoot Brigade* was chosen one of *School Library Journal*'s Best Young Adult Books, 1982.

WRITINGS—Novels, except as indicated: *The Treaty of Medicine Lodge* (nonfiction), University of Oklahoma Press, 1966; *The Court-Martial of George Armstrong Custer,* Scribner, 1976; *Arrest Sitting Bull,* Scribner, 1977; *A Creek Called Wounded Knee,* Scribner, 1978; *Winding Stair,* Holt, 1979 (published in England as *The Winding Stair Massacre,* Allen & Unwin, 1980); *Elkhorn Tavern,* Holt, 1980; *Weedy Rough,* Holt, 1981; *The Barefoot Brigade* (self-illustrated), Holt, 1982; *Season of Yellow Leaf,* Holt, 1983; *Gone the Dreams and Dancing,* Holt, 1984; *Roman,* Holt, 1986; *Hickory Cured,* Holt, 1987. Contributor of articles and reviews to periodicals, including *Kansas Historical Quarterly* and *Journalism Quarterly.*

ADAPTATIONS: "The Court-Martial of George Armstrong Custer" (television film), "Hallmark Hall of Fame," NBC-TV, 1978, (cassette) Books on Tape, 1979.

WORK IN PROGRESS: Two nineteenth-century based novels.

SIDELIGHTS: ''Writing has always been a hobby for me. When I was fifty and retired I started writing. Since I was a freshman in high school, I've enjoyed descriptive writing and developing characters. But most of all, just telling a good story. A lot of what I wrote just for fun when I was younger, I later incorporated into novels.

''From my earliest recollection, I have been a history buff. Especially as it deals with the nineteenth-century frontier in the United States. This really began when my family lived in Ft. Smith, Arkansas between the years 1927 and 1933. Ft. Smith had been a pretty wild frontier town and was just across the river from what had been the Cherokee Nation until 1907 when all of that area became part of the state of Oklahoma.

''Traveling around the country and the world as a member of the army, my interest in history increased. I did a lot of research, writing everything down and using it later when I began to write seriously. My ideas for novel plots began to develop during this time. My first was a story of an Arkansas regiment that served with Lee in the Civil War. I started nurturing that plot in 1951. It became a novel in 1982, *The Barefoot Brigade*.

''My mother's family had been residents of the Ozark hills of northwest Arkansas since two generations before the Civil War.

In that instant, I felt his gaze touch me. I had never looked into such eyes before. ■ (Jacket illustration by Wendell Minor from *Gone the Dreams and Dancing* by Douglas C. Jones.)

I heard a lot of stories from many of them about how things were in that area in the nineteenth century. I began to visualize story ideas from that time and place as early as 1958. The first novel on related subjects appeared in 1980 with *Elkhorn Tavern*.

''When I got my master's degree and later became a member of the faculty at the University of Wisconsin, research opportunities increased tenfold and I was able to fill out data and material for all my frontier story ideas.

''I write historical novels which I research as thoroughly as possible so that I can set my fictional characters down in a real situation. I try to make all my stories ring clear for the time and place in which they occur, to include how things look, smell, taste, sound and feel from the touch of your fingers.

''Before I left high school I began to cultivate a good memory for what I'd seen and what I had read. Not dates and weather reports and other such things that can always be checked in published reference material. But how things looked and smelled and sounded, the general 'mood' of a place and time. This memory for such things was enhanced in the army when it was required that as an infantry officer I needed to evaluate terrain at a glance to see where the trees were and the hills and the valleys and how the sun or a full moon cast shadows across it.

''I tried to learn early what the possibilities of the English language are, how to use it correctly, how to make a listener or a reader understand *exactly* what I meant in any description or introspection or viewpoint.

''Now that I am no longer a musician, a college professor, a high school teacher, a painter, or a soldier, all of which I have been at one time or another, I write. And when I have a theme working in my head, I write every day. It is an irresistible impulse.

''However, even at my peaks of enthusiasm for an on-going story, I can only write for about three-and-a-half to four hours a day. And then I am drained, physically and emotionally, and must stop and cook a pot of chili or some such thing and get a good night's sleep before going at it again.

''My interests include people and what they do to each other. The evil ones as well as the good ones.

''My advice to any young person who wants to be a writer is to be sure that you are *driven,* that your life will never be complete without it. And in the meantime, get a good job doing something else or you might starve to death. And if you're a good speller, so much the better. If not, don't worry about it. Just get a good dictionary and learn exactly how to use it!''

Some of Jones' works have been published in England, Norway, Denmark and Mexico.

HOBBIES AND OTHER INTERESTS: Cooking, growing potted plants.

FOR MORE INFORMATION SEE: New York Times Book Review, November 21, 1976, December 11, 1977, November 19, 1978, October 28, 1979, November 16, 1980, October 3, 1982, December 11, 1983; *Newsweek,* December 20, 1976; *Best Sellers,* April, 1977, December, 1977; *Chicago Tribune Book World,* November 5, 1978, December 28, 1980, October 25, 1981; *Los Angeles Times Book Review,* November 11, 1979; *Washington Post,* December 20, 1979; *Los Angeles Times,*

October 1, 1980; *Washington Post Book World,* October 5, 1980; *School Library Journal,* January, 1981.

JOOSSE, Barbara M(onnot)   1949-

PERSONAL: Born February 18, 1949, in Grafton, Wis.; daughter of Robert E. (a banker) and M. Eileen (a homemaker) Monnot; married Peter C. Joosse (a psychiatrist), August 30, 1969; children: Maaike Sari, Anneke Els, Robert Collin. *Education:* Attended University of Wisconsin—Stevens Point, 1966; University of Wisconsin—Madison, B.A., 1970; graduate studies at University of Wisconsin—Milwaukee, 1977-80. *Home and office:* 2953 Kettle Moraine Dr., Hartford, Wis. 35027.

CAREER: Associated with Stephan & Brady, Madison, Wis., 1970-71; Waldbillig & Besteman, Madison, copywriter, 1971-74. *Member:* Society of Children's Book Writers. *Awards, honors:* Picture Book Award from the Council of Wisconsin Writers, 1983, for *The Thinking Place,* and 1985, for *Fourth of July; Fourth of July* was exhibited at the Bologna International Children's Book Fair, 1985.

WRITINGS—For children: *The Thinking Place* (illustrated by Kay Chorao), Knopf, 1982; *Spiders in the Fruit Cellar* (illustrated by K. Chorao), Knopf, 1983; *Fourth of July* (illustrated by Emily A. McCully), Knopf, 1985; *Jam Day* (illustrated by E. A. McCully), Harper, 1987; *Better with Two* (illustrated

BARBARA M. JOOSSE

by Catherine Stock), Harper, 1988; *Presenting Anna* (illustrated by Gretchen Mayo), Harper, 1988; *Dinah's Mad, Bad Wishes* (illustrated by E. A. McCully), Harper, 1989. Contributor of articles and stories to text books and periodicals, including *Milwaukee, Chicago Tribune, Cricket,* and *Instructor.*

WORK IN PROGRESS: "More easy-to-read books, several picture books and another novel for children. I find that each of these genres taps a different area of creativity. There are stories I can tell in one that don't suit themselves to another. In addition, I have several completed picture books and one novel that have not yet received commitment from a publisher, though, of course, I expect it at any moment. They are: *Mama, Do You Love Me?* (a picture book), *Suzanna's Dance* (a picture book), *The Dream Machine* (an easy-to-read book), and *Pieces of the Picture* (a novel for middle-to-upper grades)."

SIDELIGHTS: "I have always wanted to be a redhead and writer. I tried dying my hair but I looked like a brunette with dyed hair. Writing fit more naturally.

"Even after my college creative writing professor told me I'd be better off in journalism.

"Even after my journalism professor told me I'd be better off in creative writing.

"With those doors seemingly closed, I became an advertising copywriter. They're the people who get ideas for ads, write the words, and work with the illustrators. It was fun work— a chance to practice my craft and be paid to do it.

"But it felt flat after a time, so when my first child was born I was happy to give it up. Maaike was born in 1974. I jumped into motherhood with both feet, and practically drowned in it.

"We lived on top of a remote hill in the country, a setting that was serene when it was a respite from a very active job, but that echoed with loneliness when there *was* no outside job. The days were incredibly long. I didn't allow myself to watch soap operas, but "Star Trek" became the light at the end of my daily tunnel. I rocked and rocked and rocked. Maaike cried, I clenched my teeth. I loved her dearly, but I couldn't adjust to the lack of adult contact, ideas and lunches out.

"My emotions were so powerful, and the changes so great, that the only medium strong enough to contain them was poetry. They say that writing for therapy is not good writing. They—amorphous, heard-but-not-seen devils that they are— are right. My poetry was far too raw to be of any meaning to someone else.

"But any writing is useful writing. It helps you learn the craft, and keeps the words moving. James Hazard, a creative writing professor at the University of Wisconsin—Milwaukee, says that if you listen to your writing, it will tell you what to do. Mine did.

"It told me I was not a poet.

"But Maaike, now three, had turned into a real person—full of humor and compassion, with all the twists and turns of an intricate character.

"Maaike was not a simple child. I decided, however, that she was *material.* I would be a children's writer, and use the things I saw every day. How perfect! I enjoyed staying home with Maaike, and was looking forward to a new baby (Anneke).

I am five, which is old enough to do a lot of things if my parents would let me. ■ (From *Fourth of July* by Barbara M. Joosse. Illustrated by Emily Arnold McCully.)

As a children's writer, I could be a professional mother *and* a professional-something-else. I would be my own boss.

"And who was more suited than I? I was sensitive, wasn't I? And a bit eccentric. I had a typewriter. What else did I need?

"I decided to be a children's writer with all the naiveté of a child deciding to be an astronaut or a cowboy. I was blissfully unaware of how few writers succeed in this field. I've been told, probably by the amorphous 'they,' that children's literature is the most difficult field to break into.

"So here was my plan: enroll in the master's degree program in creative writing at University of Wisconsin—Milwaukee; hire a babysitter two mornings a week to spend writing; research publishers; and get dressed before ten every morning (it was satisfying to check at least one thing off my list every day).

"That first year was exhilarating. Writing was so much fun. It was a kick to try on different characters, as I might a dress. Sometimes I was preoccupied, but my family was usually understanding. When Anneke was ten months and crawling, I let her and our dog out of the back door. I set the dog in the sandbox and grabbed Anneke's collar to chain her up. Anneke patiently waited for me to come to my senses.

"Within a year, I had written ten stories. With real objectivity, I thought they were all endearing, bright, warm and witty. I sent out my manuscripts, one at a time, to five publishers. Perhaps they would begin to recognize my name and decide I was a Writer of Promise. After a manuscript came back four times, I would rewrite it and send it again.

"There are two reasons, I think, that those manuscripts were not purchased. First, it's a matter of reaching the right editor at the right time. Also, my stories hadn't evolved properly. I

now find I need to rewrite a manuscript several times over the period of a year or more. I need some time between rewrites to give my subconscious a chance to work, and to give me objectivity.

"But I knew I was close. I had several letters from editors who had held manuscripts and considered them for a time. I knew these were near misses. But they were, in the final tabulation, misses.

"Then a wonderful, visionary editor of good taste and genius finally spotted Promise. She said Knopf was very interested in one of my manuscripts. She said Knopf had only to determine the budget before they would purchase my story. Nothing positive, of course, but very hopeful. Could they please hold on to my manuscript just a bit longer?

"But of course!

"My visionary editor was fired. The new editor was polite, but distant. There were a few manuscripts, she felt, that held vague possibilities, if I cared to rewrite them.

"I reworked one of the manuscripts, and sent it in. She offered to buy it.

"It took another eighteen months to publish *The Thinking Place.* Because each word in a children's book must be powerful and believable, there were many rewrites." [Barbara Joosse, "How Do You Print So Small?," *Milwaukee*, May, 1984.¹]

"I like to write about real children. Children do so many heroic things every day. When a child does something that's very difficult for her to do, she is a hero. I like to dramatize that 'every day heroism' in my stories."

"My children offer material for new books every day. Sometimes people ask how I think of the things in my books. I

Grandpap's world-famous biscuit recipe is a secret. ■
(From *Jam Day* by Barbara M. Joosse. Illustrated by
Emily Arnold McCully.)

don't. My children do. But they also make it difficult to write.
Somebody's paper-bag mask that's due in half an hour, somebody's dirty diaper, somebody's soccer match and everyone's
hunger always seem more pressing than a story.

"My stories are an amalgam of my children, their friends, and
me. When I write a story, I *am* the child in the story. When
I'm finished, I am its mother. It's as difficult to send a manuscript into the cruel world as it is to put a kindergartner on the
bus for the first time.

"My stories are about children you know. They dramatize the
fears and battles, the wisdom and triumphs that mark growing
up as surely as the penciled 'growth lines' on the kitchen wall.
I try to write with humor, while maintaining dignity, because,
to a child, these events are very serious matters.

"I remember, because I was once a child.

"If there was anything unusual about my childhood, it is that
it was ordinary. Not boring, because no childhood is boring.
But definitely secure. We lived in the same house on Sunset
Court in Grafton, Wisconsin, until I was in high school. Then
we moved two blocks away. My parents were always *there*.
Forever, without question.

"Because I wasn't ill, or constantly moving, or enduring a
family separation, I was free to concentrate on the meaty issues
of growing up: braving the spiders in the fruit cellar, compet-

ing with a neighbor whose white tennis shoes stayed white,
coping with the disappointment of hard-earned 'jumping shoes'
that didn't work.

"These are the things—monumental incidentals—that I write
about. And, because my childhood memories are not oversha-
dowed by major traumas, I am able to recall them with clarity."[1]

"My own children really help me with my work. Watching
them gives me lots of ideas. When Maaike was four she put
candy corn in our dishwasher and was unrepentent; that gave
me the idea for *The Thinking Place*. When I sent a Christmas
picture of my children to Kay Chorao, she made Elizabeth in
The Thinking Place and *Spiders in the Fruit Cellar* look like
my Anneke."

"Little bits of real people and places are woven throughout
my stories. I have noticed some reluctance in my family to
reveal things. Now, when I ask nine-year-old Maaike about
her day, she will ask furtively, 'Why do you want to know?'
She's afraid I'll use it in a book."[1]

"My children have also become careful critics of my work,
helping me when they don't like a character or an ending.
They've even helped critique the artwork, discovering important details that adults passed over."

"I love to write for children. They are the very best audience.
They are capable of great leaps of imagination and compassion, and they are ruthlessly honest.

"Children are not above saying they don't like a book, even
when it's yours. When I want to test a working manuscript, I
will read it to a group of five-year-olds. If there is a lot of
wiggling when I read, the book stinks. If somebody gasps
when my character is in trouble, it's good.

"To write, I climb a ladder to a loft in my bedroom. It's very
cozy up here—low ceilings, small windows, all my favorite
books. When I start a story I begin by imagining the main
character. I wait until she is so clear that I hear her whispering
in my ear.

"Then the story begins."[1]

"I live in the country, solidly planted in the midwest. The
midwest—geography, values, pace—is an important feature in
my stories. *Fourth of July* takes place in my hometown, Grafton, and includes landmarks from that town. *Jam Day* takes
place in Washington County, where I live now. Both novels
are set in Door County, Wisconsin, my favorite vacation place.

"I really love to write! Few things are more thrilling than
creating new people and places and making them come to life.
I take great satisfaction in knowing I've touched children's
lives.

"Of special interest to me is the bond between the 'reader'
and the 'listener' of picture books. Picture books are often
read aloud by someone a child cares about very much. I want
these two—through a shared reading experience—to understand each other better, and love each other more.

"Because a picture book is often read so many times, I want
to make sure that it has several levels of experience. I want it
to have music and poetry, psychology and growth, lively dia-
logue and good images. When a story is read many times it
becomes a real part of the 'listener's' life. I want it to be a
worthwhile part, cozy and secret like a treehouse."

HOBBIES AND OTHER INTERESTS: Reading, jogging, baking, and hiking.

FOR MORE INFORMATION SEE: Barbara Joosse, "How Do You Print So Small?," *Milwaukee*, May, 1984.

KEITH, Eros 1942-

PERSONAL: Born June 24, 1942, in England. *Education:* Attended Art Institute of Chicago, Denver University and University of Chicago. *Address:* 105 West 73rd St., New York, N.Y.. 10023.

CAREER: Painter; author and illustrator. Has worked previously as a color transparency retoucher, an usher at the Chicago Symphony Hall, for a package-design firm, and in advertising. *Exhibitions:* Shepard Gallery, N.Y., 1969; K & F Studio (one-man), Evergreen, Colo. *Awards, honors:* Lewis Carroll Shelf Award for children's literature, 1971, for *Undine;* illustrator of 1974 Newbery Award book, *The Slave Dancer* by Paula Fox.

WRITINGS—All for children; all self-illustrated: *A Small Lot,* Bradbury, 1968; *Rrra-ah,* Bradbury, 1969; *Bedita's Bad Day,* Bradbury, 1971; *In the Land of Enchantment: A Panorama of Fairy Tales,* Bradbury, 1972; *Nancy's Backyard,* Harper, 1973; *The Biggest Noise,* Harper, 1974; *The Obstinate Land,* Crowell, 1977.

Illustrator; all for children: Friedrich de la Motte Fouqué, *Undine,* retold by Gertrude C. Schwebell, Simon & Schuster, 1957; Elizabeth Janeway, *Ivanov Seven* (ALA Notable Book; *Horn Book* honor list), Harper, 1967; Virginia Hamilton, *The House of Dies Drear* (ALA Notable Book), Macmillan, 1968;

EROS KEITH

(From *The King's Falcon* by Paula Fox. Illustrated by Eros Keith.)

Jean Lee Latham, *Anchor's Aweigh: The Story of David Glasgow Farragut,* Harper, 1968; Paula Fox, *The King's Falcon,* Bradbury, 1969; Mary Malone, *Actor in Exile: The Life of Ira Aldridge,* Crowell-Collier, 1969; Leo Tolstoy, *Twenty-Two Russian Tales for Young Children,* selected and translated by Miriam Morton, Simon & Schuster, 1969.

Angela Carter, *The Donkey Prince,* Simon & Schuster, 1970; A. Carter, *Miss Z, the Dark Young Lady,* Simon & Schuster, 1970; Robert Moery, *Kevin,* Bradbury, 1970; Marian Murray, *Plant Wizard: The Life of Lue Gim Gong,* Crowell-Collier, 1970; Sherry Kafka, *I Need a Friend,* Putnam, 1971; Miriam Young, *Peas in a Pod,* Putnam, 1971; M. Morton, compiler and translator, *The Moon Is Like a Silver Sickle: A Celebration of Poetry by Russian Children,* Simon & Schuster, 1972; P. Fox, *The Slave Dancer,* Bradbury, 1973; Margaret Hodges, reteller, *The Other World: Myths of the Celts,* Farrar, Straus, 1973; Catherine Sefton, *In a Blue Velvet Dress,* Harper, 1973 (Keith was not associated with earlier edition); Carol Lee Lorenzo, *Mama's Ghosts,* Harper, 1974; Jerome Beatty, *From New Bedford to Siberia: A Yankee Whaleman in the Frozen North,* Doubleday, 1977; F. N. Monjo, *A Namesake for Nathan: Being an Account of Captain Nathan Hale by His Twelve-Year-Old Sister, Joanna,* Coward, 1977; Joan Aiken, *The Faithless Lollybird,* Doubleday, 1978; Rita Golden Gelman and Warner Friedman, *Uncle Hugh: A Fishing Story,* Harcourt, 1978. Also illustrator of jackets for records and books.

ADAPTATIONS: "Nancy's Backyard" (filmstrip with cassette), Listening Library.

SIDELIGHTS: Born June 24, 1942 in England. "My grandparents were probably the most important influences. My grandmother was a wonderful storyteller—to this day, I can remember a number of her tales. My grandfather, who always had high hopes for me, was also an extraordinarily talented

Pluto stepped over the threshold in a direct but courteous manner.... He was somehow larger than dream or nightmare. ■ (From *The House of Dies Drear* by Virginia Hamilton. Illustrated by Eros Keith.)

person, and it was primarily through him that I came to love music and dance.

"When I was seven or eight, my parents, grandparents and I relocated to the U.S. My initial stay, however, was relatively short, as I was sent back to England to attend a military prep school in Manchester. I was chronically and severely asthmatic and, it was later discovered, I had had a mild case of tuberculosis, as well. The English climate did me no favors. My return to Denver to live with my family cleared up my asthma. Denver, of course, has long been a renowned treatment center for those with respiratory ailments. To someone who has never suffered such problems, it may be hard to imagine the elation an asthmatic feels upon drawing a good, deep breath. It is not something we take for granted. For the first time in my life I was able to play sports, and came to particularly enjoy tennis.

"We lived in a large townhouse. The basement was my studio in which I spent most of my time drawing and painting. It was *my* space and I considered it sacred. My parents used part of the basement for storage, and I found some fabulous things there. They had crates of old books, some wretched, I'm sure, but tantalizing all the same. And there were some veritable 'jewels'—two volumes of original prints by Charles Dana Gibson, for example, whose work I still cherish. Gibson, creator of the Gibson Girl, was so witty and his humor, particularly when aimed at upper-class Philistines, was wonderfully snide.

"Most of the work I did in my studio then was charcoal or oil. These, as opposed to water color and pastel, were considered by my friends and me 'classy,' very 'sophisticated' mediums. I painted everything except people. I never, never made images of people in those days. And I never used models, but worked entirely from my imagination. Even when I did landscapes, I worked indoors.

"I also took music and dance lessons. I went through just about every instrument. I play the harpsichord extremely well, consider myself a lousy pianist, and still nourish dreams of one day becoming an organist. My parents owned two fine antique organs, one of which originally came from a theater in Denver. I've never played a grand organ, however. What a thrill that would be. My dance classes were mostly in ballet and tap. I would dance for my grandfather with our servants. Eventually I had trouble in dance class because I kept trying to do it *my way* instead of their way. To this day ballet bores me to death. I still love music, however, and am an opera fanatic. My favorite composer is Richard Strauss. I also like Brahms quite a lot.

"I was a disaster in school. I always did everything I wasn't supposed to do. The idea of writing *my* name in penmanship classes with someone else's letters appalled me, so I would make up my own letters.

"Still, my teachers recognized that I wasn't a dummy—in fact, they considered me precocious. At fourteen, I won a scholarship for a summer art trip to Europe—mostly in Paris. The trip was very frustrating for me because all we could do was sketch. There was no time to paint. At the time, I did not consider sketching to be art. Also, we camped, which I despised.

"Denver was very sophisticated in education and the arts. In one of their programs, if you achieved a certain score on a particular test, you could go to the University of Chicago or UC Berkeley after your sophomore year. I tested well, and went to Chicago.

"I loved Chicago. Everyone was nice to me, and I was immediately accepted. I even enjoyed studying, which all my life had been a chore. As a college student I also took classes at the Art Institute of Chicago. Among other things, I came to realize the value of sketching. One of my teachers at the Institute would have us do a series of time-limited sketches. We could pick our medium and our subject. We'd have fifteen seconds in which to execute the first sketch, thirty seconds for the second, a minute for the third, and so on, up to about fifteen minutes. We kept flipping the pages sketching the same

(From *Twenty-Two Russian Tales for Young Children* by Leo Tolstoy. Illustrated by Eros Keith.)

subject. It was a fascinating and very valuable exercise. Not only was I forced to work fast, but forced to gradually slow down. I became conscious of *how* I saw, what I looked at first, what I came back to. In a very real sense, we see in layers. This was a revelation to me.

"In Chicago, there was a lot of great art to look at and study. Artists whose work I particularly love are Matisse, Courbet, Bonnard and Cézanne. I learned something very important from Matisse. He would sometimes work on a painting for several years. If he hit a trouble spot, he would put the canvas away and let the problem 'percolate' subliminally while he worked on other things. He didn't consider the unfinished painting a failure, but recognized that the time wasn't right for completing it. Each painting does not have to come from *one* inspiration, or one uninterrupted wave. Until I learned that, my impulse was to burn what I couldn't finish or throw it away.

"To earn spending money, I made decorated blown eggs, which I sold at the University gift shop. I was very much into Blake at the time, and the illustrations I did on the surface of the eggs were 'Blake-ish.' I used pen and ink. It's true that egg shells are fragile, but you cushion them in your hand as you draw, and come to know the right amount of pressure to apply. I used to do about seven eggs a week. And every week I sold them all for forty-five dollars. When I stop to think of how many eggs I blew in Chicago, I get dizzy!

"Well, well, well," said the man again. "He does have fits, doesn't he?" ■ (From *Ivanov Seven* by Elizabeth Janeway. Illustrated by Eros Keith.)

"After college, I came to New York where I immediately had a couple of extraordinarily lucky breaks. First, I was offered the chance to exhibit my paintings at the Shepard Gallery. Second, I was introduced to Ursula Nordstrom, the influential and very talented children's book editor at Harper & Row. I was very fortunate to work with her and F. N. Monjo, also editor at Harper & Row. I illustrated his *A Namesake for Nathan*. Monjo was a brilliant man from whom I learned a great deal. He was so meticulous in his research, wrote so beautifully and really encouraged the artists and writers he believed in. Ursula, too, was independent in her tastes and gave her artists and writers the freedom they needed to *really* work.

"Of the books I have written as well as illustrated, my auto-biographical *Nancy's Backyard* is my favorite. I wanted bright, clear colors for this book, and as luck would have it, we had lots of trouble achieving this, particularly with the greens. They kept fading in reproduction. The blues were a problem, too. Blue is the weakest color in the spectrum and if you're using water color, as I was for this book, the delicacy of the medium exacerbates the difficulty. We finally got it right, but only after lots of trial and error.

"I am primarily a visual person, and even when I am writing a story, I work from images. For example, in a scene where I know a given character will have a certain feeling, I see the character's facial and bodily expression and work from that. Later I fill in the words.

"Writing is much harder for me than illustrating. I revise like crazy before I show a story to anyone. I feel on much firmer ground with my art work and am therefore less open to suggestions about that from editors and art directors. And when illustrating, I work very spontaneously. Consequently, I prefer mediums that are relatively 'free,' like water color and pen and ink. I have even used ballpoint pen for book illustrations.

"*The Moon Is Like a Silver Sickle*, an anthology of poems written by sensitive and incredibly gifted children in the Soviet Union, was a very special book to illustrate. Children are more aware and sophisticated than given credit. Editor Miriam Morton smuggled the poems out of Russia along with Tolstoy's *Twenty-Two Russian Tales for Young Children*, which I was also pleased to illustrate."

In addition to writing and illustrating children's books, Keith sculpts. "My sculptures tend to be architectural. It's not so much because they're large—generally they are not—but because of the way they inhabit and contain space. I work mostly in papier mâché. I have a series in that medium I call 'weirdo people,' which is pretty much what the name implies. Recently I became fascinated with avocado skins and was trying to figure out how to petrify them. Then it hit me: they can be freeze dried to retain their original shape. So now I have a series of sculptures made of embellished freeze-dried avocado skins. Don't ask me *why* I wanted to work with avocado skins. I am not trying to 'make a statement' with my sculpture—I just get these ideas and follow them to the end."

For a number of years Keith has also run a commercial color transparency retouching studio, providing a highly specialized service to publications like *Vogue, New Yorker, New York Times Magazine,* and *Economist,* among others. "This is for extremely high-quality color work. There are only about ninety people in New York who can do it. It entails covering the transparency, which is laid on a treated copper, silver or gold plate, with a frisket to protect the parts you don't want touched. Then you cut through the frisket with a very fine stylus, perhaps one four-hundred-thirtieth of an inch. You work layer by delicate layer. This technique gives you colors with extraordinarily dynamic plays of light.

"I have worked lots of jobs, from usher at Chicago's Symphony Hall to sportscaster in Australia. I play quite a good game of tennis, though I'm by no means championship material, and I enjoyed sitting in the box spouting my opinions for the TV audience. I was also a soccer commentator, but not in the U.S. My style is too laid back for the American sports scene, and besides, most U.S. commentators were at one time world-class athletes, which I never was.

"Somehow or other, the jobs I've done have enriched my art and writing. My creative projects are my most important work, and children's books are very special. A picture book must be a marriage of images, language and rhythm. It's a lovely form, and deliciously challenging."

——*Based on an interview by Marguerite Feitlowitz*

FOR MORE INFORMATION SEE: Saturday Review, March 21, 1970; *Christian Science Monitor,* May 7, 1970; Doris de Montreville and Elizabeth D. Crawford, editors, *Fourth Book of Junior Authors and Illustrators,* H. W. Wilson, 1978; Lee Kingman and others, compilers, *Illustrators of Children's Books: 1967-1976,* Horn Book, 1978.

KELLEHER, Victor   1939-

BRIEF ENTRY: Born July 19, 1939, in London, England. Lecturer, professor, author. While completing an extensive university education in South Africa, Kelleher became a junior lecturer of English at the University of Witwatersrand in Johannesburg. An avid traveler, he later lectured in another South African city as well as at universities in New Zealand and Australia. Since 1976 he has been a faculty member at the University of New England in Armidale, Australia. According to Kelleher, his writing evolved from an "attempt to assuage feelings of nostalgia" after leaving South Africa in 1973. Among his publications for adults are *Voices from the River, The Beast of Heaven,* and a volume of short stories titled *Africa and After.* Kelleher's award-winning juvenile works include *Forbidden Paths of Thual* (Penguin/Kestrel, 1979), winner of the 1982 West Australian Young Readers' Book Award; *Master of the Grove* (Penguin/Kestrel, 1982), named Australian Children's Book of the Year by the Children's Book Council of Australia; and *The Hunting of Shadroth* (Penguin/Kestrel, 1982), which received the West Australian Young Readers' Special Award in 1983. Kelleher has also contributed short stories and critical articles to several journals; in 1978 he was the recipient of the Patricia Hackett Prize for short fiction. Aside from writing, his interests include making pottery, working with silver, and running. *Home:* 8 Belinda Place, Armidale, New South Wales 2350, Australia.

FOR MORE INFORMATION SEE: Twentieth-Century Children's Writers, 2nd edition, St. Martin's Press, 1983; *The Oxford Companion to Australian Literature,* Oxford University Press, 1985; *The Writers Directory: 1986-1988,* St. James Press, 1986.

I remember, I remember,
The house where I was born,
The little window where the sun
Came peeping in at morn.
                                        —Thomas Hood
                        (From *I Remember, I Remember*)

KENEALY, James P.   1927-
(Jim Kenealy)

PERSONAL: Born June 4, 1927, in Dorchester, Mass.; son of William V. and Margaret (McConville) Kenealy; married; children: Nancy, Mike, Deane. *Home:* R.D. 1, Rensselaer, N.Y. 12144.

CAREER: WQBK-AM Radio, Albany, N.Y., outdoor editor, 1972—. Owner of J. P. Kenealy Associates (marine and environmental consultants). Director of Rensselaer Boys' Club. *Military service:* U.S. Navy, 1944-46. *Member:* Outdoor Writers of America.

WRITINGS—All under name Jim Kenealy: *Boating from Bow to Stern,* Dodd, 1967; *Better Fishing for Boys,* Dodd, 1969; *Better Camping for Boys,* Dodd, 1973. Author of outdoor column in *Knickerbocker News,* 1973—. Contributor to state and national magazines.

WORK IN PROGRESS: Hunting and Fishing in New York State, for Donlevy Press.

KLAITS, Barrie   1944-

PERSONAL: Born July 2, 1944, in Biloxi, Miss.; daughter of Harold A. and Ruth (Ross) Gelbhaus; married Joseph Klaits (a university teacher of history), September 5, 1965; children: Frederick, Alexander. *Education:* University of Minnesota, student, 1965-66; Barnard College, A.B., 1966. *Home:* 6563 Walnut Grove, Columbia, Md. 21044.

CAREER: Minnesota Mathematics and Science Teaching Project, Minneapolis, Minn., writer, 1966-67. Guest researcher at L'Institut de Paléontologie of Muséum National d'Histoire Naturelle (Paris, France), 1967-68, 1971. Founder of Troy (Mich.) Citizens for Recycling; co-founder of Elizabeth Lake Association. *Member:* American Association for the Advancement of Science. *Awards, honors: When You Find a Rock* was chosen one of Child Study Association of America's Children's Books of the Year, 1976.

WRITINGS: (With Zachariah Subarsky, Elizabeth Reed, and Edward Landin) *Living Things in Field and Classroom,* University of Minnesota Press, 1969, revised edition, 1972; (editor with husband, Joseph Klaits) *Animals and Man in Historical Perspective,* Harper, 1974; *When You Find a Rock: A Field Guide* (juvenile; illustrated with photographs by Pelle Cass), Macmillan, 1976. Contributor to paleontology journals, including *Mammalia* and *Journal of Paleontology.* Contributor to *New York Kids' Catalogue,* Doubleday, 1979.

SIDELIGHTS: "I love my family and I love the earth. Accompanying my husband to Paris for his historical research projects, I found myself wondering about the movements of fourteen-million-year-old rhinoceroses. Museum directors there graciously helped me to pursue my questions. Home with children now, I contemplate the pebbles which the glaciers delivered to our doorstep. It's fun helping children to discover the marvelous stories in everyday stones. It's exciting to interpret for them recent scientific findings. Trying to express all of these things on paper is my favorite challenge."

We are by nature most tenacious of those things which we notice in childhood, just as the flavor with which new vessels are imbued remains in them.
                                        —Seneca

KRULL, Kathleen 1952-
(Kathleen Cowles, Kathryn Kenny, Kevin Kenny)

PERSONAL: Born July 29, 1952, in Fort Leonard Wood, Mo.; daughter of Kenneth (an artist's representative) and Helen (a counselor; maiden name, Folliard) Krull. *Education:* Lawrence University, B.A. (magna cum laude), 1974. *Office:* 845 Agate St., San Diego, Calif. 92109.

CAREER: Harper & Row Publishers, Inc., Evanston, Ill., editorial assistant, 1973-74; Western Publishing, Inc., Racine, Wis., associate editor, 1974-79; author of books for children, 1975—; Raintree Publishers Ltd., Milwaukee, Wis., managing editor, 1979-82; Harcourt Brace Jovanovich, senior editor, 1982-84; free-lance editor and consultant, 1984—. Speaker at writers and librarians conferences and workshops; keynote speaker and editor-in-residence at Society of Children's Book Writers annual conference, 1983; teacher at University of Wisconsin—Milwaukee, and University of California at Los Angeles. *Member:* Society of Children's Book Writers. *Awards, honors: Sometimes My Mom Drinks Too Much* was named an Outstanding Social Studies Trade Book by the joint committee of the Children's Book Council and the National Council for Social Studies, 1980; Chicago Book Clinic Award, 1980, for *Beginning to Learn about Colors;* New York Art Directors Club Award, 1980, for *Beginning to Learn about Shapes;* numerous awards and honors for books acquired and edited while at Raintree and Harcourt Brace Jovanovich.

WRITINGS—Juvenile: Cityscape: A Changing New Providence, Harcourt, 1987.

"Beginning to Learn about" series; all with Richard L. Allington; all published by Raintree: *Beginning to Learn about Colors* (illustrated by Noel Spangler), 1979; . . . *Shapes* (illustrated by Lois Ehlert), 1979; . . . *Numbers* (illustrated by

Tom Garcia), 1979; . . . *Opposites* (illustrated by Eulala Conner), 1979; . . . *Hearing* (illustrated by Wayne Dober), 1980; . . . *Looking* (illustrated by Bill Bober), 1980; . . . *Tasting* (illustrated by N. Spangler), 1980; . . . *Smelling* (illustrated by Lee Gatzke), 1980; . . . *Feelings* (illustrated by Brian Cody), 1980; . . . *Touching* (illustrated by Yoshi Miyake), 1980; . . . *Thinking* (illustrated by T. Garcia), 1981; . . . *Writing* (illustrated by Y. Miyake), 1981; . . . *Reading* (illustrated by Joel Naprstek), 1981; . . . *Talking* (illustrated by Rick Thrun), 1981; . . . *Spring* (illustrated by Lynn Uhde), 1981; . . . *Summer* (illustrated by Dennis Hockerman), 1981; . . . *Winter* (illustrated by John Wallner), 1981; . . . *Autumn* (illustrated by Bruce Bond), 1981; . . . *Letters* (illustrated by T. Garcia), 1982; . . . *Words* (illustrated by Ray Cruz), 1982; . . . *Stories* (illustrated by Helen Cogancherry), 1982; . . . *Science* (illustrated by James Teason), 1982; . . . *Time* (illustrated by Y. Miyake), 1982; . . . *Measuring* (illustrated by N. Spangler), 1982.

Juvenile; under pseudonym Kathleen Cowles; all published by Western: *The Bugs Bunny Book,* 1975; *The Seven Wishes,* 1976; *Golden Everything Workbook Series,* 1979; *What Will I Be? A Wish Book,* 1979.

Juvenile; under pseudonym Kathryn Kenny (house pseudonym): *Trixie Belden and the Hudson River Mystery,* Western, 1979.

Juvenile; under pseudonym Kevin Kenny: (With Helen Krull) *Sometimes My Mom Drinks Too Much* (illustrated by H. Cogancherry), Raintree, 1980.

Contributor to *Word Guild.* Piano arranger of Margaret Cusack's *The Christmas Carol Sampler,* Harcourt, 1984. Also editor and piano arranger for *Songs of Praise* (illustrated by Tomie de Paola), Harcourt, 1987.

WORK IN PROGRESS: More music books; two novels; another Trixie Belden book.

I see many shapes in winter. ■ (From *Beginning to Learn about Winter* by Richard L. Allington and Kathleen Krull. Illustrated by John C. Wallner.)

Autumn brings special feelings. ■ (From *Beginning to Learn about Autumn* by Richard L. Allington and Kathleen Krull. Illustrated by Bruce Bond.)

SIDELIGHTS: An editor as well as author of children's books, Krull comments on her editorial philosophy. "In writing or editing a manuscript, the very most important thing to me is good writing, or a manuscript's literary merit. No amount of creative editing, brilliant artwork, superior design and production work, or advertising and promotion campaigns can save what is essentially a weak idea in the first place. The manuscript comes first. Everything that happens to it afterward is secondary. Writing books for children, like any other kind of writing, is a *craft*.

"As for personal preferences I think that the ability to arrange words on paper in such a way as to make a person laugh is one of the greatest talents a writer can have. I also like manuscripts that make me cry, or that make me *feel* anything. I am attracted to books about traumas that kids experience—sensitive, multi-dimensional treatments of sex, religion, divorce, alcohol, drugs, violence, death, handicaps. Another thing I'm partial to is music—anything to do with the field of music or that has strong rhythm in its words or plot devices. I like books that are imaginative and original, that to my knowledge have not been done before. Thoroughness, clarity, integrity, sincerity, and factual accuracy are other things I look for.

"Something that is important to me is whether kids in the Midwest will appreciate a manuscript. I think of a recent study reporting that Iowa has more books per capita checked out of the library than any other state in the country. I think about Iowa as I'm evaluating an idea."

FOR MORE INFORMATION SEE: Kathleen Krull, "Why Edit for Children?," *Word Guild,* February, 1978; "New Children's Book Deals with Alcoholism," *Milwaukee Sentinel,* November 14, 1980; *Follett Library Book Newsletter,* winter, 1981; *Society of Children's Book Writers Bulletin,* March/April, 1985; "Thirty-Three Questions an Editor Asks before Signing Up a Book" *Authors Guild Bulletin,* winter, 1985; "Trixie Headed for Coast," *Defensor Chieftan* (Socorro, New Mexico), June 19, 1986; *Wisconsin Authors Alliance Newsletter,* September, 1986.

KUSHNER, Donn   1927-

PERSONAL: Born March 29, 1927, in Lake Charles, La.; son of Sam (in lumber business) and Lily (Donn) Kushner; married Eva Milada Dubska (a professor of French literature and university president), September 15, 1949; children: Daniel, Roland, Paul. *Education:* Harvard University, B.Sc., 1948; McGill University, M.Sc., 1950, Ph.D., 1952. *Religion:* Jewish. *Home:* 289 Clemow Ave., Ottawa, Ontario, Canada K1S 2B7. *Office:* University of Ottawa, Department of Biology, 30 Somerset St. East, Ottawa, Ontario, Canada K1N 6N5.

CAREER: Writer, 1944—; Forest Insect Laboratory, Sault Sainte Marie, Ontario, research scientist, 1954-61; National Research Council of Canada, Ottawa, Ontario, research scientist, 1961-65; University of Ottawa, Ontario, associate professor of biology, 1965-67, professor, 1967—. Visiting scientist at National Institute for Medical Research, Mill Hill, London, England. *Member:* American Society for Microbiology; American Society of Biological Chemists; Canadian Society of Microbiologists (vice-president, 1979-80; president, 1980-81); Canadian Society of Children's Authors, Illustrators and Performers; Writer's Union of Canada. *Awards, honors:* Children's Book of the Year Award from the Canadian Library Association, 1981, for *The Violin-Maker's Gift;* received the Ottawa Biological and Biochemical Society Award, 1986.

DONN KUSHNER

WRITINGS: (Editor) *Microbial Life in Extreme Environments,* Academic Press, 1978; *The Violin-Maker's Gift* (juvenile; illustrated by Doug Panton), Macmillan (Canada), 1980, Farrar, Straus, 1982; *The Witness and Other Stories,* Borealis Press, 1981; *Uncle Jacob's Ghost Story* (juvenile), Macmillan (Canada), 1984, Holt, 1986; *A Book Dragon* (juvenile), Macmillan (Canada), 1987, Holt, 1988. Contributor of articles to scientific journals and stories to literary magazines, including *Fiddlehead, Antagonish Review, Alphabet, Inscape, Viewpoints,* and *Canadian Humanities Association Bulletin.* Reviewer for children's scientific books for *Canadian Children's Literature.* Co-editor of *Canadian Journal of Microbiology,* 1977-83; former member of editorial board, currently North American editor, *Archives of Microbiology,* 1984—.

WORK IN PROGRESS: Scientific research on the physiology of bacteria that live in extreme environments; *The Christmas Tree Watcher* ("a sort of retelling of *The Bremen Town Musicians*"); *Life on Mars; The Dinosaur Duster; The Cat Shop.*

SIDELIGHTS: "Though a professional scientist and an academic, I have been writing stories since I was fifteen and telling them much longer than that. The stories have only made it to small literary magazines. The 'children's books' seem to do better. I add the quotation marks because (like many children's writers) I didn't set out to write books 'aimed at' a particular 'market,' but to tell a story that I liked. I aim towards the contrapuntal in my writing (I am a keen amateur musician and have played the violin and viola in chamber music groups for years), so that a major theme may be under the surface, in the mind of the main character. Thus, in *The Violin-Maker's Gift,* Gaspard, the violin-maker, silently expresses his love and feeling of loss for the little bird he gave away even after he realizes it is a magical creature.

"In *Uncle Jacob's Ghost Story,* the story of Jacob who came to the New World to leave the superstitions of the Old World behind (only to find that the superstitions and some old friends have followed him) is mixed with the *telling* of the story by two old men to a boy: as the story progresses, we realize that the spirits in the story have come back to have their story told.

"Both of these stories deal with the past, and with memories; so does an unpublished one, *The Christmas Tree Watcher,* a story remembered by a Canadian soldier doing peace-keeping in the Middle East; here, however, the story line is more direct. In *A Book Dragon* the story line is indeed direct: perhaps I am being influenced by reviewers who like my writing style and imagination, but have difficulty 'placing' my stories as being for children or adults. Still, since children do seem to like the stories, it doesn't really disturb me that adults do too. On the contrary.

"Children as young as seven years have told me they like my first book very much, and I hope that somewhat older children will feel the same about my second book. Whatever their complications, they are lively stories with some interesting characters and attractive animals, and (I have been told) the reader never knows what to expect next.

The bird began to walk up and down the work-bench, leaving faint tracks in the shavings. ■ (From *The Violin-Maker's Gift* by Donn Kushner. Illustrated by Doug Panton.)

"My first 'science fiction' book, *Life on Mars,* deals with why the Viking landers didn't discover it; this is a 'peacenik' treatment.

"As to my relation between my interests in science and literature, about which I'm sometimes asked: biological research requires imagination too, in seeing previously unsuspected relations between different phenomena, in having an instinct which questions will bring new and surprising answers. Generally, however, the matter dealt with in scientific research is much simpler than that dealt with in fiction.

"My own children have served as audiences while my stories were being written and have encouraged me by asking for more. Now that I have grandchildren, I look forward to a new audience. One of them, Nathan, already is making up stories of his own, and has given me the idea for a good story about a balloon. His and his brother's interest in dinosaurs inspired *The Dinosaur Duster* which is for quite young children. Also in progress is *The Cat Shop* another animal fable about cats (and other animals), artists, and the balance between real quality and public image."

The Violin-Maker's Gift has been translated into Dutch, German, French and Polish. *Uncle Jacob's Ghost Story* has been translated into German.

FOR MORE INFORMATION SEE: Washington Post Book World, May 9, 1982.

LAGER, Marilyn   1939-

PERSONAL: Born June 29, 1939, in Bronx, N.Y.; daughter of Sol (a stockbroker) and Sylvia (an administrator; maiden name, Goodstein) Trauner; married Eric Lager (a physician), December 20, 1959; children: Karen, Jennifer, Robert. *Education:* Smith College, B.A., 1960; Drexel University, M.L.S., 1975. *Home:* 1138 Woodbine Ave., Narberth, Pa. 19072. *Office:* Friends' Central School, 68th and City Line Ave., Philadelphia, Pa. 19151.

CAREER: Miquon School, Miquon, Pa., librarian, 1975-86; Friends' Central School, Philadelphia, Pa., librarian, 1986—. *Member:* American Library Association, Independent School Teachers Association of Pennsylvania, Pennsylvania Library Association.

MARILYN LAGER

WRITINGS: Sigmund Freud, Doctor of the Mind (juvenile; illustrated by husband, Eric Lager), Enslow, 1986.

WORK IN PROGRESS: Travel articles.

SIDELIGHTS: ''In my high school yearbook, I listed my interests as 'psychology and reading.' With the publication of my book, *Sigmund Freud, Doctor of the Mind,* I feel both interests were fulfilled and a wish realized!''

LAMPERT, Emily 1951-

PERSONAL: Born April 26, 1951, in Boston, Mass.; daughter of David (a businessman and Ayshire breeder) and Irma M. (in antiques business) Lampert. *Education:* Boston University, B.A., 1973. *Politics:* Independent. *Home:* Meredith Farm, Topsfield, Mass. 01983. *Office:* Wenham Cross Antiques, 232 Newbury St., Boston, Mass. 02116.

CAREER: La Ruche, Inc., Boston, Mass., manager, 1979-83; Rose and Magpie, Marblehead, Mass., co-owner, 1983-85; Wenham Cross Antiques, Boston, co-owner, 1985—. *Awards, honors: A Little Touch of Monster* was exhibited at the Bologna (Italy) International Children's Book Fair, 1985.

EMILY LAMPERT

WRITINGS: The Unusual Jam Adventure (juvenile), Atlantic Monthly, 1978; *A Little Touch of Monster* (juvenile; illustrated by Victoria Chess), Atlantic Monthly, 1986.

WORK IN PROGRESS: Ralph and Walrus, a juvenile; *Tepler and Munro,* a children's story about a retired lion tamer and a retired lion.

SIDELIGHTS: ''I grew up on a dairy farm, the middle of five children, and the sight of fields and woods, the peace and privacy and magic one has from living in the country is as necessary to me as breathing. My favorite writers as a child were all British, authors like E. Nesbit, Lewis Carroll, and Kenneth Grahame. Reading them transported me to other worlds, and when I came to the end of a book it was pure grief to find myself back in the real world! When I sit down to write, I never picture my characters in any setting but that of the Victorian English countryside.

''I have wanted to be a writer since the age of thirteen, when I first read E. E. Cummings, but I longed then to be intensely deep and difficult to understand. Now I just want to make people laugh.

''I never know when I am going to get an idea and even when I have one I never know what is going to happen next. I am not very prolific with my writing, and sitting down at the typewriter makes me nervous, like going to the dentist. I am always afraid that nothing will come out (of course at the dentist I'm afraid something *will*). Discipline is definitely necessary.

''I do not intend to put any messages in my stories, although sometimes they get there. I just want my words to charm. Somehow, when successfully done, the right combination of rhyme and rhythm and nonsense can act like a spell, can cause a door to open to some other magic place. And if and when it does—escape!''

HOBBIES AND OTHER INTERESTS: Animals.

LANDIS, J(ames) D(avid) 1942-

BRIEF ENTRY: Born June 30, 1942, in Springfield, Mass. Publishing executive and author. After receiving his B.A. from Yale College in 1964, Landis became an assistant editor for Abelard Schuman. In 1967 he went to work for William Morrow & Co., where he has since held the positions of editor, senior editor, editorial director, and senior vice-president. In 1985 Landis was named publisher and editor-in-chief of Morrow's Beach Tree Books; previously, he served as publisher of Quill trade paperbacks. Landis is the recipient of the 1973 Roger Klein Award for editing and, in 1977, was named an Advocate Humanitarian. He is the author of four novels for young adults: *The Sisters Impossible* (Knopf, 1979), its sequel, *Love's Detective* (Bantam, 1984), *Daddy's Girl* (Morrow, 1984), and *Joey and the Girls* (Bantam, 1987). Landis is working on two additional novels, one of which is titled *Judy the Obscure.* *Office:* c/o William Morrow & Co., Inc., 105 Madison Ave., New York, N.Y. 10025.

FOR MORE INFORMATION SEE: Who's Who in America, 44th edition, Marquis, 1986.

Children have neither past nor future; they enjoy the present, which very few of us do.

—Jean de La Bruyere

Le GUIN, Ursula K(roeber) 1929-

PERSONAL: Surname pronounced "Luh-Gwin;" born October 21, 1929, in Berkeley, Calif.; daughter of Alfred Louis (an anthropologist) and Theodora (a writer; maiden name, Kracaw) Kroeber; married Charles Alfred Le Guin (a historian), December 22, 1953; children: Elisabeth, Caroline, Theodore. *Education:* Radcliffe College, B.A., 1951; Columbia University, M.A., 1952. *Residence:* Portland, Ore. *Agent:* Virginia Kidd, 538 East Hartford St., Milford, Pa. 18337.

CAREER: Writer. Part-time instructor in French at Mercer University, Macon, Georgia, 1954-55, and University of Idaho, Moscow, 1956; former department secretary, Emory University, Atlanta, Georgia; has run writing workshops at University of Washington, Seattle, 1971-73, Pacific University, Forest Grove, Oregon, 1971, Portland State University, Oregon, 1974, 1977, and 1979, University of Reading, England, 1976, and for the Arts Council of Australia, Melbourne, 1975. Creative consultant to Public Broadcasting Service in 1979 on the production of "The Lathe of Heaven," adapted for television from her novel of the same title. *Member:* Authors League, Writers Guild, Science Fiction Writers Association, Science Fiction Research Association, Science Fiction Poetry Association, National Organization for Women, National Abortion Rights Action League, Women's International League for Peace and Freedom, Phi Beta Kappa.

AWARDS, HONORS: Fulbright fellowship, 1953; *Boston Globe-Horn Book* Award for text, 1969, for *A Wizard of Earthsea;* Nebula Award from the Science Fiction Writers Association, 1969, and Hugo Award from the International Science Fiction Association, 1970, both for best novel, both for *The Left Hand of Darkness;* Newbery Honor Book, 1972, for *The Tombs of Atuan;* National Book Award finalist, 1972, for *The Tombs of Atuan,* and 1977, for *Orsinian Tales; The Farthest Shore* was chosen one of Child Study Association of America's Children's Books of the Year, 1972, and *Very Far Away from Anywhere Else,* 1976; National Book Award for Children's Books, 1973, for *The Farthest Shore;* Hugo Award from the International Science Fiction Association, for best novella, 1973, for *The Word for World Is Forest;* Hugo Award nomination from the International Science Fiction Association, Nebula Award nomination from the Science Fiction Association, and *Locus* Award, all 1973, all for *The Lathe of Heaven;* Hugo Award from the International Science Fiction Association for best short story, 1974, for "The Ones Who Walk Away from Omelas"; *The Dispossessed: An Ambiguous Utopia* was chosen one of the American Library Association's Best Young Adult Books, 1974, and *Very Far Away from Anywhere Else,* 1976.

Guest of Honor, World Science Fiction Convention, 1975; Nebula Award from the Science Fiction Writers Association for best novel, Hugo Award from the International Science Fiction Association for best novel, Jupiter Award for best novel, and Jules Verne Award, all 1975, all for *The Dispossessed: An Ambiguous Utopia;* Nebula Award from the Science Fiction Writers Association for best short story, and Jupiter Award for best short story, both 1975, for "The Day before the Revolution"; Nebula Award nomination from the Science Fiction Writers Association, and Jupiter Award, both 1976, both for short story "The Diary of the Rose"; D.Litt., 1978, from Bucknell University; Gandalf Award as "Grand Master of Fantasy," 1979; Balrog Award nomination for best poet, 1979; Lewis Carroll Shelf Award, 1979, for *A Wizard of Earthsea; Malafrena* was selected one of New York Public Library's Books for the Teen Age, 1980, *The Left Hand of Darkness,*

URSULA K. Le GUIN

1980, 1981, and 1982, *Interfaces,* 1981, and *The Beginning Place,* 1981 and 1982.

WRITINGS—Novels, except as indicated: *Rocannon's World* (also see below; bound with *The Kar-chee Reign* by Avram Davidson), Ace Books, 1966; *Planet of Exile* (also see below; bound with *Mankind under the Lease* by Thomas M. Disch), Ace Books, 1966; *City of Illusions* (adult; also see below), Ace Books, 1967; *A Wizard of Earthsea* (juvenile; first volume of Earthsea trilogy; ALA Notable Book; *Horn Book* honor list; illustrated by Ruth Robbins; also see below), Parnassus, 1968; *The Left Hand of Darkness,* Ace Books, 1969.

The Tombs of Atuan (juvenile; second volume of Earthsea trilogy; ALA Notable Book; illustrated by Gail Garraty; also see below), Atheneum, 1971; *The Lathe of Heaven,* Scribner, 1971; *The Farthest Shore* (juvenile; third volume of Earthsea trilogy; illustrated by G. Garraty; Junior Literary Guild selection; also see below), Atheneum, 1972; *From Elfland to Poughkeepsie* (lecture), Pendragon Press, 1973; *Wild Angels* (poems), Capra, 1974; *The Dispossessed: An Ambiguous Utopia,* Harper, 1974.

The Wind's Twelve Quarters (short stories), Harper, 1975; *Dreams Must Explain Themselves* (critical essays), Algol Press, 1975; *The Word for World Is Forest* (novella; originally published in collection *Again, Dangerous Visions;* also see below), Berkley Publishing, 1976; *Very Far Away from Anywhere Else* (juvenile; ALA Notable Book; *Horn Book* honor list), Atheneum, 1976 (published in England as *A Very Long*

Way from Anywhere Else, Gollancz, 1976); *Solomon Leviathan's Nine Hundred Thirty-First Trip Around the World* (illustrated by Alicia Austin), Puffin, 1976, Cheap Street, 1983; *Orsinian Tales* (short stories), Harper, 1976; (editor) *Nebula Award Stories XI* (anthology), Gollancz, 1976, Harper, 1977; *The Earthsea Trilogy* (includes *A Wizard of Earthsea, The Tombs of Atuan,* and *The Farthest Shore*), Gollancz, 1977; *The Language of the Night: Essays on Fantasy and Science Fiction,* Putnam, 1978; *Three Hainish Novels* (contains *Rocannon's World, Planet of Exile,* and *City of Illusions*), Doubleday, 1978; *Malafrena,* Putnam, 1979; (with Theodora K. Quinn) *Tillai and Tylissos,* Red Bull Press, 1979; *Leese Webster* (juvenile; illustrated by James Brunsman), Atheneum, 1979.

The Beginning Place (juvenile), Harper, 1980 (published in England as *Threshold,* Gollancz, 1980); (editor with Virginia Kidd) *Interfaces* (short stories), Grosset, 1980; (editor with V. Kidd) *Edges* (short stories), Pocket Books, 1980; *The Eye of the Heron and Other Stories* (novella; published in collection *Millennial Women;* also see below), Panther (London), 1980, Harper, 1983; *Hard Words and Other Poems,* Harper, 1981; *The Compass Rose* (short stories), Harper, 1982; *Adventures in Kroy,* Cheap Street, 1982; (with Hank Pander), *In the Red Zone,* Lord John Press, 1983; *The Visionary* (bound with *Wonders Hidden* by Scott R. Sanders), McGraw, 1984.

Always Coming Home (with cassette; illustrated by Margaret Chodos; music by Todd Barton), Harper, 1985; *King Dog: A Screenplay* (bound with *Dostoevsky: A Screenplay* by Raymond Carver and Tess Gallagher), Capra, 1985; *Buffalo Gals and Other Animal Presences* (stories and poems), Capra, 1987;

(From *Always Coming Home* by Ursula K. Le Guin. Illustrated by Margaret Chodos.)

Wild Oats and Fireweed (poetry), Harper, 1987; *A Visit from Dr. Katz* (juvenile), Atheneum, 1987; *Catwings* (juvenile), Orchard, 1988.

Contributor: Damon Knight, editor, *Orbit 5,* Putnam, 1969; Harry Harrison and Brian Aldiss, editors, *Best SF: 1969,* Putnam, 1970; Terry Carr and Donald A. Wollheim, editors, *World's Best Science Fiction,* Ace Books, 1970; Robin Scott Wilson, editor, *Those Who Can,* Mentor, 1970; D. Knight, editor, *Orbit 6,* Putnam, 1970; James Blish, editor, *Nebula Award Stories 5,* Doubleday, 1970; Samuel R. Delaney and Marilyn Hacker, editors, *Quark #1,* Paperback Library, 1970; Editors of *Playboy* magazine, *The Dead Astronaut,* Playboy Press, 1971; Robert Silverberg, editor, *New Dimensions 1,* Doubleday, 1972; R. S. Wilson, editor, *Clarion II,* Signet, 1972; Harlan Ellison, editor, *Again, Dangerous Visions,* Volume I, Doubleday, 1972.

R. Silverberg, editor, *New Dimensions III,* Doubleday, 1973; Editors of *Playboy* magazine, *The Best from Playboy,* number 7, Playboy Press, 1973; R. S. Wilson, editor, *Clarion III,* Signet, 1973; D. Knight, editor, *Orbit 14,* Harper, 1974; T. Carr, editor, *Universe 5,* Random House, 1974; Editors of *Galaxy* magazine, *The Best from Galaxy,* Volume II, Award, 1974; Michel Parry, editor, *Dream Trips,* Panther, 1974; R. Silverberg and Roger Elwood, editors, *Epoch,* Berkley Pub-

(Jacket illustration by Ruth Robbins from *A Wizard of Earthsea* by Ursula Le Guin.)

Himpí: a small animal resembling a large guinea pig. ■ (From *Always Coming Home* by Ursula K. Le Guin. Illustrated by Margaret Chodos.)

lishing, 1975; R. Silverberg, editor, *The New Atlantis and Other Novellas of Science Fiction*, Hawthorn, 1975; Edward Blishen, editor, *The Thorny Paradise*, Kestrel Books, 1975; Pat Rotter, editor, *Bitches and Sad Ladies*, Harper's Magazine Press, 1975; James Baen, editor, *The Best from Galaxy*, Volume III, Award, 1975; James Gunn, editor, *Nebula Award Stories X*, Harper, 1975.

Pamela Sargent, editor, *More Women of Wonder*, Vintage, 1976; T. Carr, editor, *The Best Science Fiction of the Year #5*, Ballantine, 1976; Peter Nicholls, editor, *Science Fiction at Large*, Gollancz, 1976, Harper, 1977; Jack Dann and Gardner Dozois, editors, *Future Power*, Random House, 1976; Lee Harding, editor, *The Altered I: An Encounter with Science Fiction*, Norstrilia Press (Carlton, Australia), 1976, Berkley Windhover, 1978; Kaye Webb and Treld Bicknell, editors, *Puffin's Pleasure*, Puffin, 1976; G. Dozois, editor, *Best Science Fiction Stories of the Year*, Sixth Annual Collection, Dutton, 1977; Kenneth Melvin, Stanley Brodsky, and Raymond Fowler, Jr., editors, *Psy Fi One*, Random House, 1977; R. V. Cassill, editor, *The Norton Anthology of Short Fiction*, Norton, 1978; V. Kidd, editor, *Millennial Women*, Delacorte, 1978; Alice Laurance, editor, *Cassandra Rising*, Doubleday, 1978; Robert Boyer and Kenneth Zahorski, editors, *Dark Imaginings*, Delta, 1978.

Author of postcard short story, Post Card Partnership, 1975, and of short story, *The Water Is Wide*, Pendragon Press, 1976; author of recordings for Alternate World Recordings, 1976, and Caedmon Records, 1977. Contributor to *Sword & Sorcery Annual*, 1975. Contributor of short stories, novellas, essays, and reviews to numerous science fiction, scholarly, and popular periodicals, including *Fantastic, Parabola, Science-Fiction Studies, Western Humanities Review, New Republic, Redbook, Playgirl, Playboy, New Yorker, Foundation*, and *Omni*.

ADAPTATIONS: "Guilan's Harp and Intracom" (recording; based on her short stories of the same titles), Caedmon, 1978;

"The Lathe of Heaven" (television movie), starring Kevin Conway, Bruce Davison, and Margaret Avery, PBS-TV, 1979; "The Tombs of Atuan" (filmstrip with record or cassette), Newbery Award Records, 1980; "The Ones Who Walk Away from Omelas" (based on short story of the same title), performed as a drama with dance and music at the Portland Civic Theatre, 1981; (audio cassette) "The Left Hand of Darkness" (abridged and read by author), Warner Audio, 1986.

SIDELIGHTS: **October 21, 1929.** Born in Berkeley, California. "My father was a professor at the University of California at Berkeley, and our summer house, an old, tumble-down ranch in the Napa Valley was a gathering place for scientists, writers, students, and California Indians. Even though I didn't pay much attention, I heard a lot of interesting, grown-up conversation.

"What I did pay close attention to were tales. My father occasionally told us stories around a fire; stories he had heard from Indians in their native language. He translated them into very impressive renditions of rolling skulls and other such horrifying things.

"My mother kept many collections of myths around the house. The ice and fire of Norse mythology were my special favorites and were much unlike the Greeks whose interests revolved around sex—so boring to me at the time. All that running off

The riverbanks grew lower, farther away, more shadowy. ■ (Jacket illustration by Jon Weiman from *The Eye of the Heron and Other Stories* by Ursula K. Le Guin.)

with another man's girl was not very appealing to my imagination. The Norse, on the other hand, were always hitting each other with axes and so on—much more up a kid's alley, I would say.

"I wrote my first story at the age of nine about a man persecuted by invisible evil elves. Speculative fiction. My parents encouraged anything we did and took us seriously. They didn't make a big fuss over our creative efforts, but respected it and gave us time and a place in which to work.

"My closest brother and I used to save our quarters to buy *Astounding Stories*. We'd laugh a lot over the stories, because most of them were junk. At twelve I submitted one of my science fiction pieces to them only to have it promptly rejected. It was all right with me. It was junk. At least I had a real rejection slip to show for it.

"I read everything I could—no holds barred. I was very impressed by the age of twelve with the 'Inner Lands' of Toldees, Mondath, and Arizim, bounded to the east by desert, to the south by magic, to the west by a mountain, and to the north by the polar wind in Lord Dunsay's *A Dreamer's Tale*. In spite of my familiarity with legends and myths, Dunsay came to me as a revelation." [Based on an interview by Rachel Koenig.[1]]

"What I hadn't realized, I guess, is that people were still making up myths. One made up stories oneself, of course; but here was a grownup doing it, for grownups, without a single apology to common sense, without an explanation, just dropping us straight into the Inner Lands. Whatever the reason,

the moment was decisive. I had discovered my native country." [Ursula Le Guin, *The Language of the Night: Essays on Fantasy and Science Fiction*, edited by Susan Wood, Berkley, 1982.[2]]

1951. Received a B.A. from Radcliffe, graduating Phi Beta Kappa. "I never thought I wanted to become a writer; I always thought I was one. The big question was how could I earn a living at it? My father wisely suggested I get some training in a money-making skill so that I would not have to live off my writing. He was quite right, because I would not have been able to support myself with my writing for at least another twenty years. With this in mind, I decided to work toward a higher degree in Romance languages and teach.

"I received an excellent intellectual education at Radcliffe. Though Harvard and Radcliffe were far from coed at the time, women students were essentially attending Harvard classes. I'm grateful to Harvard/Radcliffe for a splendid education and for the wonderful companionship of the students I met. But I've had to *unlearn* a great deal of what I learned there. We were taught a sense of being *better* than other people. And yet, girls were taught to think that they were not as valuable as boys. I've had to fight against both these attitudes in myself—one is so easily influenced and malleable at eighteen."

1952-1953. M.A. from Columbia University, graduating Phi Beta Kappa. "I started my Ph.D. program in French and Italian Renaissance Literature and after two years, I received a Fulbright Fellowship. En route to France aboard the Queen Mary, I met Charles Le Guin. We had a shipboard romance and as the French have developed bureaucracy into a way of

I will tell that journey. It was a small journey many years ago. It is a journey of the still air. ∎
(Jacket photograph by John Wagner from *Always Coming Home* by Ursula K. Le Guin.)

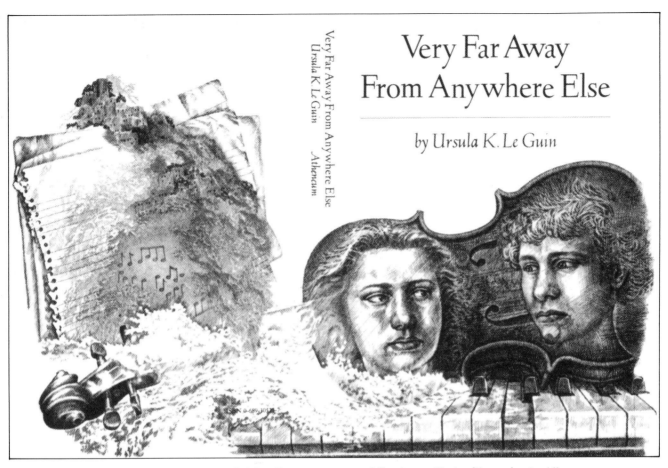

It was five days after my birthday. I was seventeen and five days. ■ (Jacket illustration by Allen Davis from *Very Far Away from Anywhere Else* by Ursula K. Le Guin.)

life, spent our first six months trying to marry. The rest of the time, we had a ball.

"When we returned to the States, my husband took up a teaching job and finished his doctorate in history at Emory University in Atlanta. While he was taking his degree, I dropped mine. We thought we really didn't need two Ph.D.s in one family, so I worked as a secretary and taught French. Wherever we were, I picked up such part-time jobs and spent the rest of my time writing.

"Between 1951-1961 I wrote five novels, four of them about Orsinia, an imaginary country in central Europe, and one set in San Francisco. I published poetry [now collected in *Wild Angels,* 1974] but did not have any luck with my novels, which were rejected by several publishers who found them 'remote.' Of course, they were intended to be remote. I had hit upon a way of 'distancing' my material from the reader, to make room for the imagination. My novels did not fit into any ready-made category and this perhaps made it difficult for them to find publication. I was very isolated at the time, and had no idea that my novels were related to the field of science fiction. When I became aware of Philip Dick, Cordwainer Smith and other science fiction writers, I thought to myself, 'Hey, this stuff is just as crazy as what I'm doing.' I knew where my work might fit in. I made my first sale, a short story called 'April in Paris,' a time travel fantasy based on my knowledge of medieval France, to the pulp magazine *Fantastic.* I was paid all of thirty dollars for it, and they said send more. I was thrilled.''

Her first science fiction stories and three novels, *Rocannon's World* (1966), *Planet of Exile* (1966), and *City of Illusions* (1967) were published. The novels, along with *The Left Hand of Darkness* (1969) and novella *The Word for World Is Forest* (1976) are set in the Hainish universe and therefore referred to as "The Hainish Cycle." A series of independent works which share a common historical background, they reflect Le Guin's interest in anthropology and extrasensory perception. Critics have referred to "The Hainish Cycle" as Le Guin's apprentice works, leading to the more mature *The Left Hand of Darkness* and *The Dispossessed.*[1]

"The first science fiction story I wrote that begins to break from the trivial became the source and prologue for the little novel *Rocannon's World.* I was beginning to get the feel for the medium. In the next books I kept on pushing at my own limitations and at the limits of science fiction. That is what the practice of art is, you keep looking for the outside edge. When you find it you make it a whole, solid, real, and beautiful thing; anything less is incomplete. These books were certainly incomplete, especially *City of Illusions,* which I should not have published as it stands. It has some good bits, but is only half thought out. I was getting vain and hasty.

"There is a lot of promiscuous mixing going on in *Rocannon's World.* We have NAFAL and FTL spaceships, we also have Brisingamen's necklace, windsteeds and some imbecilic angels. We have an extremely useful garment called an impermasuit, resistant to 'foreign elements, extreme temperatures, radioactivity, shocks and blows of moderate velocity and weight such as swordstrokes or bullets' and inside which the wearer would die of suffocation within five minutes. The impermasuit is a good example of how fantasy and science fiction *don't* shade gracefully into one another. A symbol from collective fantasy—the Cloak of Protection (invisability, etc.)—is decked out with some pseudoscientific verbiage and a bit of vivid description and passed off as a marvel of future technology. This can be done triumphantly if the symbol goes deep enough (Wells' *Time Machine*), but if it's merely decorative or convenient, it's cheating. It degrades both symbol and science; it confuses possibility with probability and ends up with neither.''[2]

Traveled to England with husband and children on sabbatical trip in 1968. The first of her ''Earthsea'' trilogy, *A Wizard of Earthsea,* was published. ''I think probably the best put together book I've written is *A Wizard of Earthsea*. It moves with the most clarity from beginning to end.

''I was asked to write a book for young adults by Parnassus Press, which printed the first edition of *A Wizard of Earthsea*. It was my first *request* from a publisher. Parnassus published many children's books and editor Herman Schein wanted to branch into young adult books. He asked me to write for the eleven-to-seventeen age range. I said, 'Gee, that scares me.' The fact that he was willing to accept my hesitation and still try somehow released me, and soon I started the book. *Wizard* . . . was written as a young adult book. I have no apologies

It was like waking, like waking from deep sleep in quietness, when the self belongs wholly to the self. ∎
(Jacket illustration by Griesbach Martucci from *The Beginning Place* by Ursula K. Le Guin.)

(From *The Tombs of Atuan* by Ursula K. Le Guin. Illustrated by Gail Garraty.)

about that. Many wonderful novels have been written for that age group. YA is a completely neglected field of literature. I do get annoyed when people use these sorts of categories *against* the writers or readers of genre fiction. In terms of what inspired me, I suppose I could say it was the opportunity to go back through adolescence and figure out what was happening to me during my own. It was a reliving transposed into imaginative terms. For writers of children's and young adult books, their own childhood and adolescence is available to them and alive to the extent that it is still a problem which has to be worked through.''[1]

''The most childish thing about *A Wizard of Earthsea,* I expect, is its subject: coming of age. Coming of age is a process that took me many years; I finished it, so far as I ever will, at about age thirty-one; and so I feel rather deeply about it. So do most adolescents. It's their main occupation, in fact.

''I did not deliberately invent Earthsea. I am not an engineer, but an explorer. I discovered Earthsea. . . . For some weeks or months I let my imagination go groping around in search of what was wanted, in the dark. It stumbled over the Islands and the magic employed there. Serious consideration of magic, and of writing for kids, combined to make me wonder about wizards. Wizards are usually elderly or ageless Gandalfs, quite rightly and archetypically. But what were they before they had white beards? How did they learn what is obviously an erudite and dangerous art? Are there colleges for young wizards? And so on.'' [Ursula K. Le Guin, *Dreams Must Explain Themselves,* Algol Press, 1975.[3]]

Regarding the geography of Earthsea, ''The story of the book is essentially a voyage, a pattern in the form of a long spiral. I began to see the places where the young wizard would go. Eventually I drew a map.

''. . . *Naming* has been the essence of the art-magic as practiced in Earthsea. For me, as for the wizards, to know the name of an island or a character is to know the island or the person . . . I worked in collaboration with a wizard named Ogion for a long time trying to 'listen for' his name, and making certain it really was his name. This all sounds very mystical and indeed there are aspects of it I do not understand, but it is a pragmatic business too, since if the name had been wrong the character would have been wrong—misbegotten, misunderstood.

''Much the same holds for the bits of invented languages in the trilogy. . . .

''The trilogy is, in one aspect, about the artist. The artist as magician. The Trickster. Prospero. That is the only truly allegorical aspect it has of which I am conscious. If there are other allegories in it please don't tell me: I hate allegories. A is 'really' B, and a hawk is 'really' a handsaw—bah. Humbug. Any creation, primary or secondary, with any vitality to it, can 'really' be a dozen mutually exclusive things at once before breakfast.

''Wizardry is artistry. The trilogy is then, in this sense, about art, the creative experience, the creative process. There is always circularity in fantasy. The snake devours its tail. Dreams must explain themselves.''[3]

''Along in **1967-68** I finally got my pure fantasy vein separated from my science fiction vein by writing *A Wizard of Earthsea* followed by *The Left Hand of Darkness,* and the separation marked a large advance in both skill and content. Since then I have gone on writing, as it were, with both the left and the right hands; and it has been a matter of keeping on pushing out towards the limits—my own and those of the medium.''[2]

Ursula Le Guin. (Drawing by Margaret Chodos.)

"With *The Left Hand of Darkness,* I felt I was beginning to hit my stride as a writer. I had certainly learned my trade as far as science fiction is concerned by the time I wrote the novel. My three earlier novels weren't nearly as ambitious, in either ideas or in the amount of emotion I was able to put into them. Because I knew my craft when I wrote *The Left Hand of Darkness,* I was able to put my heart in the book. It is a novel full of feeling, and it was an interesting idea to invent androgynes.

"Working on the American Playhouse screen adaptation of the book gave me a chance to correct some of the big, fat mistakes I made in the novel. I didn't stretch the language enough to accommodate the idea of a hermaphroditic people. In the book, all the Gethenians are called 'he.' In the screenplay, I got away from that masculine tinge which colors the book. In 1967, while I was writing *The Left Hand of Darkness,* nobody had discussed the sexist implications of the pronouns. It was before the women's movement became interested in gender bias in language—the fact that 'he' is supposedly 'universal' and therefore embraces woman. It doesn't, as a matter of fact. I have thought about how I might have solved it in the novel, had I been more enlightened at the time. Making up a pronoun would make for very difficult reading. In a long, intense novel, I think you'd get sick to death of it. I have only come up with one solution that pleases me—the possibility that there might be alternate chapters—'he' in one, 'she' in the next. Keep the reader jolly well confused.

"At the time I wrote the book, the feminist movement was just beginning. The book is contemporary with Kate Millett and other feminist theorists. I was playing with similar ideas, and dealing with the then topical question, 'What is the difference between a man and a woman? The *real* difference?' We felt if we could only identify differences, we could find out why society treats men and women so differently. In *Left Hand of Darkness* I set up a thought experiment, as I call it. I made up a people who were physiologically no different from each other and then proceeded to see what would happen. Then, of course, I threw in Genly Ai, the poor hapless earth man, because one must always have a traveler to utopia in such a novel.

"The League of All Worlds grew out of my earlier books. All my science-fiction books are set in the same universe, the same future history, as they call it. I'm not very careful about my invented time frames—I lose a thousand years here and there! Once you have invented a universe, it's much easier to stick to it than to reinvent a new universe for each book. The League of All Worlds was a rather naive idea when I first came up with it. By the time I got to *The Left Hand of Darkness,* I had thought it out a little more carefully. The idea of course grew out of my experience as a young person growing up during the years of the founding of the United Nations. It also grew out of and is connected to my gradual loss of faith—a loss of faith we've all experienced in the prospect of a world government. Because of space flight, I had to invent an instantaneous form of communication to insure linkage in my invented universe. But that was fudging, because you can't go faster than life. If it takes you 450 years to travel to the next planet, how are you going to have any sort of political communication with them? The whole thing seemed like such a wild fantasy—the degree of which began to get beyond me.

"I have never undertaken formal scientific studies in order to write science-fiction, but I have certainly had to keep up with

(Jacket illustration by Michael Mariano from *Malafrena* by Ursula K. Le Guin.)

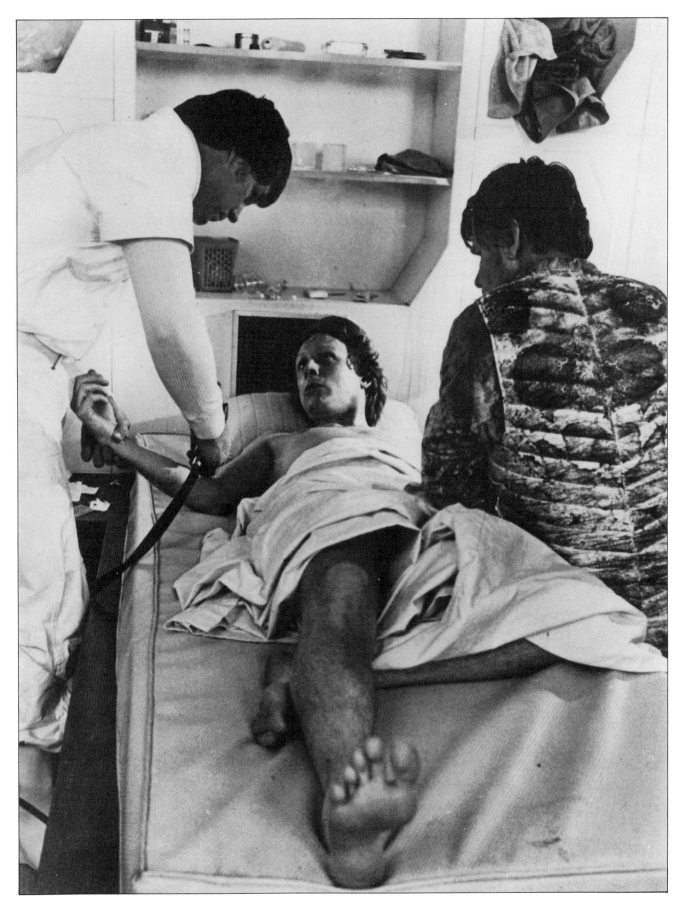

(From the television movie "The Lathe of Heaven," starring Bruce Davison. Presented on PBS-TV, January 9, 1980.)

modern astronomy and cosmology. There are wonderful books that explain it to the lay person. I also read quite a bit on geology, on sleep and dream research, among other things I happen to be interested in.

"*The Word for World Is Forest* deals with dream states, and so does *The Lathe of Heaven,* which is based totally on dreams. I would say to young people that you cannot write science fiction unless you are at least *interested* in some kind of science. My interests tend toward anthropology and psychology, but that is science, too. It doesn't have to be physics—but if you don't like science, don't write science fiction!

"The science fiction community is all over the world. They write about each other and print amateur and professional magazines and hold a whole continuous network of conferences. It is a real community. It can sometimes be claustrophobic, but it's a wonderful phenomenon, in particular for young writers who tend to be isolated. Even as a new writer the s.f. community criticizes your work, writes letters of appreciation and publishes arguments in magazines concerning your fiction. And there is, of course, the Science Fiction Writers Association, of which I was a founding member, soon after writing professionally in that genre. The initial meetings were a very exciting forum for meeting other writers for the first time."[1]

1972. Awarded the Newbery Honor Book Citation for *The Tombs of Atuan.* "The subject of [the book] is, if I had to put it in one word, sex. There's a lot of symbolism in the book, most of which I did not, of course, analyze consciously while writing; the symbols can all be read as sexual. More exactly, you could call it a feminine coming of age. Birth, rebirth, destruction, freedom are the themes."[3]

1974. *The Dispossessed* published and awarded the Nebula and Jupiter awards. "Though I hate for any feeling or opinion of mine to be put in the permanent present tense, I do find anarchism the most interesting kind of political theory. When I found out that anarchism wasn't terrorism, but a great pacifism, as prefigured in early Taoist thought and expounded on by Shelley and Kropotkin, Goldman and Goodman, I wallowed in it for years. I read everything I could get my hands on. *The Dispossessed* grew out of that. At the time, no anarchist utopia had ever been written, which startled me. Then I found out (this was the mid-seventies) that apparently no utopia had ever been written by a woman! Now, thanks to the feminist movement, we have recovered *Herland* (1915) by Charlotte Perkins Gilman, among others. But the feminist utopias had been dropped completely, never reprinted, or referred to. At the time, not knowing that other women had written utopias, I felt it almost a *duty* to do so. Still, I had a male protagonist. But in terms of my present feeling about anarchism, I would say yes, as a body of theory, I do continue to fall back on anarchism when I try to explain what happens politically.

"I have cast my voice into male protagonists, and if a woman writer does that as much and as often as I did for years, you are making a statement. The statement is that men are the people who do things, and that women are the people who sit home and wait. I knew that, to some extent, while I was writing those books, but I couldn't cope with it. People who came to me as main characters were men. One has only a certain amount of control over fiction. When a character comes to you with authority and says, 'There is a novel in me,' you can't do something like change his sex, because the operation will be fatal. Alone perhaps I could never have written central female characters, but thanks to a lot of other women, I became free of the necessity to use men as my main character.

"Only one of my earlier books, *The Tombs of Atuan* has a female main character [Arha]. But since the late seventies, I've had either androgynous characters, or a woman main character. I'm not knocking my early books, but I am happy to have finally become free of that compulsion. I do feel it as freedom. There's a whole new world to write about. Our entire literary tradition gives us the impression that only men write and that only the perceptions and actions of men are worth writing about. Within the last ten years, feminist literary criticism, theory, and presses have been bringing us back to our own female tradition. We *do* have a tradition. And it's becoming more and more visible. It has been exciting for me to rediscover authors like Sarah Orne Jewett and Mary Wilkins Freeman—marvelous American writers. Where were they all my life?''

Le Guin once said that had she been free, as male writers are, of the task of childbearing and child rearing, she would feel impoverished in some way. "I try to cope with this topic. I wrote a thirty-page paper on the issue. I certainly don't want to sound smug or arrogant toward men and women who cannot or do not want to bear children. Nobody *should,* nobody *has* to bear children. But I do want to point out that having children is not, as Freud supposed, an equivalent or a replacement for writing books. Creation and procreation are two different things. It is difficult, given our society, to do both together. You must have some sort of help. My husband was my help. Without a work-sharing spouse, you have to rely on childcare or live in a more tribal, communal, extended family situation. The incredible life commitment involved in having children will of course enrich your life and your art. What I find really immoral and wicked is the kind of belief that my generation espoused: babies or books: Not both! What that says to me is writing is a man's job. What I say is, writing is also a *woman's job.* And that means a fully fulfilled woman.''

Le Guin is a visual writer. "I don't see things as in a film and then stop and describe them. I am *there*—as in a dream. I don't hear voices, as Joan of Arc did. The voices flow directly from the source of writing. I call it 'hearing' because the attitude of mind and body that one is in while writing is *like* listening. Writing is also very similar to being in a trance state. I don't need special conditions to get into this writing state. I simply go to my room at seven or eight in the morning and sit down at the desk with some paper! After all, I have been at it for years and years now. I've learned to use any desk, any paper, any pen. I write straight through a first draft; I go from A to Z. Then I do it all over again. Except in *Always Coming Home* which was put together much differently. It was hard to find the final structure. I kept thinking, 'Oh Lord . . . this book doesn't *have* any shape.' Of course the book does have shape, but a strange one. I am pleased with it now.''

Always Coming Home is Le Guin's critically acclaimed multimedia portrait of a society which "might be going to have lived" on the American Pacific coast. The book, consisting of narratives, history, customs, and poetry of her invented Kesh people, is unified by the first-person narrative of a woman named Stone Telling. The text features original drawings by archaeological illustrator Margaret Chodos of Kesh animals, tools, musical instruments, dwellings and sacred symbols, as well as maps, charts, tables and a 501-word Kesh-English dictionary. Boxed with the book is a cassette of Kesh poetry and music. "How did the music evolve? You can only do so much with words. It's nice to branch out a bit. I simply wished I could *hear* the music of the Kesh, as I had begun to hear their poetry. While working on a radio play, I met Todd Barton, a young composer. I liked very much the music he had composed for my play, and I had a warm feeling about him.

Finally, I gathered up my courage and asked him if he would be interested in trying to write some music for a nonexistent people? Well, he just jumped at the chance. When we attempted to register the music with the U.S. Copyright Office, we were accused of claiming credit for ethnic folk songs! I had to patiently explain that none of the songwriters would even be born for thousands of years.

"It was Todd who introduced me to artist Peggy Chodos, who made the illustrations. The three of us worked very closely. I made a copy of the manuscript for each of them, so that they could find out what I had found out about the Kesh. In the early stages of our working together, both Todd and Peggy would send me their work. At first they would ask, 'Is this the way you imagined it?' Usually it was, but not always. I remember in one instance telling Todd, when he had come quite close to capturing the Kesh, 'This is not the Kesh people, it must be one of their neighbors.'"

In *Always Coming Home,* Le Guin has created a variety of voices which span all age groups. "I wanted to achieve the complexity an opera has. Critics have often pointed up the correlation between musical structure and my literary structures. Interesting, because I am musically ignorant. Dance has always been a metaphor in my work, as has weaving and pottery. Words are such strange things to work with. As a writer, you are always looking for concrete metaphors which reflect the process the mind undergoes while writing. The oral quality in *Always Coming Home* grew out of that impulse. It's very important to me because the *spoken* word is not in your mind, it is an *event.* I long for the *event* quality that music or oral storytelling or dance or theater has."

Several reviewers placed *Always Coming Home* in a "postnuclear holocaust" world, calling Le Guin an "anthropologist of a post-nuclear world," a title to which she vehemently objects. "There is not a holocaust presented in the book. I see the Kesh as probably having grown and developed over thousands of years. I want to emphasize that I would *never* write a book that said we could survive a nuclear holocaust. It frightened me when those reviewers announced that *Always Coming Home* was a 'post-holocaust' book. I have written to them, asking that they publicly correct that description, because I think it is in fact *dangerous* to believe that we could survive a major atomic war. We're going to have enough trouble surviving what we are doing to the earth right now!"

When asked why she has chosen to portray the plant and animal life of her invented worlds with so much familiarity, rather than bestowing them with alien qualities, Le Guin responded: "If everything in a novel or a story is very alien and high-tech, it reflects the writer's preoccupations, and means that the writer's primary interest is in that kind of description and imagination. My principal interest is basically the emotions of the people. If I were to make everything too alien, for one thing, I would have to spend most of the book describing, thereby subordinating the emotions. I also want the reader to experience the world of the novel. If I am describing a dog or some made-up animal, I want the reader to feel the fur. I want to be tactile, and if I were to get too far away from anything we know, the engagement I demand of the reader would be impossible. This ties me down and limits me from any really wild imaginings, but I'm happy to be limited. Tolkien is the master of this. Nobody has the least trouble visualizing or feeling anything he describes, because he knows how to evoke our familiar mythology, and because his imagination just works that way.

"Clarity and simplicity are permanent virtues in a narrative. That doesn't mean over-simplifying. Incredibly complicated scenes may be going on in a novel, and to make the work permanently interesting, things *must* be complex. But they need not trouble the surface, and that is the mark of a really good writer."

Writing is given permanence, according to Le Guin, if "like any piece of art, it is pleasing to the mind and to the sense of beauty, that is to say, aesthetically pleasing. It sounds strange to call a novel, 'beautiful,' but it is when it is right. There must be an emotional depth and complexity, qualities which keep any art work alive. Some books are very short-lived in the memory of the reader; others, one keeps coming back to. For example, as I reread Virginia Woolf's books, they are new to me. As I get older, they get larger and larger."

From a social standpoint, she feels that much science fiction has been regressive and unimaginative. "An absolutely classic example of this is a popular film like 'Star Wars,' wherein it is assumed that the crudest form of government, an *empire,* will continue to exist, and wherein it is also assumed that the only option we have is continuous aggression—warfare becomes the main occupation of mankind. It is also assumed that the alien is hateful and inferior, even when cute and furry like the co-pilot in 'Star Wars' who is obviously meant to be an inferior being. As for women, there is one princess and a couple of nurses in the entire 'Star Wars' universe. If that isn't regressive I don't know what is! One of the early socialists said that the status of women in a society is a pretty reliable index of the degree of civilization reached by that society. If this is true, 'Star Wars' universes are going back to some form of barbarism. There are fleets of books based on these mindless assumptions. Much bad fantasy plays the same game, taking a vaguely generic medieval world and acting out power battles between wizards and princes. It's escapism."[1]

"The question involved here is the question of the 'Other,' the being who is different from you, in its sex, or in its annual income, or in its way of speaking and dressing and doing things, or in the color of its skin, or the number of its legs and heads. In other words, there is the sexual alien, the social alien, the cultural alien, and finally, the racial alien. . . . If you deny any affinity with another person or being, if you declare it to be wholly different from yourself—as man has done to woman, class has done to class, and nation has done to nation—you may hate it, or defy it, but in either case, you have denied it its spiritual quality and its human reality. You have made it into a thing in which the only possible relationship is a power relationship, and thus you have fatally impoverished your own reality. You have, in fact, alienated *yourself.* I would like to see the barbarian ideal evident in much American science fiction replaced by a little human idealism." [Ursula Le Guin, "American SF and the Other," *Science-Fiction Studies,* edited R. D. Mullen and Darko Sullivan, Gregg Press, 1976.[4]]

Her younger daughter, a specialist in women's studies and a feminist, has greatly influenced Le Guin's recent readings. She spent a summer engrossed in the formidable *Norton Anthology of Women's Literature,* a cover-to-cover experience which left her reeling and very excited by the idea of a woman's language. "Women have to learn to talk their own language. By which I mean that we must not talk with men's tongues. Men have spoken for us, and we've accepted that. This won't do any longer—we must learn to speak for ourselves, and men must learn to listen. . . . But there have been other periods when there have been many major women novelists—all through the 20th century. The men get kept as literary figures, the women, except for a few, get forgotten. That's what I mean by listening.'' [Miriam Berkley, ''Ursula K. Le Guin,'' *Publishers Weekly*, May 23, 1986.⁵]

Le Guin published a short story in *Playboy* magazine in the late sixties and allowed them to identify her as ''U. K. Le Guin.'' It amused her at the time, but now feels she made a mistake. Those were hard times for women in science fiction, but times have changed and science fiction has become especially important for women. ''Women are using it to explore and make propositions about the whole role and position of men and women in society.''⁵

FOR MORE INFORMATION SEE—Books: Theodora Kroeber, *Alfred Kroeber: A Personal Configuration*, University of California Press, 1970; Philip Rawson and Laszlo Legeza, *Tao: The Eastern Philosophy of Time and Change*, Avon, 1973; Robert Scholes, *Structural Fabulation: An Essay on Fiction of the Future*, University of Notre Dame Press, 1975; Edward Blishen, editor, *The Thorny Paradise: Writers on Writing for Children*, Kestrel, 1975; George Edgar Slusser, *The Farthest Shores of Ursula Le Guin*, Borgo, 1976; *Authors in the News*, Volume I, Gale, 1976; R. D. Mullen and Darko Sullivan, editors, *Science-Fiction Studies*, Gregg Press, 1976; Dennis Butts, *Good Writers for Young Readers*, Hart-Davis, 1977; Paul Walker, *Speaking of Science Fiction: The Paul Walker Interviews*, Luna, 1978; Doris de Montreville and Elizabeth D. Crawford, editors, *Fourth Book of Junior Authors and Illustrators*, H. W. Wilson, 1978; D. L. Kirkpatrick, editor, *Twentieth-Century Children's Writers*, St. Martin's, 1978, 2nd edition, 1983; *Contemporary Literary Criticism*, Gale, Volume VIII, 1978, Volume XIII, 1980, Volume XXII, 1982; *Children's Literature Review*, Volume III, Gale, 1978; Joseph D. Olander and Martin H. Greenberg, editors, *Ursula K. Le Guin*, Taplinger, 1979; Joseph W. DeBolt, editor, *Ursula K. Le Guin: Voyager to Inner Lands and to Outer Space*, Kennikat, 1979.

Virginia Haviland, editor, *The Openhearted Audience: Ten Authors Talk about Writing for Children*, Library of Congress, 1980; *Dictionary of Literary Biography*, Volume VIII, Part 1: *Twentieth-Century American Science Fiction Writers*, Gale, 1981; Ursula K. Le Guin, *The Language of the Night: Essays on Fantasy and Science Fiction*, Berkley Publishing, 1982; Elizabeth Cummins Cogell, *Ursula K. Le Guin*, G. K. Hall, 1983; James W. Bittner, *Approaches to the Fiction of Ursula K. Le Guin*, University Microfilms International, 1984.

Periodicals: *Horn Book*, April, 1971, October, 1971, June, 1973; *Top of the News*, April, 1971; *Christian Science Monitor*, November 11, 1971; *Writer*, July, 1973, February, 1981; *Algol*, November, 1973, summer, 1975; *Hollins Critic*, April, 1974; Paula Brookmire, ''She Writes about Aliens—Men Included,'' *Milwaukee Journal*, July 21, 1974; *Biography News*, October, 1974; Charles Bigelow and J. McMahon, ''Science Fiction and the Future of Anarchy,'' *Oregon Times*, December, 1974; Gene Van Troyer, ''Vertex Interviews Ursula K. Le Guin,'' *Vertex*, December, 1974; Barry Barth, ''Tricks, Anthropology Create New Worlds,'' *Portland Scribe*, May 17-25, 1975; *Science-Fiction Studies*, November, 1975; *Signal*, January 19, 1976; *New Republic*, February 7, 1976, October 30, 1976; *Publishers Weekly*, June 14, 1976, May 23, 1986; *English Journal*, October, 1977; *MOSAIC X/2*, winter, 1977; Dorothy Gilbert, ''Interview: Ursula K. Le Guin,'' *California Quarterly*, spring/summer, 1978; ''Ursula K. Le Guin,'' *Wilson Library Bulletin*, October, 1978; *Horizon*, January, 1980; *Time*, February 11, 1980, October 14, 1985; ''Meet Your Author: Ursula K. Le Guin,'' *Cricket*, September, 1981; *Los Angeles Times*, September 5, 1982; Anne Fadiman, ''Ursula K. Le Guin: Voyager to the Inner Land,'' *Life*, April, 1986.

Collections: University of Oregon Library, Eugene, Oregon.

LEIBOLD, Jay 1957-

BRIEF ENTRY: Born October 15, 1957, in Denver, Colo. Leibold graduated from Williams College in 1980; the following year, he secured a position as editorial assistant at Farrar, Straus & Giroux, Inc. He is the author of six books for middle-grade readers in Bantam's ''Choose Your Own Adventure'' series, including *Grand Canyon Odyssey*, *Spy for George Washington*, and *The Antimatter Formula*. Leibold, whose ''primary interest is writing fiction,'' has also written reviews for *San Francisco Chronicle Book Review*, *Bloomsbury Review*, and *New Art Examiner*. Home: 46 Albion, San Francisco, Calif. 94103.

LEIGHTON, Margaret (Carver) 1896-1987

OBITUARY NOTICE—See sketch in *SATA* Volume 1: Born December 20, 1896, in Oberlin, Ohio; died June 19, 1987. Author of books for young readers. As a child, Leighton loved to make up stories, often writing down and illustrating the fairy tales she so vividly imagined. Her school years were spent in Cambridge, Massachusetts, and, during her father's teaching sabbaticals, in France and Switzerland. After graduating from Radcliffe College in 1918, she worked for a publishing house until 1921 when she left to marry Herbert Leighton. Following her husband's untimely death in 1935 and the family's subsequent move to California, Leighton began writing books for young readers. She based her first published work, *The Secret of the Old House*, on the imagined adventures of her own four young children. Leighton produced such works as *Twelve Bright Trumpets*, *Judith of France*, *The Sword and the Compass*, *Voyage to Coromandel*, *The Story of Florence Nightingale*, and *The Story of General Custer*. She earned several honors throughout her career, including a Commonwealth Club of California Silver Medal for *The Singing Cave* in 1945, and the 1959 Dorothy Canfield Fisher Memorial Book Award for *Comanche of the Seventh*. In 1971 the Southern California Book Council honored Leighton for her comprehensive contribution of lasting value to children's literature.

FOR MORE INFORMATION SEE: More Junior Authors, H. W. Wilson, 1963; *Authors of Books for Young People*, 2nd edition, 1971; *Authors and Writers Who's Who*, 6th edition, Hafner, 1971; *Contemporary Authors*, Volumes 9-12, revised, Gale, 1974; *Who's Who of American Women*, 14th edition, Marquis, 1984. Obituaries: *School Library Journal*, September, 1987.

LeROY, Gen

PERSONAL: Born in Highland Park, N.J. *Residence:* New York, N.Y.

CAREER: Author. Has worked as a model and designer of book jackets. *Awards, honors:* New Jersey Authors Award, New Jersey Institute of Technology, 1976, for *Emma's Dilemma*, 1978, for *Hotheads; Cold Feet* was selected one of American Library Association's ''Best Books for Young Adults,'' 1979.

WRITINGS—Juvenile fiction: *Bridget*, Harper, 1973; *Emma's Dilemma*, Harper, 1975; *Hotheads*, Harper, 1977; *Cold Feet* (sequel to *Hotheads*), Harper, 1979; *Billy's Shoes* (illustrated by J. Winslow Higginbottom), McGraw-Hill, 1981; *Lucky Stiff!* (illustrated by J. W. Higginbottom), McGraw-Hill, 1981.

Other: (With Anna Pump) *The Loaves and Fishes Cookbook*, Macmillan, 1985.

LEVINE, Abby 1943-

BRIEF ENTRY: Born September 27, 1943, in New York, N.Y. Editor and author of books for young readers. Levine received her B.A. and M.Ed. degrees from Cornell University in the early 1960s. She spent many years as a free-lance editor and, from 1980 to 1981, was employed at the University of Pittsburgh Press. Since 1983 she has been a member of the editing staff at Albert Whitman Co. In Levine's first book, *Sometimes I Wish I Were Mindy* (A. Whitman, 1986), written with Sarah Levine, a small girl compares her family's material wealth with that of her friend, Mindy. *Booklist* hailed the authors' approach to their subject matter: "The Levines could have taken the easy way out by stereotyping Mindy as a brat, but they didn't; she seems perfectly likable which makes the narrator's grappling with her own envy all the more believable." Levine is currently at work on two picture books, to be published by A. Whitman, one of which is titled *What Did Mommy Do Before You? Home:* 9509 Ridgeway Ave., Evanston, Ill. 60203.

LEVINSON, Riki

PERSONAL: Born in Brooklyn, N.Y.; daughter of Samuel E. (a cantor) and Anna S. (an insurance broker; maiden name, Blau) Friedberg; married Morton Levinson (an attorney; deceased); children: Gerry (daughter). *Education:* Cooper Union School of Arts and Sciences, four-year certificate, 1943. *Religion:* Jewish. *Home:* New York, N.Y. *Office:* E. P. Dutton, 2 Park Ave., New York, N.Y. 10016.

CAREER: Free-lance designer, 1945-70; Western Publishing Co., Inc., New York City, design and manufacturing manager of Education Division, 1970-72; E. P. Dutton, New York City, art director, 1972—, assistant publisher, 1986-87, associate publisher, 1987—. *Member:* American Institute of Graphic Arts, Authors Guild, Cooper Union Alumni Association. *Awards, honors:* Many graphic awards as a free-lance designer and art director; Parents' Choice Award for Literature from the Parents' Choice Foundation, one of *Booklist*'s Children's Editors' Choices, a Notable Children's Trade Book in the Field of Social Studies by the joint committee of the National Council of Social Studies and the Children's Book Council, named a notable book by the American Library Association, and a *Redbook* Top Ten Picture Book, all 1985, all for *Watch the Stars Come Out; I Go with My Family to Grandma's* was chosen a Notable Children's Trade Book in the Field of Social Studies, and one of Child Study Association of America's Children's Books of the Year, both 1986, and a Jefferson Cup Award honor book in the Field of U.S. History and Historical Fiction from the Virginia Library Association, 1987.

WRITINGS—Juvenile: *Watch the Stars Come Out* (ALA Notable Book; Reading Rainbow feature selection; illustrated by Diane Goode), Dutton, 1985; *I Go with My Family to Grandma's* (illustrated by D. Goode), Dutton, 1986; *Touch! Touch!* (illustrated by True Kelley), Dutton, 1987; *DinnieAbbieSister-r-r!* (illustrated by Helen Cogancherry), Bradbury, 1987; *Our Home Is the Sea* (paintings by Dennis Luzak), Dutton, 1988.

ADAPTATIONS: "Watch the Stars Come Out" (filmstrip with cassette; audiocassette), Miller-Brody, 1986.

RIKI LEVINSON

WORK IN PROGRESS: Early in the Morning and *Me! Baby!*, both for Dutton; a sequel to *DinnieAbbieSister-r-r!; The Black Horse Inn*, a novel for older children.

SIDELIGHTS: "I write about family. Family is the most important part of my life, and I find it a warm and personal experience to write about it.

"It is reassuring, to me, that children don't change, no matter when they live.

"Being part of a very large family with many, many cousins, gives me lots to draw from when I write. I have four brothers, two older, and two younger—each quite different from the other. My red-headed mother was the most loving and the liveliest person in our family. Although we were quite poor she made our childhood fun.

"In high school my favorite classes were geometry and English, particularly creative writing. I wrote for that class but never outside of it.

"Drawing was a natural thing for me from a very young age. But I did not think it interesting enough in high school—it was too easy. Yet when I wanted to go to college, and there was no money to pay for it, I tried for Cooper Union at the suggestion of my art teacher. Cooper Union was, in effect, a scholarship school. At Cooper Union I found a direction that suited me well, and since that time I have been in art.

to Grandma's.

(From *I Go with My Family to Grandma's* by Riki Levinson. Illustrated by Diane Goode.)

"Until September of 1983 I had never written a story since high school. One day I told my husband that I had an idea for a story but that I didn't know how to write. And he said, 'Don't worry about writing—just put it down.' My very first story was *Watch the Stars Come Out*.

"When the words and sounds fill my head, and I can't stop myself, I sit down and write."

Watch the Stars Come Out has been published in England, Spain, France, Sweden, and Germany. *I Go with My Family to Grandma's* and *Touch! Touch!* have been published in England.

HOBBIES AND OTHER INTERESTS: Natural history, especially animal behavior; architecture, particularly old homes and ancient cultures; the sea.

FOR MORE INFORMATION SEE: New York Times Book Review, March 29, 1987.

MacDONALD, Suse 1940-

BRIEF ENTRY: First name sounds like "news"; born March 3, 1940, in Evanston, Ill. Author and illustrator of children's books. After attending Chatham College for two years, MacDonald completed her B.A. at the State University of Iowa in 1962. Through the years, she has been employed as executive secretary for the picture editor of United Press International and illustrator of textbooks for Caru Studios; from 1969 to 1976, she and her husband Stewart headed their own drafting company in South Londonderry, Vermont. When her youngest child entered school, MacDonald decided to pursue a long-lived interest in illustrating books. She commuted between Boston and Vermont for four years to attend art school,

and eventually enrolled in a course on children's book writing and illustrating at Radcliffe. MacDonald's first book, *Alphabatics* (Bradbury, 1986) is designed to meet the needs of small children who are first learning their letters by relating the shape of each letter in the alphabet to an object. The letters evolve into articles with which children are familiar, making the learning process both concrete and visually appealing. *School Library Journal* described the book as "imaginative, original, and bound to strike a creative note in children." In 1987 *Alphabatics* was selected as a Caldecott honor book and received the Golden Kite Award. It was also a 1986 Junior Literary Guild selection and appeared on *Booklist*'s "Editor's Choice" and *School Library Journal*'s "Best Books of the Year" lists. MacDonald's forthcoming book, *Numblers,* uses the same format to teach children about numbers through visual effects. *Office:* P.O. Box 25, South Londonderry, Vt. 05155.

MAIDEN, Cecil (Edward) 1902-1981

PERSONAL: Born May 3, 1902, in Southport, Lancashire, England; died December 1, 1981, in Centerville, Mass.; naturalized Canadian citizen; later came to the United States; son of James Edward and Emily (Memory) Maiden; married Elizabeth Walters, December 5, 1953; children: Elizabeth Lynne, Marcus, Miles. *Education:* Attended University of Reading, England. *Religion:* Christian Scientist. *Residence:* Centerville, Mass. *Agent:* Shirley Burke, 370 East 76th St., Suite B-704, New York, N.Y. 10021.

CAREER: Has worked as advertising copywriter in London, England; film writer for Twentieth Century-Fox; motion picture director, editor and writer for Universal Studios; and staff writer for Disney Studio. *Military service:* Royal Air Force, served during World War II.

(From *Speaking of Mrs. McCluskie* by Cecil Maiden. Illustrated by Hilary Knight.)

WRITINGS: One Class Only, J. Murray, 1932; *Five to the Horizon*, P. Davies, 1933; *Song of Nefertiti*, Knox Publishing, 1943; *Here I Stay*, J. Murray, 1955; *Jonathan Found*, Crowell, 1957 (published in England as *Image and Likeness*, J. Murray, 1957); *Harp into Battle* (fiction), Crowell, 1959.

Beginning with Mrs. McBee (juvenile; illustrated by Hilary Knight), Vanguard, 1960; *The Beloved Son* (historical novel), Dodd, 1962; *Speaking of Mrs. McCluskie* (juvenile; Junior Literary Guild selection; illustrated by H. Knight), Vanguard, 1962; *The Molliwumps*, Viking, 1967; *The Borrowed Crown* (juvenile fiction), Viking, 1968; *Malachi Mudge*, McGraw, 1968; *A Song for Young King Wenceslas* (juvenile fiction), Addison-Wesley, 1969; *The Man before Morning*, Christian Herald Books, 1977.

HOBBIES AND OTHER INTERESTS: Photography, ship lore, gardening.

MANGO, Karin N. 1936-

PERSONAL: Born January 11, 1936, in Riga, Latvia; daughter of Manfred R. (a British civil engineer) and Helen (a broadcast monitor; maiden name, Libertal) Nowak; married Anthony Mango (a retired senior official of the United Nations), February 27, 1960; children: Alexander Nicholas, Helen Natalie. *Education:* University of Edinburgh, M.A. (with honors), 1958; Pratt Institute, M.L.S., 1975. *Home and office:* 189 Dean St., Brooklyn, N.Y. 11217. *Agent:* McIntosh and Otis, Inc., 310 Madison Ave., New York, N.Y. 10017.

CAREER: George G. Harrap & Co., London, England, assistant head of education department, 1958-60; McGraw-Hill Book Co., New York City, education correspondent, 1960; Long Island Historical Society, Brooklyn, N.Y., part-time librarian, editor, and research assistant, 1975-79; R. R. Bowker, New York City, free-lance copy editor, proofreader, 1979-82; Simon & Schuster, Inc., New York City, free-lance editor, indexer, 1979-87; Suzanne Pathy Speak-Up Institute, New York City, part-time staff writer, editor, 1981-86; free-lance writer, 1986—. *Member:* American Printing History Association, Self Help for Hard of Hearing People, Inc. (member of Manhattan chapter executive board, 1985—), Brooklyn Botanic Garden, British Association for the Hard of Hearing, Beta Phi Mu.

WRITINGS—Juvenile, except as noted: Cantering Through (illustrated by Dick Robinson and Joan Robinson), Harrap, 1951; *The Children's Book of Russian Folktales* (illustrated by Jenetta Vise), Harrap, 1961; *The Children's St. Francis* (illustrated by J. S. Goodall), Harrap, 1963; *New York Holiday*, Harrap, 1971; *Armor: Yesterday and Today* (illustrated by Judith Hoffman Corwin), Messner, 1980; *A Various Journey* (young adult novel), Macmillan, 1983; *Mapmaking* (illustrated by J. H. Corwin), Messner, 1984; *Somewhere Green* (young adult novel), Macmillan, 1987; *Codes, Ciphers, and Other Secrets*, F. Watts, 1988.

Editor; for adults: Marguerite V. Doggett, *Long Island Printing: A Checklist of Imprints, 1791-1830*, Long Island Historical Society, 1979; (editor) *Calendar of Manuscripts of the Revolutionary Period in the Collections of the Long Island Historical Society*, Long Island Historical Society, 1980. Author of column in *Speak-Up Newsletter*. Contributor to *World Book Encyclopedia*, and of articles to periodicals, including *Self Help for Hard of Hearing People Journal, Hark*, and *A Positive Approach*.

KARIN N. MANGO

WORK IN PROGRESS: Just for the Summer, a young adult novel set in New Hampshire; *Collectibles for Kids*, young adult nonfiction; *The Dramatic Life of Tessa Yardley*, a young adult novel set in New York and England.

SIDELIGHTS: "Some of the most influential events in my life took place before I was really aware of them. I came to England as a baby, just before World War II. We were bombed out of our house in London, and I was evacuated to the countryside. I was an only child and lived with different families, learning to adapt to different environments. I spent most of the war, however, in a hostel; my mother was a language monitor with the BBC (British Broadcasting Corporation) and my father was in the army, with the Royal Engineers, abroad. The hostel was a country manor house in beautiful surroundings, and I wrote my first book, *Cantering Through*, with that as a setting. It was published when I was fourteen. I remember taking the galleys to school and self-consciously correcting them at break. I could have done it at home, of course, but I was so proud of those unwieldy long sheets. Later I saw the book actually displayed in a bookshop window—and then it fell over, and I didn't have the courage to go in and tell the owner. Every day, on my way to school, there it was, flat on its face.

"*A Various Journey*, a novel for young adults, is set in the more normal provincial town atmosphere in which I spent my teenage years. The story grew out of classic teenage problems and anxieties, but the heroine's wartime experiences color the story. I think you can only write fiction from a basis of experience.

"I also write for children on nonfiction topics. I have lived in New York for most of my adult life because my husband worked for the United Nations there. New York provides access to just about anything one wants to know. I have written books on subjects as varied as armor, mapmaking, and St. Francis of Assisi.

"Local history has always interested me, and my second young adult novel is set in the brownstone renovation area of Brooklyn where I live.

"I worked for a while at the Long Island Historical Society in Brooklyn, editing two books. The first was on local nineteenth-century printers and stimulated my interest in printing and private presses; my current young adult novel has a printing background. But the work I enjoyed most at the Historical Society was locating and researching their Revolutionary manuscripts and making a chronological list—a calendar—of their holdings. I hunted through the archives of the landmark building from attic to cellar; I handled land deeds, shopping receipts, war documents, and manuscripts actually written by such people as Benedict Arnold and Benjamin Franklin.

"Over the past ten years I have become deaf. I write for the hearing-impaired for several organizations and media. I write to inform and also to entertain and amuse. The hearing impaired tend to withdraw and become isolated and depressed as their ability to communicate with the normal world decreases. I try to use my own experiences to encourage them to rejoin the world and to use all available help including the many new aids and assisting devices that are being developed.

"I love to travel. I also love the theater, though nowadays I have to read the play in advance in order to follow it on the stage. Music is out, but there is so much to see: art, books—including collecting them—and in the country, when taking long walks."

McGUIRE, Leslie Sarah   1945-
(Louisa Britton, Leslie Burton, Dorothy Eyre, Sarah Keyser, Sarah Leslie, Shari Robinson, David Strong)

PERSONAL: Born January 18, 1945, in New York, N.Y.; daughter of Timothy Strong and Virginia Wenderoth (Hastings) McGuire; married Daniel Max, April 10, 1971; children: David. *Education:* Barnard College, A.B., 1966. *Politics:* Democrat. *Religion:* Episcopalian. *Home:* 420 Riverside Dr., New York, N.Y. 10025. *Office:* Platt & Munk Publishers, 51 Madison Ave., New York, N.Y. 10012.

CAREER: Guild for the Blind, New York City, public relations assistant, 1966-67; Public School #165, New York City, teacher of special reading, 1967-69; Platt & Munk Publishers, New York City, editor, 1969-77. *Member:* Barnard Club. *Awards, honors: The Poky Little Puppy and the Lost Bone* was chosen one of Child Study Association of America's Children's Books of the Year, 1986.

WRITINGS—Children's books under name Leslie McGuire; published by Platt, except as noted: *Farm Animals,* 1970; *Birds,* 1970; *Forest Animals,* 1970; *Fish,* 1970; *Wild Animals,* 1970; *Water Life,* 1970; *You: How Your Body Works,* 1974, revised edition published as *Susan Perl's Human Body Book,* 1977; *Pebbles and Bamm-Bamm: The Little Helpers,* Tuffy Books, 1980; *Dino's Happy and Sad Book,* Tuffy Books, 1980; *Fred Flintstone's Counting Book,* Tuffy Books, 1980; *Yogi Bear's Animal Friends,* Tuffy Books, 1980; *Huckleberry Hound Takes a Trip,* Tuffy Books, 1980; *Barney's Picnic,* Tuffy Books, 1980; *This Farm Is a Mess* (self-illustrated), Parents Magazine Press, 1981; *Miss Mopp's Lucky Day* (illustrated by Jody Silver), Parents Magazine Press, 1982; *Scooter Computer and Mr. Chips in the Computer in the Candy Store* (illustrated by John Costanza), Golden Press, 1984; *My Pop-Up Farm,* Golden Books, 1985; *My Pop-Up Zoo,* Golden Books, 1985; *Rainbow Bright and the Big Color Mix-up,* Golden Books, 1985; *My Pop-Up Mother Goose,* Golden Books, 1985; *Bialosky's Best Behavior* (illustrated by Tom Cooke), Western, 1986.

Children's books under name Sarah Leslie: *Who Invented It and What Makes It Work?,* Platt, 1976; *Seasons,* Platt, 1977; *The Curious Little Kitten Plays Hide-and-Seek* (illustrated by Maggie Swanson), Golden Books, 1985; *The Poky Little Puppy and the Lost Bone* (illustrated by Jean Chandler), Golden Books, 1985; *The Saggy Baggy Elephant and the New Dance* (illustrated by Frank Rehkiewicz), Golden Books, 1985.

(From *Bialosky's Best Behavior* by Leslie McGuire. Illustrated by Tom Cooke.)

Children's books under pseudonym Louisa Britton: *The Bible Story Picture Book: Stories from the Old and New Testaments*, Platt, 1975.

Children's books under pseudonym Leslie Burton: *Growing Up in Nature*, Platt, 1971; *Parade of Seasons*, Platt, 1971; *Nature's Helpers*, Platt, 1971; *Children Here, Children There*, Platt, 1971.

Children's books under pseudonym Dorothy Eyre: *Petrouchka: From an Old Russian Legend*, Platt, 1971; *Rainbow Bright Saves Spring* (illustrated by Roy Wilson), Golden Books, 1985.

Children's books under pseudonym Sarah Keyser: (Adapter) James Kruess, *The Zoo That Grew*, Platt, 1970; *Numbers Are Things*, Platt, 1971; *Up, Down, All Around*, Platt, 1971; *Pop Up Circus Book*, Platt, 1973; *Pop Up Construction Book*, Platt, 1973; *Who Lives Here?*, Platt, 1973; *Gregg Finds an Egg*, Platt, 1973.

Children's books under pseudonym Shari Robinson: *Numbers, Signs, and Pictures: A First Number Book*, Platt, 1975, published as *A First Number Book* (illustrated by Sal Murdocca), Grosset, 1981.

Children's books under pseudonym David Strong: *The Magic Book*, Platt, 1977. Also author of *Magic Tricks*, Platt.

Adult: (With Beatrice Lewis) *Making Mosaics*, Drake, 1973.

SIDELIGHTS: "I am a painter, and have decided to use this talent as well as my writing to further my career. I believe that, as an illustrator, I can bring a lot more to my children's books than I could before."

McMULLAN, Kate (Hall) 1947-
(Kate Hall McMullan, Katy Hall)

PERSONAL: Born January 16, 1947, in St. Louis, Mo.; daughter of Lee Aker (a physician) and Kathryn (a teacher and flight attendant; maiden name, Huey) Hall; married James Burroughs McMullan (an illustrator), June 9, 1979; children: Leigh Fenwick. *Education:* University of Tulsa, B.S., 1969; Ohio State University, M.A., 1972. *Home and office:* 88 Lexington Ave., Apt. 12E, New York, N.Y. 10016. *Agent:* Sheldon Fogelman, 10 East 40th St., New York, N.Y. 10016.

CAREER: Magnolia School District, Los Angeles, Calif., teacher, 1969; Long Beach School District, Los Angeles, teacher, 1969-71; U.S. Department of Defense, Washington, D.C., schoolteacher in Hahn, West Germany, 1972-75; Harcourt, Brace, Jovanovich, Inc., New York, N.Y., editor, 1976-78; free-lance writer, 1978—. Consultant to *Let's Find Out* magazine, 1982—; member of Friends of Madison Square Park, New York City. *Member:* Authors Guild. *Awards, honors:* Children's Science Book Award Honor Book from the New York Academy of Sciences, 1981, for *Magic in the Movies*.

WRITINGS—Juvenile; under name Kate McMullan: *The Mystery of the Missing Mummy*, Scholastic, 1984; (adapter) Robert Louis Stevenson, *Dr. Jekyll and Mr. Hyde* (illustrated by Paul Van Munching), Random House, 1984; *The Great Ideas of Lila Fenwick* (illustrated by Diane De Groat), Dial, 1986; *Great Advice from Lila Fenwick*, Dial, 1988.

Juvenile; under name Kate Hall McMullan: *How to Choose Good Books for Kids*, Addison-Wesley, 1984.

KATE McMULLAN

Juvenile; under name Katy Hall: *Nothing but Soup*, Follett, 1976; (with Lisa Eisenberg) *Chicken Jokes and Puzzles*, Scholastic, 1977; (with Jane O'Connor) *Magic in the Movies: The Story of Special Effects*, Doubleday, 1980; (with L. Eisenberg) *A Gallery of Monsters*, Random House, 1980; (with L. Eisenberg) *Pig Jokes and Puzzles*, Scholastic, 1983; (with L. Eisenberg) *Fishy Riddles* (illustrated by Simms Taback), Dial, 1983; (with L. Eisenberg) *101 Bug Jokes*, Scholastic, 1984; *Garfield: Jokes, Riddles, and Other Silly Stuff* (illustrated by Mike Fentz), Random House, 1984; *Garfield: The Big Fat Book of Jokes and Riddles* (illustrated by M. Fentz), Random House, 1984; (with L. Eisenberg) *Buggy Riddles* (illustrated by S. Taback), Dial, 1986; (with L. Eisenberg) *101 School Jokes*, Scholastic, 1987; (with L. Eisenberg) *Grizzly Riddles*, Dial, 1988.

Editor of *Early Bird*, 1982.

ADAPTATIONS: "Fishy Riddles" (cassette), Live Oak Media, 1985.

WORK IN PROGRESS: Snakey Riddles, with Lisa Eisenberg, to be published by Dial; a novel set in the Ozarks of Missouri.

SIDELIGHTS: "Some of my warmest memories of childhood are of my mother reading aloud to me. As a sixth grade teacher in the early 1970s, I rediscovered the pleasure of children's books—this time as the reader—and left teaching to study children's literature at Ohio State University. After graduating with a master's degree, I went back to teaching, reading aloud—and writing.

"As a quick glance at my book titles indicates, humor has been a large part of my writing, especially the work I do with my partner, Lisa Eisenberg. We very much enjoy visiting schools

Why are fish so smart?

They are always in schools.

(From *Fishy Riddles* by Katy Hall and Lisa Eisenberg. Illustrated by Simms Taback.)

and swapping riddles with first, second, and third graders. Our series of easy-to-read riddle books is popular with kids, as well as librarians and teachers, because the controlled vocabulary makes the books accessible to beginning readers, and the punch lines provide good motivation for reading.

"During the past two years I have begun to write middle grade novels based on my childhood experiences in the Midwest and my years as a teacher. The books deal with issues that many ten- and eleven-year-olds have to confront, such as up-and-down friendships and the pleasures and pains of growing up. I find that, in writing these books, I am drawn back to the books I encountered when I was in fifth or sixth grade, *A Tale of Two Cities* or *The Adventures of Tom Sawyer*, and I enjoy weaving aspects of these books into my own stories. I believe that the pleasure I have derived from reading good books has been my main motivation for wanting to write them myself."

HOBBIES AND OTHER INTERESTS: Gardening, birding, reading.

When the voices of children are heard on the green
And laughing is heard on the hill,
My heart is at rest within my breast
And everything else is still.

—William Blake

MERIWETHER, Louise 1923-

PERSONAL: Born May 8, 1923, in Haverstraw, N.Y.; daughter of Marion Lloyd and Julia Jenkins; married Angelo Meriwether (divorced); married Earl Howe (divorced). *Education:* New York University, B.A.; University of California at Los Angeles, M.S., 1956. *Home:* New York, N.Y.

CAREER: Worked as a legal secretary in New York and California, 1950-61; *Sentinal,* Los Angeles, Calif., reporter, 1961-64; Universal Studios, Univeral City, Calif., story analyst, 1965-67; free-lance writer, 1967—. *Member:* Authors Guild, Watts Writers Workshop, Harlem Writers Guild.

WRITINGS—All published by Prentice-Hall, except as noted: *Daddy Was a Number Runner* (novel), 1970; *The Freedom Ship of Robert Small* (juvenile; illustrated by Lee J. Morton), 1971; *The Heart Man: Dr. Daniel Hale Williams* (juvenile), 1972; *Don't Ride the Bus on Monday: The Rosa Parks Story* (juvenile; illustrated by David Scott Brown), 1973; (contributor) Mary Helen Washington, editor, *Black-Eyed Susans,* Anchor Press, 1975. Contributor of short stories and articles to periodicals, including *Antioch Review, Negro Digest,* and *Essence.*

SIDELIGHTS: In *Black-Eyed Susans,* Meriwether wrote: "After the publication of my first novel, *Daddy Was a Number Runner,* I turned my attention to black history for the kindergarten set, recognizing that the deliberate omission of Blacks from American history has been damaging to the children of both races. It reinforces in one a feeling of inferiority and in the other a myth of superiority."

Meriwether's next three books were biographies of Robert Small, a slave who piloted a Confederate ship into Yankee waters and

LOUISE MERIWETHER

earned a promotion in the Union Army, Daniel Hale Williams, a black heart surgeon who performed the first successful open-heart surgery, and Rosa Parks.

FOR MORE INFORMATION SEE: Ebony, September, 1966, July, 1970; *Saturday Review of Literature,* May 23, 1970, December 11, 1971; *Jet,* November 12, 1970; *New York Times Book Review,* June 28, 1970; *New Yorker,* July 11, 1970; *Kirkus Reviews,* June 15, 1972, December 15, 1973; *The Ebony Success Library,* Volume 1: *1000 Successful Blacks,* Johnson, 1973; Mary Helen Washington, editor, *Black-Eyed Susans,* Anchor Press, 1975; Theressa G. Rush and others, *Black American Writers: Past and Present,* Scarecrow, 1975; *In Black and White,* Gale, 1980.

MILLER, Frances A.   1937-

PERSONAL: Born October 15, 1937, in New York, N.Y.; daughter of F. Everett (an Episcopal minister) and Frances (Reyburn) Abbott; married John David Miller (an international businessman), December 20, 1958; children: Kirsten Elizabeth, John Abbott, Dana Frances, David Williams. *Education:* Wellesley College, B.A., 1959; California State University, Hayward, teaching credential, 1976; attended San Jose State University, 1987—. *Politics:* Independent. *Religion:* Episcopalian. *Home:* 50 Deer Meadow Lane, Danville, Calif. 94526. *Office:* Australian Connection, P.O. Box 341, Danville, Calif. 94526.

CAREER: Reading tutor and volunteer worker at public schools in Oakland and San Ramon, Calif., 1966-75; Bret Harte Junior High School, Hayward, Calif., reading and English teacher, 1976-77; Adult Literacy Program, Sydney, Australia, member of executive board, 1979-83; writer and public speaker, 1983—. *Member:* National Writers Club (professional member), So-

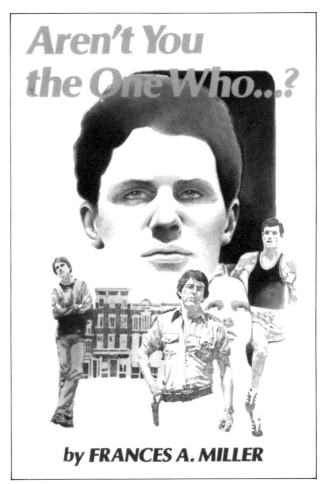

(Jacket illustration by Dennis Luzak from *Aren't You the One Who. . .?* by Frances A. Miller.)

ciety of Children's Book Writers, National Council of Teachers of English, Assembly on Literature for Adolescents; National Association for Young Writers Inc., Children's Book Council of Australia, Adult Literacy Council of New South Wales (life member), California Media and Library Educators Association, Bay Area Young Adult Librarians, Authors Guild, Pi Lambda Theta. *Awards, honors: The Truth Trap* was chosen one of New York Public Library's Books for the Teen Age, 1981, and received the California Young Reader Medal from junior and senior high school readers throughout California, 1985; *Aren't You the One Who . . .?* was nominated for the Iowa Teen Award, 1986.

WRITINGS—Young adult: *The Truth Trap,* Dutton, 1980; *Aren't You the One Who . . .?,* Atheneum, 1983; *Losers and Winners* (sequel to *Aren't You the One Who . . .?*), Fawcett, 1986; *How's It Going, Nick?,* Quercus, 1987; *Eliza Pinckney,* Quercus, 1987; *George Washington,* Quercus, 1987; *Andrew Jackson,* Quercus, 1987; *John Hancock,* Quercus, 1987; *Mark Twain,* Quercus, 1987.

WORK IN PROGRESS: Summer to Remember (tentative title), a young adult novel; *Say Something in Australian* (tentative title), an adult account of the author's life in Australia.

SIDELIGHTS: ''I grew up in a variety of places—New Jersey, Vermont and New Hampshire, Florida, and the Panama Canal Zone—but the one I think of as home was seventy-five acres of woods, fields, and freedom in lower New York state. There

FRANCES A. MILLER

my three older cousins (male), my older sisters, younger brother, and I all enjoyed independence of a kind that I tried to recreate for my own children. Books, radio, and our own imaginations were the big entertainers. My children grew up with television but inherited their parents' love for reading as well, and over the years we've done a lot of sharing and talking about people and ideas we've found in books. In fact, one way or another, children and/or books have been part of my life for as long as I can remember.

"I went to a girls' boarding school and a women's college, working summers in day camps, overnight camps, and one glorious year in a tiny public library where I got to read all the new books before anyone else even knew they were there. I graduated from Wellesley College in 1959, already married, and had our first daughter one month after my twenty-second birthday. By the time she was in the first grade, she had two younger brothers and a sister, and a big audience for her favorite read-aloud story, *Are You My Mother?*

"From the day our oldest child started kindergarten until the year our youngest turned nine, I went to school with them—tutoring their classmates in math and reading, helping in the libraries, running paperback book fairs, and cheering them and their friends at everything from Little League to swim team, horse shows to band concerts. I found being a mother the toughest, most challenging job I'd ever had, and I loved it—well, ninety percent of the time. (Whenever we all get together these days, my now grown children love to reminisce about that other ten percent.)

"A turning point came in 1974, when I spent two days a week as a paid library aide in an elementary school, and three days as a volunteer in a high school reading lab. I also lay awake nights getting acquainted with a character named Matt Mc-Kendrick. By the end of that school year, I had made up my mind to become a reading specialist, and Matt was on paper for the first time. I took him with me that summer to the family cabin in New Hampshire, where my nephews and nieces read the manuscript in relays, urging each other to read faster so the next one in line could have the page, and demanding to know what happened to Matt after the book had ended. I wondered about that myself, so the second book came into being, and the third and fourth ones as well, long before the first one was published.

"Why so many books about the same characters? Perhaps because people don't stop growing and changing in real life, and I didn't want to leave readers with the impression that Matt's life—or theirs—is ever over because of one wrong choice. Perhaps because I have such admiration for the human spirit—its ability to survive everything from daily put-downs to tragic mistakes, and its infinite capacity for compassion and generosity. Perhaps because I believe that everyone is important, everybody is 'somebody,' and I haven't heard that said often enough lately.

"At about the same time the books were taking shape, I started on my three-year goal of becoming a reading specialist. Two thirds of the way there, I was sidetracked by my husband's job, which took all of us to Australia for a two-year adventure that turned into a six-year love affair with a fascinating continent and some wonderful people. While there, I tutored adult non-readers and rewrote the books about Matt McKendrick and the four Schuylers (my own four children thinly disguised) many times. We returned to California in December, 1983, and from 1984 to 1988 I coordinated the 'Aussie Books for Kids' exhibit—a book-sharing project of the Children's Book Council of Australia—as it toured schools and libraries in the

U.S. In 1987 I began work on the MLS degree (yet another way of sharing books), and spearheaded the 'Happy Birthday, Australia!' project—a celebration of Australia's 1988 bicentennial with a gift of books to her children from schools, libraries, and individual Oz fans from all over America.

"My first book, *Truth Trap,* was published in 1980 to reviews that ranged from wonderful to terrible. In the next four years it was chosen as an ALA Best Book for Young Adults, remaindered by its hardcover publisher, and reprinted in paperback. In 1985 it won the California Young Reader Medal. The second and third books were published in 1983 and 1986. All three books have been the 'best book I ever read . . .' for good readers of all ages (the oldest ninety-four, the youngest 'nine and three quarters'), and have been used by reading teachers to turn reluctant and non-reading teenagers on to reading in intermediate schools, high schools, and juvenile court schools. While the good reviews are greatly appreciated and the bad ones make me shout and slam doors, it is the letters from readers which tell me that the sleepless nights, the eight hours a day at the typewriter, the rejections, the revisions, and the on-going struggle to capture the images inside my head and heart and share them with readers, are all worth it. One of my favorite letters is from a teenager in a reading lab: 'I've never read a book before in my whole life, but I read *The Truth Trap* and I really liked it. I think you made me get interested in reading. Now I'm reading *Aren't You the One Who . . .?* I really like your stories. Thanks.'

"Another favorite is from a high school student: 'I have read your book, *The Truth Trap* and it really touched me a lot. Every time I picked up the book, I could not put it down and the only time I stopped reading was when I had to go to bed.'

"'This book caught my attention because I have never read a book that had so much feeling and love in it. Also, this really does happen to young kids, Mrs. Miller. As I read the book it seemed so real that it seemed to be nonfiction.'

"'I am a kid myself, and I know how Matt felt some of the times in his problem, like being accused of something that he didn't do and people don't understand him because they don't know him well enough.'

"'Mrs. Miller, in this book most of the things that occur are happening today somewhere. I think that if people take time to judge people in how they look inside instead of their outside then they would not have as many problems. Please keep writing great books like *The Truth Trap* and add lots of feeling in them. I don't usually enjoy reading books but I was at a local library and I saw this book. Then I read the back and it really fascinated me a lot and that's when I started reading and I could not put it down. . . .'

"And a third is from a book-loving thirteen-year-old: '. . . *The Truth Trap* was the one I just read. At first I thought it was going to be a corny "teen" book, but soon after starting it, I was pleasantly surprised. This author credits teenagers with the most depth of character I have ever seen. The feelings of the main character could be shared by any kid in America, and I think that portraying kids as they see themselves and not as adults see them is the hardest thing for a writer to do and she accomplished it well. This book brought out a lot of emotions in me. It was written so that no one can feel anything but empathy for Matt. I read the book in one night. Even though it was a school night and it took me until two a.m., it was worth it. I just couldn't put it down.

"'I can't wait to start the other one and any other of her books I can get my hands on! . . .'

"Readers like these are the reason writers like me keep on writing."

HOBBIES AND OTHER INTERESTS: Photography, backpacking, working part time in a bookstore, exploring the U.S., dogs, family.

MILTON, Joyce 1946-

PERSONAL: Born January 12, 1946, in McKeesport, Pa.; daughter of Joseph Kent (a steelworker) and Elsie (a librarian; maiden name, Wilson) Milton. *Education:* Swarthmore College, B.A., 1967; Pratt Institute of Technology, M.L.S., 1969. *Home:* 60 Plaza St., Brooklyn, N.Y. 11238.

CAREER: New York Public Library, New York City, librarian, 1967-69; Walden School, New York City, librarian, 1969-71; *Kirkus Review,* New York City, young adult editor, 1971-77; free-lance writer, 1977—. *Awards, honors: Here Come the Robots* was selected as an Outstanding Science Trade Book for Children by the National Science Teachers Association and the Children's Book Council Joint Committee, 1981, and a Notable Children's Trade Book in the Field of Social Studies by the joint committee of the National Council for Social Studies and the Children's Book Council, 1982; *A Friend of China* was selected one of New York Public Library's Books for the Teen Age, 1982.

WRITINGS: Sunrise of Power: Ancient Egypt, Alexander and the World of Hellenism (adult), Harcourt, 1979; (with Rafael Steinberg and Sarah Lewis) *Religion at the Crossroads: Byzantium and the Turks,* Harcourt, 1979; *Tradition and Revolt: Imperial China, Islands of the Rising Sun* (adult), Harcourt, 1980; *Controversy: Science in Conflict* (young adult), Messner, 1980; *A Friend of China* (young adult; biography of Agnes Smedley), Hastings House, 1980; *Here Come the Robots* (juvenile; Junior Literary Guild selection; illustrated by Peter Stern), Hastings House, 1981; (with Jane O'Connor) *The Dandee Diamond Mystery* (juvenile; illustrated by Daryl Cagle), Scholastic, 1983; *Save the Loonies* (young adult; Junior Literary Guild selection), Four Winds Press, 1983; *Ruthie the Robot* (juvenile), Scholastic, 1983; (with Ronald Radosh) *The Rosenberg File: A Search for the Truth* (adult), Holt, 1983; *Secrets of the Mummies* (juvenile; illustrated by Dolores R. Santoliquido), Random House, 1984.

Dinosaur Days (juvenile; illustrated by Richard Roe), Random House, 1985; *Don Quixote (Miguel de Cervantes)* (young adult), Barron, 1985; (with Ann L. Bardach) *Vicki,* St. Martin's, 1986; *Marching to Freedom: The Story of Martin Luther King Jr.,* Dell, 1987; *George Washington,* Dell, 1988. Also author of *Christopher Columbus: A Punch-and-Play Storybook* (illustrated by Margaret A. Hartelius), Scholastic. Contributor to poetry magazines, including *Southern Review, New York Quarterly,* and *Beloit Poetry Journal.*

SIDELIGHTS: "I am basically a writer of popular/journalistic historical works; my primary fields of interest are history of science and technology, Eastern Europe, and history of U.S. politics, especially left-wing movements. The book on the Rosenberg case is a thorough historical study of the subject based on recently released government documents as well as extensive interviews with principals who have never before spoken for publication."

Milton grew up in Clairton, Pennsylvania. "Perhaps because I was growing up in a factory town, my early interests were rather escapist. I loved reading about faraway places, outdoor adventures, and the lives of kings and queens. In my senior year of high school I was offered an engineering scholarship but turned it down because I considered science and technology very dull and unromantic. It was only much later that I came to realize how fascinating both of these subjects could be."

After attending Swarthmore College and Pratt Institute, Milton worked as a librarian and editor before she began writing full-time. "In the meantime, I developed an avid interest in bird watching, mostly as the result of my desire to find an outdoor activity that could be pursued in New York's city parks and in New Hampshire, where I spend part of each summer. Through my activities with several environmental action groups, I also began to follow new developments in such fields as genetic research, energy planning, and wildlife conservation. My first book for young adults, *Controversy: Science in Conflict,* grew out of this research.

"When this book was completed, I began to look for a subject that could communicate some of the excitement of science to younger children. I decided to write about robots because the robot is a wonderful example of a concept that was born in the realms of art and literature and only much later became a scientific reality. I wanted to write a book that would appeal to all children, even those who do not consider themselves future scientists.

"Another of my goals was to capture the fun of technology without suggesting that new inventions are going to usher in a utopia or lead to the solution of all our social problems. I hoped to present a balanced view of the impact of the new robots. For the majority of adults, the robot is still a novelty, but today's children will grow up in a world which will no doubt have been revolutionized by the revolution in working robots and other intelligent machines. In addition to presenting information, *Here Come the Robots* is intended to encourage young readers to think about their own future role in deciding what roles the robots of tomorrow will play."

MOORE, Lilian 1909-

PERSONAL: Born March 17, 1909, in New York, N.Y.; daughter of Aaron and Sarah (Asheron) Levenson; married Sam Reavin, 1969; children: (first marriage) Jonathan. *Education:* Hunter College, B.A., 1930; graduate study at Columbia University. *Home:* Kerhonkson, N.Y. 12446.

CAREER: Writer. Has worked as elementary school teacher in New York City; staff member of New York City Bureau of Educational Research, beginning 1937; Scholastic Book Services, New York City, editor of Arrow Book Club, beginning 1957, editor of special book project (history and biography series), 1968-69. Has worked as editor of easy reader series in Wonder Books Division of Grosset & Dunlap, New York City, and as series editor for Thomas Y. Crowell, New York City. *Member:* Council on Interracial Books for Children (founding member), PEN, Authors Guild. *Awards, honors: Old Rosie, the Horse Nobody Understood* was selected one of *New York Times* Best Books of the Year, 1960; *Just Right* was selected one of Child Study Association of America's Children's Books of the Year, 1968, *Junk Day on Juniper Street, and Other Easy-to-Read Stories,* 1969, *Sam's Place, To See the World Afresh,* 1974, and *See My Lovely Poison Ivy, and Other Verses about Witches, Ghosts and Things,* 1975; *Sam's Place* was included in the American Institute of Graphic

Arts Children's Books Show, 1973; National Council of Teachers of English Award for Poetry for Children, 1985, in recognition of her poetry for children.

WRITINGS—All for children: (With Leone Adelson) *Old Rosie, the Horse Nobody Understood* (Junior Literary Guild selection; illustrated by Leonard Shortall), Random House, 1952; (with L. Adelson) *The Terrible Mr. Twitmeyer* (Junior Literary Guild selection; illustrated by L. Shortall), Random House, 1952; *The Important Pockets of Paul* (illustrated by William D. Hayes), McKay, 1954; *Daniel Boone* (biography; illustrated by William Moyers), Random House, 1956; *Wobbly Wheels* (illustrated by B. Krush), Abingdon, 1956; *The Snake That Went to School* (illustrated by Mary Stevens), Random House, 1957; *Once Upon a Holiday* (illustrated by Gioia Fiammenghi), Abingdon, 1959; *Tony the Pony* (illustrated by Wesley Dennis), Whittlesey House, 1959.

Bear Trouble (illustrated by Kurt Werth), Whittlesey House, 1960; *Everything Happens to Stuey* (illustrated by M. Stevens), Random House, 1960; *Too Many Bozos* (illustrated by Susan Perl), Golden Press, 1960; *A Pickle for a Nickel* (illustrated by S. Perl), Golden Press, 1961; *Once Upon a Season* (illustrated by G. Fiammenghi), Abingdon, 1962; *Little Raccoon and the Thing in the Pool* (illustrated by G. Fiammenghi), Whittlesey House, 1963; (with L. Adelson) *Mr. Twitmeyer and the Poodle* (illustrated by L. Shortall), Random House, 1963; *Papa Albert* (illustrated by G. Fiammenghi), Atheneum, 1964; *Little Raccoon and the Outside World* (illustrated by G. Fiammenghi), Whittlesey House, 1965; *The Magic Spectacles, and Other Easy-to-Read Stories* (illustrated by Arnold Lobel), Parents Magazine Press, 1966; *I Feel the Same Way* (poems; Junior Literary Guild selection; illustrated by Robert Quackenbush), Atheneum, 1967; *Just Right* (illustrated by Aldren A. Watson), Parents Magazine Press, 1968; *I Thought I Heard the City* (poems; illustrated by Mary Jane

Dunton), Atheneum, 1969; *Junk Day on Juniper Street, and Other Easy-to-Read Stories* (illustrated by A. Lobel), Parents Magazine Press, 1969.

The Riddle Walk (illustrated by John Pucci), Garrard, 1971; *Little Raccoon and No Trouble at All* (illustrated by G. Fiammenghi), McGraw, 1972; (reteller) *The Ugly Duckling by Hans Christian Andersen* (illustrated by Mona Barrett), Scholastic Book Services, 1972; (compiler with Lawrence Webster) *Catch Your Breath: A Book of Shivery Poems* (illustrated by Gahan Wilson), Garrard, 1973; *Sam's Place: Poems from the Country* (illustrated by Talivaldis Stubis), Atheneum, 1973; *Spooky Rhymes and Riddles* (illustrated by Ib Chisson), Scholastic Book Services, 1973; (editor) Hans Christian Andersen, *The Ugly Duckling and Two Other Stories* (illustrated by Trina Schart Hyman), Scholastic Book Services, 1973; (compiler with Judith Thurman) *To See the World Afresh* (poems; ALA Notable Book), Atheneum, 1974; (with Remy Charlip) *Hooray for Me!* (illustrated by Vera B. Williams), Parents Magazine Press, 1975; *Little Raccoon and Poems from the Woods* (illustrated by G. Fiammenghi), McGraw, 1975; *See My Lovely Poison Ivy, and Other Verses about Witches, Ghosts, and Things* (Junior Literary Guild selection; illustrated by Diane Dawson), Atheneum, 1975; (compiler) *Go with the Poem*, McGraw, 1979.

Think of Shadows (poems; illustrated by Deborah Robison), Atheneum, 1980; *Something New Begins* (poems; ALA Notable Book; illustrated by M. J. Dunton), Atheneum, 1982; *Little Raccoon Takes Charge* (illustrated by Deborah Borgo), Western Publishing, 1986; *Little Raccoon's Nighttime Adventure* (illustrated by D. Borgo), Western Publishing, 1986; *I'll Meet You at the Cucumbers*, Atheneum, 1988.

SIDELIGHTS: Born in New York City. "I still can't walk into a children's library without a rush of love. I remember my neighborhood library on Tremont Avenue in the Bronx. I would come back with an armful of books—reading all the way home. I have always wondered who was watching out for me while nose in book, I made my way. How full of promise that library was! I remember my excitement upon coming into the library and spying the *one* Andrew Lang fairy book I had yet to read, the title etched in gold. The drama of waiting on line with other children, all of me wishing that that gold fairy book would stay on the shelf until I got there! I'm sure my pleasure in teaching children to read is related to the great joy reading brought to me in my childhood.

"Although I lived in the city I also took great joy in the summers I spent in what was then a more rural part of the city. I remember fields of clover, the daisy chains we made and the knee high grass in which we could almost hide. It seems to me that I was forever after looking for that lovely field. Though I am a city person, there has always been a part of me that has yearned for the country. I started out with a flower pot on my windowsill. Then I had a back yard in which I madly planted flowers in city soot. At last I came to *Sam's Place*, my husband's farm in upstate New York. I've always wanted to make things grow, and live with the light of the sky in the country.

"I grew up in New York's world of infinite promise, went to its schools, was nourished by its human diversity, took for granted its intellectual excitement, and found there a richly satisfying work life."

Moore attended Evander Childs High School where many of her classmates were gifted students who later went "out into the world and did important things."

LILIAN MOORE

This strange black truck was taking her where she would never see her family again! ■ (From *The Terrible Mr. Twitmeyer* by Lilian Moore and Leone Adelson. Illustrated by Leonard Shortall.)

"When did I become a writer? I can't remember when I didn't in some way think of myself as one. One of my earliest memories is of sitting on a big metal box outside a hardware store on the street where I lived. There was a group of kids around me—the friends with whom I went roller skating and sledding—and there I was telling them a series of yarns. I can still remember saying 'to be continued tomorrow!' I wrote the plays I put on in the summers I worked as a camp counselor, and of course, I guess like everyone else, I had half a novel in my drawer that it took me years to throw out!" [Lee Bennett Hopkins, *Books Are by People,* Citation Press, 1969.[1]]

Attended Hunter College and did graduate work at Columbia University. "Back then, girls didn't have many career alternatives. In high school I had liked the idea that I might become a lawyer. I was a member of my high school debating team, which traveled to different schools, much like a varsity football team. But becoming a lawyer then could only be fantasy. Those of us who *had* to make a living, and quickly, became teachers. Hunter College turned us out in droves. It was in college that I first came to love poetry, the Romantics: Shelley, Keats and Blake as well as Dryden and Pope.

"I was graduated from college during the middle of the Depression. I was on a list of teachers waiting for job appointments for eight years. During that time, I worked as a substitute teacher, and with delinquent students in a school for truants where a reading clinic had been set up. Once the Bureau of Educational Research began to recognize that I had an aptitude for teaching children to read, I was assigned special work in reading clinics. We turn corners without knowing it. I had always hoped I would end up teaching college English—Marlowe and Shakespeare—but from that point on I became a reading specialist.

"After my son was born in 1950, I left the school system. In 1957, I went to work at Scholastic Book Services and became the first editor of the Arrow Book Club.

"This was one of the most satisfying things I ever did, helping to launch the first quality paperback book program for elementary school children. It was a job that brought together my experience as a teacher, my interest in children's books, my work as a writer, and my downright pleasure in the endearing middle-grader. Imagine making it possible for these youngsters to choose and buy good books for the price of comics! It was years before I could even simmer down . . . even now I remember the endless wonderful letters from children and teachers. They made it clear we were irrigating a drought area and raising a whole new crop of readers. Whatever I may have contributed to this program was due in part to my almost total recall of the children I had known and taught. They seemed to haunt me and were specters at my side, vigorously approving or disapproving books we chose for them."[1]

Moore has been an editor of early readers for Grosset & Dunlap's "Wonder Books," a series of over sixty books. She wrote the following eleven "Wonder Books" under the pen name of Sara Asheron: *Will You Come to My Party?; Surprise in the Tree; Laurie and the Yellow Curtains; The Surprise in the Story Book; Little Gray Mouse and the Train; How to Find a Friend; Little Gray Mouse Goes Sailing; Little Popcorn; The Three Coats of Benny Bunny; Fraidy Cat; Funny Face at the Window.* "These books are meant to help the young reader discover what a delightful experience reading can be. . . . [They] have been planned to help all young readers grow—in their pleasure in books and in their power to read them."

Moore believes "children who read will often begin naturally to write. When Jean Paul Sartre noted he had been a great plagiarist in childhood he pointed out something very significant about all young writers. As one reads and absorbs, one is influenced and shaped. When one makes those first attempts at writing, one is often imitative because the unconscious is a *natural* plagiarist! This is the way one develops and grows into originality. This is why I believe that the indiscriminate publication of poetry written by children is counter productive. Children's writings should not be treated as if it were finished, 'grown up' poetry—the seriousness with which this immature writing is handled can actually inhibit creativity. Too often it becomes a subtle *demand* on children to write and to produce things *adults* like."

**He just had to stop—
and look.**

■ (From *Little Raccoon and the Thing in the Pool* by Lilian Moore. Illustrated by Gioia Fiammenghi.)

There was something that Red Fox wanted—something he wanted very much. ■ (From "Wait for a Windy Day" in *The Magic Spectacles and Other Easy-to-Read Stories* by Lilian Moore. Illustrated by Arnold Lobel.)

Moore served as a reading consultant to the magazine *Humpty Dumpty* from its first issue in October, 1952. She wrote the "beginning to read" stories which the magazine featured every month, "Ten months a year, for eight years. I was all eyes and ears during that time. Everything I saw children do, everything I heard them say, went into a story. Many of these stories were simple versions—first drafts—of my later books, including *The Little Raccoon* stories.

"The animals in my books are surrogates for children, and by that I do *not* mean animals dressed in children's clothes! The character of the animal must be animal-like, but the emotional content reflects a child's development. If a character is a raccoon, for example, he should *not* eat pizza! He should eat crayfish. *Little Raccoon and the Thing in the Pool* is really a story that is meant to be like a child's first experience of going to the store alone. And *Little Raccoon and the Outside World*

Danny kept Bozo the Frog in his room and took good care of him. ■ (From *Too Many Bozos* by Lilian Moore. Illustrated by Susan Perl.)

The two little girls sat, quiet and happy, beside their Papa. ■ (From *Papa Albert* by Lilian Moore. Illustrated by Gioia Fiammenghi.)

reflects the feelings of a child who might be coming home after a long day at school.

"I've always been interested in young children. To listen to young children speak as they explore their experience is like the morning of the world. The language of young children is to me a constant enchantment, and I have drawn a lot of my material from the extraordinary things I've heard children say. I've also gone to children for practical help. For example, I ran up against a problem while writing *Everything Happens to Stuey*. The character inadvertently used invisible ink on his homework, but I had no idea how to make the words reappear. I asked my son, eight years old at the time, and he said, 'Use a radiator.' I did! In fact, the entire book was influenced by my young son, and his friends on whom I eavesdropped constantly.

"There was a long poetry hiatus in my life. One day, I said to my friend, poet Eve Merriam, 'I don't know any modern poets! Can you recommend some to me?' Eliot's *The Wasteland* had come and gone and never touched me. I was still back with Romantics, Shelley and Keats. Not a bad place to be, but I was curious. Eve suggested I browse, and the first poet I discovered was Denise Levertov. I was so inspired by her work that I began to read poetry again."

In 1967 *I Feel the Same Way*, a book of poetry for children, was written at the suggestion of Moore's editor, Jean Karl, at Atheneum. "As I worked on it, I found myself getting in touch with my own memories of childhood and reliving early feelings. As a result, the book took on a quality different from my earlier verses for children. It was so exhilarating to write these poems, that I went on writing poetry.

"When you hear a poem that sounds exactly right—when the words and the feelings seem inevitably to belong together—it is easy to believe that the poem, particularly if it is a poem for children—sprang full blown from the brow of the poet. Most of the poets I know work hard. The grain of sand that's supposed to irritate the creative center and produce a pearl often produces just the irritation. Lines that are supposed to dance sometimes drag their iambic feet. Words that were supposed to reflect light remain maddeningly dim. Or a cliché pops up that must be uprooted like a noxious weed. Then it's back to the typewriter, or the ball-point pen, or the pencil with a good eraser. And another wastebasket to fill."

Understanding the limited experiences of children, Moore does not censor her poems, but hopes that someone will help the child "take them in." "If a poem works, it has to work for *me*. If it works for me, than I have said what I meant to say. I don't feel that a poem must be *taught* to a child—but it is often useful to *activate* the experience of the poem and then let it enhance the experience. For example, teachers often have lessons on seeds and how things grow. Why shouldn't a poem like my 'Yellow Weed' be part of this experience? That would delight me—to see poetry used in an *active* way."

"To me a poem is like a balloon on a string. What you get out of it depends on how tall you are, how long the string is. Something there for everyone." [Joan I. Glazer, "Profile: Lilian Moore," *Language Arts*, Volume 62, number 6, October, 1985.[2]]

"When I'm writing a poem, I feel as if I'm working all the time. . . . I like the *echo* of words more than rhyme . . . much testing and revising seems to be done in my head. . . . As I'm working on a version I've done, I read the poem to myself but not aloud. I hear it. I hear everything that's wrong with a line inside my head.

"Do you know who helps the most? Other poets. When I need a response, I turn to my friends—Judith Thurman, Eve Merriam, Beatrice de Regniers. . . . Poets help each other wonderfully. For instance, we'd been through a severe dry spell here and the line came to me, 'Roots have forgotten the taste of rain.' I told a poet friend, 'I'm really stuck on this line. I can't go forward.' She said, 'Why don't you back into it?' I said, 'Of course!' And that's what I did, backed into it. It worked as the last line of 'Dry Spell.' That's how poets help one another—by listening seriously and taking seriously the problems in structuring a poem."[2]

"What I would love to see happen with poetry for children— is to have poetry become as much a part of their lives as cereal in the morning. Poetry should not be 'breathy,' or read in a special voice and saved for special occasions. How great if it were part of a child's day, at school and at home! Poetry can enhance and deepen the teaching of nature, science—it can be a comfort, where children can find their own feelings. There is almost no aspect of life, in or out of the classroom that can't

in some way be enhanced by poetry. That is one reason I like to edit anthologies—to help make poetry more available.

"The kind of program I envision would help children to express their own feelings in poems. Out of this quantity would come quality. I know what we are competing with: television, video games, and of course, the lack of _adult_ interest in and experience of poetry. Some adults fear that poetry is a special language they can't understand. But adults could grow along with their kids, couldn't they? By the time one has a few years of experience with poetry, one becomes naturally discriminating and can detect forced rhyme, and sentimentality—the greatest sin in poetry for children—substituting what I call a 'greeting card emotion' for real feeling and observation.

"How do I stay away from these 'greeting card' traps in my own writing? Vigilance. Eternal vigilance.''

Moore, who has worked extensively with authors on manuscripts over the years, compares editing to sculpture. "I love to perfect language. This is the basis of my pleasure in editing. Authors who have worked with me have often said the experience was enriching. Imagine taking a piece of writing to someone who will work on it with the same love as the author.

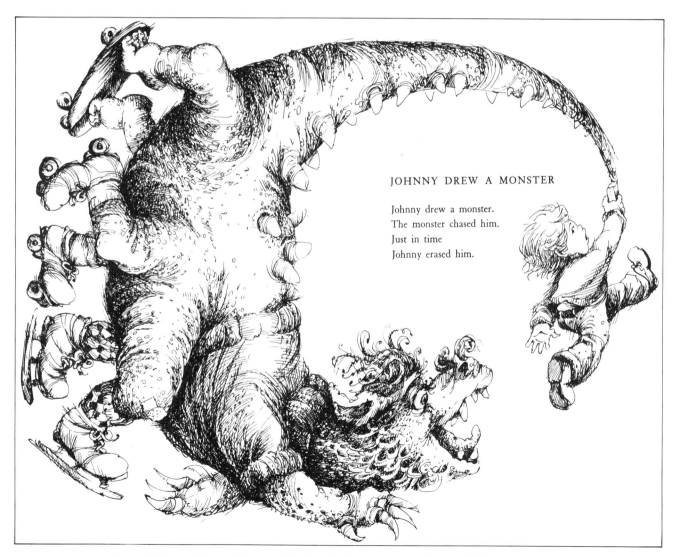

JOHNNY DREW A MONSTER

Johnny drew a monster.
The monster chased him.
Just in time
Johnny erased him.

(From "Johnny Drew a Monster" in _See My Lovely Poison Ivy and Other Verses about Witches, Ghosts and Things_ by Lilian Moore. Illustrated by Diane Dawson.)

My advice to writers was simple: Good writing is clear thinking and honest feeling, murky feeling produces sentimentality, and muddy thinking produces muddy language. This is no different from the way I work on my own poetry. If a line jounces or bucks, I reshape it, as if I were working on a piece of pottery—until I achieve a line that flows for me without interruption.''

Moore recently refused a request from a South African publisher to reprint her *Little Raccoon* books. ''I wrote the publisher saying, 'It has always been a source of deepest pleasure for me to know how much children have loved these books. Some day, when apartheid is only a terrible memory, when all children can freely have access to these books, I should be proud and happy to have you publish them.' ''

Moore was active in the anti-Vietnam war movement, the civil rights movement, and has worked with a support group for the Sanctuary movement. ''The anthology I compiled with Judith Thurman, *To See the World Afresh,* describes the intensity of the poet at this particular moment in history.''

During the Moore-Thurman collaboration, their ''sensibilities meshed. I kept Judith rooted to poems that I felt would be accessible to a wide range of young people. Judith in turn educated me to a deeper appreciation of new poems.''

For relaxation, Moore enjoys chamber music and gardening, although she admits that ''relaxation isn't a problem when you love the work you do. I had a wonderful time finishing my most recent book, *I'll Meet You at the Cucumbers.* In some ways it's a retelling of the city-country mouse fable and it contains many 'autobiographical touches.' My country mouse, Adam, loves the country just as much as my husband does. 'Who would leave this green and pleasant place?' Adam asks. (Sam feels the same way!) Adam Mouse writes down his thoughts and learns when he gets to the city that they are poems. 'Do people like poets?' Adam asks. 'I'm not sure,' his friend, Amanda Mouse replies, 'But they need them.' ''

——Based on an interview by Rachel Koenig

Moore's works are included in the de Grummond Collection at the University of Southern Mississippi.

HOBBIES AND OTHER INTERESTS: ''Almost any good chamber music,'' biking, ice skating, reading, cooking, gardening, travel.

FOR MORE INFORMATION SEE: New York Times, November 23, 1952; *New York Herald Tribune Book Review,* April 26, 1959; *New York Times Book Review,* November 9, 1969, April 29, 1979; Lee Bennett Hopkins, editor, *Books Are by People: Interviews with 104 Authors and Illustrators of Books for Young Children,* Citation Press, 1969; Martha E. Ward and Dorothy A. Marquardt, *Authors of Books for Young People,* 2nd edition, Scarecrow, 1971; *Booklist,* February 1, 1976; Doris de Montreville and Elizabeth D. Crawford, editors, *Fourth Book of Junior Authors and Illustrators,* H. W. Wilson, 1978; Judith Gleason, ''That Lingering Child of Air—Children's Poetry,'' *Parnassus,* 1980; Joan I. Glazer, ''Profile: Lilian Moore,'' *Language Arts,* October, 1985.

Child! do not throw this book about;
Refrain from the unholy pleasure
Of cutting all the pictures out!
Preserve it as your chiefest treasure.

——Hilaire Belloc

NOVAK, Matt 1962-

BRIEF ENTRY: Born October 23, 1962, in Trenton, N.J. From 1979 to 1983, Novak worked as a puppeteer for Pegasus Players and then spent one year as an animator at Walt Disney World in Orlando, Florida. After receiving his B.F.A. from the School of Visual Arts in 1985, he began teaching at both the Parsons School of Design and St. Benedict's Preparatory School. Novak's career as an author and illustrator of children's books began out of his desire ''to impart my amazement of nature's beauty to children.'' *Rolling* (Bradbury, 1986) illustrates the course of thunder as it rolls over a landscape, frightening a small boy and a crowd of animals. ''The scenes are filled with exuberant motion expressed in swirling clouds, racing animals, and wide-eyed faces,'' noted *Booklist.* In Novak's second book, *Claude and Sun* (Bradbury, 1987), the title characters daily attend to such solar pleasures as light, warmth, and beauty. ''Claude. . .is a playful caricature of his namesake, Claude Monet,'' again noted *Booklist,* ''and Novak's striking illustrations imitate the famous artist's impressionistic style.'' *School Library Journal* agreed, adding that ''within this very simple storyline is a multi-faceted art lesson on French impressionism.'' *Address:* P.O. Box 686, Hoboken, N.J. 07030.

Polly knew that the chances of his coming home again were small. ■ (Jacket illustration by Joseph A. Smith from *The Ship from Simnel Street* by Jenny Overton.)

OVERTON, Jenny (Margaret Mary) 1942-

PERSONAL: Born January 22, 1942, in Cranleigh, Surrey, England; daughter of John French (a schoolmaster) and Joyce Margaret (Botting) Overton. *Education:* Girton College, Cambridge, B.A. (with honors), 1964, M.A., 1966. *Agent:* Raines & Raines, 244 Madison Ave., New York, N.Y. 10016. *Office:* Lutterworth Press, 7 All Saints' Passage, Cambridge CB2 3LS, England.

CAREER: Cambridge University, Newnham College, Cambridge, England, appeals secretary, 1965-66, principal's private secretary, 1966-67; Aluminium Federation, London, England, assistant editor, 1967-69; Macmillan & Co., London, book editor, 1970-71; Lutterworth Press, Guildford, Surrey, England, children's book editor, 1971—. *Awards, honors: Creed Country* was selected one of Child Study Association of America's Children's Books of the Year, 1970.

WRITINGS—All juvenile: *Creed Country,* Faber, 1969, Macmillan, 1970; *The Thirteen Days of Christmas* (illustrated by Shirley Hughes), Faber, 1972, T. Nelson, 1974; *The Nightwatch Winter* (sequel to *Creed Country*), Faber, 1973; *The Ship from Simnel Street,* Greenwillow, 1986.

FOR MORE INFORMATION SEE: D. L. Kirkpatrick, editor, *Twentieth-Century Children's Writers,* St. Martin's, 1978, 2nd edition, 1983.

MARGOT M. PARKER

PARKER, Margot M. 1937-

PERSONAL: Born April 22, 1937, in Vacaville, Calif.; daughter of Herbert Walter (a banker) and Lydia (a housewife; maiden name, Seuter) Swenson; married Robert Parker (a school administrator), June 13, 1959; children: Susan Lori Parker Seifert, Jeffrey Robert. *Education:* California State University, Sacramento, B.A., 1959. *Home:* 7350 Morningside Dr., Loomis, Calif. 95650.

CAREER: Sacramento City Unified School District, Sacramento, Calif., kindergarten teacher, 1959—; author of children's books, 1984—. *Member:* National Education Association, California Teachers Association, Sacramento City Teachers Association.

WRITINGS—Juvenile: *What Is Columbus Day?* (illustrated by Matthew Bates), Childrens Press, 1985; *What Is Veterans Day?* (illustrated by M. Bates), Childrens Press, 1986.

WORK IN PROGRESS: What Is Thanksgiving Day?; What Is Martin Luther King, Jr. Day?; But What Am I?

SIDELIGHTS: "My search for illustrated books for young children that explain why we celebrate special days prompted me to write the holiday series. *But What Am I?* was inspired by an incident in my kindergarten class. A brown-haired, blue-eyed girl became frustrated when, unlike her black and Asian classmates, she could not identify the ethnic or racial group to which she belonged."

PARTRIDGE, Jenny (Lilian) 1947-

PERSONAL: Born July 25, 1947, in Romford, England; daughter of Frank Munden and Dorothy (Miles) Partridge; married Nigel Casseldine (a painter and illustrator), April 16, 1971; children: Alice, Nicholas. *Education:* Attended South East Essex Technical College, 1963-68. *Religion:* Church of England. *Home and office:* Westend Cottage, 319 Westward Rd., Ebley, Gloucestershire, England. *Agent:* Christopher Shepheard-Walwyn, 51 Vineyard Hill Rd., London S.W.19, England.

CAREER: Presentation Colour Ltd. (photographic processors), London, England, retoucher, 1967-72; Romany Studio Workshop, Ebley, England, founder and artist, 1972—. *Awards, honors:* Critici in Erba Award from Bologna Children's Book Fair, 1981, for *Mr. Squint.*

WRITINGS—Self-illustrated children's books; all British editions published by World's Work: *Mr. Squint,* 1980; *Colonel Grunt,* 1980, Holt, 1982; *Peterkin Pollensnuff,* 1980, Holt, 1982; *Hopfellow,* 1980, Holt, 1982; *Grandma Snuffles,* 1981, Holt, 1983; *Dominic Sly,* 1981, Holt, 1983; *Harriet Plume,* 1981, Holt, 1983; *Lop-Ear,* 1981, Holt, 1983; *Oakapple Wood Stories,* 1982; *A Tale of Oakapple Wood,* 1983.

SIDELIGHTS: "Writing the Oakapple Wood books was a secondary response, as I had been illustrating for some time before it was put to me to try to write stories around my illustrations. At first I found the idea daunting but after several false starts I discovered that the very way I felt about my drawings seemed to add credence to the characters. They existed, and with them the legend of Oakapple Wood, all from the very first pen and ink sketches springing into animated life. I saw the stories take form before me, and in this way the characters almost told their own tales, using me as a willing medium. Oakapple Wood is a real place to me, and there is a warmth of feeling each time I visit it and its many inhabitants, who have become my very good friends since their creation some years ago.''

HOBBIES AND OTHER INTERESTS: Wildlife.

PETRIE, Catherine 1947-

PERSONAL: Born October 22, 1947, in Elkhorn, Wis.; daughter of Landon Ellery (in truck and car rentals) and Mary (maiden name, Neuman) Petrie; married Keith Yurica (an accountant), June 24, 1982. *Education:* Attended Wheaton College, Wheaton, Ill., 1965-68; University of Wisconsin—Whitewater, B.S., 1969, M.S.E., 1972; graduate study at University of California, Los Angeles, 1981—. *Politics:* Republican. *Religion:* Christian. *Home:* Route 2, Petrie Rd., Lake Geneva, Wis. 53147.

CAREER: Reading consultant in Pine Ridge, S.D., 1970-72, Edgewater, Colo., 1972-78, San Dimas, Calif., 1978-80, and Lake Geneva, Wis., 1980-81; Professional Tour Consultants, Inc., Lake Geneva, owner and director, 1981—. Co-sponsor of Food Day in Denver, Colo., 1978. *Member:* American Association of University Women (representative to the United Nations).

WRITINGS—Juvenile; all published by Childrens Press: *Hot Rod Harry* (illustrated by Paul Sharp), 1982; *Sandbox Betty* (illustrated by Sharon Elzaurdia), 1982; *Joshua James Likes Trucks* (illustrated by Jerry Warshaw), 1982; *Seed*, 1983; *Night*, 1983; *Rain*, 1983.

SIDELIGHTS: In *Joshua James Likes Trucks*, Petrie uses an eighteen-word vocabulary in summing up young Joshua's taste in trucks. *Hot Rod Harry* also has a limited vocabulary, at twenty-nine words, and *Sandbox Betty* relies on rhyme and repetition, telling its story in three-to-five word sentences.

''I have degrees in elementary education and reading. I have ten years teaching experience as a reading consultant. I wrote beginning-to-read books for my nephew and niece who, at four and five years old, were ready to read, but lacked appropriate reading materials for those initial efforts.

''I have traveled extensively, recently returning from six months in Africa with my husband.''

PLOWDEN, David 1932-

PERSONAL: Born October 9, 1932, in Boston, Mass.; son of Roger Stanley and Mary (maiden name, Butler) Plowden; married Pleasance Coggeshall, June 20, 1962 (divorced, October, 1976); married Sandra Schoellkopf, July 8, 1977; children: (first marriage) John Stanley, Daniel Coggeshall, (second marriage) Philip Schoellkopf, Karen Calkins. *Education:* Yale University, B.A., 1955. *Residence:* Winnetka, Ill.

CAREER: Photographer and writer, 1962—. Great Northern Railway, Willmar, Minn., assistant to trainmaster, 1955-56; Illinois Institute of Technology-Institute of Design, Chicago, Ill., visiting associate professor, 1978-80, associate professor, 1980-86; University of Iowa, School of Journalism and Mass Communications, Iowa City, Iowa, lecturer, 1984—. *Member:* American Society of Magazine Photographers.

EXHIBITIONS—One man: New York Public Library, Hudson Park Branch, New York, N.Y., 1962; The Suffolk Museum, Stony Brook, N.Y., 1962; First Federal Savings & Loan Association, New York, N.Y., 1964, Queens, N.Y., 1964; Columbia University, New York, N.Y., 1965; Smithsonian Institution, Washington, D.C., 1970-71, summer/fall, 1975, Performing Arts Division, summer, 1976; The Neikrug Gallery, New York, N.Y., December, 1972; Lincoln College, Lincoln, Illinois, 1973; Bryant Library, Roslyn, N.Y., January, 1976; The International Center of Photography, New York, N.Y., February, 1976; The Half Hollow Community Center, Dix Hills, N.Y., 1976; Port Washington Library, Port Washington, N.Y., 1977; The Congress of the Laity, Los Angeles, Calif., February, 1978; Santa Fe Gallery of Photography, Santa Fe, New Mexico, March, 1979; Evanston Art Center, Evanston, Illinois, May, 1979; Witkin Gallery, New York, N.Y., June-July, 1979, November, 1981; Cincinnati Art Academy, Cincinnati, Ohio, June, 1979.

Gilbert Gallery, Ltd., Chicago, Ill., March-April, 1980, October, 1981; Columbia College Galleries, The Chicago Center for Contemporary Photography, Chicago, Ill., September-October, 1982; The Federal Hall Museum, National Park Service, New York, N.Y., October-November, 1982; University of Virginia, College of Architecture, Charlottesville, Virginia, October, 1982; Drew University, Madison, N.J., November, 1982; The California Museum of Photography, University of California, Riverside, Calif., November, 1982-January, 1983; Purdue University/Calumet, Hammond, Indiana, February, 1984; Susan Spiritus Gallery, Newport Beach, Calif., March-April, 1984; Westtown School, Westtown, Pa., December, 1984; Rhode Island School of Design, Providence, R.I., March, 1985; Chicago Historical Society, Chicago, Ill., April-July, 1985; University of Maryland, Baltimore, Catonsville, Md., April-June, 1985; Cleveland Children's Museum, Cleveland, Ohio (permanent exhibition), 1986; Martin Gallery, Washington, D.C., February-March, 1987; Kunstmuseum Luzern, Lucerne, Switzerland, August/September, 1987; Grand Rapids Art Museum, Grand Rapids, Michigan, February-March, 1988.

Group exhibitions: Metropolitan Museum of Art, New York, N.Y., 1967; Kodak Gallery, New York, N.Y., 1976; The Walker Art Center, Minneapolis, Minnesota, 1976-1977; University of Colorado, travelling exhibition, 1977; Currier Gallery of Art, Manchester, N.H., 1978; The Whitney Museum, New York, N.Y., January-February, 1979; Evanston Art Center, Evanston, Ill., November-December, 1979; Friedens Gallery, New York, N.Y., fall, 1982; Milwaukee Center for Photography, Marquette University, Milwaukee, Wis., June, 1983; Art Institute of Chicago, Chicago, Ill., summer, 1983, July-September, 1987; State University of New York, traveling exhibition, 1986; Arts Center College, Danville, Kentucky, September-November, 1986.

Permanent collections: Art Institute of Chicago, Chicago, Ill.; California Museum of Photography, University of California, Riverside, Calif.; Center for Creative Photography, University of Arizona, Tucson, Arizona; Chicago Center for Contemporary Photography, Columbia College, Chicago, Ill.; Chicago Historical Society, Chicago, Ill.; Library of Congress, Washington, D.C.; Smithsonian Institution, Washington, D.C.; J. B. Speed Art Museum, Louisville, Kentucky; University of Maryland, Catonsville, Maryland.

AWARDS, HONORS: Guggenheim fellowship, 1968; Smithsonian Institution special research grant, 1970-71; Benjamin Barondess Award, 1970, for *Lincoln and His America: 1809-1865;* Dept. of Transportation and the Smithsonian Institution

David Plowden. (Photograph by *The Grand Rapids Press.*)

grant, 1975-76; *Tugboat* was selected one of Child Study Association of America's Children's Books of the Year, and one of *New York Times* Outstanding Children's Books, both 1976, and was included in the Children's Book Showcase of the Children's Book Council, 1977; Wilson Hicks Award, 1977, for "Outstanding Contributions to Still Photography"; 57th Annual Exhibition Merit Award, 1978, from the Art Directors Club; *Boston Globe-Horn Book* nonfiction honor book, 1979, for *The Iron Road;* Art Directors' Club of New Jersey Fifteenth Annual Awards Gold Medal, 1979; *The Hand of Man on America* was chosen one of New York Public Library's Books for the Teen Age, 1980.

WRITINGS—All with own photographs: *Farewell to Steam*, Greene, 1965; (editor) *Lincoln and His America: 1809-1865*, foreword by John Gunther, Viking, 1970; *The Hand of Man on America*, Smithsonian Institution Press, 1971; *The Floor of the Sky: The Great Plains*, Sierra Club, 1972; *Commonplace*, Dutton, 1974; *Bridges: The Spans of North America*, Viking, 1974; *Tugboat* (ALA Notable Book), Macmillan, 1976; *Steel*, Viking, 1981; *An American Chronology: The Photographs of David Plowden* (ALA Notable Book), Viking, 1982; *Industrial Landscape*, Norton, 1985; *A Time of Trains*, Norton, 1987.

Photographer: Mab Wilson, *Gems*, Viking, 1967; Samuel Robinson Ogden, *America the Vanishing*, Greene, 1969; Patricia Coffin, *Nantucket*, Viking, 1971; Nelson P. Falorp, *Cape May to Montauk*, Viking, 1973; Berton Roueche, *Desert and Plain, the Mountains and the River*, Dutton, 1975; Richard Snow, *The Iron Road: A Portrait of American Railroading*

(*Horn Book* honor list; ALA Notable Book), Four Winds, 1978. Has also illustrated with photographs, *The Freeway City*, U.S. Government, 1968. Photographs are also included in "The States and the Nations" series, published jointly by Norton and the American Associations for State and Local History: *New Jersey*, 1977; *North Dakota*, 1977; *South Dakota*, 1977; *Vermont*, 1979; *New York*, 1981.

Photographs have also been included in: *With Heritage So Rich*, Random House, 1966; *The Evolution of the Machine*, Van Nostrand, 1968; *Bridges, Canals and Tunnels*, Van Nostrand, 1968; *The Beautiful Country*, Viking, 1973; *Mr. Jefferson, Architect*, Viking, 1973; *Reusing Railroad Stations*, Educational Facilities Institute, 1974; *America's Forgotten Architecture*, Pantheon, 1976; *History Cast in Metal*, Cast Metal Institute, 1976; *Railroads in America*, American Heritage, 1977; *Wayne County: The Aesthetic Heritage of a Rural Area*, Publishing Center for Cultural Resources, 1979; *Bruce Catton's America*, Doubleday, 1979; *The Art of Photography*, Life Library of Photography, 1981; *Three Centuries of Notable American Architects*, American Heritage, 1982; *The Gallery of World Photography, Photography—As Fine Art*, Shueisha Publishing, 1982; *The Gallery of World Photography, the City*, Shueisha Publishing, 1983; (also author of introduction) *The Gallery of World Photography, the Country*, Shueisha Publishing, 1983. Contributor of articles with photographs to periodicals, including *American Heritage, Life, Smithsonian, Audubon, Fortune, Horizon*, and *Architectural Forum*.

WORK IN PROGRESS: A book on rural and small town culture in Iowa, funded by the State Historical Society of Iowa and the Iowa Humanities Board through a grant from the National Endowment for the Humanities, to be published by Norton.

SIDELIGHTS: Plowden, who has spent most of his life documenting America with a camera, claims that his first camera lens was a window. ''I was born in Boston and grew up in a place on the East River. Through my bedroom window I could watch the boats travel up and down. I remember when my father left for work, he would wave a newspaper at me from the top deck of his boat, and even after he turned to a tiny speck and was gone, I would watch for hours. How could you see anything like that and know nothing about perspective?'' [Mike Arents, ''Plowden: Image Maker,'' *Grand Rapids Press,* April 24, 1983.¹]

Plowden, who received a B.A. degree in economics from Yale University in 1955, studied photography first with O. Winston Link in New York City. He then studied with Minor White and Nathan Lyons in Rochester, N.Y., and was an assistant to George Meluso in 1960-62. From 1962 he has been a self-employed photographer. Commissions include those from: Columbia University (1962-66); The Smithsonian Institution (1975); United Church of Christ (1976); New York Botanical Gardens and Society (1978); State Historical Society of Iowa (1987); and the Iowa Humanities Board and the National Endowment for the Humanities (1987-88). Plowden was one of twelve photographers selected for inclusion in the portfolio, *In Chicago,* which was published by the Art Institute of Chicago in commemoration of the city's sesquicentennial year, 1983. ''I was [also] an associate professor at the Institute of

(From *Industrial Landscape* by David Plowden. Photograph copyright © 1985 by David Plowden.)

(From *Desert and Plain, the Mountains and the River: A Celebration of Rural America* by
Berton Roueché and David Plowden. Photograph by David Plowden.)

Design, 1978-84 and was awarded tenure in 1982. I have been
a lecturer at the University of Iowa, School of Journalism and
Mass Communications since 1984.''

As a photographer, teacher, author and illustrator, Plowden
has travelled throughout the United States, photographing mainly
small towns and ''man-made America.''¹ He lives with his
wife and four children in Winnetka, Illinois.

HOBBIES AND OTHER INTERESTS: ''Aside from my work,
my family is the only other real interest in my life. Railroads,
baseball, and fishing could be considered distant runners.''

FOR MORE INFORMATION SEE: U.S. Camera Annual, 1963,
1964; *Library Journal,* October 7, 1970; *Smithsonian,* June,
1971; *Popular Photography,* June, 1971, June, 1973; *Time,*
November 19, 1973; *Photography Annual,* 1976; *Modern Photography,* January, 1977; *Scene,* March/April, 1977; *Photograph Collectors' Guide,* New York Graphic Society, 1979;
American Photographer, July, 1980, July, 1982; *Contemporary Photographers,* Macmillan, 1981; *Historic Preservation,*
summer, 1982; Mike Arents, ''Plowden: Image Maker,'' *Grand*

Rapids Press, April 24, 1983; *American Land Forum Magazine,* winter, 1983, spring, 1986; *USAIR,* February, 1985; *Chicago Tribune,* April 12, 1985.

POWERS, Bill   1931-

PERSONAL: Born February 3, 1931, in Brooklyn, N.Y.; son
of Robert (a steelworker) and Delia (Thompson) Powers; married Suzy Martin, October 26, 1965 (divorced, 1970); children: Michael, James. *Education:* Attended Pratt Institute, 1956-
58, and Mexico City College, 1959. *Home* 72 Barrow St.,
New York, N.Y. 10014. *Agent:* Elaine Markson, 44 Green-
wich Ave., New York, N.Y. 10010.

CAREER: Free-lance commercial artist in New York City,
1956-65; Second Story Players, New York City, theatrical
director, 1965-68; free-lance writer and photographer, 1969—.
Military service: U.S. Air Force, 1951-55; became sergeant.
Member: American Society of Magazine Photographers.
Awards, honors: Obie Award from *Village Voice,* 1967, for
excellence in off-Broadway and off-off-Broadway productions.

WRITINGS—Juvenile: Break Him Down!, F. Watts, 1977; *The Weekend* (illustrated with photographs by Meryl Joseph), F. Watts, 1978, new edition (illustrated with photographs by G. Richardson Cook), Dell, 1984; *Flying High* (self-illustrated with photographs), F. Watts, 1978; *Love Lost, and Found*, F. Watts, 1979; *A Test of Love* (illustrated with photographs by Bill Aron), F. Watts, 1979; *Behind the Scenes of a Broadway Musical* (self-illustrated with photographs), Crown, 1982.

Illustrator—all written by Donald Honig; all published by F. Watts: *Breaking In*, 1974; *Playing for Keeps*, 1974; *The Professional*, 1974; *Coming Back*, 1974; *Running Harder*, 1976; *Going the Distance*, 1976.

WORK IN PROGRESS: ''Sweet Arsenic,'' a film script.

RABINOWITZ, Sandy 1954-

PERSONAL: Born October 22, 1954, in New Haven, Conn.; daughter of Harold W. (an artist) and Kiki (a designer; maiden name, Harris) Rabinowitz; married; children: one daughter. *Education:* Parsons School of Design, certificate of illustration, 1975. *Home:* Carmel Rd., Bethany, Conn. 06525.

CAREER: Author and illustrator of children's books, 1975—.

WRITINGS—Juvenile; self-illustrated: The Red Horse and the Bluebird, Harper, 1975; *What's Happening to Daisy?*, Harper, 1977; *A Colt Named Mischief*, Doubleday, 1979; *How I Trained My Colt*, Doubleday, 1981.

Illustrator: Lynn Hall, *The Something-Special Horse*, Scribner, 1985.

WORK IN PROGRESS: The Nature of Wild Horses, a self-illustrated children's book.

SIDELIGHTS: ''I am a full-time horsewoman. I illustrate and write children's books in order to buy hay and grain. My experiences with my animals inspire my stories, and my horses are references for my illustrations. I am at ease writing for children because I am a perpetual child myself.''

SANDY RABINOWITZ

RADIN, Ruth Yaffe 1938-

BRIEF ENTRY: Born October 8, 1938, in Hartford, Conn. Author of books for young readers. Radin received a B.A. from Connecticut College in 1960 and an M.S. from Southern Connecticut State College in 1963. She held several occupations after college, including elementary school teacher, librarian, and reading specialist. Radin's first book, *A Winter Place* (Atlantic/Little Brown, 1982), is geared primarily for four- to six-year-olds and tells the story of a family's ramble through farm country, past a town, and finally, up to snow-covered mountains where a frozen pond creates a rink for skaters. Radin and illustrator Mattie Lou O'Kelley have achieved such a degree of harmony in their work that, according to *Publishers Weekly*, ''it appears like the creation of one dedicated and extraordinarily talented person, so tuned-in are the colorful pictures to the story.'' *A Winter Place* was named both an ALA Notable Book and a Reading Rainbow Book. Radin's next work, *Tac's Island* (Macmillan, 1986), accounts the evolving summer friendship of two boys on an island off the coast of Virginia. *School Library Journal* called this work for middle-grade readers a ''quiet and gently humorous book,'' while *Booklist* commented that ''the story's simple lines and pleasant mood make it a nice choice for reluctant readers . . . who should easily identify with the protagonists and the setting.'' Forthcoming books by Radin include *Tac's Turn* and *High in the Mountains*, both to be published by Macmillan.

RANSOM, Candice F. 1952-
(Kate Kenyon)

PERSONAL: Born July 10, 1952, in Washington, D.C.; daughter of Thomas Garland Farris (a builder) and Irene Lightfoot (a housewife; maiden name, Dellinger); married Frank Wesley Ransom (a satellite engineer), February 14, 1979. *Education:* Attended high school in Oakton, Va. *Home:* 14400 Awbrey Patent Dr., Centreville, Va. 22020. *Agent:* Frank W. Ransom, P.O. Box 936, Centreville, Va. 22020. *Office:* P.O. Box 936, Centreville, Va. 22020.

CAREER: Computer Sciences, Silver Spring, Maryland, secretary, 1973-77; writer, 1980—. *Member:* Society of Children's Book Writers, Children's Book Guild of Washington, D.C. *Awards, honors:* Finalist, Gold Medallion Award from the Romance Writers of America, 1985.

WRITINGS—Juvenile; all published by Scholastic except as noted: The Silvery Past, 1982; *Amanda*, 1984; *Susannah*, 1984; *Kathleen*, 1985; *Emily*, 1985; *Breaking the Rules*, 1985; *Blackbird Keep*, Silhouette, 1986; *Sabrina*, 1986; *Nicole*, 1986; *Cat's Cradle*, Silhouette, 1986; *Thirteen*, 1986; (under pseudonym Kate Kenyon) *The Day the Eighth Grade Ran the School*, 1987; *Kaleidoscope*, Crosswinds, 1987; *Fourteen and Holding*, 1987; *Fifteen at Last*, 1987; *Going on Twelve*, 1988; *My Sister the Meanie*, 1988; *My Sister the Traitor*, 1989; *My Sister the Creep*, 1989.

Contributor of articles and stories to magazines, including *Seventeen, Rural Living, Jack and Jill, Ebony Jr!, Country, Country Living, Insight, Cat Fancy, Scholastic Voice, Listen, Writer's Digest, Single Parent, Highlights for Children* and *Lutheran Women*.

WORK IN PROGRESS: A sequel to *Susannah* (as yet untitled); a young adult novel called *Ask Me No Questions;* a pre-teen novel called *She's Penelope, I'm Prune;* and a middle-grade novel called *The Junkyard Class*.

CANDICE F. RANSOM

SIDELIGHTS: "My first novel, pencilled on the long bus ride home from school at the age of seven, began with the immortal lines, 'It was dark. Everything was silent. Then in rustling leaves. . . .' The books I wrote in elementary school were feeble imitations of Nancy Drew or *Lassie Come Home*, in which I was always the main character. As a lonely child growing up in rural Fairfax County, I wrote to while away long evenings, and who else would I rather have read about having wonderful adventures than myself?

"During the sixth grade, my best friend and I spent recess periods tunneling out tangles of honeysuckle and wisteria that were wrapped thick around dogwood trees growing along the perimeter of the playground. Hidden in our 'Honeysuckle Hideout,' we spied on an old man's house high on the hill, scratched our poison ivy, and collaborated on a mystery novel. Those were the golden years, when writing was fun, effortless.

"In high school, I worried that I had a severe case of arrested development. While other kids were passing around *The Green Berets*, with page 388 marked, I was still reading *The Borrowers*. My English teacher set me straight. 'You're going to be a children's writer,' she said. Relieved that I was not living my life in reverse like Merlin in *The Once and Future King*, I set out to fulfill her prophecy. The summer I was sixteen, I wrote a children's novel on my new typewriter and mailed poetry off to the *New Yorker*, a writer at last. That same year, my first poem was published (alas, not in the *New Yorker*), but the novel was lost in the mail, en route to Harper and Row, who never realized how lucky they were.

"After high school, I went to work as a secretary, but I still yearned to be a children's writer. Whenever I walked into the children's room of a library, memories of myself at nine, wide-eyed and thrilled to be in a roomful of books, overpowered me to the point where I thought I'd faint. I *had* to write. And I did.

"Now that my dream has come true, I often reflect what a strange world I inhabit, trapped between the floors of childhood and adulthood—not really *there,* but not really *here* either.

"Much of my material comes from within, drawn from my own past, which I remember vividly. A lot of my childhood interests have carried over into my profession. It came as no great surprise to me that my first published novel was a mystery, since I had devoured dozens as a child. A grown-up love for history has led to the discovery of a new passion, writing historical novels for young people.

"Best of all, I am able to recapture that shivery feeling of anticipation I once had whenever I turned to the first page of a new library book. Only now the pages are blank, waiting for me to fill them."

HOBBIES AND OTHER INTERESTS: Reading children's books and collecting original art from children's picture books.

ROBERTS, Nancy Correll 1924-

PERSONAL: Born May 30, 1924, in South Milwaukee, Wis.; daughter of Milton Lee (a chemist) and Maud (MacRae) Correll; married Bruce Stuart Roberts (a free-lance photographer), February 27, 1957 (divorced); children: Nancy Lee, David Correll. *Education:* Attended Centre College, 1942-44; University of North Carolina, B.A., 1947; University of Miami, graduate study, 1947-48. *Religion:* Presbyterian. *Home:* 3600 Chevington Rd., Charlotte, N.C. 28226.

CAREER: Scottish Chief, Maxton, N.C., editor and publisher, 1953-57; free-lance writer. President, Maxton (N.C.) Development Corp., 1954-55. Town commissioner of Maxton, 1952-56. *Awards, honors: Where Time Stood Still: A Portrait of Appalachia* was chosen by the *New York Times* editorial board as one of the outstanding children's books of 1970.

WRITINGS—Illustrated with photographs by Bruce Roberts: *An Illustrated Guide to Ghosts and Mysterious Occurrences in the Old North State,* Heritage House, 1959, 2nd edition, McNally & Loftin, 1967; *Ghosts of the Carolinas,* McNally & Loftin, 1962, 2nd edition, 1967; *David,* John Knox, 1968; *Sense of Discovery: The Mountain,* John Knox, 1969; *A Week in Robert's World: The South,* Crowell-Collier, 1969; *The Governor,* McNally & Loftin, 1972; *The Goodliest Land: North Carolina,* Doubleday, 1973; *The Faces of South Carolina,* Doubleday, 1976; *Appalachian Ghosts,* Doubleday, 1978; *Southern Ghosts,* Doubleday, 1979; *Ghosts and Specters of the Old South,* Sandlapper, 1984.

With B. Roberts; illustrated with photographs by B. Roberts: *Where Time Stood Still: A Portrait of Appalachia,* Crowell-Collier, 1970; *This Haunted Land,* McNally & Loftin, 1970; *Ghosts and Specters: Ten Supernatural Stories from the Deep South,* Doubleday, 1974; *Ghosts of the Wild West,* Doubleday, 1976; *America's Most Haunted Places,* Doubleday, 1976; *You and Your Retarded Child* (adult), Concordia, 1977.

Other: *Help for the Parents of a Handicapped Child,* Concordia, 1981; *South Carolina Ghosts: From the Mountains to the*

NANCY CORRELL ROBERTS

Coast, University of South Carolina Press, 1983; *Haunted Houses: Tales from 32 American Homes* (illustrated with photographs), Globe Pequot, 1988.

SIDELIGHTS: Roberts' first book came about because of the encouragement of writer, Carl Sandburg. She went on to write twenty widely acclaimed books about ghosts, folktales and handicapped children. Her first book led to a career of supersleuthing all over the U.S. interviewing subjects and recording first-hand ghost story accounts. Some of her best known titles are: *America's Most Haunted Places, Southern Ghosts, Appalachian Ghosts, Ghosts of the Wild West* (a finalist for the Spur Award), *South Carolina Ghosts: From the Mountains to the Coast* and *Haunted Houses* (February, 1988). *Southern Living Magazine* has termed her a "custodian of the twilight zone." Roberts is a frequent speaker on the supernatural, enjoys leading writing workshops for students and, when not absorbed in work on a book or magazine story, her hobbies are photography and hiking.

History is so interwoven with her stories that Roberts was awarded one of the annual Certificates of Commendation from the National Association of State and Regional History.

FOR MORE INFORMATION SEE: New York Times Book Review, November 9, 1969; Dorothy A. Marquardt and Martha E. Ward, *Authors of Books for Young People,* 2nd edition supplement, Scarecrow, 1979; *Southern Living,* December, 1979.

ROFES, Eric Edward   1954-

PERSONAL: Surname is pronounced "*Row*-fess"; born August 31, 1954, in Manhasset, N.Y.; son of William Lopatin (an archivist) and Paula Ruth (a business manager; maiden name, Weinstein) Rofes. *Education:* Harvard University, B.A. (cum laude), 1976. *Religion:* Jewish. *Agent:* Helen Rees Literary Agency, 308 Commonwealth Ave., Boston, Mass. 02116. *Home:* 5801 Lindenhurst Ave., Los Angeles, Calif. 90036.

CAREER: Fayerweather Street School, Cambridge, Mass., teacher, administrator, and co-director, beginning 1978. Delegate to the White House Conference on Families, 1980; area board member of Massachusetts Department of Social Services, 1980-81; member of the Massachusetts Committee for Children and Youth (member of board of directors of Project Assist, chairman of board of directors of Project Aware); member of board of directors of *Gay Community News. Member:* Gay Men's Professional Group of Boston, Boston Area Gay and Lesbian Schoolworkers (founder), Gay Harvard Alumni (director). *Awards, honors: The Kids' Book of Divorce* was selected one of New York Public Library's Books for the Teen Age, 1982; *The Kids' Book about Death and Dying* was chosen one of Child Study Association of America's Children's Books of the Year, 1985, and was a Notable Children's Trade Book in the Field of Social Studies by the National Council for Social Studies and the Children's Book Council, 1986.

WRITINGS: (Editor) *The Kids' Book of Divorce: By, for and about Kids,* Lewis Publishing, 1981; *"I Thought People Like That Killed Themselves": Lesbians, Gay Men, and Suicide,*

ERIC EDWARD ROFES

Grey Fox, 1982; (editor) *The Kids' Book about Parents*, Houghton, 1984; (editor) *The Kids' Book about Death and Dying: By and for Kids*, Little, Brown, 1985; *Socrates, Plato and Guys Like Me: Confessions of a Gay Schoolteacher*, Alyson, 1985; *Gay Life*, Doubleday, 1986; *The Kids' Book of Sex*, Rawson, 1987. Contributor of articles to periodicals, including *Gay Community News, Radical Teacher, The Advocate*, and *Guardian*.

WORK IN PROGRESS: An anthology of gay men's writings.

SIDELIGHTS: "I am engaged in two major areas of writing: books for children, which I write in collaboration with children, and books about a broad range of political issues, including social service issues, gay liberation, feminism, and progressive politics. I am a gay man very much involved in youth advocacy work and expect to continue this work for many years."

The Kids' Book about Parents "was a class project at the Fayerweather Street School in Cambridge, Mass. . . . We met three days a week for one hour. In the beginning of the year we brainstormed all the things we wanted to put in a book about parents. When we decided on the subjects—things like homework and chores, being an only child, rules and punishments, being part of a stepfamily—the students had writing assignments. They also acted out the topics and shared experiences with each other.

"I took all the written material and synthesized it. Then we all went over it together. Sometimes we'd decide we had to change the material because someone would say, 'That doesn't sound like what I said.' The kids took the pictures and helped with the editing and proofreading." [Sylvia Sachs, "Open Up to Us, Kids Advise Parents in Their Book," *Pittsburgh Press*, May 5, 1984.]

FOR MORE INFORMATION SEE: Newsweek, June 8, 1981; *Boston Globe*, April 18, 1984, April 25, 1984; Sylvia Sachs, "Open Up to Us, Kids Advise Parents in Their Book," *Pittsburgh Press*, May 5, 1984.

ROSEMAN, Kenneth David   1939-

BRIEF ENTRY: Born May 10, 1939, in Washington, D.C. In 1965 the National Association of Temple Educators awarded Roseman an Emanuel Gamoran Prize for his monograph entitled "Dramatic Moments in Jewish History." He completed his rabbinical and Ph.D. studies at Hebrew Union College—Jewish Institute of Religion in 1972, remaining on campus through 1974 to serve as dean and instructor in Jewish American history. From 1974 to 1976 Roseman directed the Institute for Jewish Life, an affiliate of the Council of Jewish Federations and Funds based in New York. Since 1976 he has been rabbi of Temple Beth-El in Madison, Wis., and has served in a number of organizations, including the Association of Attending Clergy at Madison General Hospital. Roseman's books for young readers reflect his belief that history is not a predetermined sequence of events, but the assimilation of choices made by many individuals. His works offer several choices which invite the reader to help formulate the Jewish protagonist's life story. All published by the Union of American Hebrew Congregations, Roseman's titles include *The Cardinal's Snuffbox, All in My Jewish Family*, and *The Melting Pot: An Adventure in New York*, which, according to *School Library Journal*, "provides a fun way to learn and deserves a place in Hebrew schools and larger secular collections." *Escape from*

the Holocaust is the most current title in the series. *Home:* 117 Shiloh Dr., Madison, Wis. 53705.

FOR MORE INFORMATION SEE: Who's Who in World Jewry: A Biographical Dictionary of Outstanding Jews, Olive Books of Israel, 1978; *Who's Who in American Jewry*, Standard, 1980; *Contemporary Authors*, Volume 110, Gale, 1984.

SACHS, Judith   1947-
(Emily Chase, Petra Diamond, Rebecca Diamond, Jocelyn Saal, Jennifer Sarasin, Antonia Saxon)

PERSONAL: Born February 13, 1947, in New York, N.Y.; daughter of E. Milton (a physician) and Naomi (a social worker; maiden name, Diamond) Sachs; married Anthony Bruno (a writer), February 6, 1982; children: Mia Miriam. *Education:* Brandeis University, B.A., 1968. *Politics:* "Liberal-ish." *Religion:* Jewish. *Home and office:* 404 Burd St., Pennington, N.J. 08534. *Agent:* Andrea Cirillo, Jane Rotrosen Agency, 318 East 51st St., New York, N.Y. 10022.

CAREER: Saturday Review Press, New York City, associate editor, 1970-73; Arbor House Publishing Co., New York City, managing editor, 1973; Delacorte Press, New York City, senior editor, 1973-77; Hawthorn Books, New York City, senior editor, 1977-79; free-lance writer and editor, 1979—. *Member:* Editorial Freelancers Association, Authors Guild.

WRITINGS—Young adult; under pseudonym Rebecca Diamond: *Summer Romance*, Silhouette, 1982.

Young adult; all under pseudonym Jocelyn Saal; all published by Bantam: *Dance of Love*, 1982; *Trusting Hearts*, 1982; *Running Mates*, 1983; (with Margaret Burman) *On Thin Ice*, 1983.

JUDITH SACHS

Young adult; under pseudonym Jennifer Sarasin; all published by Scholastic: *Spring Love,* 1984; *The Hidden Room,* 1984; *Acting Up,* 1988.

"Cheerleaders" series; young adult; all under pseudonym Jennifer Sarasin; all published by Scholastic: *Splitting,* 1985; *Cheating,* 1985; *Living It Up,* 1986; *Taking Over,* 1987; *Together Again,* 1987; *Talking Back,* 1988; *Getting Serious,* 1988.

"The Girls of Canby Hall" series; young adult; all under house pseudonym Emily Chase; all published by Scholastic: *The Big Crush,* 1985; *With Friends Like That,* 1985.

Adult romance novels: (With husband, Anthony Bruno, under joint pseudonym Antonia Saxon), *Paradiso,* Silhouette, 1983; (with A. Bruno, under joint pseudonym Antonia Saxon) *Above the Moon,* Silhouette, 1984; (under pseudonym Petra Diamond) *Confidentially Yours,* Jove, 1984; (under pseudonym Petra Diamond) *Night of a Thousand Stars,* Jove, 1985; (under pseudonym Petra Diamond) *Play It Again, Sam,* Jove, 1986.

Screenplays: (With A. Bruno under name Judith Sachs) "Smoky Joe's High Ride," released by HPS Productions, 1984; (with A. Bruno under name Judith Sachs) "Just Another Friday Night," released by HPS Productions, 1984. Also author of radio scripts on home decorating.

Ghostwriter: Theodore Rubin, *Dr. Rubin, Please Make Me Happy,* Arbor House, 1978; Bob Teague, *Live and Off-Color: The News Biz,* Addison Wesley, 1982; Fay Eckstein and Warren Eckstein, *Pet Aerobics,* Holt, 1984; F. Eckstein and W. Eckstein, *Understanding Your Pet,* Holt, 1985; Suzanne Brangham, *House-Wise: The Smart Person's Guide to Buying, Renovating and Selling Real Estate at an Enormous Profit,* Clarkson Potter, 1987.

Contributor to *Career Choices for Students of Art,* Walker, 1985. Contributor to magazines and newspapers, including *On Film, Harper's, New York Times, Miami Herald,* and *Backpacker.*

WORK IN PROGRESS: Rites of Spring, a novel about a doctor and a surgeon—he Romanian Jewish, she Gentile—in New York and Romania, 1906-40, to be published by Pocket Books.

SIDELIGHTS: "I grew up in Manhattan in the fifties and sixties. I was a real city child, the daughter of a physician. Achievement was praised highly, any interest was worthy of pursuit if it would 'get you somewhere in life.'

"Because of my parents' difficult marriage, I used my imaginative life as a substitute for real family life. My teenage years, I think, were the most formative. The adolescents I write about are often parts of me, struggling to find out how to become an adult. I became involved in theater when I was a teenager, because playing parts provided a way to explore myself. Later, I became a writer so that I could play all the parts and write the script as well.

"My best friend and I would make up situations and act them out then. We trusted each other implicitly, and never feared being made fun of. As a writer, now, I realize how important that time was for me—I was allowed to take risks with my imagination, to put down characters and ideas, no matter how silly or improbable, and have them count as something.

"I didn't really do a great deal of creative writing in high school or college, but saved experiences, jotted down notes, observed keenly. I became an actress, and then an editor, I

suppose, to displace myself a little bit from the creative act. But finally, I discovered, my real love was in getting my thoughts down on paper and sharing them with others. And so, I switched professions and became a writer. A friend was becoming involved in a new line of books specifically for young adults and asked if I could write one quickly, in a few months. I took a deep breath and agreed. I've been doing it ever since.

"My mother's father was a doctor. The novel I am currently writing, as well as the next one I have planned, relies heavily on the authority of the physician in America—how he evolved to be the god-like character everyone trusted. However, doctors can hurt as well as heal, which is what makes the vocation such an interesting double-edged one."

HOBBIES AND OTHER INTERESTS: Travel, music (formerly a choral singer), quilting.

SACHS, Marilyn (Stickle) 1927-

PERSONAL: Born December 18, 1927, in Bronx, N.Y.; daughter of Samuel (an insurance salesman) and Anna (Smith) Stickle; married Morris Sachs (a sculptor), January 26, 1947;

He stopped, even though Frances kept tugging at him.
■ (From *Marv* by Marilyn Sachs. Illustrated by Louis Glanzman.)

children: Anne, Paul. *Education:* Hunter College (now Hunter College of the City University of New York), B.A., 1949; Columbia University, M.S. in L.S., 1953. *Politics:* "Changing constantly." *Religion:* Jewish. *Address:* 733 31st Ave., San Francisco, Calif. 94121.

CAREER: Writer of children's books. Brooklyn (N.Y.) Public Library, children's librarian, 1949-60; San Francisco (Calif.) Public Library, part-time children's librarian, 1961-67. *Member:* American Jane Austen Society, English Jane Austen Society, PEN, Authors Guild, Society of Children's Book Writers, SANE (Society Against Nuclear Energy), ACLU (Association Civil Liberties Union).

AWARDS, HONORS: Outstanding Books of the Year Award, *New York Times,* 1971, for *The Bears' House,* and 1973, for *A Pocket Full of Seeds;* Best Books of the Year Award, *School Library Journal,* 1971, for *The Bears' House,* and 1973, for *The Truth about Mary Rose;* National Book Award, finalist, 1972, for *The Bears' House;* Jane Addams Children's Book Honor Award, 1974, for *A Pocket Full of Seeds;* Silver Pencil Award, Collective Propaganda van het Bederlandse Boek, Netherlands, 1974, for *The Truth about Mary Rose,* and 1977, for *Dorrie's Book;* Austrian Children's Book Prize, 1977, for *The Bears' House;* Garden State Children's Book Award, 1978, for *Dorrie's Book; A Summer's Lease* was chosen one of *School Library Journal*'s "Best Book for Spring," 1979, and received the South Carolina Young Adult Book Award, 1985; *Fleet-Footed Florence* was selected as a "Children's Choice"

by the International Reading Association, 1982; Association of Jewish Libraries Award, 1983, for *Call Me Ruth; The Fat Girl* was chosen one of American Library Association's Best Books for Young Adults, 1984; Christopher Award, 1986, for *Underdog.*

WRITINGS—All published by Doubleday, except as noted: *Amy Moves In* (illustrated by Judith Gwyn Brown), 1964; *Laura's Luck* (illustrated by Ib Ohlsson), 1965; *Amy and Laura* (illustrated by Tracy Sugarman), 1966; *Veronica Ganz* (ALA Notable Book; illustrated by Louis Glanzman), 1968; *Peter and Veronica* (Junior Literary Guild selection; illustrated by L. Glanzman), 1969.

Marv (Junior Literary Guild selection; illustrated by L. Glanzman), 1970; *The Bears' House* (illustrated by L. Glanzman), 1971; *The Truth about Mary Rose* (illustrated by L. Glanzman), 1973; *A Pocket Full of Seeds* (ALA Notable Book; illustrated by Ben Stahl), 1973; *Matt's Mitt* (illustrated by Hilary Knight), 1975; *Dorrie's Book* (illustrated by daughter, Anne Sachs), 1975; *A December Tale,* 1976; *A Secret Friend* (Junior Literary Guild selection), 1978; *A Summer's Lease,* Dutton, 1979.

Bus Ride (illustrated by Amy Rowen), Dutton, 1980; *Class Pictures,* Dutton, 1980; *Fleet-Footed Florence* (illustrated by Charles Robinson), 1981; *Hello . . . Wrong Number* (illustrated by Pamela Johnson), Dutton, 1981; *Beach Towels* (illustrated by Jim Spence), Dutton, 1982; *Call Me Ruth* (Junior

MARILYN SACHS

It's impossible to act cutesie when you're nearly five feet ten and wear a size 9 shoe. ■ (Jacket illustration by Helen Cogancherry from *Almost Fifteen* by Marilyn Sachs.)

Literary Guild selection), 1982; *Fourteen* (Junior Literary Guild selection), Dutton, 1983; *The Fat Girl*, Dutton, 1983; *Thunderbird* (illustrated by J. Spence), Dutton, 1985; *Underdog* (Junior Literary Guild selection), 1985; *Baby Sister*, Dutton, 1986; *Almost Fifteen*, Dutton, 1987; *Fran Ellen's House*, Dutton, 1987.

Play: *Reading Between the Lines*, Children's Book Council, 1971.

Contributor to *New York Times* and *San Francisco Chronicle*.

ADAPTATIONS: "Veronica Ganz" (filmstrip with record or cassette and books), Insight Media Programs, 1975.

SIDELIGHTS: Born **December 18, 1927** in Bronx, New York. "I was a very skinny, cowardly kid. There were lots of bullies on our block and I never learned to stand up to them. They'd take advantage of me until my older sister came to my rescue, bash a few heads, and I would beat a hasty retreat. The only place I felt safe was our neighborhood branch library where I spent as much time as I could. I was not weak in the sense of not knowing what I wanted to do or not having the determination to do it, rather it was that I was not at all confrontational, particularly if the confrontations became physical. It's the weaklings who grow up to become writers, not the bullies. Of this I am sure.

"My teachers and librarians were impressed with my reading habits because I devoured the classics. It wasn't so much that my tastes were particularly 'refined,' or that I was exceptionally 'advanced,' but that I had no desire to read stories set in the present. I knew from an early age that I would be a writer. Reading and writing always seemed to me to go together. I wrote for the school newspapers and magazines from as far back as elementary school.

"Our mother died when I was twelve. My father, who eventually remarried, did not believe that girls needed an education. My sister and I had to fight him very hard on this. Both of us held jobs throughout high school, and I left home at seventeen in order to go to college.

"I was an English major at Hunter College and knew that someday I would be a writer. But when I graduated, I didn't seem to have much to write about, so I took a job with the Brooklyn Public Library as a children's librarian. We were 'missionaries' as much as librarians. I worked on a bookmobile that went all over Brooklyn and I told stories in parks, playgrounds, housing projects, and hospitals. The Brooklyn system was extraordinary. Not only was the collection excel-

"What's your name, anyway?..."
"Judy Koppelmacker. What's so funny?"
■ (From *Bus Ride* by Marilyn Sachs. Illustrated by Amy Rowen.)

lent, but the librarians were models of professionalism and dedication. I loved my job and stayed ten years.

"During this time I wrote *Amy Moves In*. I was young, impressed with myself and absolutely astonished when no one offered to immediately publish it. I was also astounded at the amount of criticism and suggestions I got from editors who returned the manuscript. A number of them said they would consider buying the book if I made certain revisions. I had no idea publishing worked that way. By today's standards, *Amy Moves In* is a very mild book. But back then, apparently it wasn't mild enough. Amy's perfectly nice father doesn't work, and that was one problem. Editors asked that I find him some suitable employment. They wanted all the other 'loose ends' tied up. As though life were neat and tidy. I couldn't make changes I didn't believe in, so the manuscript sat in my desk drawer for ten years.

"I moved with my husband and two children to California where I worked in the San Francisco Public Library. Out of the blue, someone I had worked with in Brooklyn wrote to tell me that she was now an editor with Doubleday and would I please send the novel I had written so very long ago. Two weeks later, one of those 'impossible days' where everything that could go wrong did, there was a letter in my mailbox

"It's a letter," Mary Rose said loftily, "from *our* Papa." ■ (From *Veronica Ganz* by Marilyn Sachs. Illustrated by Louis Glanzman.)

accepting my book for publication. I remember telling my children, who had been acting up all day, that I was 'going to be an author,' to which my daughter replied, 'You don't have the time.' Well, I did too have time! Knowing that I had a book coming out was tremendously inspiring, and I have had a book published just about every year since.

"My working process is pretty much the same for every book. The first stage is always research. I prolong this phase as long as I possibly can, reading everything I can get my hands on. When I was doing a book on Joan of Arc I even looked at court records of her trial. After my library work is done, I do a first draft by hand and go through it very quickly to get the whole book roughed out. I then type, make corrections, and send this draft to my daughter, whose criticism I value highly. I've done this for years, and for years she's wanted me to put more sex in my books. What can I say? First drafts usually take me about three months, sometimes less. The corrected draft goes to my editor who generally returns it with suggestions for revisions. I usually spend a month or less on revisions."

Sachs is routinely praised for her handling of ambiguity and for the strong social consciousness she brings to her books. "Basically I like losers. Most of my protagonists are characters who don't 'fit in,' who are struggling hard to find out who they are, or who are fighting for an ideal. That's not to say that my protagonists are perfect. Far from it. Peter in *Peter and Veronica,* for example, is trying so hard to counter what he perceives as his parents' bigotry against gentiles that he goes too far in the other direction. He goes out on a limb to ensure that Veronica is invited to his Bar Mitzvah when to have been the only gentile at the affair would have made her feel very ill-at-ease. Before one goes around helping people, one must make sure that it is help people want.

"I have done a lot of political work in my time. I was active in the Civil Rights Movement, in the fight against the war in Vietnam, against the proliferation of nuclear arms, etc. etc. We 'social conscious types' have to be careful that we don't take ourselves too seriously. Yes, of course, we want to make the world a better place, but we should bear in mind that a sense of humor goes a long way toward achieving that goal. To that end, I do sometimes poke fun at activist characters who in some measure may be 'foils' for myself.

"One of my favorite characters is Marv. Two kids in the book are brilliant, but only Marv's sister, who gets the highest grades in her class and has a scholarship to a prestigious college, is generally recognized as such. Her achievements are not only conspicuous but predictable. She always has her nose in a book, hasn't time for ordinary mortals, and hasn't the merest hint of a sense of humor. Marv, on the other hand, always inventing things and building fantastical structures, is considered a little weird, particularly by his elder sister. But to my mind, Marv is the real genius. He sets out on his own to execute ambitious projects of his own devising. Marv is a dreamer. And I believe that genius frequently feeds on dreams.

"*Call Me Ruth* is a book that owes a lot to my immigrant heritage. My grandmother came to this country from Russia at the turn of the century. As with the father in the novel, my grandfather had come over first to earn the money to bring over the rest of his family. My mother, like Ruth, was born on the other side. Fanny, who in the novel is Ruth's mother, is based in part on my grandmother. The struggle between Fanny and Ruth is essentially their conflict over what it means to be an American. Ruth wants desperately not to be a 'greenhorn.' Her mother interprets this as a desire to shed her heritage like so much dirty clothing.

"America was supposed to have 'streets paved with gold.' I remember my grandparents talking about their expectations of America as a land of ideals, but what it came down to was cold cash, which wasn't so easy to earn. Sweatshops with dangerous working conditions were run by rapacious bosses. The Lower East Side was overcrowded. Bear in mind that many immigrants came from small villages in the countryside and had little, if any, exposure to city life. Such living conditions were a shock, to say nothing of a threat to health. In the old country, people knew what the dangers were; in America no one knew what to expect, and this drove many to desperation and early deaths.

"For *Call Me Ruth*, I used not only my own family history but sources made available to me by the International Ladies Garment Workers. Because the characters in my novel worked in textile sweatshops I needed to know a great deal about the details of that life. I spent days and days reading about early textile strikes, many of which were led by women. I was also able to talk with a very elderly woman who had participated in some of those strikes and had written a monograph on early efforts to organize textile workers. The 1911 strike figures largely in *Call Me Ruth*.

"*A Pocket Full of Seeds* is based on an interval in the life of Fanny Krieger, a friend of mine. Fanny, a French Jew, was trapped in France during World War II. Her family was rounded up by the Gestapo while Fanny was out visiting friends and eventually died in Auschwitz. Fanny lived in hiding and then was brought to America by a cousin. Originally, her cousin didn't want to get involved in her problems. After suffering a heart attack, however, he reconsidered the suggestion of a friend that God would look kindly on him if he were to do something that could save the young girl's life. So he brought her to America unbeknown to his family. There was a lot of bitterness about this newcomer. Here she had narrowly escaped the Nazis, was in a foreign country where she didn't speak the language and where even members of her own family didn't want her. It was very hard on her, but Fanny is an admirable woman and repaid the evils with kindness. I tried to deal with the fear people sometimes have of those they perceive as different, and the cruelty that is often born of that fear.

"For *A Pocket Full of Seeds*, I interviewed Fanny at length about her experiences in France and did a lot of reading about France during the occupation. I needed all kinds of details—what people wore, what they ate for breakfast, what the subtle social dynamics in a village caught in a web of fear and peril were. Jews, of course, were terrified of being sent to concentration camps and dealt with that possibility in a number of ways: by hiding, by fleeing, by joining the Resistance, and some, by hiding their Jewishness. There were non-Jews who sheltered Jews; others collaborated with the Germans; still others tried to walk a fine line of cooperation with the occupying Germans, but not to the degree of becoming vulnerable to accusations of collaboration. These were nightmarish times, and I tried in my book to capture the complexities and contradictions in both attitudes and actions.

"After the book came out, Fanny and I went around to schools giving talks to students a little younger than she was during the Second World War. She explained how the Nazis came and took her parents away and went around looking for her as well. Confused, the kids asked, 'Why? What did you do?' 'We hadn't done anything,' she would reply. 'We were Jews.' 'Yes, but what did you *do*?' 'Our crime, if you want to call it that, was that we were Jews.'

"Could you tell him please that Angie called, and I'll call him tomorrow about 8:30." ■ (From *Hello... Wrong Number* by Marilyn Sachs. Illustrated by Pamela Johnson.)

"It was hard for the kids to understand this. They seemed to assume that if one was arrested one was guilty. I was very disturbed at this apparent assumption that the authorities—governments, police, the military—are right until proven wrong. We must exercise vigilance over our governments and social institutions. It is not easy explaining the Holocaust to children, but we must. The only way to prevent future holocausts is to examine those that have already happened."

Several of Sachs' books have been banned by local school systems. "I have also received hate mail from parents and teachers. I once had a mother picket her local school protesting the presence of *Dorrie's Book*. This actually turned out to be very good for me. The faculty, principal and school board all read the book and came to the conclusion that it deserved a spot on their school library shelves. There was lots of discussion and the book undoubtedly got more attention in that town than it otherwise would have. The photograph of the mother picketing hangs in my office to this day. I must say I think it's good when parents take an interest in what their kids read. Reading is terribly, terribly important. I always respond to people who would censor my books, either in person or by mail, unless their letters are abusive. I am one hundred percent against the censorship of books. As censorship remains a hotly contested issue, those of us who feel strongly about it have a responsibility to speak out.''

When she is not working, Sachs reads voraciously. ''My favorite writer is Jane Austen. I'm a member of both the American and English Jane Austen Societies. I never travel without a copy of at least one of her novels. Her books are treasures of detail. She has such a wonderfully subtle sense of humor and as a stylist, she is unparalleled.

''For about eleven years I have been part of a women's reading group. We read only books by women. I think, that like many women of my generation, I was educated (brainwashed!) to believe that the great writers were men, and that the work of women writers was inherently 'minor.' For my part, I think that books by women tend to be richer in details of everyday life than books by men. A male teacher once said to me, 'In every book you write there is something about food.' I was startled because I hadn't been aware of that. But if you think about it, food is enormously important. Particularly during childhood. There are specific foods we associate with our day-to-day family life as well as holidays. The thought of a particular food can summon memories from long, long ago. And need we mention Proust and his 'Madeleine'?

''Even though some of my books deal with the larger issues like prejudice and power, as in *The Fat Girl*, I feel that the everyday details of life come through strong and clear as well. I'm not always sure of the larger truths but I do believe in the preciousness of all the little everyday matters that enrich most of our lives. And humor—what a blessing laughter is! I'm proud of my funny books like *Veronica Ganz, Fourteen* and *Almost Fifteen*, and I try, even in my more serious books, always to balance pain with laughter. I learned this from Charlie Chaplin. Whenever things begin to get a little heavy or mushy in his movies, a flower pot or a bag of garbage will fall out of a window and hit someone on the head.

''Books brought me great comfort as a child and still do. For many people, books are a place to go when things get tough. They can close doors as well as open them. I like to feel that I'm part of that continuing chain.''

——*Based on an interview by Marguerite Feitlowitz*

Sachs' works are included in the Kerlan Collection at the University of Minnesota.

HOBBIES AND OTHER INTERESTS: Walking, reading, and good company.

FOR MORE INFORMATION SEE: Times Literary Supplement, October 16, 1969; *Library Journal,* June 15, 1970, September, 1970; *New York Times Book Review,* November 7, 1971, August 19, 1979, September 20, 1981; *Publishers Weekly,* January 8, 1973; *Children's Literature Review,* Volume II, Gale, 1976; Doris de Montreville and Elizabeth D. Crawford, editors, *Fourth Book of Junior Authors and Illustrators,* H. W. Wilson, 1978; D. L. Kirkpatrick, *Twentieth-Century Chil-*

dren's Writers, St. Martin's Press, 1978, 2nd edition, 1983; *Los Angeles Times Book Review,* December 28, 1980; *Washington Post Book World,* July 12, 1981.

SAMACHSON, Joseph 1906-1980 (John Miller, William Morrison, Brett Sterling)

OBITUARY NOTICE—See sketch in *SATA* Volume 3: Born October 13, 1906, in Trenton, N.J.; died June 2, 1980, in Chicago, Ill. Chemist, educator, and author. Samachson devoted much of his career to chemical research, serving as a chief chemist at hospitals in both New York and Illinois. He taught as an assistant professor of biochemistry at the University of Illinois for eight years, after which time he joined the faculty at Loyola University as clinical professor of oral biology. Other accomplishments by Samachson include self-employment as a science writer, translator of technical articles, and contributor of individual works to scientific journals and general magazines. As a writer of fiction under the pen names John Miller, William Morrison, and Brett Sterling (a house pseudonym), Samachson collaborated with his wife, Dorothy, on a number of books. Two of their works, *Gold Digging* and *The Fabulous World of Opera*, were named Junior Literary Guild selections. Samachson's combined writings include such titles as *Let's Meet the Theatre, Masters of Music, The Russian Ballet and Three of Its Masterpieces, Murder of a Professor, Mel Oliver and Space Rover on Mars*, and *The Tenth Planet*, which is also the twelfth volume in the ''Captain Future'' paperback novel series.

FOR MORE INFORMATION SEE: Contemporary Authors, Volumes 17-20, revised, Gale, 1976; *Science Fiction and Fantasy Literature,* Volume 2: *Contemporary Science Fiction Authors II,* Gale, 1979. Obituaries: *New York Times,* June 12, 1980.

SCHONGUT, Emanuel 1936-

PERSONAL: Born May 19, 1936, in Monticello, N.Y.; son of Henry and Celia (Taub) Schongut. *Education:* Pratt Institute, B.F.A., 1958, M.F.A., 1961; graduate study, Pratt Graphic Art Center, 1957-58, and Art Students League, 1960-61. *Home address:* P.O. Box 247, Main St., Mountaindale, N.Y. 12763. *Agent:* Vicki Morgan, 194 Third Ave., New York, N.Y. 10003.

CAREER: Artist, author and illustrator of books for children. Worked at Pratt Institute, Brooklyn, N.Y. as an art instructor. Has also designed and illustrated book jackets. *Awards, honors: John Henry McCoy* was chosen one of Child Study Association's Children's Books of the Year, 1971; *Stone Man, Stone House* was selected for the American Institute of Graphic Arts Children's Book Showcase, 1971-72.

WRITINGS—For children; all self-illustrated; all edited by Kate Klimo; all published by Simon & Schuster, 1983: *Catch Kitten; Hush Kitten; Look Kitten; Play Kitten; Wake Kitten.*

Illustrator; all for children: Isaac Asimov, editor, *Tomorrow's Children: Eighteen Tales of Fantasy and Science Fiction*, Doubleday, 1966; Kurt Kläber, *The Outsiders of Uskoken Castle*, translated by Lynn Aubry, Doubleday, 1967; Eileen Rosenbaum, *The Kidnapers Upstairs*, Doubleday, 1968; Lillie D. Chaffin, *John Henry McCoy*, Macmillan, 1971; Anne Merrick Epstein, *Stone Man, Stone House*, Doubleday, 1972; Betty

EMANUEL SCHONGUT

Boegehold, *What the Wind Told*, Parents Magazine Press, 1974; Georgess McHargue, *Elidor and the Golden Ball*, Dodd, 1973; Seon Manley and Gogo Lewis, compilers, *Baleful Beasts: Great Supernatural Stories of the Animal Kingdom*, Lothrop, 1974; S. Manley and G. Lewis, compilers, *Bewitched Beings: Phantoms, Familiars, and the Possessed in Stories from Two Centuries*, Lothrop, 1974; S. Manley, *The Ghost in the Far Garden and Other Stories*, Lothrop, 1977; G. McHargue, *The Talking Table Mystery*, Doubleday, 1977; Jenny Hawkesworth, *The Lonely Skyscraper*, Doubleday, 1980; Mary Stewart, *A Walk in Wolf Wood: A Tale of Fantasy and Magic*, Morrow, 1980, revised edition, 1984. Also contributor of artwork to periodicals, including *Ingenue, Harper's, New York, Esquire, Redbook, Cosmopolitan,* and *McCall's.* Designed posters for Mobil ''Masterpiece Theatre'' and record album covers for RCA and CBS.

SIDELIGHTS: Born May 19, 1936, in Monticello, N.Y. ''I guess there was never any question that I would grow up to be an artist. I was 'the artist in the family,' the kid in school who was always drawing. When I was about nine, I won a 'Draw Me' contest advertised in a popular magazine, which entailed copying the head of a dog or a soldier (this was during World War II) and sending it in to the sponsor. The winner would get to go to a fancy art school. Well, as it turned out, the winner could indeed go, but at his parents' expense. I remember a representative of the contest coming to visit my parents and putting a lot of pressure on them. I'm happy to say they didn't give in—it was a shady deal.

''I grew up near Mountaindale [N.Y.]. We owned a farm with a big barn with chickens and goats. My father worked primarily as a waiter in restaurants and hotels in New York City. In the summer, we took in paying guests, and he worked with my mother in the farm/hotel business.

''When I was about six, the family moved to New York City. My sister, who was twelve years older than I, was graduating high school and it was thought that her opportunities would be better in the city. For three years we lived in the Bronx, which then was 'countrified' when compared with Manhattan.

But I remember it as being very confining and rather barren. I refused to be enrolled at the school. The principal took me to all the classrooms in every grade, saying, 'Emanuel, pick one. You may be in *any* class you wish.' But I didn't like any of them and wouldn't make a selection. So he made a deal with me: I could stay out of kindergarten provided I signed a contract *promising* that I would attend first grade the following year.

''School wasn't quite as bad as I had expected it would be. The worst thing was the predictability of it—having to go to the same place every day at the same time. To the extent that I could, I drew instead of doing class work.

''When I was nine, we moved back to the country. Odd as it may seem, I had more friends out there than in the city. I guess because I lived closer to kids in my class. By the time I was in fifth or sixth grade I absolutely knew that drawing was serious business. I was lucky to have had the same art teacher all through junior high and high school. He recognized that I was not only talented but serious and went out of his way to introduce me to art books. Botticelli was one of the first artists to make a deep impression on me. I was aware of Rembrandt and Picasso, but I don't think they had much of an influence on my work.

''I also spent a lot of time reading. English was my favorite subject after art. I loved folk tales from all over the world. The Brothers Grimm were favorites. My sister had some il-

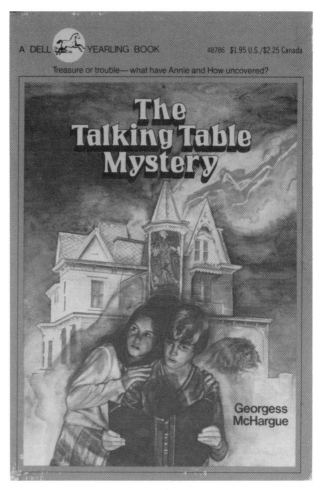

(Jacket illustration by Emanuel Schongut from *The Talking Table Mystery* by Georgess McHargue.)

lustrated primers and study books I loved to pore over. Maude and Miska Petersham were among the best illustrators. They did mostly line drawings with colored fill and were able to get a full color affect from using just two colors—blue and orange, for example. I have tried to do that myself, unsuccessfully, alas. As a boy, I copied the Petersham's illustrations; as an adult I have collected illustrated school books from the thirties, and their work figures largely in my collection.

"After high school—in the mid-fifties—I went to Pratt. The first year was introductory, and everyone pretty much took the same courses. In the second year I began taking commercial art and advertising courses. After a semester I realized that that wasn't for me—I wasn't very interested in photography and devoted my energy to illustration and graphic arts. My favorite classes were figure drawing. Teacher Richard Lindner had the most influence on me. He was still doing fairly realistic work at that time and even doing illustrations for magazines like *Seventeen*. I also studied with Fritz Eichenberg, renowned for his strong 'Prussian' personality. He wasn't as authoritarian as one was led to expect, but he was extremely demanding, especially if he didn't approve of what you were doing, or if you disagreed about something, he could come down on you with a crushing force. I took book illustration with him. One of our assignments was to do an illustrated autobiography. The text could be minimal and I remember doing a lot of leaf prints (I guess to denote my childhood in the country) for that project. I also did an illustrated book of *The Song of Songs*. This

John Henry sat down and hugged the dog to him. ▪
(From *John Henry McCoy* by Lillie D. Chaffin. Illustrated by Emanuel Schongut.)

was a difficult project. As I had elected to make etchings, I had to write out the text backwards on the etching plates. I also made illustrations for poems by Baudelaire.

"My years at Pratt were very, very happy. For the first time in my life I was surrounded by people as obsessed with art as I was. Upon graduation I had a portfolio full of etchings and not much idea of what I would do next. I landed a couple illustration jobs with magazines after which I promptly went back to Pratt to get a masters degree so I could teach. Not only did this keep the 'real world' at bay for a while, but I learned a lot, particularly from the students. As a grad student, I was assistant teacher of undergraduates. This was during the sixties and I was very impressed with the independence of mind of the undergraduates—if they were told to do a black and white line drawing, they did it in purple. They had a clear idea of what they wanted and needed to explore and went ahead and did it. We submitted more readily to authority. The curriculum for the masters degree included repertorial drawing, which consisted of going to a different place every week and making sketches. We went on the Staten Island Ferry, to Chinatown, and a host of neighborhoods.

"By this time I had some friends who were art directors for publishing houses. Through them, I began getting work illustrating book covers and magazine articles. I started working pretty steadily for *New York* magazine, whose founder, Milton Glazer, started Push Pin Studio, an affiliation of graphic artists. Push Pin had a signature style—flat surface, bold colors, urbane sophistication. It was very prestigious to be affiliated with it. It had practical advantages as well because the studio's work was in demand and because it held well-publicized exhibits. I was represented by Push Pin for about five years until the studio merged with another. And then, an art director at Doubleday for whom I'd been doing covers, offered me a picture book. While studying with Eichenberg, it had occurred to me that picture books would be a lot of fun, but I never—and still do not—wish to be 'typecast' exclusively as illustrator of children's books. I prefer illustrating fantasy to other types of books. I also love doing album covers; record companies give you so much freedom with regard to style, medium and colors. And because I do a lot of editorial illustrations, I enjoy doing posters and the chance to work large-scale.

"My favorite illustrating mediums are pencil and water colors. Pencil is easy to work with and allows changes with no problem. It can also look like other, more difficult mediums, rendering opacity associated with pen and translucency associated with wash. Water color, too, is extremely versatile, giving light, airy shades or a dense build-up. Working with water colors can be tricky, but for some reason I seem to have a natural feeling for them, and always have had.

"My working process is painstaking. My favorite time to work is at night. During the day I am more easily distracted. I always work with the television on. I can labor over a detail for several days—I won't let it go until it's right. I start off with a rough sketch, which I refine on layers of tracing paper. I trace and re-trace at every stage, all the way through the finishes. I am having a bit of a crisis now that the particular paper which I had been using is no longer available—it is very thin, yet strong and able to stand up to erasure, water and pressure. This pure linen English paper was made from castoff shirt collars from the days when men wore detachable collars. Because they no longer make shirts that way, the paper has become a 'dinosaur.' I am rapidly coming to the end of my supply. My back-up paper is also English and is also very strong, but more irregular than my linen favorite. In fact, it is so irregular that I cannot use it for water colors.

(From *Elidor and the Golden Ball* by Georgess McHargue. Illustrated by Emanuel Schongut.)

"I am beginning now to write my own children's books. My stories always begin with images, which come to me in a variety of ways. I recently saw a picture of a sea horse in *National Geographic*. Something about it grabbed me, and so it's going in the book I'm trying to write." The "Kitten" books were done for Walker Books of London and published in the U.S. by Simon & Schuster.

When he is not working, Schongut enjoys making pottery. "Pottery is a very recent interest for me, and I use the medium in a fairly eccentric way. I use the clay as a canvas. The shape of the object determines the kind of images I make on its surface. And here, too, I use tracing paper. I rough out an image, refine it via tracings and then trace it onto the pottery object. It's fun, I get to work in both two and three dimensions on one piece.

"I have also recently joined a figure drawing group. Four of us meet once a week, chip in to pay for a model and spend hours drawing. We have had the good fortune of getting an exceptional model. The woman, a karate student, does fantastic moves and can hold difficult positions for a long time. She becomes an extraordinary *structure,* not just a body in space.

The wolf...lifted his grey head towards the moon, and once more let out that long, terrible howl. ■ (From *A Walk in Wolf Wood: A Tale of Fantasy and Magic* by Mary Stewart. Illustrated by Emanuel Schongut.)

"I am a great collector. I never throw anything away. I collect children's books from the turn of the century illustrated by Kay Nielsen, Arthur Rackham, Edmund Dulac, Margaret Tarrent, among others. My house is filled with magazines—*National Geographic, Smithsonian, Metropolis, European Travel*—a most eclectic mix. I also love foreign magazines, particularly Italian and Japanese. The Japanese have very small illustrations scattered in dense banks of print. Thumbnail they might be, but these pictures tell you everything you need to know. Extraordinary. I don't have a clipping file as such, because I can never bring myself to cut up magazines. It seems so violent, somehow.

"Like most anyone who is crazy about images, I also love film. Fellini and Antonioni are my favorite directors. The recent 'boom' of Australian film is also very interesting to me. I just got a VCR and often work to old movies. When I see an extraordinary image, I often take a polaroid and then make an illustration.

"I don't do a lot of traveling, but I do love England and make a couple of trips every year. It's commonplace to say that London is a 'civilized' city, but it's true. And I find the English countryside so very congenial. I have a close friend from Pratt who lives there as a 'proper English eccentric,' a prototype I can easily relate to!

"I live in the rambling old house my family lived in. Although I'm tempted to move to England or California, there is something very compelling about the Catskill area. It's beautiful country, for one thing. Too, this region was once filled with thriving resorts. Now, a lot of those hotels, motels, and bungalow colonies have fallen into disuse. Eyesores according to many people, but I think they're wonderful. To me, they're like ruins of an all but vanished civilization. They cast a spell."

——*Based on an interview by Marguerite Feitlowitz*

FOR MORE INFORMATION SEE: Martha E. Ward and Dorothy A. Marquardt, *Illustrators of Books for Young People,* 2nd edition, Scarecrow, 1975.

SEGOVIA, Andrés 1893(?)-1987

OBITUARY NOTICE: Name originally Andrés Segovia Torres; born February 21, 1893 (some sources say February 18, 1894), in Linares, Andalusia, Spain; died of a heart attack, June 2, 1987, in Madrid, Spain; buried in San Isidro Cemetery, San Isidro, Spain. Classical guitarist, musical educator, and author. Segovia, widely acclaimed as one of the twentieth century's greatest musicians, enjoyed an almost eighty-year career playing classical guitar. Essentially self-taught, he made his professional debut at age fifteen (some sources say sixteen) in Granada, Spain. Received with enthusiasm, he then appeared in Madrid and Barcelona, Spain and in 1919 performed on tour in South American cities. In 1924 a fellow countryman and musician, cellist Pablo Casals, arranged for Segovia to make his Paris debut. The concert advanced his career considerably; within four years he embarked on his first tour of the United States, beginning at the Town Hall in New York City. Segovia's unique blend of lyrical expressiveness and dazzling technique earned him a Grammy Award in 1958. In 1967 he was honored by the Spanish Government with a Gold Medal for Meritorious Work. Segovia made adaptations of classical works and his own transcriptions available to succeeding generations of classical guitarists whom he also influenced through classroom instruction. With George Mendoza, he was the author of *Andrés Segovia, My Book of the Guitar: Guidance for the Young Beginner.* In 1976 an English translation of Segovia's memoirs appeared in print, titled *Andrés Segovia: An Autobiography of the Years 1893-1920.*

FOR MORE INFORMATION SEE: Current Biography, H. W. Wilson, 1964; Andrés Segovia, *Andrés Segovia: An Autobiography of the Years 1893-1920,* Macmillan, 1976; George Clinton, compiler and editor, *Andrés Segovia: An Appreciation,* Musical New Services, 1978; *Contemporary Authors,* Volume 111, Gale, 1984; *Who's Who in the World,* 8th edition, Marquis, 1986. Obituaries: *Chicago Tribune,* June 4, 1987, June 5, 1987; *New York Times,* June 4, 1987; *Times* (London), June 4, 1987; *Washington Post,* June 4, 1987; *Facts on File,* June 6, 1987; *Newsweek,* June 15, 1987; *Time,* June 15, 1987.

SEIDLER, Tor 1952-

PERSONAL: Born June 26, 1952, in Littleton, N.H.; son of John M. (an investor) and Jean (an actress; maiden name, Burch) Falls. *Education:* Stanford University, B.A., 1972. *Home:* 121 West 78th St., New York, N.Y. 10024. *Agent:* Harriet Wasserman, 137 East 36th St., New York, N.Y. 10016.

CAREER: Harcourt, Brace, Jovanovich, New York City, freelance contributor to Language Arts program, 1976-78; writer, 1978—. *Awards, honors:* Fiction Award from Washington State

TOR SEIDLER

Writer's Day, 1980, for *The Dulcimer Boy; Terpin* was named one of *New York Times*'s Outstanding Children's Books of the Year, 1982.

WRITINGS—Juvenile: *The Dulcimer Boy* (illustrated by David Hockney), Viking, 1979; *Terpin,* Farrar, Straus, 1982; *A Rat's Tale* (illustrated by Fred Marcellino), Farrar, Straus, 1985; *The Tar Pit,* Farrar, Straus, 1987. Contributor of articles and reviews to art magazines.

WORK IN PROGRESS: A novel set in New York City.

SIDELIGHTS: "I started trying to write children's books after working on elementary school readers for a language arts program at Harcourt, Brace. I always liked children's literature. My step-father used to tell terrific bedtime stories to my older brother and me. He made up 'episodes' which featured animal characters whose foibles were, in fact, ours. I like to alternate working on a children's book with adult fiction, but so far my two attempts in the latter area remain unpublished.

"I've been writing pretty much regularly for eleven years and every once in a while I think I'm beginning to get the hang of it, but most of the time I really wonder.

"I love living in New York City, though I often wish I could afford to escape more often. I seem to get to Europe about every two years."

SLOANE, Eric 1910(?)-1985

PERSONAL: Name originally Everard Jean Hinrichs; name changed about 1930; born February 27, 1910 (some sources say 1905), in New York, N.Y.; died of a heart attack, March 6, 1985, in New York, N.Y.; son of George Francis (a wholesale meat broker) and Marietta (O'Brien) Hinrichs; married several times. *Education:* Attended Art Students League, Yale University, 1929, New York School of Fine and Applied Art, 1935, and Massachusetts Institute of Technology. *Residence:* Cornwall Bridge, Conn.

CAREER: Artist, author, and meteorologist. Traveled across country, painting shop signs during the 1920s; painter of landscapes and cloudscapes, beginning 1939; designed exhibit, "Hall of Atmosphere," for American Museum of Natural History, New York, N.Y., 1949; designed murals for International Silver Co., Meriden, Conn., Morton Salt Co., Chicago, Ill., and National Air and Space Museum, Washington, D.C. Lecturer on cloudforms and meteorology, beginning 1940—; director of Weatherman of America, beginning 1950. First weatherman to appear on television. *Member:* National Academy of Design, Salmagundi Club, Wings Club, Dutch Treat Club (New York), Lotos Club. *Awards, honors:* Leadership award from Freedom Foundation of Valley Forge, 1964; Gold Medal from Hudson Valley Art Association, 1964; Gold Medal from National Academy of Design.

WRITINGS—All self-illustrated: *Clouds, Air and Wind,* Devin-Adair, 1941; *Camouflage Simplified,* Devin-Adair, 1942; *Gremlin Americanus: A Scrap Book Collection of Gremlins,* B. F. Jay, 1942; *Skies and the Artist: How to Draw Clouds and Sunsets,* Art Books for All, 1950; *Weather Book,* Little, Brown, 1952, published as *Eric Sloane's Weather Book,* Hawthorn, 1977; *American Barns and Covered Bridges,* Funk, 1954; *Almanac and Weather Forecaster,* Little, Brown, 1955; *Our Vanishing Landscape,* Funk, 1955, reissued, Ballantine, 1975; *American Yesterday,* Funk, 1956; *Book of Storms,* Duell, Sloan

ERIC SLOANE

& Pearce, 1956; *How You Can Forecast the Weather*, Fawcett, 1957; *The Seasons of America Past*, Funk, 1958.

Return to Taos: A Sketchbook of Roadside Americana (foreword by Bruce Catton), Funk, 1960; *Look at the Sky!*, Duell, Sloan & Pearce, 1961, revised and enlarged edition published as *Look at the Sky . . . and Tell the Weather*, World, 1970, published as *Look Up at the Sky and Tell the Weather*, Hawthorn, 1979; *Diary of an Early American Boy, Noah Blake, 1805* (young adult), Funk, 1962, reissued, Ballantine, 1977; *ABC Book of Early Americana: A Sketchbook of Antiquities and American Firsts* (juvenile), Doubleday, 1963; *Folklore of American Weather*, Duell, Sloan & Pearce, 1963; *A Museum of Early American Tools*, Funk, 1964; *A Reverence for Wood*, Funk, 1965; *The Sound of Bells* (juvenile), Doubleday, 1966; *An Age of Barns*, Funk, 1967, new edition published as *An Age of Barns: A Special Natural History Bonus*, 1976; *The Cracker Barrel*, Funk, 1967; *Eric Sloane's Don't: A Little Book of Early American Gentility* (adapted from *Don't: Manual of Mistakes and Improprieties Prevalent in Conduct and Speech* by Oliver Bell Bunce, Appleton, 1883), Funk, 1968; (with Edward Anthony) *Mr. Daniels and the Grange*, Funk, 1968; *The Second Barrel*, Funk, 1969.

I Remember America (autobiography), Funk, 1971; *Eric Sloane's Do: A Little Book of Early American Knowhow*, Walker, 1972; *The Little Red Schoolhouse*, Doubleday, 1972; *The Spirits of '76*, Walker & Co., 1973, published as *Spirits of Seventeen Seventy-Six*, Ballantine, 1976; *Recollections in Black and White*, Walker, 1974, enlarged edition, Crowell, 1978; *Eric Sloane's Sketchbook Calendar for 1979*, Crowell, 1978; *For Spacious Skies: A Meteorological Sketchbook of American Weather*, Crowell, 1978; *The Legacy*, Crowell, 1979. Also author of *Your Body in Flight*, 1943.

Collections: *Americana* (contains Volume I: *American Barns and Covered Bridges*, Volume II: *American Yesterday*, and

Volume III: *Our Vanishing Landscape*), Funk, 1957; *Eric Sloane's Double Barrel* (contains *The Cracker Barrel* and *The Second Barrel*), Funk, 1969; *Three By Sloane* (contains *The Diary of an Early American Boy, Noah Blake, 1805, A Museum of Eary American Tools*, and *A Reverence for Wood*), Funk, 1969; *The Do's and Don'ts of Yesterday* (contains *Eric Sloane's Don't: A Little Book of Early American Gentility* and *Eric Sloane's Do: A Little Book of Early American Knowhow*), Walker, 1972; *School Days* (contains *ABC Book of Early Americana: A Sketchbook of Antiquities and American Firsts* and *The Little Red Schoolhouse*), Doubleday, 1973.

Author of syndicated column, "It Makes You Think." Contributor of articles to periodicals, including *Popular Science Monthly, Nature, Science Digest, Outdoor Life, American Heritage, Better Homes and Gardens, Field and Stream, American Artist, Popular Mechanics*, and to Army and Navy manuals.

SIDELIGHTS: Sloane, whose original name was Everard Jean Hinrichs, was born at the beginning of the century in New York City. His father, a wealthy wholesale meat broker, owned homes in New York and New Jersey. "I was born into a home of the least artistic taste. Decoration consisted of a plaster-cast bust of Abraham Lincoln and two wall plaques of matching Indian heads; there was an oak-framed duo of litho-chromed 'Cupid Awake' and 'Cupid Asleep'; and on the wall behind an overstuffed couch there was a long, narrow print of a foxhunt with a frame that included a horse's bit and an imitation riding crop. I was probably reborn when I left home and began thinking for myself.

"One advantage of my having been raised in an inartistic family was that no one accused me of having talent; that sort of thing often frightens otherwise creative children into becoming business people. Discovering your own ability or reason for being is one of the rare and inspiring privileges of life, a deeply moving and a necessarily personal experience." [Eric Sloane, *I Remember America*, Funk, 1971.[1]]

The future artist did poorly in school, preferring instead to frequent the workshop studio of a neighbor, artist Herman Rountree. "The father of my first love, the girl next door, had inspired me to become an artist for he was one of the more successful black and white illustrators of that time. He did pictures for *Field and Stream* magazine, but his greater income came from doing pen and ink catalog illustrations for Butterick Patterns. I remember his robust ladies posed in long underwear and children in shorts, shirtwaists and panty waists. A page full of those drawings took him less than a day to do but they made for him as much money as the average man earned in a whole month. When other daddies had their breakfasts and were well on their way to work, Herman Rountree in his plus-four knickers and tweed cap, was out walking with his pipe and his dog before the day's work. That, I decided, was not work at all; it was a beautiful way of life, and so a good pen and ink artist I'd become. The artist delights himself to the extent of wanting nothing else in life but the privilege of expressing himself, so I am forever thankful for my decision. Now that I look back, I guess I was less in love with the girl next door than I was admiring of her father, for he was my secret hero.

"Generally speaking, the day of the hero belongs to the past. Today is an age when apprenticeship is looked upon as condescending, old-fashioned and according to present union ethics, against the law. Following in the footsteps of another, when I was a boy, was the wise and proper thing to do and the world was delightfully rich with all sorts of heroes. There were people to admire in politics, favorite writers, inspiring actors and artists whose techniques were worth practicing. Artist Herman Rountree's Butterick Patterns were not so inspiring to me but his *Field and Stream* covers and animal drawings certainly were, and my first decision was to become a nature artist. I recall collecting a file of his published work (art students called that a 'morgue') hoping to acquire his technique at nature art. But alas my abilities were not most suited to animal drawing; I remember having such difficulty with drawing horses' legs that I usually compromised by having my animals standing in high grass. Twenty-five dollars a week for doing lettering and simple commercial art seemed a better way for me to start, and I answered that ad.

''My first job, however, did not last very long but I do remember being impressed by the vast amounts of black ink and white paint being used at that time and wondering if instead

of drawing, I should not go into *that* business. Ink had always fascinated me; it seemed to have a wonderful aura of decision, finality and permanence.

''. . . As a child I had experimented with ink-making, trying early American methods with squeezed walnut hulls, indigo juice, madder, fruit acids and charred potato skins (or lamp soot) to produce a black. The manufacture of ink was already an interesting challenge, so either brave or stupid or simply young, I contacted manufacturing chemists and soon mixed what seemed to be a good waterproof black ink. Then I arranged to buy white showcard paint wholesale, so that I might be in both the black and white manufacturing business. I designed cartons and registered the name 'Nig' (for my black ink) and 'Chink' (for my Chinese white). Those made two great trade names then, but obviously would not be very popular now.

(From *Diary of an Early American Boy, Noah Blake, 1805* by Eric Sloane. Illustrated by the author.)

"My adventure into commerce, however, was short; I learned that the businessman and artist are two entirely different people. 'Nig' and 'Chink' never reached the public market and I was left with a thousand printed cartons and my first batch of waterproof black ink which I stored in a dozen cases of discarded Moxie bottles. . . ." [Eric Sloane, *Recollections in Black and White,* Crowell, 1974.[2]]

1920s. Still a teenager, Sloane drove across the United States, earning a substantial income painting shop signs along the way. "I was not the first artist to start as a lowly sign painter. Many of the early American painters began by doing tavern signs; furthermore it seemed to be a great way for a young fellow to see the country. The old-timers, of course, went by foot or on horseback and by comparison, in my Model-T, I traveled in grand style. A canvas awning which stretched from the auto top to the ground made a fine tent at night and, although it was before the invention of the rumble seat, there was still room in back for everything a young artist could want for his studio. If it had not been for my great supply of black ink, I might have specialized in pencil-sketching. But being frugal had its compensation, for to this day I still seem to think in black and white, in pen and ink.

"The idea of sketching the countryside, as I sign painted my way across the United States, was inspired by a twin-volume set given to me by my father, called *Picturesque America.* Done in pen and ink and steel engraving, Hudson River school artists had therein compiled a portfolio of drawings that dramatized the American scene; their presentations were so different and startling that most of my boyhood nightmares were enacted from pages of that book. There was something dramatic and haunting about them.

"The trick, it seems, was not to draw a landscape as one might see it from the comfort of any conventional viewpoint; instead, the artist climbed to a dizzy position aloft and looked down upon the scene. Then to add to the tenseness he would put tiny figures in a precarious position, ready to slip and fall into space. A balanced rock scene would be enhanced by the figure of a man sleeping peacefully and unconcerned under it; a simple town panorama would be viewed from the very top of a church spire; no cliff was complete without a couple of people standing inches from doom and one felt an immediate urge to shout out and warn them to stand back. This trick of the Hudson River school of art made each landscape an unforgettable experience. Besides inspiring me to do black and white sketches of the American scene, I am sure it also influenced my interpretation of the dramatic in both thinking and writing. I still have those two volumes and I still find enjoyment and fascination in its unusual presentations."[2]

Sloane avoided the major cities along his cross-country route, preferring to ply his sign-painting trade in small towns and villages throughout America. "My studios, as I progressed south and west of Pennsylvania, were destined to be what we now call 'motels.' That word had not yet been invented, but one stopped instead at a 'cabin camp.' For one dollar you were entitled to clean sheets, a tiny stove equipped with corn husks (which started at once and gave a most satisfying heat) and the use of a communal washhouse and toilets in an outside stall. My first 'studio' was near Intercourse, Pennsylvania, where I was asked to do a roadside sign for them: 'Clean beds, Intercourse Cabin Camp.' I think I reworded that sign. For a dollar a day, these motels of yesteryear made excellent places for me to stay long enough to do posters and signs for the

(From *A Reverence for Wood* by Eric Sloane. Illustrated by the author.)

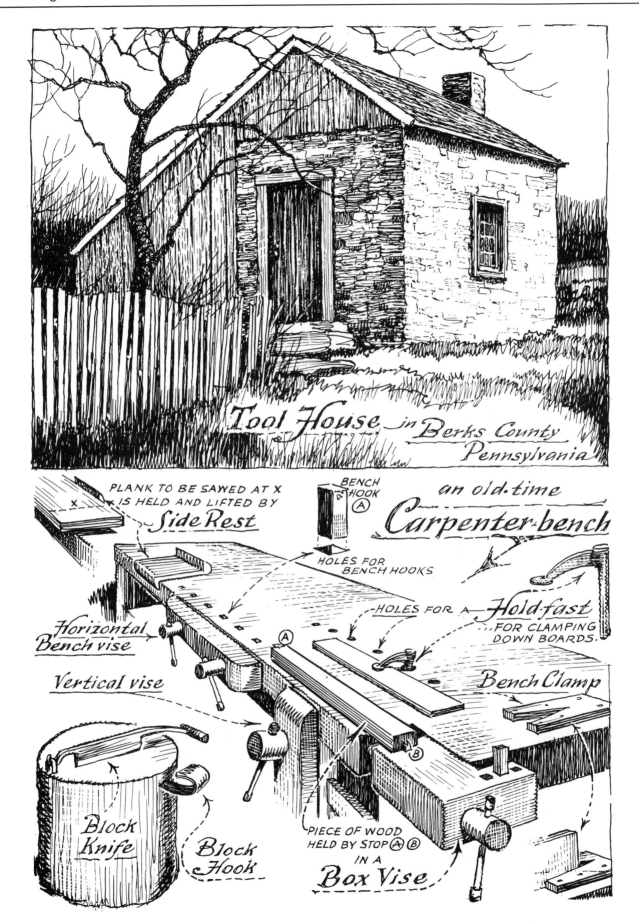

(From *A Museum of Early American Tools* by Eric Sloane. Illustrated by the author.)

community and ready myself for the next adventure along the road.

". . . The smaller the community, the more signs were needed, and an itinerant sign painter could enter a tiny midwest village in the morning and leave by evening some fifty dollars richer, which was really something in those days. The result of having to travel backroad and around civilization was priceless luck for anyone looking for rural Americana.

"From New Orleans, my mobile sign shop headed west and soon reached another Bohemia of that day at Taos, New Mexico, where I settled long enough to finish off my entire supply of black ink. I even sold some of it to the Indians and you can still find occasional Taos pottery decorated with my home-made ink.

"I set up a little sign shop on the outskirts of Taos, at 'Kiker's Cabin Camps' on the road to Cimmaron Canyon, where the Taos Indians frequently danced for the tourists. The dance leader named Juanito Luhan taught me dance steps and some of their songs well enough to become their impresario. I made posters and announcements, and we went as far as Raton and Pueblo, entertaining at fairs and theaters. But most of all I recall making a hoop for Juanito's young nephew; the Indians had never seen such a toy but little Bobby had ideas other than rolling it along with a stick—he began to *dance* with it. And that, believe it or not, was the origination of the well-known 'ancient American Indian hoop dance.' Now they use as many as six hoops in this dance.

"With my base at Taos, my Model-T took me to deserted mining places, abandoned missions, ghost villages and the ruins of ancient New Mexican culture, an area which provided endless subjects for drawings. The black and white technique was perfect for depicting that blasting sunlight and devouring shadow so typical of the bright western landscape. Western

artists who paint in color *on location* are frequently blinded by the intense sunlight, resulting in hazy pastel scenes that seemed bathed in mist, quite the opposite of the true western vision which is crystal clear and where even distant mountains loom distinct.

"My pen and ink drawings sold quickly to tourists and provided me with money for the paints that wooed me away from monochrome and started me on a half-century of painting in color with oils."[1]

1929. Returning East, Sloane spent a year at the Yale School of Fine Arts and joined the Art Students League of New York. ". . . At art school, I found my lessons disappointing and unrewarding and I decided that perhaps analyzing art itself and writing a paper on the subject of drawing might give me better results than my trying to learn anything from teachers. Presumptuous upstart that I must have been, there nevertheless was worthwhile thought in my unusual theory that primarily, art deals in *shapes* rather than *outlines,* and therefore the very first thing an art student should do is learn to see the world about him only in *shapes,* forgetting outlines.

"It must have exasperated my professors that I refused to use my stick of charcoal in the orthodox manner (like a pencil) to outline drawings with its point. Instead, I laid the stick flat upon the paper and scrubbed in large masses of shadow and created major shapes of light: details and outlines were added almost reluctantly afterward. I considered art a reflection of life itself; and in life, after all, overall observation, planning and purpose should come first while details should be considered later. An inspired revolutionist was I.

"My schooling was obviously short-lived so I left my studies to set about trying to see the world in shapes. A portrait study, or a still life or landscape scene held no promise at all for me unless it was first an interesting composition of *shapes.* A

a Dissatisfied American, 1902 style.

(From *American Yesterday* by Eric Sloane. Illustrated by the author.)

(From *American Yesterday* by Eric Sloane. Illustrated by the author.)

barn, for example, might be completely unsuitable to paint at midday (casting little or no shadow), but in the early morning or in the late afternoon when it was transformed into a composition of triangles of shadow and rectangles of light instead of just an outlined barn, that same structure became an exciting and irresistible subject. . . .

"I was convinced that the students who learned to ignore outlines and see everything in shapes would at once become an artist even before he tried his hand at drawing. Art school, with its outlining first and adding shading later of vases and plaster casts and skinny men in jockstraps, was not for me. Leonardo da Vinci said, 'The boundary of bodies is the least of all things. O painter, do not surround your bodies with lines!'

"My manuscript on this subject never did reach the publishing stage but the album of pen and ink illustrations, which were involved, led me off into a lifetime adventure in black and white that has ever since been my constant enjoyment."[2]

1930s. Influenced by John Sloan, one of the realistic painters of the American "Ash Can School," he renamed himself Eric Sloane. "When I was a young art student in New York City I was privileged to sit at a luncheon table with George Luks and John Sloan while they discussed recognition. 'If only a young painter might work for twenty-five years or so, learning and improving his style, but using an assumed name and selling just for expenses,' observed Luks. 'Then after he felt his work was really ready, he could start anew with his true name, increasing his price tenfold . . . perhaps that would be an answer. So many painters at middle age find themselves haunted by the inferior work of their youth. Some of my own early work sickens me!'

"John Sloan laughed. 'Just last week,' he said, 'I bought one of my earlier sketches from a collector, only for the purpose of destroying it. A good idea might be to work the required time without signing your name at all. Or to destroy all of your early work, as fast as you do it.'

"I didn't forget that conversation and I thought a lot about it during the next week of art classes. Perhaps I could work under an assumed name until my work satisfied me completely! Anyway, my real name, Everard Jean Hinrichs, was a difficult

name for people to remember. Most everyone pronounced the Dutch name 'Hinrichs' like the German 'Heinrich,'" and those were the strained postwar years when anything German was unpopular. Why not a simple name like 'Eric Sloan'?

"I did a quick sketch of Luks and Sloan at the table and I signed it 'Eric Sloan.' Then, just to be different, I added an 'e' to the 'Sloan.' It looked fine. Where the 'Eric' came from, I don't recall; but I remember being pleased that it was the middle four letters of the word 'American,' and so I kept it.

"I really intended to use the assumed name of Eric Sloane only until my painting reached some point of perfection. But in time I learned that no painter of worth is ever satisfied; I have yet to do a piece of work which couldn't in some way be improved. I am still, thank God, a student, dissatisfied with my work, and I still sign it 'Eric Sloane.'

"I shall always feel I received some sort of heritage from John Sloan and I apologize for having added the 'e.' But now that I have earned an N.A. [National Academy of Design membership] to add to the name, I feel better about it; I've even stopped wondering about ever returning to my real name of Everard Jean Hinrichs. Secretly, I'm afraid that should I go back to that name, I'd fall into dust like a mummy that has been preserved only by being protected from the air of the outside world.

"Like John Sloan, I have often been haunted by samples of my early work. One sketch that I gave to a waiter as a tip during the lean years came back to me many years later when I found it in a gallery and bought it. Painted on Masonite board, it made a bright and strange flame in my fireplace, and I felt much better for having burned it. I still buy back my early works (if the prices are right) for the sole purpose of destroying them.

"Somehow or other I have always detested the idea of keeping samples of one's work. I've known so many art students who 'just happen to have a portfolio of sketches' with them, and who 'would really enjoy a criticism.' I'm sure if you carry your early work around with you long enough, you will finally fall in love with it, but to me, the idea is a bit like carrying around some old candy from a cooking school class and asking chefs to taste it and pass on its merits. My advice to any art

(From *Recollections in Black and White* by Eric Sloane. Illustrated by the author.)

Eric Sloane with wife, Ruth, and dog, Spook.

student is to paint fast and furiously, and then sell, hide, or destroy everything done during the first ten years. In my case I wish it had been forty years.''[1]

1939. Began painting ''cloudscapes.'' ''It was Wiley Post who first interested me in the idea of painting the sky. On practice robot flights in the *Winnie Mae* he would sometimes take me along; with his one eye he would pick out the wonders of clouds and explain the mechanics of weather. 'Some day,' said Wiley, 'a fellow will come along and paint nothing but the sky itself. Where else can you find higher mountains? Look at that cumulonimbus over yonder—twice the height of the Matterhorn and twice as beautiful. Where else but up here could you see a better landscape of clouds?'

'''What you mean is a *cloudscape,*' I said. 'And I wouldn't be surprised if the first fellow to try painting cloudscapes turns out to be me.'

''My first cloudscape was a painting of the thunderhead I saw that day from the *Winnie Mae,* and I hung it in the Roosevelt Field Inn (that old airport is now a vast shopping center). The canvas was a menacing portrayal of a cumulonimbus such as few people other than flyers had ever seen. I felt certain no one would wish to buy so dread and mysterious a picture, so I put a 'For Sale'' tag on it with what I thought was an outlandish price. But someone who was familiar with the subject did buy it: a check arrived from a Miss Amelia Earhart.

''The experience of looking *down* at the clouds was a brand-new twentieth-century happening; yet since I first coined the word 'cloudscape' nearly fifty years ago, few painters have chosen to paint that scene. With the plains more vast than those on earth, mountains that would dwarf the Alps, and canyons as much as two miles deep, the cloudscape can be a powerfully moving subject.

''I remember my first business card. It identified me as an 'aviation artist.' People with enough money to own their own planes had the money to buy paintings of them, so business was good. But as time went by, the sky took up more room in my pictures and the airplanes became tinier, until I was finally content to paint just plain sky. People would ask, 'Where's the plane?' Or my friends would say, 'You mean you paint *clouds*—just plain sky?' That *did* it. I had chanced upon the career with the least competition—I would be a sky painter!''[1]

1940. Sloane's fascination with clouds led to an in-depth study of meteorology. ''My decision to paint the sky prompted me to learn first what the sky was all about. And the best way to learn, I decided, was to write a book about it. At least that was my way, so I began writing. I called that first book *Clouds, Air and Wind,* and the fact that I was actually learning meteorology while I wrote about it turned out to be doubly valuable, for later the reader learned the subject along with me. 'You don't talk down to your audience' was the comment of the Army Air Force when they accepted the book as a weather manual. 'It is almost as if you were learning the subject as you wrote the book,' they said. How right they were!''[1]

1949. ''Five more books about weather followed. I even tried my hand at being the first weatherman on TV, but I still didn't feel I had become a master of skyscapes. I remember going to the American Museum of Natural History in New York. 'What do you have here about the atmosphere?' I asked. 'I want to learn more about the sky.' The guard didn't think there was any such exhibit, but he sent me to the curator's office.

'''This isn't an aviation museum,' I was told. 'We have nothing at all on meteorology. Our exhibits are entirely confined to natural history.'

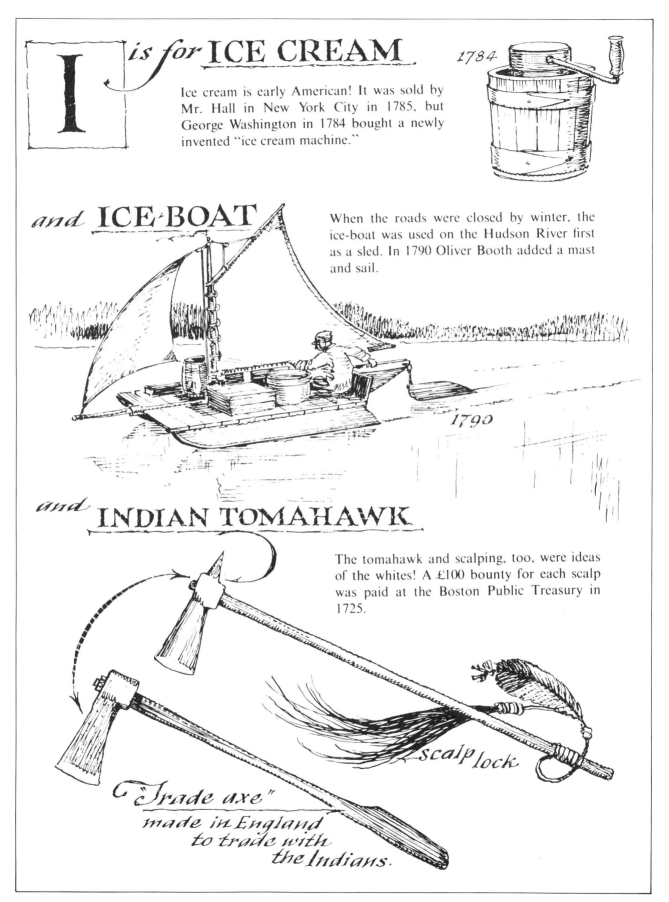

I is for ICE CREAM

1784

Ice cream is early American! It was sold by Mr. Hall in New York City in 1785, but George Washington in 1784 bought a newly invented "ice cream machine."

and ICE-BOAT

When the roads were closed by winter, the ice-boat was used on the Hudson River first as a sled. In 1790 Oliver Booth added a mast and sail.

1790

and INDIAN TOMAHAWK

The tomahawk and scalping, too, were ideas of the whites! A £100 bounty for each scalp was paid at the Boston Public Treasury in 1725.

scalp lock

*"Trade axe"
made in England
to trade with
the Indians.*

(From *ABC Book of Early Americana: A Sketchbook of Antiquities and American Firsts* by Eric Sloane. Illustrated by the author.)

''I reminded him that all natural history happened to be confined to atmosphere—that the moon has no natural history simply because it lacks atmosphere. 'The most important thing you should have here,' I said, 'is a Hall of Atmosphere.' The curator's attitude made me feel unwelcome. 'Sorry, young fellow,' he said curtly, 'we are limited in funds at the present time. Therefore we do not contemplate any new displays like that. Good day.'

''I still think you should have a Hall of Atmosphere,' I insisted. 'I'll see if I can find you the money to build one.' And I left. I'm sure they were glad to be rid of me.

''I then went to a neighbor of mine, William Willetts, and told him about my problem. 'I'd like you to introduce me to your friend Trubee Davison, who's the head of the museum and seems to be quite a man. I think I can interest him in a Hall of Atmosphere.' Bill heard me out. 'I have an even better idea,' he said. 'I've been wanting to create some sort of memorial for my son Prentice who was killed in an air crash. Why don't I donate the money for your Hall of Atmosphere?' We shook hands on it.

''Bill transformed his squash court into a studio workshop, and I began building three-dimensional models of weather phenomena. Our little company needed a weather-sounding name but I never liked the ancient misleading word *meteorology* which started when people thought meteors caused the weather. So I invented the word *airology* (which has since become a proper scientific word) and 'Airology Workshop' became a busy little factory. There were soon Plexiglas cold and warm fronts and tornadoes and hurricanes. Lightning flashed, winds blew, and simulated rain fell from plastic clouds. I wanted movement in the displays, so I used those circular fans I had seen in artificial fireplaces (the heat of an electric light bulb turns tiny fins to create the illusion of flickering flames). Within a year or so the Willets Memorial was installed in the museum as the very first Hall of Atmosphere anywhere.

''But that was long ago. The fiber clouds soon turned black from the impurities in New York's air, and the fan-light motion was later replaced by electric-motor-driven illumination effects. I suppose if I went back to see my brainchild now, I would find it quite different from the original.''[1]

Antique weather instruments became another new interest. Before long, Sloane was collecting a wide variety of relics, including farm and weather implements and wood working tools. His collection eventually became so large that he contributed a number of artifacts to the Sloane-Stanley museum of Early American Tools in Kent, Connecticut. ''There's no doubt about it: one thing leads strangely to another. It seemed appropriate for me as a weatherman to collect weather vanes, so I began collecting them before they reached the expensive antique market. Even with my limited income, I managed at that time to gather enough of them to make walking about my home a problem. Finally I gave up keeping the clumsy finials with the north, east, south and west initials and just collected the decorative statuary. I recall buying one old barn (to use the siding to make frames for my paintings) for one hundred dollars; the weather vane on it had sold the week before for three hundred! It later sold to a folklore museum for three thousand dollars. . . .''[1]

Sloane's interest in the past led to an exploration of history and a score of books on pre-industrial America, which he researched, wrote and illustrated. ''Most of my lifetime has been spent in painting and writing, with the steadfast purpose of either reviving or retrieving certain worthwhile things of

the American past, yet always without being bitter about present-day devastation. Perhaps my nostalgic dreams did hide an occasional bitterness, but the richness and pleasure derived from rekindling earlier times overcame it. I think I simply left animosity and criticism to the angry young men of my time. But now, in good and patriotic cause, I ask the right to become an angry *old* man, because in my heart for a long while there has been a small voice of despair for the survival of America which I believe deserves to be heard at this time.

''As far as our beautiful countryside is concerned, that particular part of the American heritage has already gone wherever we have 'developed' it. The urge to become rich at the expense of the land, to commercialize the countryside at the expense of the landscape, is a recognized national trait. The winds of change certainly have reached tornadolike speed in devastating our landscape.

''The challenge for the survival of America is currently much greater than it was when our country began because now we are confused millions instead of a dedicated few. Moderation, peace, decency, freedom, discipline, devotion to country, reverence for God—almost everything on which our nation was originally founded, are suddenly on trial: the real danger is that we tolerate it.''[1]

1964. Given the Leadership Award of the Freedom Foundation of Valley Forge. Among his many accomplishments, Sloane held the distinction of being the person who initiated the custom of ringing bells throughout the nation on July 4th. ''. . . Life without tradition can only produce art without memory; both suffer from amnesia.

''Those who have lost sight of their past are condemned to relive it, and it seems that this rule, according to history, applies to nations as well as to individuals. Living only in the *past* produces the disease of nostalgia; living only in the *present* produces irresponsibility; living only in the *future* is impossible because the future is yet to be. The real art of living, I believe, is blending equally the past, present, and concern for the future. And real art, it seems to me, should reflect this principle.''[1]

March 6, 1985. Died of a heart attack in New York City. ''My love affair with the American countryside began less than fifty years ago, yet very little of what I knew then remains untouched or unspoiled. But I am thankful for having known it, and glad that I can recollect bits of it and pass them on. Such is the gratifying privilege of being writer and painter.''[1]

FOR MORE INFORMATION SEE: Publishers Weekly, September 20, 1941; *San Francisco Chronicle*, November 25, 1954, November 27, 1958, December 13, 1960; *New York Times*, December 11, 1955; *Christian Science Monitor*, December 15, 1955, January 31, 1972; *New York Herald Tribune Lively Arts*, January 19, 1961; *Time*, January 18, 1963; *New Yorker*, November 30, 1963; *American Artist*, March, 1965, July, 1976, June, 1977; *Reader's Digest*, June, 1966, March, 1972; *Sunday News* (New York), January 15, 1967; Lee Kingman and others, compilers, *Illustrators of Children's Books: 1957-1966*, Horn Book, 1968; *Chicago Sunday Tribune*, December 11, 1969; Eric Sloane, *I Remember America*, Funk, 1971; *Conservationist*, October, 1972; *Current Biography Yearbook*, H. W. Wilson, 1973; E. Sloane, *Recollections in Black and White*, Walker, 1974; S. K. Oberbeck, ''Treasure of Tradition,'' *Newsweek*, January 27, 1975. Obituaries: *Newsday*, March 8, 1985; *New York Times*, March 8, 1985; *Los Angeles Times*, March 9, 1985; *School Library Journal*, May, 1985.

SMITH, Emma 1923-

PERSONAL: Born August 21, 1923, in Newquay, Cornwall, England; married R. L. Stewart-Jones, 1951 (died, 1957); children: one son, one daughter. *Agent:* Curtis Brown Ltd., 162-168 Regent St., London W1R 5TA, England.

CAREER: Free-lance writer. *Awards, honors:* Atlantic Award, 1947; John Llewellyn Rhys Memorial Prize, 1949, for *Maidens' Trip;* James Tait Memorial Prize, 1950, for *The Far Cry;* Black Memorial Prize, 1950; *New York Herald Tribune*'s Children's Spring Book Festival honor book, 1964, for *Out of Hand; Boston Globe-Horn Book* honor book, and Carnegie Medal commendation, both 1973, both for *No Way of Telling.*

WRITINGS: Maidens' Trip (adult novel), Putnam, 1949; *The Far Cry* (adult novel), MacGibbon & Kee, 1949, Random House, 1950; *Emily: The Story of a Traveller* (juvenile; illustrated by Katherine Wigglesworth), Nelson, 1959, published as *Emily the Traveling Guinea Pig,* Astor-Honor, 1960; *Emily's Voyage* (juvenile; illustrated by Irene Haas; *Horn Book* honor list), Harcourt, 1962; *Out of Hand* (juvenile; illustrated by Antony Maitland), Macmillan, 1963, Harcourt, 1964; *No Way of Telling* (juvenile; ALA Notable Book), Atheneum, 1972; *The Opportunity of a Lifetime* (adult novel), Doubleday, 1980. Also author of short stories.

FOR MORE INFORMATION SEE: Martha E. Ward and Dorothy A. Marquardt, *Authors of Books for Young People,* 2nd edition, Scarecrow, 1971; D. L. Kirkpatrick, editor, *Twentieth-Century Children's Authors,* St. Martin's, 1978, 2nd edition, 1983; James Vinson, editor, *Contemporary Novelists,* 3rd edition, St. Martin's, 1982.

ROBERT PAUL SMITH

SMITH, Robert Paul 1915-1977

PERSONAL: Born April 16, 1915, in New York, N.Y.; died January 30, 1977, in New York, N.Y.; son of Joseph Elkin (a manufacturer) and Esther (Breckstone) Smith; married Elinor Jane Goulding (an artist and writer), February 7, 1940; children: Daniel Paul, Joseph Robert. *Education:* Columbia College (now University), B.A., 1936. *Agent:* Monica McCall, 667 Madison Ave., New York, N.Y. 10022.

CAREER: Author. Wrote continuity for radio for the Columbia Broadcasting System, beginning 1936. *Awards, honors: Jack Mack* was chosen one of American Institute of Graphic Arts Children's Books, 1958-60.

WRITINGS: So it Doesn't Whistle, Harcourt, 1941; *The Man with the Gold-Headed Cane,* Holt, 1943; *The Journey,* Holt, 1943; *Because of My Love,* Holt, 1946; *The Time and the Place,* Simon & Schuster, 1952; (with Max Shulman) *The Tender Trap,* Random House, 1955, three-act play under the same title (first produced on Broadway at the Longacre Theatre, October 13, 1954), Dramatists Play Service, 1956; "*Where Did You Go?*" "*Out.*" "*What Did You Do?*" "*Nothing.*" (illustrated by James J. Spanfeller), Norton, 1957; *How to Do Nothing with Nobody, All Alone by Yourself* (illustrated by wife, Elinor Goulding Smith), Norton, 1958; *Where He Went: Three Novels,* Viking, 1958; *Translations from the English* (illustrated by Roberta Macdonald), Simmon & Schuster, 1958; *And Another Thing* (poems), Norton, 1959.

Jack Mack (juvenile; Junior Literary Guild selection; illustrated by Erik Blegvad), Coward, 1960; *Crank: A Book of Lamentations, Exhortations, Mixed Memories and Desires, All Hard or Chewy Centers, No Creams,* Norton, 1962; *How to Grow Up in One Piece,* Harper, 1963; *When I Am Big* (juvenile; illustrated by Lillian Hoban), Harper, 1965; *Nothingatall, Nothingatall, Nothingatall* (juvenile; illustrated by Alan E. Cober), Harper, 1965; *Got to Stop Draggin' that Little Red Wagon Around,* Harper, 1969; *Lost and Found: An Illustrated Compendium of Things No Longer in General Use* (illustrated by Gerald Gersten), Charterhouse, 1973; *Brooklyn at Play: A Social and Cultural History of Brooklyn at the Turn of the Century,* Revisionist Press, 1976. Also author of "Forget This Night," a three-act play.

ADAPTATIONS: "The Tender Trap" (motion picture), starring Frank Sinatra, Debbie Reynolds, David Wayne, and Celeste Holm, Metro-Goldwyn-Mayer, 1955.

SIDELIGHTS: Smith was born in New York City on April 16, 1915. "On my block, when I was a kid, there was a lot of loose talk being carried on . . . about how a father was supposed to be a pal to his boy. This was just another of those stupid things that grownups said. It was our theory that the grownup was the natural enemy of the child, and if any father had come around being a pal to us we would have figured he was either a little dotty or a spy. What we learned we learned from another kid. I don't remember being taught how to play mumbly-peg. . . . When you were a little kid, you stood around while a covey of ancients of nine or ten played mumbly-peg, shifting from foot to foot and wiping your nose on your sleeve and hitching up your knickerbockers, saying, 'Lemme do it, aw come on, lemme have a turn,' until one of them struck you in a soft spot and you went home to sit under the porch by yourself or found a smaller kid to torture, or loused up your sister's rope-skipping, or made a collection of small round stones. The small round stones were not *for* anything, it was just to have a collection of small round stones.

''What we knew as kids, what we learned from other kids, was not tentatively true, or extremely probable, or proven by science or polls or surveys. It was so. I suppose this has to do with ontogeny recapitulating phylogeny. We were savages, we were in that stage of the world's history when the earth stood still and everything else moved. I wrote on the flyleaf of my schoolbooks, and apparently every other kid in the world did, including James Joyce and Abe Lincoln and I am sure Tito and Fats Waller and Michelangelo, in descending order my name, my street, my town, my county, my state, my country, my continent, my hemisphere, my planet, my solar system. And let nobody dissemble: it started out with me, the universe was the outer circle of a number of concentric rings, and the center point was me, me, me, sixty-two pounds wringing wet with heavy shoes on. I have the notion, and perhaps I am wrong, that kids don't feel that way any more. Damn Captain Video! And also, I am afraid, damn 'The Real True Honest-to-God Book of Elementary Astrophysics in Words of One Syllable for Pre-School Use.'

''Good books were either library books or birthday presents. Bad books were fifty cents apiece, new, and were tradeable. Bad books were *The Boy Allies, The Motor Boys, Tom Swift, Sax Rohmer.* They were not read so much as devoured. There was an established rate of exchange, and it took at least three *Rover Boys*—they were, for some reason, held in much scorn in my literary circle—for even not the latest *Tom Swift.* The newest *Tom Swift* was read by three people at once, one holding the book and two saying, 'Not so fast,' or 'Come on, fa Crise sake, turn the page.'

''This lasted only until we found Jules Verne. What a surprise that was, finding out that there was somebody better than Victor Appleton—and in the library, honest, I swear, I'll show ya!

''Then an uncle of mine gave me a complete set of Mark Twain, and I was, and am, equipped for life. I started in at Volume One, and read through to the end of Volume Twenty. I concluded that there was very little else of value written down, and I went back to Volume One and started all over again. I have never stopped doing this. I was told the other evening that someone, either Thurber or Mencken, or both, looked forward to old age as sitting on a screened porch reading *Huckleberry Finn.* With, for me, maybe Louis Armstrong playing 'Beale Street Blues' in a handy grape arbor, and a jug of Paddy's Irish whiskey like it used to be, close at hand.

''However.

''I found Mark Twain, and my education as an adult began.'' [Robert Paul Smith, *''Where Did You Go?'' ''Out.'' ''What Did You Do?'' ''Nothing.''* Norton, 1958.[1]]

Smith graduated from Columbia University and went on to work for the Columbia Broadcasting System. Beginning in 1936, he wrote continuity for such radio performers as Benny Goodman, Frank Sinatra, and Guy Lombardo. He married a fellow writer, Elinor Jane Goulding, in 1940. ''. . . I have two boys of my own, I live in a suburb where three out of three fathers are up to here with catching that commuting train and

(From the movie ''The Tender Trap,'' starring Debbie Reynolds and Frank Sinatra. Produced by Metro-Goldwyn-Mayer, 1955.)

paying that mortgage and burning those leaves and shoveling that snow, and when all else is indefensible, say, 'But it's a wonderful place to raise children.' Spock and Gesell and others of that Ilg are the local deities, the school teachers speak of that little stinker from Croveny Road as 'a real challenge,' there are play groups and athletic supervisors and Little Leagues and classes in advanced finger painting and family counselors and child psychologists. . . .

''My little boy was mooning around the house the other day— it is one of the joys of being a writer that occasionally when *I* am mooning around the house because I haven't the vaguest idea of what to do about the second act, or the last chapter, or Life, or why I don't have an independent income or a liquor store or a real skill like a tool-and-die maker or a lepidopterist or a mellophone player—I can slope downstairs and trap a child. The littler boy was mooning around. I was mooning around. He had no idea what to do with himself because his room is full of woodburning kits and model ships to be made out of plastic and phonographs and looms and Captain Kangaroo Playtime Kits and giant balloons and plaster of paris and colored pencils and compasses and comic books and money. I will straighten this little bugger out, I said, I will pass on to him the ancient knowledge of his sire, I well teach him a little something about the collective unconscious, by God I will. 'Did you ever make a buzz-saw out of a button?' I opened brightly. He thought for a while, and tried to remember what a button was, and concluded that it was something like a zipper, but he didn't know what a buzz-saw was. He decided that a buzz-saw was like what I almost cut my thumb off with in the cellar and had out of the house by nightfall. 'First thing we need is a big button,' I said, and then we went into that thing about, 'I don't know where there's a button, for the love of God ask your mother, of course there's a button around the house. Where? In the button box.'

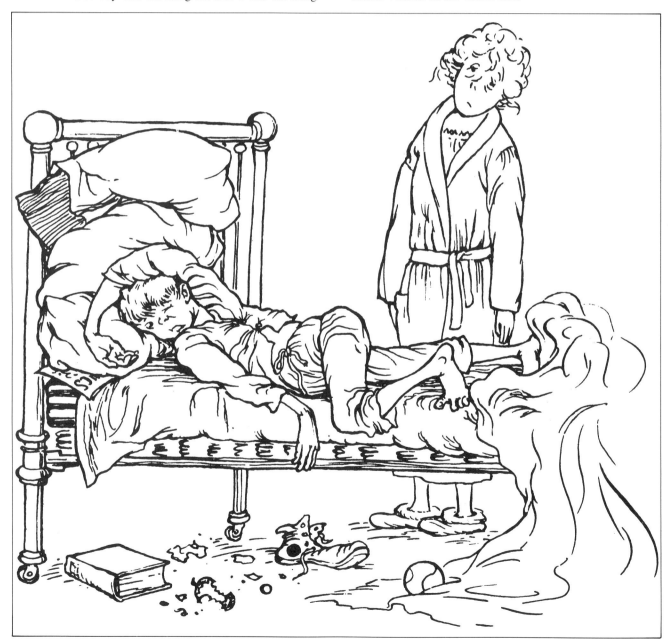

My stomach hurts...and my head and my nose and my hair, too. ■ (From *Translations from the English* by Robert Paul Smith. Illustrated by Roberta Macdonald.)

(From the stage production of "The Tender Trap," starring Kim Hunter and Robert Preston. Opened on Broadway at the Longacre Theatre, October 13, 1954.)

"That's when I found out we don't have a button box. We went to our neighbor's and after a while they found a button box. Not their button box, but one that Grandma had had. We got a big button. I strung it with a loop of silk thread, and it didn't work and the thread broke. I suppose nobody bothers making silk thread strong now, if you want strong thread you use nylon. When I was a kid, silk thread was so strong you practically cut the tip of your finger off breaking it. *That* was thread. We went to look for string, but all there was was a ball of very good string that was too thick. We went back to the neighbor with the button box and in *her* kitchen drawer there was an assortment of bits of string. We made a buzz-saw. He took it to day camp with him. The other kids thought it was a new kind of yo-yo and wanted to know where to buy one. When my kid told them his father had made it, they decided he was a liar.

"I am a good father and a dutiful husband. I have been married for . . . years. I have diapered the children, and physicked them, I have talked to them and listened to them, I have bathed them and rocked them to sleep, I have swum with them and pig-gybacked them and attended them in hospitals and restaurants and doctors' offices and airplanes and automobiles and I believe I know them very well. On the witness stand, ask me to swear what grade they are in, *for sure*, what is the color of

their eyes, *absolutely*, what is the exact height of my wife, does she prefer rutabagas to Jerusalem artichokes, *under oath*—I don't know."[1]

Smith wrote his first novel in 1941 and for the next three decades continued to earn his living writing novels, children's books, poetry in a style similar to Ogden Nash, and plays. In 1954 he collaborated with Max Schulman on "The Tender Trap," a hit play that ran for over one hundred performances on Broadway and was later adapted into a successful movie starring Frank Sinatra and Debbie Reynolds.

In 1957, Smith's book of childhood recollections, *"Where Did You Go?" "Out." "What Did You Do?" "Nothing."* sold over 170,000 copies and was on the best-seller list for almost a year. It was based on his idea that childhood should be unstructured. Smith believed that children should be allowed to lead lives with little adult supervision and expounded this belief in his "how-to" book for young people, *How to Do Nothing with Nobody, All Alone by Yourself,* which was illustrated by his wife. "Many many hours of my childhood were spent in learning how to whistle. In learning how to snap my fingers. In hanging from the branch of a tree. In looking at an ants' nest. In digging holes. Making piles. Tearing things down. Throwing rocks at things.

by Robert Paul Smith

"Where Did You Go?" "Out." "What Did You Do?" "Nothing."

How it was when you were a kid—and how things have deteriorated since.

(Jacket illustration by James J. Spanfeller from *"Where Did You Go?" "Out." "What Did You Do?" "Nothing."* by Robert Paul Smith.)

"My world, as a kid, was full of things that grownups didn't care about. My fear now is that all of us grownups have become so childish that we don't leave the kids much room to move around in, that we foolishly believe that we understand them so well because we share things with them.

"This is not only folly, it is not fair. At somebody's house one night, a harassed father who was trying to talk to grownups with his brood around, finally spoke a simple sentence of despair, 'For Gossakes, go upstairs or downstairs!'

"He was, I believe, asking for privacy. He was, I believe, entitled to it.

"I think kids are, too.

"Let them moon, let them babble, let them be scared.

"I guess what I'm saying is that people who don't have nightmares don't have dreams."[1]

Other books that Smith wrote for children include *Jack Mack*, a Junior Literary Guild selection, *When I Am Big* and *Nothingatall, Nothingatall, Nothingatall.* "I understand some people get worried about kids who spend a lot of time all alone, by themselves. I do a little worrying about that, but I worry about something else even more; about kids who don't know how

to spend any time all alone, by themselves. It's something you're going to be doing a whole lot of, no matter what, for the rest of your lives. And I think it's a good thing to do; you get to know yourself, and I think that's the most important thing in the whole world." [Robert Paul Smith, *How to Do Nothing with Nobody All Alone by Yourself,* Norton, 1958.[2]]

Smith died on January 30, 1977 in New York City at the age of sixty-one.

HOBBIES AND OTHER INTERESTS: Building model ships and reading (especially Mark Twain).

FOR MORE INFORMATION SEE: Saturday Review, September 6, 1941, June 29, 1957; *New Republic,* September 29, 1941; *Kirkus,* February 15, 1957; *Chicago Sunday Tribune,* August 23, 1959; *San Francisco Chronicle,* September 1, 1959. Obituaries: *New York York Times,* January 31, 1977; *Newsweek,* February 14, 1977.

SNOW, Richard F(olger) 1947-

PERSONAL: Born October 28, 1947, in New York, N.Y.; son of Richard B. (an architect) and Emma (Folger) Snow; married Carol Peckham (a magazine publication manager), August 25, 1979. *Education:* Columbia University, B.A., 1970. *Home:* 490 West End Ave., New York, N.Y. 10024. *Agent:* Brandt & Brandt, 1501 Broadway, New York, N.Y. 10036. *Office:* American Heritage, 10 Rockefeller Plaza, New York, N.Y. 10020.

CAREER: Magazine editor and writer. *American Heritage* (magazine), New York, N.Y., member of staff, 1970-72, as-

RICHARD F. SNOW

sociate editor, 1972-77, senior editor in book division, 1977-78, managing editor, 1979—. *Member:* Authors Guild. *Awards, honors: Freelon Starbird* was selected one of *New York Times* Outstanding Juvenile Books, and one of Child Study Association of America's Children's Books of the Year, both 1976; *Boston Globe-Horn Book* Award honor book for nonfiction, 1979, for *The Iron Road: A Portrait of American Railroading; The Burning* was selected one of New York Public Library's Books for the Teen Age, 1982.

WRITINGS: The Funny Place (poetry), J. Philip O'Hara, 1975; *Freelon Starbird: Being a Narrative of the Extraordinary Hardships Suffered by an Accidental Soldier in a Beaten Army During the Autumn and Winter of 1776* (juvenile; Horn Book honor list; illustrated by Ben F. Stahl), Houghton, 1976; *The Iron Road: A Portrait of American Railroading* (juvenile; illustrated with photographs by David Plowden), Four Winds, 1978; *The Burning* (adult historical novel), Doubleday, 1981.

WORK IN PROGRESS: A novel set in New York City in the second half of the nineteenth century.

SIDELIGHTS: "The narrator of one of Stephen Vincent Benet's novels, recalling the New York City of his youth, speaks of the horsecars and the tangle of wires on the telegraph poles and the little steam engines that pulled the elevated trains. 'I have seen books since recalling these things as quaint, and they have made me feel odd. For they assume that I knew I was living in an epoch, and, of course, I did not know.'

"Much of the challenge of writing historical fiction lies, I believe, in successfully avoiding the quaint—in recreating a past where such accessories as starched collars and trolley cars, sad irons and horsebarns are serious working tools, used by real men and women, and not just by extras borrowed for a costume drama from our familiar world of supermarkets and air shuttles. It is a truism, of course, that our forebears were much the same people as we are: they bickered with their landlords, couldn't believe the price of meat, quarrelled, fell in love, wrote bad checks, and lay awake worrying about what the future had in store for them. But looking at the old photographs, people with white-faced strangers in their boxy suits and faintly comic hats, it is sometimes hard to really believe this.

"But when the historical novelist succeeds in making us believe, he gives us a good deal more than a tour through a landscape cunningly tricked out with nickel beers and parasols. Watching recognizable people coping as best they can with events whose outcome we know offers a pleasure beyond the story the author is telling. The resource, energy, fear, or fatalism with which people alive a hundred years ago lived through their days can give us comfort in getting through ours."

FOR MORE INFORMATION SEE: Washington Post Book World, May 2, 1976; *New York Times Book Review,* May 2, 1976, December 10, 1978; *Boston Globe,* August 12, 1976; *San Francisco Chronicle,* July 26, 1981; *Saturday Review,* August, 1981; *Cleveland Plain Dealer,* August 30, 1981; *Washington Post,* September 8, 1981.

SUTTON, Jane 1950-

PERSONAL: Born May 11, 1950, in New York, N.Y.; daughter of Milton (a creative director for an advertising agency) and Freema (Balloff) Sutton; married Alan G. Ticotsky (an elementary school teacher), August 10, 1975; children: Re-

JANE SUTTON

becca, Charles. *Education:* Brandeis University, B.A. (magna cum laude), 1972. *Residence:* 11 Mason St., Lexington, Mass. 02173.

CAREER: Harlem Valley State Hospital, Wingdale, N.Y., mental health worker with retarded adults, 1972-74; *Mid-Hudson Leisure,* Poughkeepsie, N.Y., staff writer, 1974-75; Instrumentation Laboratory, Inc. (manufacturers of medical and analytical instruments), Lexington, Mass., in public relations, 1975-80; author of children's books, 1979—. Member of Lexington FISH and Citizens for Lexington Conservation. *Member:* Phi Beta Kappa. *Awards, honors: Me and the Weirdos* was selected as a Children's Choice by the International Reading Association, 1982, and received the Utah Children's Book Award, 1986.

WRITINGS—Juvenile: What Should A Hippo Wear? (illustrated by Lynn Munsinger), Houghton, 1979; *Me and the Weirdos* (illustrated by Sandy Kossin), Houghton, 1981; *Confessions of an Orange Octopus* (illustrated by Jim Spence), Dutton, 1983; *Not Even Mrs. Mazursky* (illustrated by Joan Drescher), Dutton, 1984.

Work represented in anthologies, including *Contained Reading Comprehension and Fluency Development,* Level E, edited by Dorothy M. Bogart, A/V Concepts, 1976, and *In View Of,* edited by John Molloy and Robert Ward, Joist Productions, 1976.

WORK IN PROGRESS: A novel for teenagers, *Definitely Not Sexy;* a short story, "No Room for Alex," to appear in *Cricket Magazine.*

Debbie was wearing her big brother's leather jacket, and she was carrying a motorcycle chain. ■ (From *Not Even Mrs. Mazursky* by Jane Sutton. Illustrated by Joan Drescher.)

SIDELIGHTS: "In *What Should a Hippo Wear?*, I have tried to capture the sense of awkwardness both children and adults experience when they feel they don't fit in, that they have to look or act a certain way in order to be accepted. Bertha the hippo learns that she is much better off being herself, that her true friends like her for what she is. This is a happy lesson that many of us, including myself, need to be reminded of once in a while.

"I enjoy writing for children. It's satisfying to me to invent situations they can identify with and to share whatever knowledge I have gained of the world. Also, in children's works I can express a strong moral message . . . without having to couch it in cautious language so that the modern reader can feel that he or she has read between the lines.

"*Me and the Weirdos* is probably my funniest book. It's about the feeling that one's family is embarrassing. Judging by the enthusiastic response this book has had from children in the United States and other countries, this seems to be a feeling everyone experiences at one time or another.

"I recently completed my first novel for teenagers, *Definitely Not Sexy,* and I enjoyed writing for this older age group. I have liked writing for as long as I can remember, and I was lucky that my elementary school teachers encouraged me."

HOBBIES AND OTHER INTERESTS: Bike riding, tennis, talking to children about writing.

FOR MORE INFORMATION SEE: Lexington Minute-Man, May 17, 1979, January 19, 1984.

TURLINGTON, Bayly   1919-1977

OBITUARY NOTICE—See sketch in *SATA* Volume 5: Born September 14, 1919, in Norfolk, Va.; died in November, 1977. Educator and author. During the course of his four year service in the U.S. Army, Turlington became a captain. He later taught as a professor of classical languages at the University of the South, eventually attaining the position of department head. In addition to contributing to classical journals, Turlington wrote *Socrates: The Father of Western Philosophy,* which he geared for juvenile readers.

FOR MORE INFORMATION SEE: Who's Who in America, 39th edition, Marquis, 1976; *Contemporary Authors,* Volumes 29-32, revised, Gale, 1978. Obituaries: Date of death provided by wife, Anne A. Turlington.

WATTS, Isaac   1674-1748
(I.W.)

PERSONAL: Born July 17, 1674, in Southampton, England; died November 25, 1748, in Stoke Newington, England; son of Isaac (a clothier and nonconformist schoolmaster) Watts. *Education:* Attended the Dissenting Academy, Stoke Newington, England, 1690-94. *Home:* Theobalds, Hertfordshire, England.

CAREER: Hymn writer and nonconformist clergyman. Began writing hymns shortly after finishing his schooling; tutor at Stoke Newington until 1701, at about the same time he became an assistant pastor at an Independent church in London, 1699, pastor, 1702; resigned from pastoral duties due to ill-health, devoting his remaining years to literary works. *Awards, honors:* D.D., University of Edinburgh, 1728.

WRITINGS—For children: *Divine Songs Attempted in Easy Language for the Use of Children,* [London], 1715, reprinted Oxford University Press, 1971; *Prayers Composed for the Use and Imitations of Children,* [London], 1728; *Catechisms; or, Instructions in the Principles of the Christian Religion, and the History of Scripture,* [London], 1730; *The First Set of Catechisms and Prayers; or, The Religion of Little Children,* fifth edition, [London], 1734; *The Second Set of Catechisms: A Preservative from the Sins and Follies of Childhood and Youth,* second edition, [London], 1734; *Advice to a Young Man Entering upon the World,* Religious Tract Society, circa 1830; *Logic for the Young,* edited by J. W. Gilbart, [London], 1855; *The Improved Reading Made Easy; or, First Book for Children,* [London], 1861.

Theological works: *An Essay against Uncharitableness,* [London], 1707; *A Guide to Prayer; or, A Free and Rational Account of the Gift, Grace, and Spirit of Prayer,* [London], 1715; *Sermons on Various Subjects, Divine and Moral,* three volumes, John Clark, 1721-29; *The Christian Doctrine of the Trinity,* [London], 1722; *Logick; or, The Right Use of Reason in the Enquiry after Truth,* [London], 1725; *A Defense against the Temptation to Self-Murther,* J. Clark & R. Hett, 1726; *A Short View of the Whole Scripture History,* [London], 1732 [other editions published as *Dr. Watt's Historical Catechisms,* edited by Joseph Priestley, (Birmingham), 1788; *A Catechism of Scripture History,* (London), 1849]; *The Redeemer and the Sanctifier,* [London], 1736.

Humility Represented in the Character of St. Paul, R. Ford & R. Hett, 1737; *The Doctrine of the Passions Explained and Improved; or, A Brief and Comprehensive Scheme of the Natural Affections of Mankind,* third edition, enlarged, [London], 1739; *The Improvement of the Mind; or, A Supplement to the Art of Logick* [London], 1741; *The Harmony of All the Religions Which God Ever Prescribed,* J. Bracstone, 1742; *A Faithful Enquiry after the Ancient and Original Doctrine of the Trinity,* J. Gressell, 1745; *The World to Come; or, Discourses on the Joys or Sorrows of Departed Souls at Death,* two volumes, second edition, [London], 1745, reissued, Moody, 1954.

Useful and Important Questions Concerning Jesus [and] The Glory of Christ as God-Man, J. Oswald, 1746; *The Rational Foundation of a Christian Church,* J. Oswald & J. Buckland, 1747; *Orthodoxy and Charity United,* second edition, Rogers & Fowle, 1749; *Discourses of the Love of God,* fourth edition, J. Waugh, 1760; *The Parable of the Prodigal Son: Paraphrased,* R. Thomas, 1762; *An Exhortation to Ministers,* Reiner Publications, 1970.

Poems and metrical writings: *Horae Lyricae* (poems), [London], 1706; *Hymns and Spiritual Songs,* J. Humpreys, 1707; *The Psalms of David,* John Clark, 1719; *Reliquiae Juveniles: Miscellaneous Thoughts in Prose and Verse,* R. Ford & R. Hett, 1734, C. Pierce, 1796, reprinted as *Miscellaneous Thoughts,* Garland Publishing, 1971; *A Wonderful Dream,* [London], circa 1766; (under name, Dr. Watts) *Cradle Hymn,* J. Harris, 1812 [later edition published as *The Cradle Hymn,* Illman & Pibrow, circa 1830].

Other: *The Art of Reading and Writing English,* [London], 1721, reissued, Scolar Press, 1972; *The Knowledge of the Heavens and the Earth Made Easy, or; The First Principles of Astronomy and Geography,* edited by J. Eames, [London],

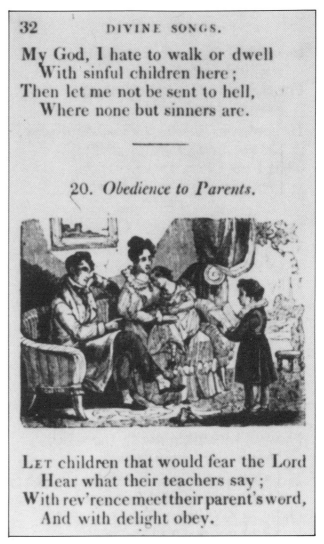

(From *Divine Songs Attempted in Easy Language for the Use of Children* by Isaac Watts.)

1726; *An Essay towards the Encouragement of Charity Schools,* John Clark, 1728; *A Treatise on the Education of Children and Youth,* second edition, [London], 1769; *Four Letters of Dr. Isaac Watts,* edited by S. A. Green, privately printed, 1898.

Selections: (Under the initials I. W.) *Philosophical Essays on Various Subjects,* R. Ford, 1733, later editions published under the author's full name; *A Collection of Hymns from Dr. Watts,* W. McAlpine, 1767; *Devout Meditations from Dr. Watts,* [London], 1803; *Nine Sermons Preached in the Years 1718-19,* [Oxford], 1812; *Extracts from the Writings of Dr. Watts,* [Boston], circa 1820; *The Psalms and Hymns of Dr. Watts,* edited by John Rippon, D. Clark, 1838 [another edition edited by Samuel M. Worcester, Crocker & Brewster, 1851]; *The Penny Watts' Hymns,* Guilford, 1867; *Childhood's Songs of Long Ago* (illustrated by Blanche McManus), E. B. Herrick, 1897.

SIDELIGHTS: **July 17, 1674.** Born in Southampton, England, the eldest of nine children of Isaac Watts, a deacon of a dissenting Protestant church and master of a popular boarding school, who was in prison when Watts was born. The Watts' family was active in the business and religious community of Southampton. ''My grandfather Mr. Thomas Watts had such

ISAAC WATTS

acquaintance with the mathematics, painting, music, and poesy, etc. as gave him considerable esteem among his contemporaries. He was commander of a ship of war 1656, and by blowing up of the ship in the Dutch war he was drowned in his youth.'' [Arthur Paul Davis, *Isaac Watts: His Life and Works,* Dryden Press, 1948.[1]]

Watts showed an early inclination toward learning, studying Latin and Greek at the age of four. ''By the art of reading we learn a thousand things which our eyes can never see, and which our thoughts would never have reached to: we are instructed by books in the wisdom of ancient ages; we learn what our ancestors have said and done, and enjoy the benefit of the wise and judicious remarks which they have made through their whole course of life, without the fatigue of their long and painful experiments. By this means children may be led, in a great measure, into the wisdom of old age. It is by ouselves with what has been done in the distant parts of the world. . . .

''But the greatest blessing that we derive from reading is, the knowledge of the holy scriptures, wherein God has conveyed down to us the discoveries of his wisdom, power, and grace, through many past ages, and whereby we attain the knowledge of Christ, and of the way of salvation by a mediator.'' [Isaac Watts, *The Improvement of the Mind,* Edwards and Knibb, 1821.[2]]

At the age of nine, Watts recorded his father's imprisonment: ''1863. My father persecuted and imprisoned for nonconformity 6 months. After that forced to leave his family and live privately in London 2 years. . . .''[1]

1690. Sent to London to study. ''It is meditation and studious thought, it is the exercise of your own reason and judgment upon all you read, that given good sense even to the best genius, and affords your understanding the truest improvement. . . .''[2]

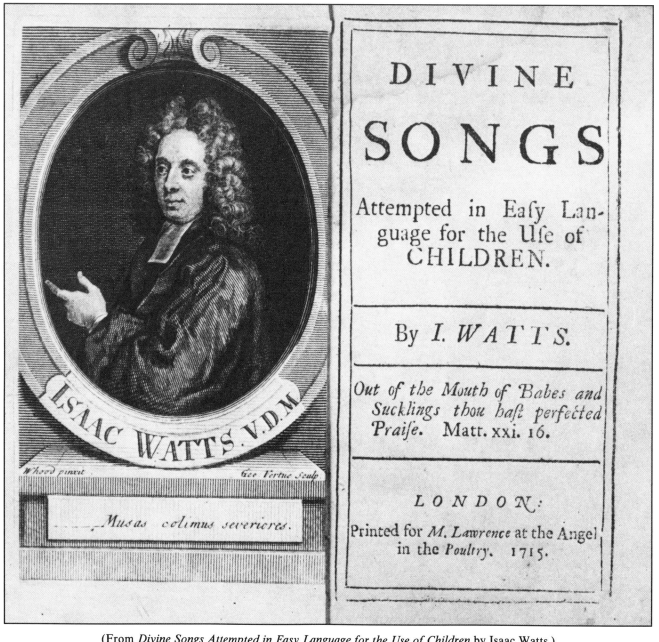

(From *Divine Songs Attempted in Easy Language for the Use of Children* by Isaac Watts.)

(From *The Cradle Hymn* by Dr. Watts.)

1694. After completing his studies in London, Watts returned to Southampton, where he spent two years in reading, meditation, and prayer. During this time he composed most of his hymns, although they were not published until 1707.

1696. Hired as a tutor for Sir John Hartopp's son, a position he retained for five years.

1698. Preached his first sermon on his twenty-fourth birthday.

1699. Named assistant to the pastor of an Independent church in London.

1702. Named pastor of the Independent church in London. He declared his acceptance in a sermon to his fellow parishioners: "You know what a constant aversion I have had to any proposals of a pastoral office for these three years, ever since the providence of God called me first among you. You know also that, since you have given me a unanimous and solemn call thereto, I have heartily proposed several methods for your settlement without me, but your choice and your affections seemed still to be settled and unmoved.

"I have objected warmly and often, my own indispositions of body, which incapacitate me for much service, and I have pointed often to three reverend divines that are members of this church, whose gifts might render them more proper for instruction, and whose age for government. These things I have urged till I have provoked you to sorrow and tears, and till I myself have been almost ashamed. But your perseverance in your choice and love, your constant profession of edification by my ministry, the great probability you show of building up this famous and decayed church of Christ, if I accept the call,

and your prevailing fears of its dissolution if I refuse, have given me ground to believe that the voice of this church is the voice of Christ by you: and to answer this call I have not consulted with flesh and blood: I have laid aside the thoughts of myself to serve the interest of our Lord.

"I give up my own ease for your spiritual profit and your increase. I submit my inclinations to my duty, and in hopes of being made an instrument in the hands of Christ to build up this ancient church, I return this solemn answer to your call, that, with a great sense of my own inability in mind and body to discharge the duties of so sacred an office, I do, in the strength of Christ, venture upon it, and in the name of our Lord Jesus I accept your call, promising in the presence of God and his saints, my utmost diligence in all the duties of a pastor, so far as God shall enlighten and strengthen me; and I leave this promise in the hands of Christ our Mediator, to see it performed by me unto you through the assistance of his grace and Spirit." [Dr. Gibbons, selector, *Life of the Rev. Isaac Watts, D.D.*, Religious Tract Society, 1799.[3]]

1712. Stricken with a "violent fever," which left him permanently disabled. "But has not my spirit been depressed by a sickly constitution, and confined to a feeble engine of flesh under daily disorders? Have I not sustained many sorrows on this account, and wasted some years among the infirmities of the body, and in painful idleness? Are there not several souls favoured with a more easy habitation, and yoked with a better partner? Are they not accommodated with engines which have more health and vigour, and situated in much more happy circumstances than mine? What then? Shall I repine at my lot, and murmur against my Creator, because he has made some

(From *The Cradle Hymn* by Dr. Watts.)

hundreds happier than I, while I survey whole nations, and millions of mankind that have not a thousandth part of my blessings?''[2]

Watts spent his convalescence at the home of his friend Sir Thomas Abney, becoming a permanent boarder at the Abney home. Although Sir Thomas died after eight years had passed, Watts remained with Abney's daughters and widow, spending the next thirty-six years with the family. He was responsible for the education of the Abney daughters.

Wrote to the members of his congregation during his prolonged illness: ''Shall I tell you the little health which I have received is chiefly owning to the perpetual change of place and air and travelling for which I enjoy such conveniencys in this worthy family. Had I stay'd in London till this time I had not been able to have ministered to you again. My moments of ease and strength are so few and incertain that I cannot appoint any hour or day, and sometimes my indispositions seize me when I most earnestly desire an hour of service as they have lately done. The last two attempts of any thing like preaching that I have made in private in this family [illegible] unexampled friendship. I would not give you any suspicion that I deprive you of my strength by employing it another way; Tho some of my friends are of opinion that such private attempts would rather encourage and hasten me towards the publick. However these last two Lord's days I did desyre to try again in the family and that in the Evening which is my best hour. But God was pleased to disappoint me both days by the return of the weak'ning fits of the headache each morning.

''My kind friends around me saw the hand of God, submitted to the disappointment, and made no Reflexion on what I had done lately in publick. They rejoyced heartily that God had indulged me so far as to serve you twice together tho' I was prevented serving them at all: And they take more sensible satisfaction in any ability God bestows upon me to minister among you than to worship in this household. I am sure they deserve a large share in my Thanks and Prayers, and I think also they zealously and sincerely seek your Interests, if my Health and Publick Ministry may be so esteemed. Tho I owe my life under God to their care and kindness, yet they desire no manner of service from me that may prevent or cut short my labours among you. It is God who cuts them short and it is God who prevents them. He is Wise and Holy, and I would learn to be patient and humble.''[1]

1715. Wrote *Divine Songs for Children,* which he sent to his London congregation. ''While I am thus waiting his will, I would be doing some work, . . . and review some of my former Labours to make them publick for your profit. As I lately made your selves a small present of a Treatise of Prayer, so I now desire your acceptance of a few Divine Songs for your young children for whom they were written. Every person that hath children under fifteen years of age capable of reading a verse will receive of my Brother Price a book for each. And may God even your God cause your family's to flourish in grace & build the church in the next generation!''[1]

Watts became famous for his pious children's verses. Many of his phrases became so popular that they were considered proverbs. Years later, Lewis Carroll borrowed Watts' phrase, 'tis the voice of the sluggard,'' in his book *Alice in Wonderland.*

1721. First volume of sermons published. Watts, although hampered by ill health, tried to visit the members of his conregation and promote Christian ideals among his parishioners. ''As fast as my health increases, you may assure yourselves it is devoted to your edification. It often grieves me to think

how poor, feeble, and short my present labours are among you, and yet what days of faintness I generally feel after every such attempt, so that I am continually prevented in my design of successive visits to you by the want of active spirits while I tarry in the city; and if I attempt to stay but a week or ten days there, I find a sensible return of weakness, so that I am constrained to return to the country air to recruit and maintain this little capacity of service.

''I bless God heartily, and you are my witnesses that, in my better seasons of health heretofore, and in the intervals of my studies, I was not a stranger to your private families, nor thoughtless of your souls' improvement.''[3]

1724. Expressed his love for his congregation in a preface to an edition of his sermons. '''Tis in the service of your souls I have spent the best period of my life, ministering the gospel among you. Two-and-twenty years are now expired since you first called me to this delightful work, and from that time my cares and labours, my studies and prayers, have been employed on your behalf. I trust they have been accepted with God, and, through his Almighty blessing, have obtained some success. As to their acceptance with you, I have too many and plain evidences to admit a doubt of it, which I have often thankfully acknowledged to God and you. Your forward kindness hath always forbid my requests, nor do I remember that you ever gave me leave to ask anything at your hands, by your constant anticipation of all which I could reasonably desire.

''While I was thus walking with you in the fellowship of the gospel with mutual delight, God was pleased to weaken my strength in the way, and thereby has given you a fairer opportunity to show the vigour of your affection under my long weakness and confinement. Your diligence and zeal in maintaining public worship in the church, under the pastoral care of my dear brother and colleague, your special days and hours of prayer for my recovery, your constant and fervent addresses to the throne of grace on my account, in your weekly solemn assemblies, and your cheerful supplies of my neccessities under so tedious an affliction, have made me your debtor in a high degree, and have strengthened the bands of my duty by adding to them the bands of your love.''[3]

1728. Received an honorary doctorate from the University of Edinburgh. Although he wrote numerous poems, he did not consider himself a poet nor an accomplished writer of his age. ''Though I have sported with rhyme as an amusement in younger life, and published some religious compositions to assist the worship of God, yet I never set myself up among the numerous competitors for a poet of the age, much less have I presumed to become their judge. . . . If I had ever been blessed with a capacity of this kind, yet there is a certain limit and period to all mortal powers. The gay colours of imagery, and the sprightly relish of verse die away and vanish in my advancing age, for I have almost left off to read or write what was once so engaging. One ought to preserve a quick sense of beauties and blemishes, and an elegant taste of sentiment and language in order to pass a judgment on the labours of the muses.

''I acknowledge your civility . . . and the respect of the gentlemen who have done me this honour. I wish, in return, I could adjudge the prizes to every one of them, for all have their peculiar merit.''[3]

Watts' life was largely spent in quiet study. A bachelor and a chronic invalid, he preferred country life to the city, avoiding London as much as possible.

November 25, 1748. Died in Stoke Newington, England. "Dying with faith and fortitude is a noble conclusion of a life of zeal and service. It is the very last duty on earth."[3]

Watts was buried in Bunhill Fields, and a monument to him was erected in Westminster Abbey.

FOR MORE INFORMATION SEE: Dr. Gibbons, selector, *Life of the Rev. Isaac Watts, D.D.*, Religious Tract Society, 1799; Isaac Watts, *The Improvement of the Mind*, Edwards and Knibb, 1821; Arthur Paul Davis, *Isaac Watts: His Life and Works*, Independent Press, 1948; R. Stevenson, "Watts in America," *Harvard Theological Review*, July, 1948; R. Stevenson, "Dr. Watts' Flights of Fancy," *Harvard Theological Review*, October 1949; Ernest Gordon Rupp, *Six Makers of English Religion: 1500-1700*, Harper, 1957; Eric Routley, *Isaac Watts: 1674-1748*, Independent Press, 1961; Harry Escott, *Isaac Watts, Hymnographer: A Study of the Beginnings, Development, and Philosophy of the English Hymn*, Allenson, 1962; Isaac Watts, *Hymns and Spiritual Songs: 1707-1748* (a study by Selma L. Bishop), Faith Press, 1962; (for children) David C. Hill, *Messengers of the King*, Augsburg, 1968.

WILSON, Jacqueline   1945-

BRIEF ENTRY: Born December 17, 1945, in Bath, England. After her two-year stint as a journalist for Thomson Newspapers in Dundee, Scotland, Wilson became a free-lance writer in 1965. Since then she has written several suspense novels for adults, including *Hide and Seek, Let's Pretend, Making Hate,* and *Snap,* all of which were published by Macmillan in the early to middle 1970s. In 1973 she contributed to *Winter's Crimes,* a periodical also printed by Macmillan. Wilson's first book for young readers, *Nobody's Perfect* (Oxford University Press, 1982), portrays a young girl in search of her biological father. According to *Bulletin of the Center for Children's Books,* the story is "written with sensitive understanding; the characterization, plot, and pace all have impact, and the treatment of relationships is realistic and perceptive." Wilson's other

novels for young readers include *How to Survive Summer Camp, Waiting for the Sky to Fall, The Killer Tadpole, The Other Side, The School Trip, Amber,* and *The Monster in the Cupboard.* She has also written radio plays such as "Are You Listening," "It's Disgusting at Your Age," and "Ask a Silly Question," broadcast on BBC between 1982 and 1984. *Home:* 1B Beaufort Rd., Kingston-on-Thames, Surrey, England.

FOR MORE INFORMATION SEE: Twentieth-Century Crime and Mystery Writers, 2nd edition, St. Martin's Press, 1985; *Contemporary Authors, New Revision Series,* Volume 17, Gale, 1986; *The Writers Directory: 1986-1988,* St. James Press, 1986.

WORTHINGTON, Phoebe   1910-

BRIEF ENTRY: Born November 29, 1910, in Wigan, Lancashire, England. Secretary, teacher, author and illustrator of books for children. After sixteen years as a secretary for firms in Liverpool, Worthington began working as a preschool teacher in 1947. During that time, she and her brother Selby produced their first book, *Teddy Bear Coalman* (F. Warne, 1948). Born of Selby's imagination during storytelling sessions with his young son, the tale involves an industrious bear who delivers coal daily, then goes home to tea and bed. Thirty years elapsed before Worthington resumed illustrating, a period which she devoted to her marriage, family, and teaching career. In 1977 she began work on illustrations for a sequel to her first book, entitled *Teddy Bear Baker.* A complete "Teddy Bear" series has resulted, featuring the title character in such roles as postman, gardener, and farmer. *Times Educational Supplement* described the books as "rightly loved" by small children, while *Booklist* noted that their "charming concessions to childlike sensibilities are what make them successful." While Worthington and her brother continued their collaboration on *Teddy Bear Postman* (F. Warne, 1981), she teamed up with sister Joan on the series' last two books. The upcoming sixth book is titled *Teddy Bear Boatman. Home:* 62 Fairfield Rd., Stockton Heath, Warrington, Cheshire WA4 2UU, England.

Cumulative Indexes

Illustrations Index

(In the following index, the number of the volume in which an illustrator's work appears is given *before* the colon, and the page on which it appears is given *after* the colon. For example, a drawing by Adams, Adrienne appears in Volume 2 on page 6, another drawing by her appears in Volume 3 on page 80, another drawing in Volume 8 on page 1, and another drawing in Volume 15 on page 107.)

YABC

Index citations including this abbreviation refer to listings appearing in *Yesterday's Authors of Books for Children,* also published by the Gale Research Company, which covers authors who died prior to 1960.

Author Index

The following index gives the number of the volume in which an author's biographical sketch, Brief Entry, or Obituary appears.

This index includes references to all entries in the following series, which are also published by Gale Research Company.

YABC—*Yesterday's Authors of Books for Children: Facts and Pictures about Authors and Illustrators of Books for Young People from Early Times to 1960,* Volumes 1-2
CLR—*Children's Literature Review: Excerpts from Reviews, Criticism, and Commentary on Books for Children,* Volumes 1-14
SAAS—*Something about the Author Autobiography Series,* Volumes 1-5

Mrs. Fairstar
See Horne, Richard Henry
Mueller, Virginia 1924- 28
Muir, Frank 1920- 30
Mukerji, Dhan Gopal
1890-1936 40
See also CLR 10
Mulcahy, Lucille Burnett 12
Mulford, Philippa Greene
1948- 43
Mulgan, Catherine
See Gough, Catherine
Muller, Billex
See Ellis, Edward S(ylvester)
Mullins, Edward S(wift)
1922- 10
Mulock, Dinah Maria
See Craik, Dinah Maria (Mulock)
Mulvihill, William Patrick
1923- 8
Mun
See Leaf, (Wilbur) Munro
Munari, Bruno 1907- 15
See also CLR 9
Munce, Ruth Hill 1898- 12
Munowitz, Ken 1935-1977 14
Muñoz, William 1949- 42
Munro, Alice 1931- 29
Munro, Eleanor 1928- 37
Munsch, Robert N. 1945- 50
Brief Entry 48
Munsinger, Lynn 1951- 33
Munson(-Benson), Tunie
1946- 15
Munves, James (Albert) 1922- 30
Munzer, Martha E. 1899- 4
Murch, Mel and Starr, Ward [Joint
double pseudonym]
See Manes, Stephen
Murphy, Barbara Beasley
1933- 5
Murphy, E(mmett) Jefferson
1926- 4
Murphy, Jill 1949- 37
Murphy, Jim 1947- 37
Brief Entry 32
Murphy, Pat
See Murphy, E(mmett) Jefferson
Murphy, Robert (William)
1902-1971 10
Murphy, Shirley Rousseau
1928- 36
Murray, John 1923- 39
Murray, Marian 5
Murray, Michele 1933-1974 7
Murray, Ossie 1938- 43
Musgrave, Florence 1902- 3
Musgrove, Margaret W(ynkoop)
1943- 26
Mussey, Virginia T. H.
See Ellison, Virginia Howell
Mutz
See Kunstler, Morton
Myers, Arthur 1917- 35
Myers, Bernice 9
Myers, Caroline Elizabeth (Clark)
1887-1980 28
Myers, Elisabeth P(erkins)
1918- 36

Myers, Hortense (Powner)
1913- 10
Myers, Walter Dean 1937- 41
Brief Entry 27
See also CLR 4
See also SAAS 2
Myller, Rolf 1926- 27
Myra, Harold L(awrence)
1939- 46
Brief Entry 42
Myrus, Donald (Richard)
1927- 23

N

Nakatani, Chiyoko 1930-
Brief Entry 40
Namioka, Lensey 1929- 27
Napier, Mark
See Laffin, John (Alfred Charles)
Nash, Bruce M(itchell) 1947- 34
Nash, Linell
See Smith, Linell Nash
Nash, Mary (Hughes) 1925- 41
Nash, (Frederic) Ogden
1902-1971 46
Earlier sketch in SATA 2
Nast, Elsa Ruth
See Watson, Jane Werner
Nast, Thomas 1840-1902 51
Brief Entry 33
Nastick, Sharon 1954- 41
Nathan, Adele (Gutman) 1900(?)-1986
Obituary 48
Nathan, Dorothy (Goldeen)
(?)-1966 15
Nathan, Robert (Gruntal)
1894-1985 6
Obituary 43
Natti, Susanna 1948- 32
Navarra, John Gabriel 1927- 8
Naylor, Penelope 1941- 10
Naylor, Phyllis Reynolds
1933- 12
Nazaroff, Alexander I. 1898- 4
Neal, Harry Edward 1906- 5
Nearing, Penny 1916- 47
Brief Entry 42
Nebel, Gustave E. 45
Brief Entry 33
Nebel, Mimouca
See Nebel, Gustave E.
Nee, Kay Bonner 10
Needle, Jan 1943- 30
Needleman, Jacob 1934- 6
Negri, Rocco 1932- 12
Neigoff, Anne 13
Neigoff, Mike 1920- 13
Neilson, Frances Fullerton (Jones)
1910- 14
Neimark, Anne E. 1935- 4
Neimark, Paul G. 1934-
Brief Entry 37
Nelson, Cordner (Bruce) 1918-
Brief Entry 29
Nelson, Esther L. 1928- 13
Nelson, Lawrence E(rnest) 1928-1977
Obituary 28

Nelson, Mary Carroll 1929- 23
Nerlove, Miriam 1959-
Brief Entry 49
Nesbit, E(dith)
1858-1924 .... YABC 1
See also CLR 3
Nesbit, Troy
See Folsom, Franklin
Nespojohn, Katherine V.
1912- 7
Ness, Evaline (Michelow)
1911-1986 26
Obituary 49
Earlier sketch in SATA 1
See also CLR 6
See also SAAS 1
Nestor, William P(rodromos)
1947- 49
Neufeld, John 1938- 6
See also SAAS 3
Neumeyer, Peter F(lorian)
1929- 13
Neurath, Marie (Reidemeister)
1898- 1
Neusner, Jacob 1932- 38
Neville, Emily Cheney 1919- 1
See also SAAS 2
Neville, Mary
See Woodrich, Mary Neville
Nevins, Albert J. 1915- 20
Newberry, Clare Turlay
1903-1970 1
Obituary 26
Newbery, John 1713-1767 20
Newcomb, Ellsworth
See Kenny, Ellsworth Newcomb
Newcombe, Jack 45
Brief Entry 33
Newell, Crosby
See Bonsall, Crosby (Barbara
Newell)
Newell, Edythe W. 1910- 11
Newell, Hope (Hockenberry)
1896-1965 24
Newfeld, Frank 1928- 26
Newlon, (Frank) Clarke
1905(?)-1982 6
Obituary 33
Newman, Daisy 1904- 27
Newman, Gerald 1939- 46
Brief Entry 42
Newman, Robert (Howard)
1909- 4
Newman, Shirlee Petkin
1924- 10
Newsom, Carol 1948- 40
Newton, James R(obert)
1935- 23
Newton, Suzanne 1936- 5
Ney, John 1923- 43
Brief Entry 33
Nic Leodhas, Sorche
See Alger, Leclaire (Gowans)
Nichols, Cecilia Fawn 1906- 12
Nichols, Peter
See Youd, (Christopher) Samuel
Nichols, (Joanna) Ruth 1948- 15
Nicholson, Joyce Thorpe
1919- 35

Stewart, Elizabeth Laing
1907- 6
Stewart, George Rippey
1895-1980 3
Obituary 23
Stewart, John (William) 1920- 14
Stewart, Mary (Florence Elinor)
1916- 12
Stewart, Robert Neil
1891-1972 7
Stewart, Scott
See Zaffo, George J.
Stewig, John Warren 1937- 26
Stiles, Martha Bennett 6
Stiles, Norman B. 1942-
Brief Entry 36
Still, James 1906- 29
Stillerman, Robbie 1947- 12
Stilley, Frank 1918- 29
Stine, G(eorge) Harry 1928- 10
Stine, Jovial Bob
See Stine, Robert Lawrence
Stine, Robert Lawrence 1943- 31
Stinetorf, Louise 1900- 10
Stirling, Arthur
See Sinclair, Upton (Beall)
Stirling, Nora B. 3
Stirnweis, Shannon 1931- 10
Stobbs, William 1914- 17
Stockton, Francis Richard
1834-1902 44
Stockton, Frank R(ichard)
Brief Entry 32
See Stockton, Francis Richard
Stoddard, Edward G. 1923- 10
Stoddard, Hope 1900- 6
Stoddard, Sandol
See Warburg, Sandol Stoddard
Stoiko, Michael 1919- 14
Stoker, Abraham 1847-1912 29
Stoker, Bram
See Stoker, Abraham
Stokes, Cedric
See Beardmore, George
Stokes, Jack (Tilden) 1923- 13
Stokes, Olivia Pearl 1916- 32
Stolz, Mary (Slattery) 1920- 10
See also SAAS 3
Stone, Alan [Collective
pseudonym] 1
See also Svenson, Andrew E.
Stone, D(avid) K(arl) 1922- 9
Stone, Eugenia 1879-1971 7
Stone, Gene
See Stone, Eugenia
Stone, Helen V. 6
Stone, Irving 1903- 3
Stone, Jon 1931- 39
Stone, Josephine Rector
See Dixon, Jeanne
Stone, Raymond [Collective
pseudonym] 1
Stone, Richard A.
See Stratemeyer, Edward L.
Stonehouse, Bernard 1926- 13
Stong, Phil(ip Duffield)
1899-1957 32
Storch, Anne B. von
See von Storch, Anne B.

Storey, (Elizabeth) Margaret (Carlton)
1926- 9
Storey, Victoria Carolyn
1945- 16
Storme, Peter
See Stern, Philip Van Doren
Storr, Catherine (Cole) 1913- 9
Story, Josephine
See Loring, Emilie (Baker)
Stoutenburg, Adrien 1916- 3
Stover, Allan C(arl) 1938- 14
Stover, Marjorie Filley 1914- 9
Stowe, Harriet (Elizabeth) Beecher
1811-1896 .... YABC 1
Strachan, Margaret Pitcairn
1908- 14
Strait, Treva Adams 1909- 35
Strand, Mark 1934- 41
Strange, Philippa
See Coury, Louise Andree
Stranger, Joyce
See Wilson, Joyce M(uriel Judson)
Strasser, Todd 1950- 45
Brief Entry 41
See also CLR 11
Stratemeyer, Edward L.
1862-1930 1
Stratford, Philip 1927- 47
Stratton, Thomas [Joint pseudonym]
See DeWeese, Thomas Eugene
Stratton-Porter, Gene
1863-1924 15
Strayer, E. Ward
See Stratemeyer, Edward L.
Streano, Vince(nt Catello)
1945- 20
Streatfeild, Noel 1897-1985 20
Obituary 48
Street, Julia Montgomery
1898- 11
Stren, Patti 1949-
Brief Entry 41
See also CLR 5
Strete, Craig Kee 1950- 44
Stretton, Barbara (Humphrey)
1936- 43
Brief Entry 35
Strong, Charles [Joint pseudonym]
See Epstein, Beryl and Epstein,
Samuel
Strong, David
See McGuire, Leslie (Sarah)
Strong, J. J.
See Strong, Jeremy
Strong, Jeremy 1949- 36
Ströyer, Poul 1923- 13
Stuart, David
See Hoyt, Edwin P(almer), Jr.
Stuart, Forbes 1924- 13
Stuart, Ian
See MacLean, Alistair (Stuart)
Stuart, (Hilton) Jesse
1907-1984 2
Obituary 36
Stuart, Sheila
See Baker, Mary Gladys Steel
Stuart-Clark, Christopher
1940- 32
Stubis, Talivaldis 1926- 5

Stubley, Trevor (Hugh) 1932- 22
Stultifer, Morton
See Curtis, Richard (Alan)
Sture-Vasa, Mary
See Alsop, Mary O'Hara
Sturton, Hugh
See Johnston, H(ugh) A(nthony)
S(tephen)
Sturtzel, Howard A(llison)
1894- 1
Sturtzel, Jane Levington
1903- 1
Styles, Frank Showell 1908- 10
Suba, Susanne 4
Subond, Valerie
See Grayland, Valerie
Sudbery, Rodie 1943- 42
Sugarman, Tracy 1921- 37
Sugita, Yutaka 1930- 36
Suhl, Yuri 1908-1986 8
Obituary 50
See also CLR 2
See also SAAS 1
Suid, Murray 1942- 27
Sullivan, George E(dward)
1927- 4
Sullivan, Mary W(ilson)
1907- 13
Sullivan, Thomas Joseph, Jr.
1947- 16
Sullivan, Tom
See Sullivan, Thomas Joseph, Jr.
Sumichrast, Jözef 1948- 29
Sumiko
See Davies, Sumiko
Summers, James L(evingston) 1910-
Brief Entry 28
Sunderlin, Sylvia 1911- 28
Sung, Betty Lee 26
Supraner, Robyn 1930- 20
Surge, Frank 1931- 13
Susac, Andrew 1929- 5
Sussman, Susan 1942- 48
Sutcliff, Rosemary 1920- 44
Earlier sketch in SATA 6
See also CLR 1
Sutherland, Efua (Theodora Morgue)
1924- 25
Sutherland, Margaret 1941- 15
Sutherland, Zena B(ailey)
1915- 37
Suttles, Shirley (Smith) 1922- 21
Sutton, Ann (Livesay) 1923- 31
Sutton, Eve(lyn Mary) 1906- 26
Sutton, Felix 1910(?)- 31
Sutton, Jane 1950- 52
Brief Entry 43
Sutton, Larry M(atthew)
1931- 29
Sutton, Margaret (Beebe)
1903- 1
Sutton, Myron Daniel 1925- 31
Svenson, Andrew E.
1910-1975 2
Obituary 26
Swain, Su Zan (Noguchi)
1916- 21
Swan, Susan 1944- 22

Author Index

W

For Reference